Prague

PRAGUE
The Heart of Europe

CYNTHIA PACES

OXFORD
UNIVERSITY PRESS

Oxford University Press is a department of the University of Oxford.
It furthers the University's objective of excellence in research, scholarship,
and education by publishing worldwide. Oxford is a registered trade mark of
Oxford University Press in the UK and in certain other countries.

Published in the United States of America by Oxford University Press
198 Madison Avenue, New York, NY 10016, United States of America.

© Oxford University Press 2025

All rights reserved. No part of this publication may be reproduced, stored in a retrieval system, transmitted, used for text and data mining, or used for training artificial intelligence, in any form or by any means, without the prior permission in writing of Oxford University Press, or as expressly permitted by law, by license or under terms agreed with the appropriate reprographics rights organization. Inquiries concerning reproduction outside the scope of the above should be sent to the Rights Department, Oxford University Press, at the address above.

You must not circulate this work in any other form
and you must impose this same condition on any acquirer.

Library of Congress Cataloging-in-Publication Data
Names: Paces, Cynthia, author.
Title: Prague : the heart of Europe / Cynthia Paces.
Description: New York, NY : Oxford University Press, 2025. |
Includes bibliographical references and index. | Summary: "This book examines the history of Prague, emphasizing the city's linguistic, religious, and architectural diversity. The Slavic Přemyslid clan converted to Christianity and fortified Prague Castle in the late ninth century. The city expanded to include Lesser Town and Old Town, and in the thirteenth century, Otakar II encouraged German traders to settle in Prague. A large Jewish community thrived despite periodic antisemitic attacks. In 1346, Emperor Charles IV moved the imperial capital to Prague. He founded the New Town, Prague University, and St. Vitus Cathedral. The execution of Prague University rector Jan Hus, a religious reformer, sparked decades of war. Rudolph II returned the imperial capital to Prague in 1576 and patronized the arts and sciences. The Thirty Years' War began in 1618 with the Second Defenestration of Prague, a Protestant rebellion against Habsburg rulers. During the Counterreformation, Prague gained its Baroque character. The German language dominated until the industrial era when rural Czech speakers migrated to Prague. Czechs took over the city government and built patriotic institutions. A sanitation project replaced the Jewish ghetto with modern boulevards. German-Jewish writers, particularly Franz Kafka, explored themes of bureaucracy and the individual. In 1918, Tomáš G. Masaryk became the president of a new state, Czechoslovakia, and remade Prague as the capital city. Functionalist architecture and experimental art movements thrived. Nazi Germany occupied Prague in 1939, and the majority of Prague's Jews were murdered in the Holocaust. The Communist Party took control in 1948. The Warsaw Pact invaded Prague 1968, ending the Prague Spring reform movement. Dissident writer Václav Havel emerged as the leader of Prague's 1989 Velvet Revolution and served as the president of Czechoslovakia and the Czech Republic"—Provided by publisher.
Identifiers: LCCN 2024062143 (print) | LCCN 2024062144 (ebook) |
ISBN 9780197554838 (hardback) | ISBN 9780197554852 (epub)
Subjects: LCSH: Prague (Czech Republic)—History.
Classification: LCC DB2626 .P34 2025 (print) | LCC DB2626 (ebook) |
DDC 943.71/2—dc23/eng/20250212
LC record available at https://lccn.loc.gov/2024062143
LC ebook record available at https://lccn.loc.gov/2024062144

DOI: 10.1093/oso/9780197554838.001.0001

Printed by Sheridan Books, Inc., United States of America

The manufacturer's authorized representative in the EU for product safety is
Oxford University Press España S.A., Parque Empresarial San Fernando de Henares,
Avenida de Castilla, 2 – 28830 Madrid (www.oup.es/en).

For Mariel and Charlotte
and
in memory of Ben Jacobs (1968–2022)

Contents

Acknowledgments — ix
A Note on Language — xi
Timeline of Prague History — xiii

Introduction: All This Is Prague — 1

1. Foundations of Prague — 10
2. The Imperial Capital of Charles IV — 35
3. Faith and Violence in Wenceslas IV's Prague — 63
4. Hussite Wars and New Dynasties — 83
5. Rudolphine Prague — 105
6. Revolt and Defeat in Habsburg Prague — 122
7. Enlightened Prague — 145
8. Creating a Czech City — 163
9. Prague in a New Century — 187
10. Prague During the Great War — 207
11. Capital of the Republic — 221
12. Prague Under Nazi Rule — 242
13. Prague Winter, Prague Spring — 264
14. Communism's Gray Zone — 286
15. Post-Communist Prague — 303

Notes — 321
Bibliography — 339
Index — 357

Acknowledgments

LIKE ALL CREATIVE endeavors, this book would not have been written without the support of many people. Special thanks to Susan Ferber and the anonymous readers engaged by Oxford University Press. Their sage advice has made the book better. The following individuals read chapters and offered critique and encouragement: Hugh Agnew, Dina Boero, Chad Bryant, Gary Cohen, Daniel W. Crofts, Holly Haynes, Ben Jacobs, Howard Louthan, Dorothy Paces, Miloslav Paces, Mariel Paces Carter, Diane Pačes-Wiles, Krystyna Pindral, David Updike, Nancy M. Wingfield, Lisa Wolverton, and members of the East Europe / Eurasia Working Group at the University of North Carolina–Chapel Hill. Katerina Čapková and Celia Donert generously shared their knowledge of Prague's Jewish and Roma communities. Thank you to the helpful staff members at Prague's archives, libraries, and museums who aided my research.

Awards from The College of New Jersey made my research and writing possible. Thank you to the Support of Scholarly Activities and Sabbatical Councils for supporting this project. Thank you also to the Dean's Office in the School of Humanities and Social Sciences, the Office of Academic Affairs, and the Department of History at TCNJ.

The Shared Space writing group at The College of New Jersey has created a community of friends and scholars who write together every week. The members share one another's triumphs and frustrations and make writing something to look forward to. This book would not have been written without this extraordinary group of women. Thank you to my friends and colleagues who believed in me and this project: Eliza Ablovatski, Chris Ault, Matthew Bender, Elizabeth Borland, James Carter, Sarah Darrow, Laura Hargreaves, Craig Hollander, Lisa Kirschenbaum, Michael Marino, Christine Marks, Robert McGreevey, Robert Nemes, Tyler Sauers, Felicia Steele, Wendy Urban-Mead, Ann Warner-Ault, Nancy M. Wingfield, and Patty Witt.

I suffered an unexpected tragedy while writing this book. My partner Ben Jacobs died suddenly in February 2022. Ben read every word I wrote, expressed enthusiasm for the project, and unfailingly gave me his love and support. His belief in me propelled me to write through my grief. Profound thanks to the entire Jacobs clan, who welcomed me into their family many years ago. Words can hardly express my love and admiration for Ben's daughters, Hannaliese Jacobs and Fiona Jacobs.

Our scholarly community lost an incomparable mentor when István Deák passed away in January 2023. His extended family of students carries on his work to understand Central Europe as a complex and diverse region. I have relied on this community's scholarship and insights throughout this project. Hopefully, István's wit and lively style have made their way into this book.

I have had the good fortune of sharing Prague with friends, students, and family while working on this book. Thank you for helping me see the city through fresh eyes, Matthew Bender, Christine Marks, Charlotte Paces-Carter, Mariel Paces Carter, David Updike, and the TCNJ students from my Holocaust and Genocide Study Tours.

David Updike entered my life late in this project. His impeccable editing skills, steadiness, encouragement, and love got me to the finish line. His unique way of seeing the world, somewhat at an angle and with all its complexities, reminds me of Prague itself.

My family has been a part of this project from the beginning. My talented sister Diane Pačes-Wiles read drafts, talked through ideas, and held me up with her gentle strength. She and her family, John, Elena, and Evan Pačes-Wiles, have shared fun and laughter in Prague's Christmas markets, parks, and pubs. My parents, Milo and Dorothy Paces, infused a sense of history in me from my earliest childhood, and their generosity has supported many trips to Prague. Thank you to my parents and my grandparents, Karel and Marie Pačes, for nurturing our Prague 10 home, the heart of my own family story.

My daughters inspire me every day, and this book is for them. Mariel Paces Carter worked as my editorial assistant over the summer of 2024. I am in awe of her literary gifts, editing skills, and ability to organize information. Charlotte Paces-Carter kept us entertained and infused our home with her unequaled joie de vivre. Our trip to Prague in 2022 healed me in ways I cannot put into words.

And to Prague—you have been my second home for over thirty years, but you continue to surprise me. Thank you.

A Note on Language

PRAGUE'S COMPLEX HISTORY has generated multiple versions of place names. Political leaders renamed streets, squares, and landmarks to commemorate historical events and public figures compatible with contemporary values. As a multilingual space, Prague place names have German and Czech versions, and many well-known sites also have English versions. My principle has been to make the book accessible to a broad readership and to balance linguistic complexity with comprehensibility. Rather than implementing a single rule, I employ the terms most familiar to a broad audience. For place names, I use familiar English names where possible—for example, Prague, Vienna, Wenceslas Square, Prague Castle, and Old Town. For places without well-known English equivalents, I use the current Czech versions, such as Vyšehrad and Žižkov. When appropriate, I provide the German place name upon first mention. I refer to the region that now corresponds to the territory of the Czech Republic as the "Bohemian Lands" or "Bohemia." These historical terms encompass Bohemia, Moravia, and a small part of Silesia. As opposed to the term "Czech Lands," using "Bohemia" acknowledges the multiethnic composition of the region throughout most of its history. The current Czech government accepts both English terms "Czech Republic" and "Czechia." I have elected to use Czech Republic throughout.

Prague's historical figures often have Czech, German, English, and other versions of their names. For saints whose names have obvious equivalents, I use the English version, for example, John of Nepomuk (instead of Jan Nepomucký or Johannes Nepomuk) and Saint Wenceslas (instead of Svatý Václav). I also use the English versions for royal and imperial leaders, such as Charles IV, John of Luxembourg, and Francis Joseph. I refer to all other historical figures by their Czech or German birth names, for example, Jan Hus, Franz Kafka, Tomáš G. Masaryk, Božena Němcová, and Václav Havel.

Czech is a difficult language to pronounce, and readers will encounter various diacritical marks, which change a letter's sound. A *haček* (hook) softens a letter's pronunciation, so, for example, an *š* sounds like the English *sh*, *č* is equivalent to *ch*, and *ě* becomes *nye*. A *c* is pronounced *ts*, as in Václav Havel. An accent mark over a vowel or *y* lengthens the sound.

The bibliography focuses on works in English and English-language translations of Czech and German texts.

Timeline of Prague History

c. early ninth century	First fortifications at Prague Castle
c. late ninth century	According to medieval chronicles, the Přemyslid duke Bořivoj and his wife Ludmila accept Christianity. Bořivoj fortifies Prague Castle and builds the church of the Virgin Mary, the first Christian church in Prague.
c. 929 or 935	Duke Wenceslas murdered and buried in Prague
1002	Bohemia becomes part of the Holy Roman Empire.
c. 1120	Cosmas begins work on *The Chronicle of the Czechs*.
1198	Bohemia elevated to a hereditary kingdom under Přemysl Otakar I
	Agnes founds Franciscan Monastery in Old Town.
1253–1278	Expansion of Bohemia under Přemysl Otakar II, who invites German settlers to Prague and grants rights to Jews. Lesser Town is founded beneath Prague Castle.
c. 1270	Old New Synagogue founded
1306	Last Přemyslid king Wenceslas III dies. John of Luxembourg elected king of Bohemia
1316	The future Charles IV, son of John of Luxembourg and Elisabeth of Bohemia, is born in Prague.
1346–1378	Reign of Charles IV. Prague becomes the capital of the Holy Roman Empire, and Charles founds Prague University, St. Vitus Cathedral, the Stone Bridge, and New Town.
1389	Massacre of Prague Jews
1409	Jan Hus becomes rector of Prague University and leads church reform movement.

1410	Astronomical clock unveiled on Old Town Hall
1415	Jan Hus found guilty of heresy and executed
1419–1437	Hussite Wars
1458–1471	Reign of Hussite king George of Poděbrady
1471–1526	Jagiellonian dynasty reigns in Bohemia. Vladislav Hall built at Prague Castle
1526	Ferdinand I of Habsburg becomes king of Bohemia, beginning three centuries of Habsburg rule.
1569–1601	Jewish Quarter flourishes under leadership of Mordechai Maisel and Rabbi Loew.
1576	Rudolph II moves the imperial court to Prague. Arts and sciences flourish.
1618	The Second Defenestration of Prague launches the Thirty Years War.
1620	Bohemian defeat at the Battle of White Mountain
1621	Execution of twenty-seven Bohemian rebels on Old Town Square
1648	Swedish retreat from Prague. End of the Thirty Years War.
1650	Marian Column erected on Old Town Square
1704–1755	St. Nicholas Church built in the Lesser Town
1740–1780	Reign of Maria Theresa. Wars of Austrian Succession. Renovation of Prague Castle
1744	Maria Theresa expels Prague's Jews.
1781 and 1782	Joseph II issues Edicts of Toleration, giving rights to Protestants and Jews.
1787	W. A. Mozart conducts the premiere of *Don Giovanni* in Prague.
1848	Prague uprising during Europe's Springtime of Nations. Pan-Slav Congress held in Prague
1881	Opening of the Czech National Theater
1888	Czech speakers gain control of the Prague Board of Aldermen.
1896	Demolition of Prague's Jewish Quarter begins.
1912	Franz Kafka publishes *Description of a Struggle*.
1914–1918	World War I. Prague faces martial law, food shortages, and workers' strikes.
1918	Czechoslovak independence declared. Tomáš G. Masaryk elected first president

1924	Death of Franz Kafka
1935	Tomáš G. Masaryk steps down. Edvard Beneš becomes Czechoslovakia's second president.
1937	Death of Tomáš G. Masaryk
1938	Sudetenland ceded to Germany in Munich Agreement. Beneš resigns. Emil Hácha forms Second Czechoslovak Republic.
1939	Nazi Germany annexes Bohemia and Moravia and occupies Prague.
1941	First deportation of Prague Jews
1942	Assassination of Nazi official Reinhard Heydrich in Prague by Czechoslovak resistance fighters
1945	Prague residents participate in the May uprising against Nazi occupiers. Red Army aids in the liberation of Prague.
1945–1948	Coalition of socialist parties forms Third Czechoslovak Republic. Beneš resumes presidency.
1948	Communist Party of Czechoslovakia takes power. Klement Gottwald becomes president. Death and funeral of Beneš
1951	Slánský Show Trial of fourteen leading Communists
1953	Klement Gottwald dies.
1955	The largest Stalin Monument in the world unveiled in Prague
1962	Stalin Monument demolished
1968	Alexander Dubček becomes general secretary of the Communist Party. Prague Spring reform movement ends with Warsaw Pact invasion of Czechoslovakia.
1969	Gustav Husák becomes general secretary of the Communist Party and leads normalization era.
1977	Charter 77 published
1979–1983	Dissident Václav Havel serves his longest prison term.
1989	Velvet Revolution topples the Communist government.
1990	Havel sworn in as president. Government launches privatization schemes.
1992	Velvet divorce of Czech Republic and Slovak Republic. Havel elected president of Czech Republic
2003–2013	Presidency of Václav Klaus

2011	Death of Václav Havel
2013–2023	Presidency of Miloš Zeman
2020	New Marian Column erected on Old Town Square
2022	Return of the Stones memorial unveiled in Žižkov's Old Jewish Cemetery
2023	Petr Pavel defeats Andrej Babiš in presidential election.

Introduction

ALL THIS IS PRAGUE

> Like berets hurled into the air
> Berets of boys, cocottes and cardinals
> Turned into stone by the sorcerer Žito
> at the great feast
> Berets with Chinese lanterns
> on the eve of St John's Day
> when fireworks go up
> Yet also like a town of umbrellas opened skyward as a
> shield against rockets
> All this is Prague
> —VÍTĚZSLAV NEZVAL, "Panorama of Prague"

IN 1936, THE writer and critic Vítězslav Nezval described a joyful Prague, where people toss their caps into the air while fireworks and lanterns illuminate the night sky. Yet, the sorcerer Žito also lurks in Nezval's Prague. The character from medieval Czech legends turns "boys, cocottes and cardinals" into statues, and Prague's revelers have only flimsy umbrellas to ward off rocket attacks. Nezval reconciles his whimsical yet ominous depiction by concluding: "All this is Prague."[1]

Prague's architectural richness and geographical beauty have inspired romantic descriptions, but they only tell a partial story. Poets and scholars have called Prague the Golden City, the City of One Hundred Spires, the Mother of Cities, and the Mistress of All Bohemia. At the height of the Cold War, the Italian Slavicist Angelo Maria Ripellino called it Magic Prague. His nostalgia for the city led him to speculate: "Now that I am far from her, perhaps forever, I catch myself wondering whether Prague really exists or whether she is not an imaginary land." His work focused on the "bewitched kaleidoscope" of early modern Prague, characterized by "the ravings of alchemists...and the philosopher's stone, Tycho Brahe and Kepler, the Golden Lane, the animal and vegetable physiognomies of Arcimboldo, Rabbi Loew and his homunculus Golem, the fearful, misshapen Ghetto, [and] the old Jewish Cemetery." Even writers who acknowledged Prague's dark side used fanciful language to describe the city. Franz Kafka called his birthplace a mother with claws, but Ripellino retorted, "She is no 'mother' (*matička*).... She is an enticer, an inconstant paramour."[2] Albert Camus surmised that an evil spirit enchanted Prague at night, but in daylight, the sun revealed "an elaborate setting that looked as if it were cut out of gold paper."[3]

Since the fall of communism in 1989, Prague has become one of the most visited cities in Europe, a magnet for tourists, students, and writers looking for inspiration. Travelers seek the magical city that inspired Mozart's playful operas and fed Kafka's haunted dreams. Intellectuals embrace the capital city where philosophers and playwrights ascended to the presidency. Whereas poets and tourists search for the city's transcendent qualities, the Prague-born scholar Peter Demetz worried that emphasizing mystery and decadence obscures "the fullness of Prague history."[4] Prague writer Ivan Klíma likewise warned, "The word 'paradox' also applies to the spirit of this city." A Holocaust survivor and dissident during the Communist era, Klíma claimed, "A Czech writer today would hesitate to write that his city was 'magical' or 'mystical'; he might even hesitate to think so." In his essay "The Spirit of Prague," Klíma acknowledged the "remarkable and stimulating blend of three cultures that lived side by side… the Czech, German, and Jewish cultures." Yet, for him, "the unfreedom, the life of servitude, the many ignominious defeats and cruel military occupations" shaped Prague's history.[5] Klíma's paradox serves as a guiding principle of this book, which examines Prague's many contradictions: central and peripheral; cosmopolitan and provincial; and progressive and intolerant.

──────── ◆ ────────

Prague is often called the heart of Europe. While not the precise geographical midpoint, the city has long served as a meeting place of cultures. Germans, Czechs, and Jews, as well as artisans and traders from all corners of Europe, have called Prague home. In the sixth century CE, the Czechs' Slavic ancestors migrated westward from the Carpathian Mountain region to Central Europe. Slavic dukes and kings controlled Prague from the ninth to fourteenth centuries, but the Bohemian region was part of the German sphere of influence for most of its history. From 1002 to 1806, Bohemia was a polity within the Holy Roman Empire (also known as the Kingdom of the Germans), and the Germanic Habsburg dynasty ruled from 1526 to 1918. The city's dominant spoken language shifted between Czech and German, while Latin once served as the language of church and state. A complicated religious history also marks Prague's identity. Byzantine and Roman influences shaped the region's early Christian practices, though Bohemia eventually adopted the Latin Catholic rite. One of Europe's earliest Protestant movements began in Prague, which also once sheltered the largest Jewish community in Europe. Today, Prague governs a rather homogeneous nation-state, the Czech Republic, which ranks as one of the most secular countries in the world.

During its long history, Prague vacillated from a center of power to a peripheral city within larger empires. It was the seat of the Bohemian duchy and the Kingdom of Bohemia. Twice it served as the leading city of the Holy Roman Empire, and it has been the capital of Czechoslovakia and the Czech Republic. In other eras, Prague was a provincial city within Austria-Hungary,

FIGURE 0.1 Map of contemporary Europe, highlighting Prague's central location.

an occupied territory of the German Third Reich, or a subordinate state within the Soviet sphere of influence. Over eleven centuries of history, Prague has experienced various forms of power: monarchic, imperial, democratic, authoritarian, and state socialist.

The fortunes of Prague's geography—a sharp bend in the Vltava (Moldau) River, a steep hill on its left bank, and a central location in Europe—created a unique canvas for historical events. A legacy of historic preservation and urban planning has allowed various styles to coexist. Romanesque, Renaissance, and Rococo buildings stand side by side on medieval squares. Baroque domes and Gothic church spires reach skyward while twisted medieval lanes open up onto spacious modern boulevards. Rather than feeling chaotic, Prague's manifold styles form a balanced aesthetic. The horizontal planes formed by the river and its bridges anchor the city's abundant spires and towers. This symmetry has made Prague an exemplar of genius loci, the spirit of place.[6] (See Color Plate 1.)

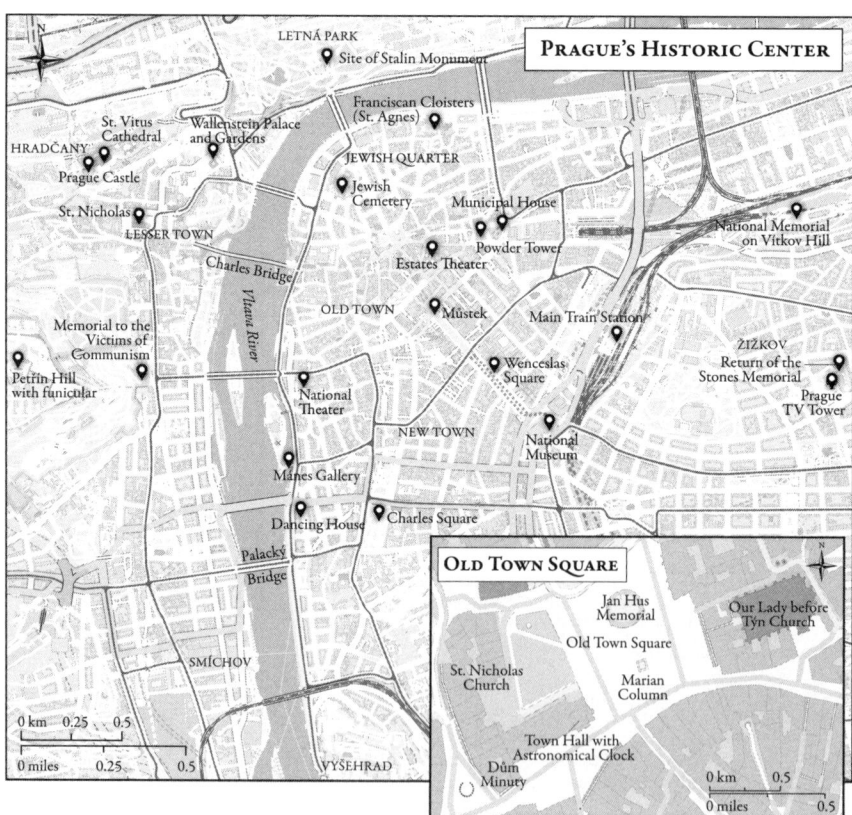

FIGURE 0.2 Major Historical Sites in Contemporary Prague.

Introduction

Prague's leaders understood this power of place and used architecture and public art to assert their authority. Czech dukes built Prague's earliest fortress on a craggy hill overlooking the river. Subsequent rulers commissioned churches and schools and founded Prague's four historical towns: Castle Town (Hradčany, Hradschin), Lesser Town (Malá Strana, Kleinseite), Old Town (Staré Město, Altstadt) with its small Jewish quarter, and New Town (Nové Město, Neustadt). In a city founded well over a thousand years ago, even its "new" town dates back nearly seven hundred years.

From the fifteenth to the nineteenth centuries, Bohemian kings rode through Prague's four historical towns en route to their coronations. The journey began at the border of the Old and New Towns, at the royal residence known as Králův Dvůr. The king's party rode through the arch of the fifteenth-century Gothic Powder Tower to process down Celetná Street

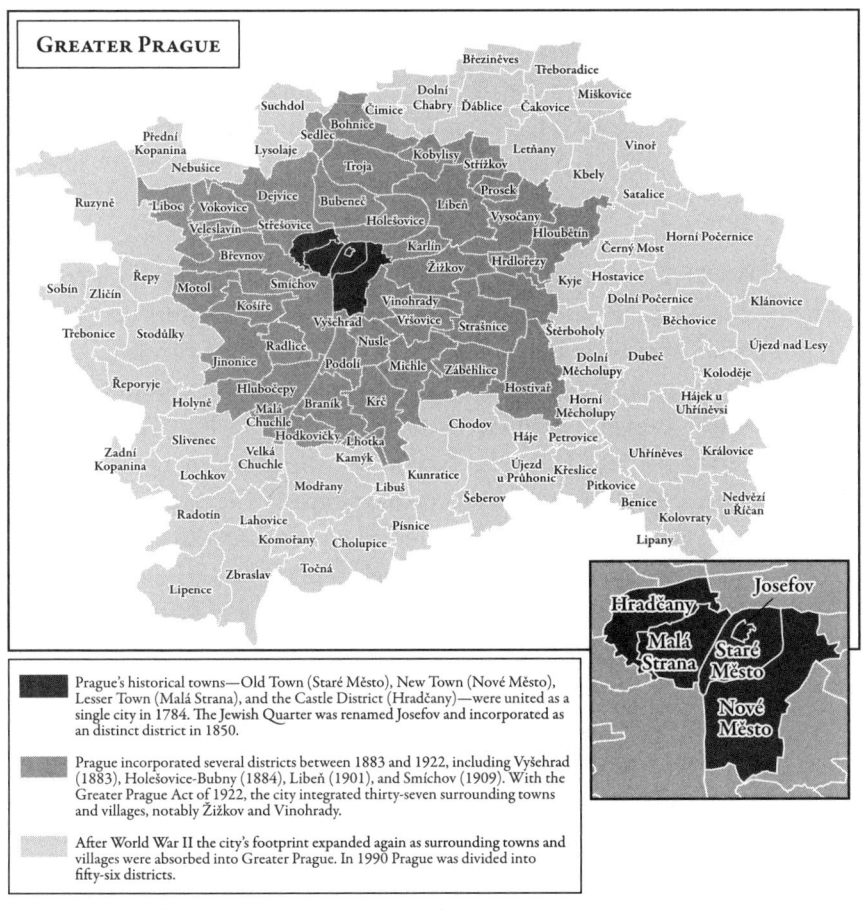

FIGURE 0.3 Map showing the expansion of Prague, 1784–1990.

(Zeltnergasse) into the Old Town Square. The king then proceeded to the Vltava River—the heart of Prague—and across the Stone Bridge (now Charles Bridge). The mayor of Lesser Town greeted the king and presented him with the keys to the city gate. The coronation party next climbed the steep path to Castle Town. Inside St. Vitus Cathedral, the archbishop of Prague bestowed the Crown of Saint Wenceslas on the new king, who pledged his loyalty to the Bohemian state.

In the twentieth century, Prague became the modern capital of a republic, and its borders expanded well beyond the historical core. The Greater Prague Act of 1921 incorporated neighborhoods, industrial districts, and independent towns into the city. As the population swelled past one million inhabitants, Prague also grew upward—multistory apartment buildings formed a fortress-like border on the city's outskirts.

In Prague, traces of the past form layers beneath the cobblestones, and disparate historical memories coexist. Charles IV founded Wenceslas Square in 1346 as Prague's Horse Market, and it has remained a center of trade and commerce for nearly seven centuries. An equestrian statue of St. Wenceslas has stood there since 1680, but the square was not renamed for Bohemia's patron saint until 1848. That year, a Catholic mass turned into a pitched battle between Czech liberals and the Austrian military. In 1918, crowds gathered on Wenceslas Square to celebrate the foundation of the Czechoslovak Republic, and two decades later, many of the same people returned to weep as Nazi German soldiers occupied their country. In May 1945, Prague's residents celebrated the arrival of the Red Army, which helped liberate the city from the Nazis. Yet, when Soviet tanks came to Wenceslas Square in August 1968, it was to stamp out the reform movement known as the Prague Spring. A few months later, university student Jan Palach protested the invasion in an act of self-immolation. The area near the National Museum, at the top of the square, became a makeshift shrine to the young man. In November 1989, thousands of Czechoslovak citizens crowded into Wenceslas Square chanting Jan Palach's name as they demanded regime change. Since then, citizens of the Czech Republic have come to the square to celebrate the 1998 Olympic gold medal in ice hockey, to protest government corruption, and to stand in solidarity with the people of Ukraine. Between these monumental events, Prague citizens and visitors shop, stroll, and dine in the heart of the city.

Traces of the past exist in all corners of Prague, much as a medieval palimpsest still holds the marks of erased texts.[7] At the turn of the twentieth century, the city of Prague destroyed much of the Jewish quarter in the name of modernity, leaving only five historical synagogues and the town hall. By this time, most Jews no longer lived in the ghetto, but traces of their rich history were lost in the rubble. Gustav Meyrink, a purveyor of horror tales who lived in the ghetto in the early twentieth century, called Prague "the city with the secret heartbeat." He wrote that the city "no longer seems real, but ghostly. Every person I know there turns into a ghost, an inhabitant of a realm that does not know death."[8] Franz Kafka walked through the ghetto construction sites to get to his elementary school and, as an adult, remarked to a friend, "Our heart knows nothing of the slum clearance which has been achieved. The unhealthy old Jewish town within us is far more real than the new hygienic town around us. With our eyes open we walk through a dream: ourselves only a ghost of a vanished age."[9] Both Meyrink and Kafka used the metaphor of a heart to contemplate Prague. Like them, the Italian writer Umberto Eco knew of the heart's dark potential. In his penultimate novel, *The Prague Cemetery*, which examines the roots of modern anti-Semitism, Eco explained, "You always want someone to hate in order to feel justified in your own misery. . . . [Y]ou can hate someone for your whole life—provided he's always there to keep your hatred alive. Hatred warms the heart."[10]

Prague's beauty can conceal the hatred that defined much of the city's past. In the early modern era, Protestants and Catholics took up arms against one another. In the nineteenth and twentieth centuries, Czech and German nationalists clashed on Prague's streets. Prague Jews shaped the city's history through their scholarly endeavors and philanthropic contributions. Yet, the Jewish community endured expulsions, violence, burdensome taxes, and blame for plagues and economic woes. For most of their history, Jews were relegated to the margins of Prague society: banned from living outside their ghetto and forbidden from pursuing certain economic and educational opportunities. Today, members of the Roma community, descendants of Vietnamese immigrants, and recent refugees experience prejudice and, at times, violence.

Prague's historical core survived World War II when relentless bombing raids decimated many other Central European cities. Still, the murder of most of Prague's Jewish population during the war destroyed no small part of the city's essence. The son of Prague Holocaust survivor Rabbi H. G. Adler explained what has been lost: "Prague remains a city of ghosts, crowded not by Jewish life, but by visitors who seek a vanished past."[11]

My relationship to Prague encompasses the personal and professional. In Prague, I learned to work as a historian, to pore through papers in chilly archives, and to contemplate the monuments, memorials, and architecture that have allured visitors, writers, and artists for centuries. It has been my object of study, and I have brought dozens of students to Prague to learn about its history, culture, and people.

Prague was also my family's home. As a child growing up in New York during the Cold War, I wondered about the mysterious place where my father was born. Little by little, I learned my family's story. My father was born during World War II when Prague was under Nazi occupation. After the Communist Party took control in 1948, the government nationalized my grandparents' small liquor manufactory, which produced cordials and sweet liqueurs in a workshop beneath the family home. My grandfather's political activities made staying in Prague impossible. The family escaped to Germany, where they lived in a displaced persons camp before sailing to New York in 1951. Remnants of my grandparents' Prague life shaped my American childhood—a needlepoint of the Charles Bridge, ginger ale served in beer glasses, and the Czech conversations of my grandparents' neighbors.

My grandfather lived to see the Velvet Revolution unfold on his television screen. In 1990, I studied in Prague and experienced the euphoria of free elections and a Rolling Stones concert advertised with the slogan "Tanks are rolling out. The Stones are rolling in." In 1991, I returned to Prague, and my grandfather visited the city for the first time in over forty years. Together, we walked to the church where he was baptized, met cousins I didn't know I had, and sipped coffees with whipped cream. I stood on Královická Street with him as he stared at his former house and business, now run-down and tired. A sign announced that the State Biological Institute occupied the former workshop space, and new families lived above. Just as Wenceslas Square contains disparate memories of the past, Prague's small neighborhoods hold layers of personal history and emotion.

My grandfather lived in or near Prague for the first forty years of his life, during which he was a citizen of six different political entities: the Austro-Hungarian Empire, the Nazi Protectorate of Bohemia and Moravia, and four distinct Czechoslovak Republics. That remarkable fact illuminates the complex history of Prague, a story this work aims to tell.

This book presents the political, cultural, and social history of Prague from the ninth to the early twenty-first centuries. Prague's famous leaders, writers, and artists feature prominently, but I also aim to give voice to the common people who have composed Prague's majority. Whenever possible, I highlight women's contributions as saints, abbesses, warriors, wealthy patronesses, politicians, artists, and writers, but I also recognize the ordinary women who worked, prayed, and raised generations of children. Artisans and workers built the city according to the visions of powerful rulers, but they did not often leave behind written records of their daily struggles. Their contributions are inscribed instead on the landscapes that have made Prague famous.

All this is Prague.

I

Foundations of Prague

A RIVER FLOWS through Europe's Central Uplands, a heavily forested region in the Alpine foothills. It travels southwest from Bohemia's Šumava Mountains and then turns sharply north. Terraces of shale, sandstone, quartz, and clay rise steeply, flanking each bank. Oceanic fossils embedded in the hillsides tell the story of glacial retreat at the end of the Great Ice Age, while knife-marked bones found in the fluvial deposits indicate that hominids have lived along the river since the Paleolithic Era, over seven thousand years ago.

Late ninth-century Frankish chronicles referred to the river as *Wilt awha*, a Germanic term meaning wild water. Eventually, the name morphed into Vltava in Czech, while German speakers began to use the name Moldau, perhaps to describe the muddy silt deposits that gave the river its murky brown hue. About 125 miles from its source, the river turns eastward but quickly corrects its path, forming a horseshoe shape. Ninth-century dukes fortified the hill above the sharp riverbend. The city that grew from there came to be known as Praha, Prag, Praga, or Prague.

Information about the region's early history is limited, but archaeological records suggest that Celts of the Boii tribe settled along the Vltava riverbanks near modern Prague somewhere between the fourth and fifth centuries BCE. Primarily agricultural, the Celts cultivated grain in the rich floodplain along the Vltava and supplemented their diet with honey and berries from the surrounding forests. The Boii influenced the development of Iron Age Central Europe and gave their name to Bohemia as well as to settlements whose names have survived as Bavaria and Bologna. An excavation site just south of modern Prague included fortifications, a metalworks, and ritual spaces, as well as anthropomorphic carvings, intricate jewelry, metal spears, pottery, glass, and gold coins. The Celts left Bohemia during the first two centuries of the Common Era, likely driven out by Roman-Germanic wars. Although nomadic German speakers settled temporarily along the river, Bohemia remained sparsely populated until the sixth century CE, when Slavic speakers migrated westward from Transcarpathia to the

Vltava River basin. Descendants of these Slavic migrants built the foundations of modern Prague on a hill above the Vltava River's left bank. Archaeologists have dated the oldest structures at Prague Castle (Prážský Hrad-Prager Burg)—a moat or ditch enclosing a fifteen-acre area and a wooden-staked palisade—to the early ninth century.

In this era, Bohemia was wedged between Great Moravia, the most powerful Slavic empire in Central Europe, and the Kingdom of the East Franks, a Germanic successor state to Charlemagne's vast territories. Scholars continue to debate where the ninth-century borders lay and the nature of Bohemia's relationship with each medieval state. Both empires influenced Bohemia's Christianization and political development. The oldest church building at Prague Castle was dedicated to the Virgin Mary and reflected Moravian architectural traditions in its simple rectangular nave and semicircular apse. The earliest known burial sites in Prague were found in the church crypt. A male skeleton lay with a warrior's sword, leading archaeologists to surmise it was the remains of an early Přemyslid duke, possibly Bořivoj's son Spytihněv. A gilded cross and a silver grape-cluster earring found near the female remains suggest the influence of Greater Moravian craft techniques, while other discoveries may point to Baltic, Viking, and East European burial traditions. Even in the early tenth century, Prague was a crossroads of cultures.[1]

Prague was not the first fortress in Bohemia, but it became the most important medieval settlement among a network of Vltava River fortifications. The narrow river valley widens significantly at Prague, forming a shallow basin that could be easily traversed by the merchants who traveled along European trade routes. Prague was a trading post on an important west–east route that extended from the Cordoban Caliphate through Regensburg, Prague, and Kraków and finally into Kievan Rus. A north–south route that connected cities from the Baltic Sea to Venice also ran through Prague. Ibrahim Ibn Ya'qūb, a traveler from Moorish Spain who was in Central Europe around 965 CE, wrote that Prague "is built with stones and limestone on the shore of a river which flows there. It is smaller than cities but bigger than villages. There is a market there in which one can buy all the goods which are necessary for travels or sedentary life. In the upper part of Prague, there is a big, fortified castle. There is a brook there, the water of which traverses the valley."[2]

Archaeological discoveries of clay and wooden ramparts, a stone fortification, and a broad, timbered road support Ibrahim's evocative description. By the late tenth century, the well-fortified Prague Castle complex functioned as a small town, housing numerous residences and three churches. Lime and stone ramparts replaced typical Slavic wooden fortifications called *gorgs*.

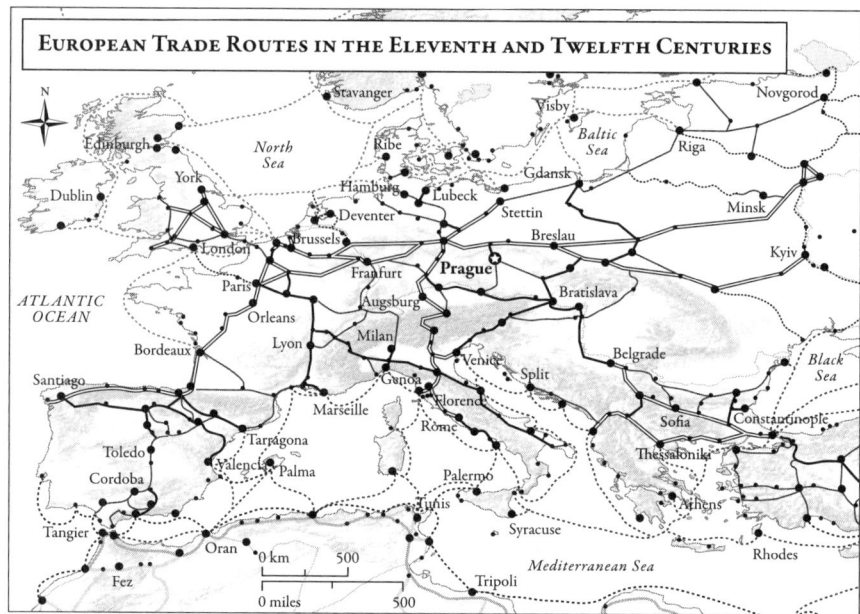

FIGURE 1.1 Prague was located near the crossroads of the major trade routes through Central Europe.

Several religious edifices were built in the ninth and tenth centuries. A cemetery, used from the tenth to the thirteenth centuries, stood just outside the castle walls. Archaeologists have remarked on the abundance of gold and silver ornaments buried with the dead, leading them to conclude that a wealthy aristocracy lived among the earliest Bohemian dukes.[3]

Below the castle, a second settlement developed along the river. Archaeologists have uncovered iron smelting furnaces from the ninth century and workshops for other metal production dating from the eleventh. The abundance of metal forges has led some scholars to conjecture that Prague's name derived from Slavic words for roasting or refining raw ore (*pražiti*, *prahnouti*) rather than threshold (*prah*), the most common supposition. Ibrahim visited the area's bustling market, which he described as "the richest place in goods. Russians and Slavs come there from Cracow with goods. Muslims, Jews, and Turks come there from the country of the Turks and bring goods.... Flour, tin, and various kinds of furs are exported from there." Ibrahim's text marked the first mention of Jews in Prague. Itinerant Jewish merchants served as intermediaries between Muslims and Christians, bringing Silk Road and Mediterranean luxury goods to Central Europe. A small Jewish community eventually settled near the market.

Ibrahim commented on local goods and touched upon the agriculture and diet of the residents. "In Prague, people make saddles, bridles, and round leather shields, which are all used in their country." He was impressed with the abundance of food: "Their land is the best in the north and the richest in food. For small change one gets enough wheat for a month." Archaeologists concur that Prague's early residents enjoyed a hearty diet that included grains, pork, beef, and dairy products.[4]

Beyond archaeological findings and scant textual evidence, much of Prague's early history is unknown. The earliest written sources that mention Prague are ninth-century East Frankish chronicles, where Bohemians appear as "wild Barbarians" and subordinates to the Frankish kings. Latin and Slavonic texts from the tenth and eleventh centuries recounted the lives of early Bohemian saints, but these hagiographies are considered formulaic, embellished, or even fabricated. The early twelfth-century Latin manuscript *The Chronicle of the Czechs* centered Prague as the dominant settlement within a Bohemian polity. The chronicle's erudite Latin prose and detailed descriptions of the Bohemian church and state make it an important, albeit unreliable, source. Written by Cosmas, a canon at the Prague Cathedral, when he was well into his seventies, the chronicle became the basis for ideas about the Bohemian state that have persisted into the twenty-first century.

Although Cosmas's foundation narratives influence ideas about Czech history and identity to this day, his claims and source base cannot be verified. Even Cosmas admitted, "Since these things are said to have occurred in ancient times, we leave it to the reader to judge whether they are fact or fiction." Cosmas described the settlement of Bohemia in biblical terms, following the great flood and the dispersal of linguistic groups from Babel. When an "honorable...simple, and righteous" group of Slavs arrived at Mount Říp, between the Ohře and Vltava Rivers, their leader reportedly declared, "This is it. This is the land that you often reminded me I promised you. A land subject to no one, filled with wild animals and fowl, wet with nectar, honey, and milk, and, as you yourselves see, delightful for living."[5]

Generations later, according to Cosmas, the nobleman Krok ruled a Czech settlement in the Bohemian forests. Krok was "exceptional for his wealth in secular things, discreet in considering lawsuits.... Like bees to their hive, so everyone...flocked to him." Krok had no sons but sired three daughters, each with an extraordinary power of healing, magic, or prophecy. The youngest, the prophetess Libuše, stepped forward to take her father's place upon his death. Cosmas described her as "younger by birth but older in wisdom...a woman among women: cautious in counsel, quick to speak, chaste in body, upright in character, second to no one in resolving the lawsuits of the people. Affable, even lovable, in all things, she adorned and glorified the feminine sex while handling masculine affairs with foresight."

Despite Libuše's attributes, Cosmas contends that male subjects resented her power. Following a land dispute that Libuše adjudicated, the disappointed plaintiff proclaimed, "O, the injuries hardly to be tolerated by men!... A woman full of cracks treats manly judgments with a deceitful mind.... They all have long hair, to be sure, but women are short on sense." Libuše's advisers warned her to take a husband to prevent a rebellion. She agreed to marry but warned her people that they faced a harsher future. "I am a woman, I live as a woman, and for that reason I seem to you to know too little. Because I do not judge you with a rod of iron and since you live without fear, you rightly look down on me. For where fear is, there is honor." She warned that a male ruler would wield power for himself and determine his subjects' futures: "some slaves, some peasants, some taxpayers, some tax collectors."

Libuše summoned her sisters, "who stirred up matching rages." That night, she entered a trance and received visions of her future husband. Cosmas explained that Libuše directed her counselors to journey beyond the mountains to a village on the Bilina River where they would find a farmer plowing a field with a pair of oxen. Libuše would take this peasant as her husband, but she warned that he "will think up many laws upon your necks and heads." Libuše's advisers set out as directed and found the farmer. They adorned him in rich cloaks to bring him to his princess bride, but the humble plowman insisted on keeping his muddied and broken boots "so that our descendants will know whence they sprang." The marriage united a mystical princess with a humble cultivator of the Bohemian earth. Because Libuše encountered him in a vision, he became known as Duke Přemysl, a Slavic word meaning "forethought." His Přemyslid descendants ruled Bohemia until 1306.

Cosmas reported that following her marriage, Libuše received another powerful revelation. "I see a burg," she told her husband and the local elders, "whose fame touches the stars, situated in a forest, thirty stades [about three miles] distant from the village where the Vltava strongly fortifies it." She sent her advisers to a rocky mountain called Petřin, "curved like a dolphin, a sea pig, stretching to the aforementioned stream.... When you come to that place, you will find a man putting up the doorway of a house in the middle of the forest.... Since even a great lord must duck under a humble threshold—the city you will build, you will call 'Prague' [Praha, from *prah*, threshold]." Libuše foretold that "two golden olive trees will grow up; they will reach the seventh heaven with their tops and glitter throughout the whole world with signs and

FIGURE 1.2 Josef Václav Myslbek's nineteenth-century statues of Libuše and Přemysl, originally designed for the Palacký Bridge, now stand in a garden at Vyšehrad, ca. 1889–1897. Photo by the author.

miracles." Libuše's advisers found the place described in her vision, and there they built Prague, a town Cosmas called "the mistress of all Bohemia."

Cosmas likewise provided an origin story for Prague's secondary fortress, Vyšehrad (High Castle), which still looms over the Vltava today. While archaeologists have dated Vyšehrad's fortifications and a royal mint to the tenth and eleventh centuries, Cosmas connected the fortress's appearance to the end of an undefined ancient period following Libuše's death. Cosmas explained, "The maidens of that land, growing up without a yoke, pursuing military arms like Amazons and making leaders for themselves, fought to gather like young soldiers and trod manfully through the forests on hunts." When the women built a fortress on the Vltava's left bank, the men, "very jealous, built a burg among the bushes on another cliff, no farther than a trumpet call." Cosmas reported that the founders called the fort Chrasteň, after the native bushes there, but "present-day men call it Vyšehrad." The cunning maidens came to the fort, plied their male foes with mead, and then attacked the slumbering group. Despite their early victories, the women warriors eventually met their defeat on Vyšehrad's slopes. Cosmas concluded, "After the death of Princess Libuše, the women of our people are under the power of men."

Following the stories of Libuše and her descendants, Cosmas turned to Bohemia's Christianization. He used dates when describing events, the first being the baptism of the Přemyslid duke Bořivoj in 894 CE. Still, he admitted that, even in this section, his "pen was blunt." According to Cosmas, Bořivoj accepted the faith while visiting the Moravian emperor Svatopluk and received the sacrament from the Byzantine missionary Saint Methodius. Bořivoj is credited with founding the first church at Prague Castle, and medieval hagiographies called him "the first builder of holy places, the assembler of priests, and the founder of the Christian faith."

Ludmila, the wife of Duke Bořivoj, appeared in medieval texts as Prague's first Christian martyr and saint. Scholars have long debated the veracity of these accounts, which include an Old Church Slavonic prologue and a tenth-century Latin hagiography. Some doubt her existence altogether and point out the similarities between her attributes and those of Slavic pagan goddess figures.[6] Regardless, Ludmila played a central role in narratives that established the primacy of the Přemyslid dynasty in Bohemian politics and Czech Christianity. According to the hagiographies, Ludmila's great accomplishment was instilling the Christian faith in Wenceslas, her grandson and heir to the throne. When Wenceslas was thirteen, his father died, and his mother Drahomíra ruled as regent for her thirteen-year-old son. Medieval hagiographers blamed Drahomíra, a converted pagan princess, for Ludmila's murder.

Ludmila's martyrdom narrative followed a common arc of piety and submission to God's will. Upon hearing of the plots against her, Ludmila took refuge in Tetín Castle, near Prague, where the dowager queen "armed herself fully with the weapons of faith." As she prayed alone one night, she "began to chant psalms zealously, having strengthened herself with the reception of the body and blood of the Lord." When assassins broke into her room, Ludmila chastised them, "What manner of sudden insanity has set you off? Are you not ashamed and do you not remember how I nurtured you like my own sons?" Ludmila begged the men to behead her so she could "bear witness for Christ by shedding her blood in the manner of martyrs." Instead, they strangled her with her own veil. Believers reported miracles following Ludmila's death. Her assassins all died shortly after the murder, and her tomb at Tetín Castle emitted beautiful illuminations and "a wondrous aroma."[7]

When Wenceslas turned eighteen in 921, he took power from his mother and sought to return his grandmother's remains to what Cosmas called the "glorious city of Prague." Upon her exhumation, Wenceslas saw that her body had not decomposed, and he "wept a torrent of tears" in gratitude for this miracle. An early hagiography described the procession from Tetín to Prague Castle: "They then met the faithful bearers who were carrying the body of Saint Ludmila.... And immediately the priests and deacons joyfully placed it on their shoulders and carried it to the castle, praising God and singing psalms and verses of praise." They laid her body in St. George Basilica, and more miracles occurred—a lame woman walked, and a blind man regained his sight, thanks to the holy woman's intercessions.

Wenceslas joined his grandmother in Christian martyrdom several years later—either 929 or 935 CE. Hagiographies asserted that Boleslav lured his brother Wenceslas to Stará Boleslav, a fortification on the Elbe River. The brothers feasted and prayed together, but Boleslav intended to murder the duke and seize power. "After the Mass, Wenceslas wished to go home to Prague. But Boleslav, pleading mournfully, implored him: 'How can you wish to depart! I have the finest ale.'" Wenceslas agreed to stay but was attacked the following morning. According to the account, when Boleslav charged at his brother and drove a lance through his torso, the duke—like other Christian martyrs—echoed Jesus's last words: "Into your hands, Lord, I commend my spirit."

Medieval writers emphasized the duke's piety, charity, and learnedness rather than political or military accomplishments. One early account noted, "If [Wenceslas] happened upon God's servants, or household bondservants, or foreigners, or happened somewhere upon those exposed to the cold, he would clothe and feed them all. If some priests were sold, he came to him and would ransom him with all he had." Cosmas claimed that Wenceslas rose "every night from his noble bed, with bare feet and only one chamberlain, [and] went around to God's churches and gave alms generously to widows, orphans, those in prison and afflicted by every difficulty, so much so that he was considered, not a prince, but the father of all the wretched."

Following his death, Wenceslas became a symbol for Prague. The early twentieth-century historian Otakar Odložilík noted Wenceslas's malleable legacy: "The course of his life was very short and rather uneventful...[yet] few were so suitable to become the heroes of medieval legends as the young prince who was pious and peaceful and who died by his brother's hand on the threshold of a church."[8] Wenceslas was posthumously credited with making peace with neighboring German states, securing Bohemia's historical borders, and Christianizing the Bohemian nation. The duke's likeness appeared in public art beginning in the eleventh century. Přemyslid coins featured Wenceslas as a knight on horseback, as did the seventeenth- and twentieth-century equestrian statues on Prague's eponymous square. A fourteenth-century Prague University seal depicted Emperor Charles IV kneeling to his patron Wenceslas, and the most elaborate chapel in the Gothic St. Vitus Cathedral was dedicated to Saint Wenceslas. Even English speakers learned about "Good King Wenceslas" from the nineteenth-century Christmas carol that focused on the saint's charitable works.

Medieval texts had to reckon with Boleslav's legacy, since he became an important Přemyslid ruler after the death of his brother. Contemporary hagiographies claimed that Boleslav immediately regretted his deed and named his son—born on the very night of the murder—Strachkvas, meaning terrifying feast. A hagiography stated, "Boleslav, acknowledging to the Lord God what a great sin he had committed, prayed to God and all the saints and sent his servants to bring the body of his brother Wenceslas from Boleslav's city to the glorious city in Prague." The martyr was laid to rest at St. Vitus Rotunda, a church commissioned by Wenceslas himself. (See Color Plate 2.)

Boleslav has been credited with cultivating Bohemia's relationship with the Roman church. Cosmas wrote that Boleslav implored Bishop Michael of Regensburg to consecrate the church his brother had built at Prague Castle. Cosmas conjectured that Michael "would scarcely have agreed to it, except he determined it to be in memory of the soul and for the salvation of his friend...now slain." His chronicle described the joyful scene: "All the devoted common folk and magnates and clergy rushed to meet the arriving bishop and received him with great honor and rejoicing in the buildings of the metropolis of Prague." Cosmas named the date of the church's consecration as September 22, 929, which is still celebrated as Saint Wenceslas's feast day.

By the time of Wenceslas's martyrdom, the Great Moravian Empire had fallen to Hungarian invaders, so Bohemia became increasingly tied to its western Germanic neighbors. Some historians credit Boleslav I with conducting a series of wars that expanded Bohemia's territory eastward into present-day Poland and Belarus. Still, it is impossible to ascertain the position of Prague and the Přemyslid family this early in history. From the tenth to the twelfth centuries, the Přemyslid dukes consolidated power over secular and ecclesiastical matters and took control of regional fortifications, taxes, tolls, and mining rights. They increasingly controlled the narrative of the region's achievements. Other powerful noble families continued to challenge the centralization of power, a trend that would continue in Bohemia for centuries.

Cosmas credited Boleslav I's children, Boleslav II and his sister Mlada, with founding religious institutions and strengthening Prague's connection to the church. According to the chronicles, Mlada traveled on a diplomatic mission to Rome to negotiate the establishment of a Prague bishopric. She returned determined to establish a Benedictine monastery for women in the city. Cosmas described Mlada as "a virgin devoted to God, learned in sacred letters…charming to talk to, a generous patron of paupers and orphans." Following their father's death, Boleslav II added a convent to the Romanesque Basilica of St. George at Prague Castle. Its nuns followed Saint Benedict's rule, venerated the Virgin Mary, and developed a cult around the memory of

FIGURE 1.3 St. George Basilica, founded 920 CE. The church has been renovated and expanded several times. A Benedictine convent was founded there in 973; the two towers were erected between 1145 and 1151; and a Baroque facade was added in the late seventeenth century. Photo by Jerzy Strzelecki, CC BY-SA 3.0 via Wikimedia Commons.

Mlada's great-grandmother, the martyr Saint Ludmila. Today, St. George's Basilica is the oldest surviving church at Prague Castle.

The Catholic Church finally bestowed Prague with a bishopric in 973 and named Thietmar (Dětmar), a Saxon priest conversant in Slavic languages, its first leader. The Bohemian church was placed under the jurisdiction of the archbishop of Mainz, an important city within the Kingdom of the East Franks. The bishopric's location at Prague Castle gave the Přemyslid dukes an advantage in mediating church-state relations and likely played a role in the family's eventual supremacy in Bohemia.

Prague's second bishop, Adalbert (Vojtěch), took office around 982. Adalbert hailed from Bohemia and belonged to the Slavníkid clan, a rival of the Přemyslids. Hagiographies described the bishop's frustration with the persistence of paganism and polygamy in Bohemia. While he met resistance to his reforms, Adalbert successfully established new religious institutions in Prague. Together with Boleslav II, Adalbert established Břevnov, Prague's first Benedictine monastery for men. Located just west of Prague Castle, Břevnov purportedly took its name from a wooden branch (*břevno*) that floated in a bubbling brook at the spot Adalbert consecrated. Archaeological evidence suggests that the first monks at Břevnov lived and prayed in temporary wooden structures, which were eventually replaced by stone residences and a Romanesque church with three naves and a crypt. Břevnov became a center of Christian learning and beer production. Until the thirteenth century, only sanctioned monasteries could brew and sell ale, and Břevnov monopolized Prague's beer production for over two centuries. The monastery thus contributed to the gastronomic and religious histories of Bohemia.

Despite this joint achievement, the Přemyslids and Slavníkids continued to feud. Cosmas reported that in 995, Boleslav II led a violent attack against the Slavníkid clan. Five of Adalbert's brothers died in the massacre, and, in fear, Adalbert left Prague. The pope granted his request to work as an itinerant missionary, but according to medieval hagiographies, Adalbert died within a few years of leaving Prague. He met his fate in the Baltic Sea town of Truso, where pagan priests murdered him and sold his body to the Polish king for its weight in gold. When news of Adalbert's fate reached Prague, a cult of followers grew around the once-unpopular bishop. He joined Wenceslas and Ludmila as an exalted Bohemian saint and protector of Prague, but his relics remained abroad.

◆

The incorporation of the Bohemian duchy into the Holy Roman Empire in the early eleventh century marked a new era for Prague. The city's history would be linked to Europe's vast Germanic empire for the next eight centuries. The Holy Roman Empire was established in 800 CE by Charlemagne, king of the Franks, who was crowned emperor by the pope. Charlemagne proclaimed he was reviving the Christian Roman Empire, and his son Louis inherited his father's titles in 814. Upon Louis's death in 840, the empire was divided among his sons. The western region, the Kingdom of the West Franks, became the centralized French kingdom, but the Kingdom of the East Franks was a looser polity composed of duchies, city-states, church lands, and other territories. East Frankish leaders chose a king from the various polities, and the pope conferred the title of Holy Roman emperor upon him. He also used the secular titles King of the Romans and King of the Germans. The Bohemian dukes paid tributes to the Holy Roman emperor and supported his military campaigns. Alliances with the German rulers likely contributed to the ascendancy of the Přemyslid clan in Bohemia.

The military successes of Přemyslid duke Břetislav I increased Prague's power. Břetislav retook Moravia from Poland in 1034 and installed his Přemyslid relatives at Moravian and Bohemian settlements. In 1039, Břetislav I attacked Poland and retrieved the remains of Adalbert and his brother Gaudencius from Gniezno, Poland's ecclesiastical capital. Polish church leaders disputed Břetislav's account and insisted that the Bohemian king had stolen the wrong body. Nonetheless, according to Cosmas, a jubilant crowd of clergy and laymen gathered at Prague's city gates and followed the triumphant duke to St. Vitus Rotunda at Prague Castle. Adalbert was interred near the remains of Saint Wenceslas, and his grave attracted pilgrims from Bohemia, Moravia, Poland, and Hungary. Prague was becoming a hub of secular power and sacred authority. To this day, both St. Vitus Cathedral in Prague and the Royal Cathedral at Gniezno claim that St. Adalbert rests there. (See Color Plate 3.)

Vratislav II, Břetislav's son and heir, continued his father's work to increase Bohemia's prestige in Central Europe. Prague's wealth attracted non-Slavic settlers, and in 1080, Vratislav granted judicial privileges to resident Jews, Germans, and Italians. In 1085, in recognition of his fierce loyalty and support in military campaigns, the Holy Roman emperor Henry IV bestowed on Vratislav the nonhereditary title of king of Bohemia.

Medieval sources credit Vratislav with strengthening Prague's secondary fortress of Vyšehrad. Cosmas's narrative suggests that Vratislav relocated his court there to gain autonomy from the Prague bishopric, led by his irascible brother Jaromír. The fraternal conflict described by Cosmas was perhaps a metaphor for church-state discord, but archaeological and church records do

FIGURE 1.4 St. Martin's Church at Vyšehrad is the largest and oldest preserved rotunda in Prague. Originally built in the late eleventh century, it was restored in the nineteenth and twentieth centuries. Photo by the author.

substantiate Vyšehrad's expansion in the late eleventh century. The new parish church, St. Martin's Rotunda, featured a unique Romanesque design with meter-thick walls, a parabolic-shaped apse, and a cupola decorated with celestial images. Vratislav also established the St. Peter and St. Paul Chapter at Vyšehrad. The non-monastic clerical college reported directly to Rome rather than to the Prague bishop. Some sources suggest that the Slavonic mass endured at Vyšehrad despite the pope's and bishops' insistence on the exclusive use of Latin.

A new marketplace sprung up below Vyšehrad, just as one had developed beneath Prague Castle a century earlier. The neighborhood attracted wealthy and diverse residents, including Jews. Cosmas claimed that Duchess Wilpirk remarked on the Jews' influence there: "You will never grow more rich nor be more glorified than in the suburb of Prague and the village of Vyšehrad. There are the Jews most filled with gold and silver, there the richest merchants from every land, there the wealthiest money changers, there the market in which the abundant spoils are more abundant than your warriors."

Cosmas's description reflected the medieval association of Jews with wealth and greed. Anti-Semitic violence spread in Central Europe during the First Crusade. In 1096, en route to Jerusalem, French and German knights massacred Jews in several Rhineland settlements—Speyer, Cologne, and Mainz—and continued east, where they attacked Prague's Jewish community. Cosmas belittled Jews who rejected conversion: "With God permitting it, they attacked the Jews and baptized them against their will, killing those who objected.... The Jews, after not many days, cast off the yoke of Christ, spurned the grace of baptism and the salvation of the Catholic faith, and again submitted their necks to the yoke of Mosaic law."

Over the next few years, many Prague Jews sought to leave Bohemia for Hungary or Poland. Yet the Přemyslid duke Břetislav II would not permit them to take their possessions abroad, claiming that Jewish property belonged to the Crown. Břetislav's soldiers ransacked Jewish homes, taking "their treasures and...whatever furniture seemed the best." Even Cosmas commented on the Jews' fate. "They left them nothing, not even a grain of corn, except what pertained to the victim alone. O, how much money was taken from the wretched Jews that day!" Despite the anti-Semitic culture that dominated Europe, Prague Jews retained important roles in the economic development of their city.

As Prague's population grew in the eleventh and twelfth centuries, large numbers of Jews and Christians alike relocated to the Vltava's right bank to escape the unsanitary, crowded conditions below the castle. Prosperous freemen and merchants moved across the river, where the flatter terrain was more hospitable for new homes and private chapels. Monastic orders and foreign communities funded houses of worship constructed from uniform stone blocks manufactured in nearby quarries. By the early twelfth century, eight new churches stood on Prague's right bank, each architecturally distinct. St. John the Baptist, erected on the riverbank between 1120 and 1122 following a devastating tornado and flood, featured a typical single-nave Romanesque design. Later in the century, the church was renovated into a small but architecturally significant building with three semicircular apses, vaulted roofs, and a tall tower.[9] Nearby stood an early twelfth-century rotunda, the Finding of the Holy Cross, constructed from small square stones. The chapel had an elaborate lantern adorned with a gold-plated crescent moon, an eight-pointed star hung from the vaulted cupola, and an ornately decorated arched frieze framed the semicircular apse. The building engineers designed the rotunda for superior acoustics by embedding ceramic bottles into the walls. The first known Czech choral anthem, "Hospodine pomiluj ny" (Lord, have mercy on us), may have been heard within its walls. The chapel's unique name likely refers to its location at the right bank's main crossroads. A more fanciful story that emerged years later described a Christian girl who had converted against her parents' wishes and was crucified and thrown into a pond upon her cross. The cross rose to the surface during a violent storm but soon disappeared again. Years later, long after the pond dried up, workers discovered a rotted wooden cross embedded in the rotunda's foundation.

Prague's rapid growth occurred in an era that archaeologists and historians call the medieval transformation. Improved tools, crop cultivation, soil enrichment, and animal husbandry enabled rural areas to support larger urbanized centers in Central Europe. During the reign of Vladislav II, Prague Castle was refortified, and in 1172, Prague's first stone bridge spanned the Vltava River. Named for Vladislav's wife, the Judith Bridge comprised twenty Romanesque sandstone arches on an oak foundation. It replaced unstable wooden footbridges and connected the flourishing economies on both sides of the river. A Jewish chronicler remarked that Vladislav had "brought with him from Italy artists, masons, and built for majesty and glory for the joyfully bustling city of Prague the great, beautiful bridge over the [Vltava] River, to which none can compare in length, width, height, strength and beauty in all the area of Ashkenaz."[10] The Judith Bridge—only the third stone bridge in Central Europe—boosted Prague's importance on European trade routes.

The city continued to develop on the right bank. A sizable Christian cemetery at Malé náměstí (Small Square / Kleiner Ring) had over 120 graves, but within two or three generations, the land was deemed too valuable for that purpose. Builders created a marketplace by layering pebbled pavement atop the gravesites. The unstable ground could not accommodate the new buildings, and the square caved in, creating a macabre site of coffins and bodies emerging from the ground. Once it was reconstructed, Malé náměstí became a trade and communication hub with at least sixty-three Romanesque houses constructed there between 1179 and 1230. The simple houses, built with wooden scaffolding and square stones, gave this Prague residential area an unprecedented uniformity. The multifunctional houses served as workshops, warehouses, and upstairs residences for those involved in local and long-distance trade. Wooden stalls, where merchants and artisans displayed their goods, stood in front of the homes. Narrow access corridors between the buildings led to rear-facing entrances and small back buildings used for storage and cooking. Three larger homes, known as palaces, belonged to Prague's wealthiest merchants or Bohemian noblemen who sought an urban residence away from their estates.

As the name "Small Square" implies, Malé náměstí could not accommodate the expanding trade sector. Foreign merchants, who sold goods ranging from Iberian pottery to West Asian glassware, required facilities such as inns, warehouses, churches, and a hospital. The area, later known as Old Town Square (Staroměstské náměstí / Altstädter Ring), was built in the eleventh century to support the growing population. German-speaking merchants called the square's administrative and customs center Ungelt, the medieval German word for tax or toll. The Prague court charged foreign merchants fees in exchange for facilities and some political and economic rights. Old Town Square benefited from urban planning. In the early thirteenth century, city officials designed the new marketplace with straight borders. Tradesmen and shopkeepers lived in houses with deep, vaulted cellars where they could store goods and tools.

By the early twelfth century, there were four distinct settlements on Prague's right bank. The largest was directly across from Prague Castle, and the three others were to the south toward Vyšehrad. The city supported an increasingly diverse economy, and the name "Prague" came to describe a bigger area than the original castle settlement. The ironworks that employed many residents moved to the city's periphery, leaving the center a safer and more pleasant environment for its inhabitants. Merchants from other regions came to Prague to sell goods and then stayed. By 1230, the right bank housed more than four thousand residents and twenty-two houses of worship. Prague had become a small medieval city and a powerful Slavic center within the mostly Germanic Holy Roman Empire.

In 1198, Duke Přemysl Otakar I declared himself the king of Bohemia and had himself crowned in Mainz, an important archbishopric within the Holy Roman Empire. By judiciously navigating feuds among various rulers within the empire, Otakar I secured unprecedented rights for Bohemia and its capital, Prague. Emperor Frederick II rewarded Otakar for his loyalty and military support by issuing the Golden Bull of Sicily, affirming Bohemia's status as a hereditary kingdom. Unlike Vladislav II a century earlier, Přemysl Otakar I could pass his royal title to his descendants. The golden bull exempted Bohemia from most obligations to the emperor, except for participation in the imperial councils.

When Přemysl Otakar I died in 1230, his son, King Wenceslas I, ascended the throne. As a hereditary king, he used the reign number "I" to distinguish himself from Duke Wenceslas, Bohemia's patron saint. Wenceslas I invested considerable resources in Prague's infrastructure, especially on the right bank. He granted town privileges to the settlements there and commissioned fortifications, city walls, and a moat to protect the profitable marketplaces and delineate a political boundary for the new Town of Prague. The walls and moat formed a semicircle that connected the Vltava in two places, and thirteen city gates regulated traffic in and out of the town. Wenceslas became a patron of religious institutions in Prague. Missionaries from monastic orders shaped Prague's religious landscape in the early thirteenth century. Monasteries served as the educational centers of medieval cities, and new institutions increased opportunities for study. Franciscan and Dominican friars arrived in the 1220s, spreading the message of poverty and service, and the Knights Templar established a residence in Prague in 1231.

The Přemyslid princess and king's sister Agnes (Anežka) established a monastic complex that dominated the right bank. Agnes was a remarkable woman who defied her family's expectations that she marry the Holy Roman emperor, Frederick II. Headstrong Agnes had other plans. Raised in a Cistercian convent in Silesia, Agnes committed to taking holy orders at a young age and insisted on leading a celibate life devoted to Christ. After the princess asked Pope Gregory IX to intervene, Emperor Frederick II graciously released Agnes from the engagement. The seventeenth-century Irish priest and historian Luke Wadding claimed that Frederick remarked, "If she had left me for a mortal man, I would have taken vengeance with the sword, but I cannot take offense because in preference to me she has chosen the King of Heaven."[11] Agnes maintained her celibacy and remained in Prague.

In 1234, King Wenceslas I donated land and funds for Agnes's project. The princess used her dowry to found a hospital and invited the Franciscan Friars Minor and the Sisters of the Poor to establish a monastery complex in Prague. The "double convent," the first cloister for both men and women north of the Alps, was devoted to caring for the indigent and the ailing. Agnes's mother, the dowager queen Constance, likewise donated and managed a large endowment to the hospital, and Wenceslas I decreed that the establishment had royal protection. Vaulted walkways connected the red-brick monastery to the Church of St. Francis, whose sandstone presbytery featured Prague's first Gothic windows. St. Francis became an important religious center for the royal family. Wenceslas I's coronation and burial, as well as Agnes's investiture ceremony, took place there. The Chapel of the Virgin Mary served as Agnes's private oratory, while the Friars Minor used St. Barbara's Chapel for daily prayers.

Agnes insisted that the monastery and convent follow the Franciscan rule to live simply. Agnes's spiritual adviser was Clare of Assisi, a close associate of Francis of Assisi and the founder of the female Franciscan order. The two abbesses corresponded for over two decades and became strong political and spiritual allies. In one letter, written in 1234, Clare remarked on Agnes's particular sacrifice. "You, more than others, could have enjoyed the magnificence and honor and dignity of the world, and could have been married to the illustrious Caesar with splendor befitting you and His Excellency. You have rejected all these things and have chosen with your whole heart and soul a life of holy poverty and destitution."[12] Agnes and Clare fought to maintain their vows of poverty, as Pope Gregory IX opposed expanding the mendicant orders. The church hierarchy feared the Franciscans' radical views and opposed their economic dependence on other institutions. While most medieval monasteries were self-sufficient, Franciscans relied on charity and even begged on the streets. Gregory conceded to Agnes's wishes, as he needed Bohemian support in his ongoing conflicts with the Holy Roman emperor, Frederick II. With pressure from Wenceslas I, the pope granted Agnes's convent the "privilege of poverty."

Agnes also founded the Knights of the Cross with the Red Star to staff her hospital. The lay brotherhood was the only native Bohemian religious order and the only male order founded by a woman. As the Knights of the Cross did not follow the Franciscan rule, they could accept property from donors and receive financial support from the pope. The knights were strong allies of the Přemyslid rulers and benefited from their close ties. In 1252, Agnes founded a second hospital and monastery near the Judith Bridge, and the Knights of the Cross with the Red Star were tasked with managing the traffic and taxation on the thoroughfare across the Vltava River. This privilege made the religious order one of the wealthiest institutions in Prague.

Wenceslas I's achievements in developing the right bank intensified the tax burden on Bohemian noble families, causing resentment among the aristocracy. In 1248, several noblemen convinced the king's younger son to depose his father and declare himself "the Young King." Following a pitched battle at Prague Castle, Přemysl Otakar II expelled his father. Wenceslas I's armies retook the throne a year later, and the two noble instigators met their fates on the wheel and the gallows. Wenceslas I soon forgave his son for his treachery, and in 1251, the king restored Otakar's title, Margrave of Moravia. Wenceslas I had lost his elder son and wanted to make amends with his remaining male heir.

Přemysl Otakar II legitimately gained the throne upon his father's death in 1254 and became the most powerful and wealthiest ruler in the Holy Roman Empire. Through prudent marriages and military successes, he expanded his territory southward to the Adriatic Sea. He held the titles king of Bohemia, Margrave of Moravia, and Duke of Austria, Styria, and Carinthia.

FIGURE 1.5 Presbytery of St. Francis Church inside the Convent of St. Agnes, Old Town. The monastery was founded by Agnes of Bohemia in 1231 and became one of the most important institutions in medieval Prague. Photo by the author.

Přemysl Otakar II elevated the Bohemian kingdom's position in Central Europe by asserting himself as the seventh imperial elector.

Otakar II's legal and economic power swelled. He became known as the King of Gold and Iron and founded over thirty towns in Bohemia and Moravia. In 1257, he chartered Prague's Lesser Town (Malá Strana, Kleinseite) by placing the various settlements below Prague Castle under a single jurisdiction. The town attracted many German speakers who established residences and businesses there. Within a few decades, the Town of Prague became known as the Old Town (Staré Město, Altstadt) to distinguish it from Lesser Town on the left bank. Otakar II contributed to Old Town building projects as well. In 1261, he added the Přemyslid family necropolis of the Holy Savior to Agnes's cloisters. Its presbytery featured a high ceiling with ribbed vaults, five Gothic windows, and sculptural adornments of saints, kings, leaves, and serpents. The mausoleum's regal architecture was modeled on King Louis IX's palace chapel in Paris, and its design reflected Přemysl Otakar II's imperial aspirations. Twice, Otakar put himself forward for the imperial crown, but his fellow electors objected to a Slavic king serving as "king of the Germans."

Přemysl Otakar II liberalized immigration laws, encouraging foreign skilled artisans and other workers to move to Bohemia. With the discovery of silver throughout the region, Přemysl Otakar needed German expertise to establish mines. Jihlava (Iglau), about eighty miles southeast of Prague, soon became one of the most prosperous mines in Central Europe. Přemysl Otakar II freed peasants from feudal obligations to local lords, created a modern rent and taxation system, and issued the first written communal law (*zemské desky*) for Bohemia. Towns received privileges to self-govern, establish civil courts, create guilds, and brew beer. Přemysl Otakar II's legal reforms weakened the rural nobility's political power and stimulated Prague's commercial economy.

Jews involved in trade benefited from the economic development and cosmopolitan ideals of Otakar's reign. By the early thirteenth century, most of Prague's Jewish community had moved to the right bank. The largest Jewish settlement developed northwest of Old Town Square. The land there, precariously close to the river and floodplain, was less desirable than other right-bank neighborhoods. Prague's first Jewish cemetery, known as the Jewish Garden, stood outside the Old Town fortifications and served several Jewish communities scattered throughout Prague.

Medieval law limited Jewish economic life. Forbidden to join Christian artisan guilds or to work for Christian patrons, Jews tended to serve their communities in jobs such as tailor, barber, baker, liquor producer, or ritual butcher. Jews' primary economic relationship with Christians involved moneylending, as the church forbade its members from participating in this practice. Jewish involvement in trade and banking enabled Prague's right bank to thrive. Jewish lenders provided low-interest loans to the Crown and the urban middle class known as burghers.

Přemysl Otakar II sought to stabilize economic relations and promote urban peace and prosperity by addressing the Jews' status in the kingdom. His 1254 charter granted Jews unprecedented rights to adjust interest rates on loans and protected them from having to conduct business on the Sabbath or during the Holy Days. Jews could hold royal court offices and could seek protection from any royal officer. To quell anti-Semitism, the king publicized Pope Innocent IV's condemnation of blood libel, a spurious accusation that Jews murdered Christian children in religious rituals. Přemysl Otakar II prohibited attacks on Jewish property, synagogues, and cemeteries and outlawed forced conversion. When local clergy and town burghers reacted against the charter, Přemysl Otakar II retorted that Jews were direct subjects of the Crown and part of the Royal Treasury. Jews paid exorbitant taxes for royal protection, but Otakar II's charter enabled the Prague Jewish community to flourish. A self-governing Jewish district within the Old Town remained outside the jurisdiction of the Christian burghers.

A unique archaeological find near Old Town Square—a man's signet ring dating from the late twelfth or early thirteenth century—hinted at the newfound economic success of individual Jews despite restrictions placed upon their community. The solid gold ring bearing the owner's Hebrew name, Moshe bar Shlomo, held an antique gem etched with an image of the Roman goddess Victoria. The owner may have worked as a rabbi, merchant, banker, tradesman, or other occupation that brought him enough wealth and prominence to purchase a beautiful, unique, and expensive adornment that doubled as a tool for signing contracts and sealing documents.[13]

Commerce was not the only reason for Jews to come to Prague. Ephraim of Regensburg, a prominent twelfth-century Jewish legal scholar, wrote, "In Prague, there are sages of sages."[14] Prague yeshivas, affiliated with local synagogues, were renowned throughout Central and Western Europe as important sites of Tosafist debate and writing. French and German rabbis joined Prague scholars to write commentaries and explanatory notes on the Talmud, the main source for Ashkenazi rituals and responsibilities. The thirteenth-century rabbi Abraham ben Azriel, also known as "the Elder of Bohemia" or by his Czech name Chladek, taught at the Prague Jewish academy. His Talmudic commentaries, *Arugat ha-Bosem* (A bed of spices), named after a passage in the Song of Solomon, are among the oldest Jewish texts that originated in a Slavic-speaking region. Ben Azriel's disciple, Isaac ben Moses of Vienna, was born in Bohemia and lived in Prague for part of his life. His treatise on halakhic law, *Or Zaru'a* (Light is sown), codified Central European Jewish liturgies and rituals and included his correspondence with important European rabbis. The text shaped Ashkenazi daily life for several centuries, as it contained valuable guidance on hunting, clothing, ritual slaughter, criminal law, and superstition. Ben Moses instructed Jewish women on their duties within marriage and family, establishing practices followed for generations. Isaac ben Moses called Bohemia "the land of Canaan," a common appellation for Eastern Europe during the Middle Ages, possibly because both Canaan and the Slavic lands were associated with slavery. His commentaries included glosses in Old Czech, suggesting that Prague's medieval Jews commonly used the Slavic tongue. Words for soap, lice, flea, shawl, and fork were rendered in Old Czech so readers would clearly understand ben Moses's directives on Jewish ritual and daily life.

Prague's Jewish quarter needed a larger synagogue to accommodate its growing population. King Přemysl Otakar II granted a permit and even allowed the community to employ the royal stonemasons, who had come from France to construct Agnes's nearby convent. The double-nave structure bore striking similarities to small Gothic monastery chapels. Because Jews could not join Prague's craft guilds, they relied on Christian architects and builders who used principles of church design. Despite his generosity, Přemysl Otakar II declared that the synagogue could not stand higher than any church in Prague. To accommodate the high Gothic vaults, the builders sank the foundation lower than the street level, so worshipers had to descend several stairs to enter the synagogue. Wooden benches for the male worshipers lined the walls. Rich in symbolism, the synagogue honored the twelve tribes of Israel with interwoven vine motifs, and twelve windows refracted sunbeams onto the bema (altar). Masters of light, the French builders installed reflective mirrors that created an ethereal candlelit glow during evening services. In the fourteenth century, the Jewish community added a high-pitched saddle roof with red brick gables, making the synagogue a stunning example of Prague Gothic architecture. The New Synagogue became the Jewish quarter's centerpiece and a striking addition to Prague's landscape.

A powerful local legend maintained that the synagogue contained stones from the Holy Land. Following the Roman attack on Jerusalem's Second Temple in the first century CE, holy angels carried its dismantled stones to Prague. There they would remain until the arrival of the Messiah when the angels would return the stones to Jerusalem and construct the Third Temple. When newer synagogues were built in subsequent centuries, the people of Prague began to call the building the Old-New Synagogue (Staronová synagoga, Altneuschul), a name it retains to this day. The name of Prague's most holy Jewish site suggested a sacred place that defied time, at once representing the old and new and the past and present.

———— ✦ ————

Přemysl Otakar II's sudden death in 1278 challenged Prague's stability and wealth for decades to come. Otakar died fighting his arch-rival, the Holy Roman emperor Rudolph of Habsburg, in a war that cost the Přemyslid dynasty all its territory outside Bohemia and Moravia. Otakar's son and heir, Wenceslas II, was only seven when his father died, enabling Otto V of Brandenburg to usurp power and hold the young prince hostage for several years. Wenceslas II was not crowned until 1297, when a lavish celebration in Prague brought together royal and church representatives from across Europe. On Petřín Hill, adjacent to the Castle District, an enormous tent lined with tapestries served as the banquet room. Royal musicians entertained the luminary guests, who ate and drank throughout the night. On the right bank, the common people and burghers enjoyed nightly dances, acrobatic performances,

FIGURE 1.6 Old-New Synagogue, Prague, ca. 1270. Altneusynagoge, Prag, William A. Rosenthall Judaica Collection—Postcards, College of Charleston Libraries, Charleston, SC, USA. Courtesy of Special Collections, College of Charleston Library.

boxing matches, and a nude road race. Wine flowed from fountains throughout the Old Town, and revelers celebrated for over a week.

Through prudent marriages and diplomacy, Wenceslas II expanded the Přemyslid territory into Poland and Hungary. The discovery of silver at Kutná Hora (Kuttenberg), fifty miles east of Prague, enriched the throne. Wenceslas II established a royal monopoly on silver, and Bohemia produced the largest output in the Holy Roman Empire, about twenty tons per year. Wenceslas issued the Prague groschen and the Prague penny, denominations soon used throughout Europe. Medieval Czech literature likewise flourished in this period; Wenceslas II's sister, Kunigunde, the abbess of St. George's convent at Prague Castle, commissioned important pieces of Czech Gothic literature, *The Prayer of Lady Kunigunde* and the magnificently illuminated *Passional of the Abbess Kunigunde*.

The political instability exacerbated a split between town and country in Bohemia. Prague was a bilingual city at the end of Přemyslid rule. The Old Town and Lesser Town burghers were primarily German speaking, owned their own homes, and earned income through commerce. Many German tradesmen imported European luxury goods—French and Italian wines, Flemish cloth, and Bavarian linens—and sold products from the surrounding countryside. Many burghers also owned shares in the region's silver mines, the most important source of Bohemian wealth.

In contrast, most Bohemian noblemen spoke medieval Czech. They owned large estates but often had property and interests in Prague too. Their political privileges gave them the right to enforce the law and to participate in the Bohemian Diet, which selected and advised the Bohemian kings. When the Přemyslid family died out, nobles filled political vacuums and looked for a new monarch who would advance their interests. These noble landowners' wealth came from the land. They hired peasant laborers or leased plots to smallholders.

Prague's population more than doubled in the thirteenth century as German immigrants and rural Czech speakers arrived in Prague. Czech-speaking farmers produced the meat, vegetables, wheat, and hops sold in the marketplaces. Other peasants sought new opportunities as artisans and day laborers in the manifold urban building projects, hoping that such work would prove more lucrative than rural labor. These peasants, artisans, and laborers tended to support their fellow Czech speakers, the native aristocracy, even though their economic interests rarely aligned. A class structure based on language began to solidify, with German-speaking burghers sandwiched between the Czech-speaking nobility and laboring classes.

Meanwhile, illnesses and political intrigue plagued the Přemyslid family and threatened to destabilize the delicate balance between Germans and Czechs, burghers and aristocrats. Wenceslas II died in 1305 at age thirty-three, and a year later, unknown assailants murdered his childless son Wenceslas III. The powerful Přemyslid dynasty, native to Bohemia, was suddenly extinguished, and a chaotic succession crisis ensued. Albrecht of Habsburg, the Holy Roman emperor, demanded Bohemia for his son Rudolph. King Rudolph was so thrifty and unpopular that Prague residents called him "the King of Porridge" (*král kaše*). When Rudolph died suddenly in 1307, the Bohemian nobles gave the crown to Henry of Carinthia, whose extravagant spending habits contrasted with Rudolph's frugality.

Old Town Prague burghers expressed increasing frustration that their political influence did not match their wealth and contributions to Prague's economic growth. They had a town council but no permit to build a town hall or to employ a scribe for record keeping. In 1309, German-speaking Prague burghers Jakob Wölfin and Nikolaus Tausendmark, in alliance with Peregrin Pusch and other wealthy owners of silver mines in Kutná Hora, moved against the Bohemian aristocracy to demand more influence in political decisions. When the Czech-speaking laborers sided with the nobility, civil war nearly broke out. To prevent further violence, the nobility gave in to some demands, including allowing the burghers' sons to marry their aristocratic daughters.

Bohemian noblemen recognized the need for stronger leadership and sought to oust the extravagant Henry of Carinthia. They turned to John of Luxembourg, son of the newly elected Holy Roman emperor Henry VII, hoping that an alliance with the empire's Western reaches would strengthen Bohemia's position in Europe. Leading Bohemian noblemen negotiated a union between fourteen-year-old John and eighteen-year-old Elisabeth Přemyslová, Wenceslas II's second daughter. The couple married in Speyer and then journeyed through Nuremberg to Prague. An entourage of Czech-speaking soldiers from the imperial army accompanied them to Prague's city gates, where John announced that he had come to invade Bohemia in Elisabeth's name. John's forces took Prague Castle on December 3, 1310, and deposed the Bohemian king, launching a new era in Prague's history.

2
The Imperial Capital of Charles IV

IN THE FOUR centuries of Přemyslid rule, Prague had grown from a small fortification above the Vltava River to one of the Holy Roman Empire's most important and wealthiest cities. By securing the Crown of the Bohemian lands, John of Luxembourg acquired the empire's only hereditary kingdom, whose capital had become famous for trade, architecture, and religious institutions. The Přemyslids had consolidated secular and ecclesiastic power in Prague, but at the beginning of the fourteenth century, the city was in a precarious situation. The dynasty's sudden extinction exposed fissures in Prague society. Church and state leaders vied for influence over the young, untested king, and conflicts erupted between noble landowners and urban dwellers, Czech and German speakers, and Christians and Jews.

For the first time in Bohemian history, a foreigner wore its crown. Although his marriage to a Přemyslid princess lent credibility to his position, the new king had to contend with a strong and suspicious Bohemian nobility that prioritized maintaining its prestige, wealth, and historic rights. John had little knowledge of Bohemia's customs and culture. The Duchy of Luxembourg stood at the western edge of the Holy Roman Empire and enjoyed a close relationship with the French kingdom and the papacy, whereas Bohemia lay in the easternmost part of the empire.

The well-traveled king found Prague distasteful and culturally backward compared to French and Italian cities. Because Prague Castle had fallen into disrepair and needed thorough renovation following a 1303 fire, the newlyweds John and Elisabeth lived on the Old Town Square at the House of the Stone Bell. The stately Gothic building was adorned with French-inspired polychromatic sculptures of lions and Bohemian patron saints. A carved stone bell hung at the building's top right corner, supposedly to commemorate John's 1310 arrival in Prague, when supporters rang the Týn church bells to welcome his army through the city gates.

The marriage between John of Luxembourg and Elisabeth Přemyslová began auspiciously. Elisabeth taught Bohemian customs to John and advised

FIGURE 2.1 The House of the Stone Bell, Old Town Square was likely a residence of John of Luxembourg in the early fourteenth century. Photo by the author.

him on cultural and political matters. She did not produce a male heir until six years into the marriage, but she did bear two healthy daughters, Margaret and Bonne. In 1316, Elisabeth gave birth to her third child, a son called Wenceslas, later known as Charles IV.[1] Although John had sired a Czech heir for the Bohemian throne, he could not shake off his moniker, "the Foreigner King." His recurrent absences from Prague and his court's cosmopolitan atmosphere provoked mistrust among the Bohemian elite. John had to return to Luxembourg for more than a year following his father's death in 1313, and he made numerous trips to his holdings in northern Italy. While some noblemen claimed that John's international outlook brought prestige to the kingdom, his opponents believed John viewed Bohemia as a revenue source for his military campaigns.

John recognized his unpopularity and negotiated a new agreement with the local nobility. He promised to dismiss all foreign advisers from his Prague court, and he affirmed the Czech nobility's right to elect their king, approve extraordinary taxation, and choose whether to participate in military campaigns. The king also transferred tax revenue to improve Prague's infrastructure. A public bath opened, and streets were paved with cobblestones and cleansed of human and animal excrement. Some convicted criminals could choose the distasteful sentence of street cleaning over a prison term.

John did not sponsor many new architectural projects, but his few contributions marked the transition to a French Gothic style that dominated fourteenth-century Prague. New buildings featured higher ceilings, vertical lines, and elaborate decor. Larger, more intricate windows introduced light as an architectural element. When a fire gutted St. James the Greater in the Old Town, John's architects transformed the Romanesque church into a long Gothic basilica with three naves. John and Elisabeth also funded the conversion of the St. Lawrence rotunda and the Knights Templar commandery into a complex for Dominican nuns. The most important secular building project during John's reign was the Gothic Old Town hall. German-speaking burghers had long petitioned the Crown for a municipal building to house offices, courts, and a small prison. John's acquiescence acknowledged the growing power of Prague's wealthy elite.

Despite these important contributions, John received criticism for bringing French customs to Prague. A contemporary chronicler lambasted the new fashion trends: "In the style of monkeys, which try to imitate everything they see, the people have…stopped wearing the clothes worn by their ancestors and now wear shortened, ill-judged dress which allows others to see their thighs and buttocks. These clothes are so tight that they can barely breathe in them."[2]

The early fourteenth century signified a new era in Prague's cultural history, marked by literary output in Church Latin, French, German, and Czech. The king's close adviser, the French scholar and composer Guillaume de Machaut, dedicated his most successful poem to John. *The Judgment of the King of Bohemia* cast the king as a wise ruler who must settle a dispute on the nature of love and grief. Machaut praised his liege:

> No man ever was in all ways so perfect
> As this man is, in both word and deed.
> Sir, his flag cries out Luxembourg,
> and he is King of Bohemia.[3]

Alongside German and French cultural influences, a Czech vernacular literature emerged during John's reign. Whereas Bohemian Germans had abundant access to reading materials from across the Holy Roman Empire, Czech-speaking nobles longed for native literature. Early Czech works included translations and adaptations of Latin and West European literature, such as the *Life of Alexander the Great* and the *Song of Roland*. Soon, original writings appeared, including Czech-language histories, legends, epics, and hagiographies of local saints.

The first historical chronicle in Czech, the *Chronicle of Dalimil*, appeared in the early fourteenth century. It advanced the values of Czech-speaking landholders, who resented Prague's German-speaking town dwellers. In one passage, a twelfth-century Bohemian duke tells his sons, "If I learn from a bird that you are leaving it up to the Germans, I will put you in a leather bag and throw it into the Vltava River!... Do not be faithful [to the Germans] and take instead a ploughman for your duke!"[4] Another Přemyslid duke in the chronicle chastised his advisers for steering him away from his preferred spouse: "Why shouldn't Božena be my wife? I would rather laugh with a noble-spirited Czech peasant woman than marry a German queen.... A German... would teach my children German. Then the people would become disunited, and the land brought to certain ruin."[5]

Although John understood the importance of investing in Prague's architecture, culture, and modernization schemes, he continued to look for fulfillment outside of Bohemia. John and Elisabeth's marriage began to disintegrate following their son's birth in 1316. John became suspicious when his advisers informed him in 1319 that his wife and several noblemen were plotting to oust him in favor of his son. His men occupied Loket Castle in Western Bohemia, where Elisabeth was staying with her children; kidnapped the young prince; and brought him back to Prague. The queen gave birth to another son, John Henry, in 1322, but the royal marriage did not improve. The following year, John insisted that seven-year-old Charles leave Prague to be educated in the French court of King Charles the Fair, his brother-in-law. The Luxembourgs customarily provided their children with a French education, but John also wanted to separate his son from his influential mother. Elisabeth—pregnant with twin daughters—left Prague. She settled with the surviving infant, Anna, just north of Prague at Mělník Castle. Elisabeth died of tuberculosis on Saint Wenceslas's feast day in 1330. Charles never saw his mother again.

In France, Charles was being prepared for the political career that awaited him in Prague. Our knowledge of Charles's childhood comes from Charles's autobiography, written decades later. Medieval rulers molded their images by commissioning written and cultural artifacts that placed them in high esteem. Later in life, Charles became a master at promoting his image as a powerful, spiritual, and learned leader. He commissioned histories of Bohemia and his Přemyslid ancestors, and he authored an autobiography that highlighted his education, religious experiences, military campaigns, and journey to becoming king and emperor. In this work, Charles credited his time in Paris as the formative experience of his youth, and he discussed his tense relationship with his father and his estrangement from his mother and the land of his birth. While he likely had assistance in composing the autobiography, it stands as a rare example of a medieval text that shared aspects of a ruler's personality and even vulnerability.[6]

In Paris, the young prince formally took the name Charles in honor of the French king, his patron, uncle, and godfather. He was wed to his young cousin Margaret of Valois when both were seven years old. Known as Blanche because of her remarkably light blond hair, the future queen did not live with Charles until she reached adolescence. Charles's close relationship with the French royal family shaped his statecraft, faith, and scholarly interests. About his uncle and mentor, King Charles the Fair, Charles later recalled, "He loved me very much, and ordered my chaplain to teach me letters a little, though he himself was ignorant of letters.... The king was no avaricious lover of gold, he had good counselors, and his court shone with a group of elder statesmen, spiritual and secular."

Charles studied Latin, French, German, and Italian and became fascinated with architecture, sculpture, literature, and theology. His broad and substantial education contrasted sharply with most European rulers. In his autobiography, written in 1350, Charles fondly remembered his schooldays. "I learned to read the hours of the glorious Virgin Blessed Mary and, understanding them a little every day, I gladly read through my boyhood." Charles's mentor Pierre Roger, a monk and esteemed theologian who held a doctorate and chair at the Sorbonne, had a profound effect on him. Following a mass celebrated by Roger, Charles wrote, "The beauty and eloquence of the abbot's sermon pleased me so much.... I ... kept wondering, 'What is it about this man that causes so much grace to flow over me?'" Thus began a lifelong friendship with Roger, who would eventually become Pope Clement VI.

Charles excelled at physical as well as intellectual pursuits. An accomplished horseman, he entered dueling and jousting tournaments, and at age fifteen, Charles joined his father in Luxembourg to round out his education with military training. He spent the next two years accompanying or representing John on his campaigns in northern Italy, Carinthia, and Alsace. Charles later recorded his youthful adventures. He escaped an attempted poisoning and then liberated the San Felice fortress in Lombardy on Saint Catherine's Day, November 25, 1322. Charles earned a knighthood and began a lifelong devotion to the martyr Saint Catherine. Despite his successes, Charles grew frustrated with his father's military campaigns and excessive expenditures. Meanwhile, the political situation in Prague needed attention.

The Bohemian nobility and Prague burghers enjoyed their freedom in John's absence, but they also feared their vulnerability to foreign encroachment without a monarch situated in Bohemia. Several leading noblemen beseeched John to come to Prague, but the king sent his son instead.

No fanfare greeted Charles on his return to Prague in 1333, after a decade away from his birthplace. He recalled in his autobiography, "I found that my mother, Elisabeth, had died some years before," and his siblings were abroad. "And thus, when we arrived in Bohemia, we found neither father nor mother nor brother nor sister nor anyone else we knew." Charles visited his mother's grave at Zbraslav, a Cistercian monastery just outside Prague, and throughout his life, he honored his mother's resting place with financial contributions and artistic commissions. He expressed frustration that he had "completely forgotten the Czech language, which we have since relearned so that we speak it and understand it like any other Bohemian."

Charles bemoaned Bohemia's disorderly state. "We found the kingdom so forsaken that there was not one castle which was free and not mortgaged together with all its royal property, so that we did not have anywhere to stay except houses in the cities just like any other citizen." Charles described Prague Castle as "desolate, in ruins, and reduced from the times of King Otakar so that it had crumbled almost to the ground," though he may have been motivated to exaggerate its condition to elevate the need for a glorious restoration.[7] Charles embraced the teachings of Saint Augustine, who viewed art and beauty as earthly representations of the divine, and the young prince strove to display his faith through public works. Of the renovations, Charles's autobiography claimed, "We raised up at great expense the great, new, and beautiful palace the way it appears to those who look on it today." Chronicler Francis of Prague agreed, calling it "a royal residence worthy of admiration, such as no one had previously seen in this kingdom. He built it...after the pattern of the residence of the French kings."[8]

Despite his keen political acumen, Charles had little real power during his first decade in Prague. His father anointed Charles the Margrave of Moravia, the traditional title for the Bohemian royal heir, but the position came with few rights or responsibilities. Charles had to prove himself worthy to the independent-minded Bohemian nobility, and he wisely emphasized his descent from the Přemyslid dynasty through his mother, Elisabeth. His autobiography asserted, "When the great council of Bohemia remembered that I belonged to the ancient house of Bohemia, they gave me help to recover the castles and royal possessions." Fulfilling a promise made by his father, Charles restored the Bohemian nobility to government offices and appointed the wealthy nobleman Peter Rožmberk as Prague's high chamberlain.

Charles had a formidable political opponent in Prague's bishop, Jan IV of Dražice. The church represented Prague's central authority until Charles's arrival. Whereas the bishop wanted to remake Prague into an episcopal center, Charles envisioned a city like Paris, which embodied royal power. Jan promoted the cult of fellow bishop Saint Adalbert, whereas Charles devoted himself to his ancestors, Saints Wenceslas and Ludmila. A fourteenth-century hagiography attributed to Charles called Ludmila the "first pearl, the first flower of Bohemia" and described Wenceslas as "the glorious prince [who] devoted himself to acts of charity and generosity."

Charles's rivals in Prague attempted to drive a wedge between the prince and his father. Charles later decried these "evil and false advisors, [who] seeking their own advantage...prevailed against us with our father.... [They] whispered, 'Lord take care. Your son has many castles in the kingdom and great following among your people; if he continues long to have this advantage, he will be able to drive you out whenever he wishes...he is much loved by the Bohemians; you, however, are a foreigner.'" In 1335, the suspicious king rescinded Charles's administrative responsibilities and confiscated his Bohemian and Moravian fortifications and castles. As Charles later wrote, "Thus, there remained for us only the title of margrave of Moravia without any powers."

Although frustrated with his lack of autonomy, Charles gained important experience in John's military campaigns and political negotiations. Together, father and son forged a peace with the Polish king and maintained their French alliances. For much of the fourteenth century, the French Crown controlled the papacy, which had moved to Avignon. In early 1341, Charles and John visited the papal court of Pope Benedict XII and met with Charles's friend and mentor Pierre Roger, who predicted that Charles would one day become Holy Roman emperor. In turn, Charles told Roger he would be the next pope. Charles later wrote, "And both came to pass."

The favorable meeting in Avignon restored John's faith in Charles. In 1341, John bestowed the title junior king (*rex iunior*) upon his son and fully entrusted him with the Bohemian government and its royal possessions. Some noblemen in the Bohemian Diet resisted the appointment, citing their right to choose the king, but others recognized the need for centralized authority.

The Luxembourg father and son spent the next few years pursuing a goal their Přemyslid predecessors never achieved: elevating the Prague bishopric to an archdiocese. The marriage of secular and church authority remained key to medieval power structures. An archbishop controlled a larger ecclesiastic region, and his court brought prestige to its locale. Moreover, the archbishop's blessing legitimized the king's secular rule. In the spring of 1344, Pierre Roger, now Clement VI, issued a papal bull that established the archdiocese of Prague.

John returned to Prague to lay the foundation stone for St. Vitus Cathedral. On November 21, 1344, Prague's first archbishop, Ernest (Arnošt) of Pardubice, led the solemn ceremony surrounded by the dean of the cathedral chapter, local priests, and Bohemian noblemen. The Gothic cathedral replaced Duke Wenceslas's tenth-century rotunda, but the patron saint's new tomb became "the ideological focal point of the cathedral."[9] Charles envisioned the cathedral as a symbol of his political legitimacy, a resting place for his Přemyslid forebearers, and the location of his growing collection of holy relics. As the seat of a kingdom and an archbishopric, Prague became one of the most important power centers in Central Europe.

With his paternal relationship healed and his succession in Bohemia assured, Charles turned to his next political goal: becoming the Holy Roman emperor. Unfortunately, the title was already held by Louis IV of Bavaria, but the Luxembourgs plotted to depose Louis and replace him with Charles. In July 1346, five of the empire's prince electors declared Louis an illegitimate ruler and elected Charles in his stead. In bestowing the secular title of King of the Romans on Charles, the electors created a crisis whereby two men claimed the throne.

A month later, on August 26, 1346, Charles joined his father in the Battle of Crécy, a campaign during the Hundred Years' War between France and England. A disastrous defeat for the French, the battle claimed the life of John, king of Bohemia. According to chronicles from the era, the ailing king, totally blind by this time, charged into the battle to die a hero's death. John spent most of his life outside Prague, but his purported last words underscored his Bohemian identity. As the English army descended on the French alliance, John exclaimed, "Far be it for a king of Bohemia to run away!"[10]

Charles, a son of Prague, would take John's place as that king of Bohemia.

———— ◆ ————

Charles left Prague as *rex iunior* but returned as the king of Bohemia and the elected king of the Germans. At age thirty, his supremacy in Central Europe was far from secure. Louis IV of Bavaria refused to relinquish his right to the Roman crown, leaving two claimants to the imperial title. Charles's disparagers called him the "pope's emperor" because his power stemmed from his alliance with Pope Clement, rather than the support of the German duchies. As most imperial cities remained loyal to Louis, Charles could not use the traditional coronation sites at Aachen or Cologne, so he instead ascended the imperial throne at Bonn in November 1346. He wore a replacement crown because Louis still possessed the original. There could hardly be a less auspicious beginning of an imperial reign.

In contrast, Charles's Prague coronation as king of Bohemia on September 2, 1347, fulfilled the monarch's passion for ritual, tradition, and celebration. Several years before his father's death, he started to plan his coronation. He rewrote the order of service for the coronation mass and commissioned a Crown of Saint Wenceslas to represent the Kingdom of Bohemia. The new crown was made of pure gold and encrusted with ninety-one gemstones, including a crystal encasing a thorn said to be from Christ's crucifixion crown. A jeweled cross and four fleurs-de-lis symbolized Charles's faith and French heritage, and a girdle belonging to Charles's wife, Blanche of Valois, formed the crown's base. Charles's devotion to Saint Wenceslas guided his aesthetic and symbolic choices throughout his reign. For a full year before the coronation, the new crown sat upon a golden bust of Wenceslas at the patron saint's tomb. He included the saint's image on countless art commissions and official documents, and he endowed the St. Vitus chapter, tasking the member priests with maintaining the cathedral and Wenceslas's burial site.

The coronation ceremonies began the night of September 1, 1347, when Charles and his court honored the ancestral Přemyslid dynasty at Vyšehrad. Fourteenth-century Bohemians believed that Libuše founded Prague at Vyšehrad, and Charles sought to connect himself to that ancient tradition. Charles wore woven bast shoes and carried a bag that had purportedly belonged to Přemysl the Ploughman, the first Bohemian duke. Cosmas, whose chronicle Charles cherished, mentioned the shoes and bags in his narrative of Libuše's betrothal: "Afterward, dressed in princely robe and royal shoes, the ploughman mounted the high-spirited horse, but not forgetful of his lot, he took with him his boots, stitched in every part from cork, and ordered them preserved for posterity. They are indeed preserved in the duke's treasury at Vyšehrad now and forever." At Vyšehrad, Charles also visited Saint Martin's Rotunda and the Chapter of Saints Peter and Paul. Fire had destroyed parts of Vyšehrad in the previous century, and Charles invested in restoring the historic area.

Charles's Vyšehrad ceremony demonstrated his connection to the humble Přemysl and the Bohemian land, but the subsequent coronation events at Prague Castle displayed a broader royal power. Charles and his entourage of knights and priests, illuminated by torchlight, journeyed from Vyšehrad to the Old Town, across the Vltava to Lesser Town, and then up to Prague Castle, where Charles's party spent the night. This path through Prague, later known as the Royal Way, became the traditional procession route for Bohemian kings.

On September 2, Charles and hundreds of dignitaries gathered in the Romanesque Basilica of St. Vitus for a mass that lasted close to four hours. Charles adapted the original Přemyslid coronation ceremony and added French traditions he learned in his youth. Prague's archbishop cloaked Charles in an ermine robe and consecrated his hands with holy oils to imitate Solomon's biblical anointing of David. The archbishop asked God to bestow unto Charles the gifts of the Hebrew kings, quoting the Book of Kings: "You exalted to royal dignity Humble David, your child, and to Solomon you gave the unspeakable gift of wisdom." Charles and his wife Blanche held scepters and golden apples to symbolize their power and purity. The abbess of Saint George Convent, established by Boleslav I's daughter Mlada in 973, administered the queen's coronation oath, thus linking Blanche to Prague's female spiritual history. As the ceremony ended, Charles returned the Crown of Saint Wenceslas to his patron saint's tomb.[11]

All of Prague reveled in Charles's coronation. A temporary wooden banquet hall, draped with luminous silks, stood on St. Gall's market square in the Old Town. The townspeople danced and drank at venues throughout the city. On the day following the coronation, Charles laid the foundation stone of Our Lady of the Snows and donated wood from the temporary banquet hall to build the church and its associated Carmelite monastery. Charles foresaw Our Lady as the spiritual center of a new town that would expand Prague beyond the riverbanks. With his tenuous hold on the imperial title, Charles invested in Prague as the undisputed seat of his kingdom.

In his coronation year, Charles also founded Na Slovanech, a Benedictine monastery on the Vltava's right bank that would revive the Old Church Slavonic liturgy. He brought monks from Bosnia, Serbia, and Croatia who could perform and teach the Slavic rituals. The monastery became known as Emmaus, perhaps because the first mass celebrated there included the gospel reading about Christ's appearance on the road to Emmaus. Locals, however, claimed that a pub called Emma's Haus once stood on the monastery site. Charles donated a rare, illuminated manuscript in Old Church Slavonic to the Emmaus library and helped fund eighty-five frescoes of Old and New Testament scenes. Unlike his predecessors, Charles succeeded in bringing the Slavic liturgy back to Prague after centuries of suppression by the Roman church. He envisioned Bohemia as a bridge that could repair the Great Schism between Eastern and Western Christianity and a central place where both the Slavic and Latin liturgies could thrive.

Good fortune came to Charles one month after his Bohemian coronation. On October 11, 1347, Louis IV suffered a massive stroke while on a bear hunt. With his imperial rival's death Charles gained wider acceptance of his election as King of the Romans. Yet his relief would not last. On August 1, 1348, Charles's wife Blanche of Valois died following a short illness. The couple had produced two daughters, but Charles desperately longed for a male heir to secure the dynasty. Less than a year later he married Anna of Bavaria of the Wittelsbach family. Not only did a marriage offer him another chance for a son, but also the union repaired some tension between Bohemia and Bavaria.

In June 1349, the imperial prince electors met in Frankfurt and re-elected Charles the King of the Romans. The following month he journeyed to Aachen with his new wife and sat upon Charlemagne's throne to receive his office's privileges. While Aachen welcomed him, he still had to use a replacement crown, as Louis IV's family had not returned the original to the imperial court. Following Charles's ceremony, Anna was crowned Queen of the Romans and, a few months later, queen of Bohemia. While Charles officially held the secular title, ongoing European rivalries meant that the pope would not anoint Charles Holy Roman emperor until 1355. Charles chose Prague as his imperial capital, where he would gather Europe's finest scholars, politicians, poets, and artists. Although Charles resided in Prague less than a third of the year, he considered it his true home and sought to transform it to an unrivaled center of commerce, statecraft, learning, and spirituality.

While famed for his intelligence and piety, Charles had another side. His detractors complained bitterly about his ostentatious behavior at dances and tournaments. His old friend Pope Clement VI admonished him in a letter dated February 25, 1348. "We have learned... that you by your clothes, which you wear too short and too close fitting, do not preserve the dignity that belongs to [you]. You also defy your dignity by taking part in fights and tournaments. We... have been astonished, and emphatically ask [you] to wear long and loose-fitting clothes..., to refrain from fights and tournaments, and to show appropriate earnestness in your actions and conduct."[12]

Charles certainly had more serious ambitions than sport. He envisioned his future Prague as a modern, organized urban center for the kingdom and empire. Originally, he planned to expand the left bank, adjacent to the Castle District, but his advisers recognized a potential public health crisis owing to the limited access to water. Prague had fared better than much of Central Europe during the 1348 Black Death epidemic, and the emperor's physician,

Gall of Strahov, wanted to stave off future outbreaks. Gall, who also taught mathematics and astronomy at the university, considered the right bank the ideal location to avoid overcrowding and tainted water sources. Beneš Krabice of Weitmil, a contemporaneous Prague historian, described Charles's leadership:

> Charles...laid the foundation stone for the New Town in Prague, and he ordered construction of a very strong wall with very high towers... and finished the whole work in two years. He also ordered gardens and vineyards to be planted around Prague, and because of these gardens and vineyards the population greatly increased. In a short time, many houses were built.[13]

Charles modeled the New Town on urban areas in northern Italy and France, and he believed a large, planned town could solve overcrowding, transportation, and sanitation concerns. New Town featured wide boulevards, and huge public squares like the Horse Market and Cattle Market (later Wenceslas and Charles Squares) supplemented or replaced the cramped Old Town shops. Here merchants could display their goods and welcome visitors. New Town was organized around monasteries and parish churches, creating neighborhoods and small communities throughout the enormous development. The Corpus Christi Chapel, located in the center of the town's largest square, showcased some of Charles's holy relics and attracted pilgrims to Prague. Gardens and vineyards formed the town's perimeter, a development that took pressure off the inner towns' need to produce food.

New Town had a predominantly Czech-speaking population, whereas German-speaking middle-class burghers dominated the Old Town. Charles's expansion project created opportunities for rural Czech speakers to settle in Prague, where they opened shops, worked as craftsmen, or labored at the manifold construction sites. Membership in Czech artisan guilds increased, particularly among goldsmiths and stonemasons. Czech-speaking painters joined the Brotherhood of St. Luke, which had several branches in Prague. Guilds combined professional, religious, and social functions, and their legal privileges protected members from replacement by foreign workers.

Charles provided a generous tax incentive to encourage settlement in New Town. Those who built homes within eighteen months of the district's founding would not pay taxes for twelve years. During the first four years, four hundred houses were constructed in New Town. To finance this enormous project, Charles "forgave" all debts to Jews, meaning that anyone who owed money to the Jewish bankers did not have to repay the loans and instead could pay a smaller tax directly to the Crown. The Jews had no recourse, as by law their property belonged to the monarch. Charles retained the Jewish community's right to self-govern their neighborhood, but the king continued to impose dress regulations and other restrictions on Prague Jews. Like other monarchs, Charles tolerated Jews' presence in the city only if it benefited the state.

Charles granted New Town burghers the right to brew beer and to hold markets. He favored Bohemian merchants and artisans—both Czech and German speakers—and imposed the "mile right," meaning that foreigners could not settle within a mile of New Town without obtaining the leading burghers' permission. Merchants' homes lined town squares. Families lived above the artisan workshops and stalls on the ground floors. At the popular establishments called *Maßhäuser* (beer houses), burghers brewed beer and sold other merchandise. The German word literally meant "measuring house," as a *Maß* (about one liter, or thirty-four ounces) designated the serving size for a beer. Many artisan workshops had small brewing operations where community members gathered. Prague workers and merchants consumed a significant amount of beer for nutrition, hydration, and pleasure. Fairly low in alcohol and high in carbohydrates and vitamins, the beers protected drinkers from Prague's unsanitary water.

New Town continued to grow and attract settlers from the countryside and abroad. By the end of Charles's reign, Prague's population of around 40,000 residents put it on par with important German cities like Nuremberg and Frankfurt, but it was considerably smaller than Paris, which had approximately 100,000 residents, and Milan, which had 125,000. While many Czech and German speakers could understand each other's language, two distinct linguistic cultures continued to develop side by side in Prague.

Charles was fluent in several languages—in addition to Czech and German, he knew French and Latin. Viewing education as central to statecraft and faith, the king yearned to establish a university in Prague modeled on the Paris Sorbonne. His Přemyslid grandfather Wenceslas II had attempted to establish a university in the late thirteenth century, but the local nobles deterred him, fearing high costs and an influx of foreigners in Prague. Charles's connection to Pope Clement ensured that he would succeed where his forebearer had failed. He received a papal charter in 1347 and officially founded the institution in 1348. The university seal celebrated Charles's role as founder: he was depicted holding the university charter and kneeling before his patron Saint Wenceslas, a tall figure in scale armor.

Prague University, modeled on the universities of Paris and Bologna, boasted several firsts, including the first in the Holy Roman Empire and the first north of the Alps. One of Charles's court chroniclers, Beneš Krabice of Veitmile, proudly stated, "There was no counterpart in all the countries of Germany." The university charter outlined Charles's plans to make Prague a European center of learning and influence: "The Bohemian kingdom…should be adorned…with a multitude of learned men.… We have decided to establish, elevate and newly create a *Studium generale* in our metropolitan and especially charming town of Prague, abounding in both a wealth of fruits of the earth and amenity of the place, so convenient and suited for such a great task."[14]

The university had four faculties—liberal arts, theology, medicine, and law—but no formal purpose-built building until a decade after its founding. Prague did not have a rich tradition of Latin education, so the new university had to lure scholars from Paris, Padua, and Bologna. A contemporary chronicler assured his readers, "The masters were sufficiently cared for; besides the food which they received from students, they had secured annual revenues."[15] The university's reputation grew swiftly, attracting students from England, France, Lombardy, Hungary, Poland, and the neighboring German polities.

In the university's first years, lectures were held in churches scattered throughout the city. The archbishop of Prague served as the university chancellor and pressured parish churches and monasteries to contribute funds. With donations, the university purchased a house in the Old Town, where students could reside and professors could hold seminars. The university organized students and faculty into nations—Bohemian, Bavarian, Polish, and Saxon—based on broad geographic identities. The Bohemian nation included Bohemians, Moravians, South Slavs, and Hungarians, while the Saxon nation included students from German states and Scandinavia. Czech speakers made up between one-sixth and one-fifth of the entire student body during the fourteenth century.

The first students lived in the private homes of their masters and paid rent, but when living expenses rose considerably, the university established communal housing for students and faculty. The chronicler Beneš Krabice described the university's acquisition of Jewish houses as the king's benevolent act: "When the lord Charles saw that the teaching greatly and excellently prospered, he gave to the university Jewish houses, and he established in them a college of masters, so that they daily lectured and disputed here." Charles founded the eponymous Carolinum (Caroline College) in 1366, within the home of a wealthy Jew named Lazarus. Architects added Gothic elements to the Old Town dwelling's facade, including an elaborate window decorated with fanciful beasts. Charles also founded All Saints College and St. Hedwig College in former Jewish homes. University records do not disclose whether the Jewish homeowners received any compensation.

Controversial religious thinkers found their way to Prague and influenced university life, even when they had no formal affiliation with the institution. Students and scholars alike sought out sermons by progressive priests and debated their ideas in university seminars. Reformers criticized the church's tax exemption, which they believed unfairly burdened the lower classes. They questioned the clergy's material wealth and advocated vernacular services to engage the congregation. Charles also believed that many priests had become derelict in their duties, and his first two archbishops, Ernest of Pardubice and John Očko of Vlašim, attempted to institute meaningful reforms.

In 1358, Charles invited the priest Conrad von Waldhauser, recently censured by the archbishop of Passau, to preach in Prague. His fiery German-language sermons criticized church corruption and the practice of selling church offices, known as simony. He accused the Franciscans and Carmelites, mendicant monastic orders that lived by collecting alms, of breaking their vows of poverty, living extravagantly, and charging exorbitant fees for funerals. While serving two of the most important churches in the Old Town, St. Gall's and Our Lady Before Týn, he became popular among university students, who requested translations of his German sermons into Latin. Conrad attracted enemies as well. The Franciscans challenged his teachings, and Prague's Carmelites brought a charge of heresy against him. Acquitted by Pope Urban V, Conrad returned to Prague and died in 1369. Beneš Krabice's praise—"a man of great erudition and still greater eloquence"— may indicate Charles's appreciation for Conrad's strict ethical code. Beneš declared, "His saintly sermons corrected the morals of the inhabitants of our country."

Jan Milíč of Kroměříž also preached reform theology from Prague's pulpits. Milíč had served as a canon at the cathedral and as a member of Charles's chancellery. However, he became disillusioned by the church's wealth and gave up his offices to live as an unaffiliated mendicant preacher in Prague. A friend and admirer of Conrad Waldhauser, Milíč preached in Czech and Latin—sometimes several times a day—in various Lesser Town and Old Town churches. After Conrad's death, he presented German-language homilies at Týn. Milíč shared Conrad's criticisms of church corruption, but he took his accusations further, even once comparing Emperor Charles IV to the Antichrist. Milíč journeyed to Rome, where Dominican inquisitors imprisoned him for heresy. As with Conrad, Charles intervened to win Milíč's release. Despite the personal attacks, Charles sympathized with Milíč's attempts to reform the clergy and improve the church he loved.

When Milíč returned to Prague, he turned his ministry to the poor, especially prostitutes. In Prague, like other medieval cities, prostitution took various forms. Prague had semiofficial public brothels in the Obora neighborhood, just outside the Lesser Town city wall, and in Hampays, between the Old Town Jewish quarter and the river. Sometimes complaints by neighbors or local priests spurred temporary closures, but city magistrates usually tolerated public brothels, and the women soon returned to work. Other women sold sexual acts for money or food, especially near the bustling Old Town St. Gall market, which housed several rowdy pubs, gambling establishments, and pawnbrokers. On Kraków Street, at the edge of New Town, some women operated out of private homes as "clandestine prostitutes."

Milíč focused his ministry near the city wall that divided the Old and New Towns. The theologian Matthias of Janov called the Venice Street brothel "the long established and most famous brothel in Prague... the worst, the most awful neighborhood."[16] With funds from Charles IV and other donors, Milíč purchased the brothel and another twenty-seven nearby houses, renaming the neighborhood "New Jerusalem." It housed a community of Catholic priests and over eighty reformed prostitutes. Although the women lived in separate cloisters, the unusual arrangement of men and women attracted gossip. Milíč's opponents brought charges of heresy against him, but Milíč died before his papal hearing. Charles transferred New Jerusalem to the Cistercian order, which established a theological college there. Any records about the fate of the converted women who took shelter at New Jerusalem have been lost.

Charles's Prague court rivaled the university district as an intellectual center for theology, church reform, literature, and law. The imperial court employed dozens of trilingual scholars and writers who used Latin, German, and Czech interchangeably. Charles encouraged translations of Latin works into Czech and commissioned the first Czech-Latin dictionary. He allowed his courtiers to pursue their own interests, yet he directed his advisers to undertake projects that forwarded his political and spiritual goals. A Czech version of *The Life of Saint Catherine*, about one of Charles's patron saints, represented an important Slavic work from Charles's court. Scholars surmise that someone from Charles's inner circle, likely John of Moravec, wrote it, working from Latin hagiographies. The author added features unique to the Czech manuscript, such as mentioning Saint Anne, Jesus's grandmother and the namesake of Charles's second and third wives and a daughter. Another

Czech-language hagiography, *The Life of Saint Procopius*, helped revive the memory of an eleventh-century Bohemian priest who, like Charles, had championed Slavic-language masses.

Charles understood the importance of favorable national histories and sought to strengthen his connection to his Přemyslid genealogy. He commissioned at least five official Bohemian chronicles, written in Latin and later translated into Czech and German, and ordered court scholars to research and incorporate all existing Bohemian chronicles, beginning with Cosmas. Beneš Krabice's *Chronicle of the Prague Church* offered the most comprehensive account of the Caroline era.

The scholarly king was also credited with writing prayers, a hagiography of Saint Wenceslas, and the introduction to a historical chronicle by John of Marignolli, a Franciscan friar and traveler from Florence. Although Charles likely did not compose it unaided, the introduction did express the king's desire "to search for all the ancient chronicles and the latest historiographical works, mostly the Bohemian ones, written in such an obscure fashion, in order to remove from them the convoluted language, cut off the superfluous information and add something useful."[17]

Charles composed his autobiography in 1350, during a yearlong convalescence following a jousting accident sustained in a tournament abroad. He was thrown from a horse and suffered a broken jaw, a disfigured face, and spinal damage. For the rest of his life, Charles's neck protruded forward and his once-athletic frame stooped quite noticeably. The king must have felt chastened that he had not heeded the advice of his friend and mentor Pope Clement VI to refrain from worldly pursuits.

The accident was only one trauma during this period of Charles's life. Anna gave birth to a son named Wenceslas in 1350, but the young prince died within a year. The queen followed in 1353 at age twenty-three, leaving Charles once again a widower without a male heir. In this era, Charles also contended with the demands of the local nobility. Members of the royal court attempted to codify and centralize Bohemian criminal law by creating the *Codex Carolinus*. The vast collection of laws ranged from the procedure to report a rape to the protection of the Bohemian forests. Some laws took a more humane approach to punishment (landowners were no longer permitted to blind or maim their unfree peasants), while others seemed arbitrary (children could not play with dice). The Bohemian nobility, as they had long done, resisted attempts to centralize the law. They preferred oral legal traditions, which allowed them discretion and local jurisdiction. Charles, frustrated by the noblemen's obstruction, announced in 1355 that the codex had been lost in

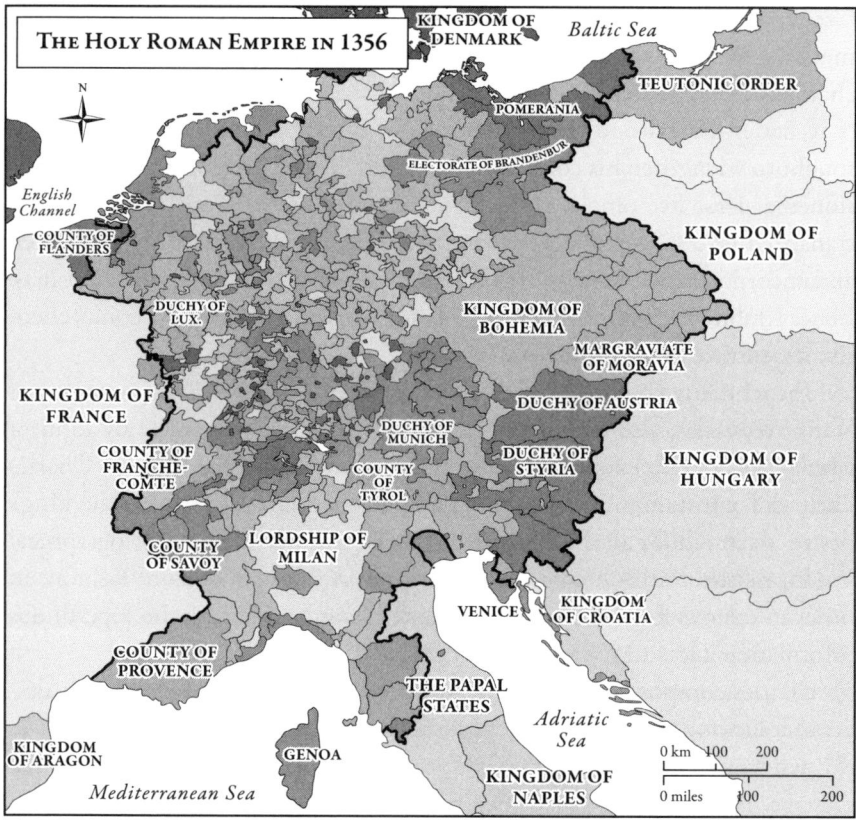

FIGURE 2.2 Map of the Holy Roman Empire in 1356, following Charles IV's golden bull.

a fire at Prague Castle. He no longer bound the nobility to follow his legal code and gave up trying to create a universal justice system for his kingdom.

Charles's court had more success with imperial law. The Golden Bull of 1356 codified the election process for the King of the Romans. It named the seven prince electors who would select the king: the archbishops of Mainz, Cologne, and Trier; the king of Bohemia; the Count Palatine of the Rhine; the Duke of Saxony-Wittenberg; and the Margrave of Brandenburg. The Wittlebachs of Bavaria and the Habsburgs of Austria were not granted electors, as Charles sought to limit the power of his most powerful rivals.

By recentering the empire in Prague, Charles created a cosmopolitan atmosphere that lured scholars and artists from abroad. The Roman tribune and orator Cola di Rienzi took refuge in Prague in 1350 and sought the emperor's help uniting the Italian states and reasserting the power of Rome. Charles swiftly dismissed the Italian's plea and turned him over to the archbishop of Prague, who imprisoned the Italian patriot. Petrarch, the famed

Italian Renaissance writer, spent a month in Prague in the summer of 1356 to continue Rienzi's mission. Petrarch left few notes on his experiences in Prague but expressed his admiration for the city in a letter to the archbishop: "I declare not to have seen anything less barbarian and more human than the emperor and the noblest men around him.... They are reputable and honorable men who deserve acknowledgement, in fact so mellow and urbane that it makes one think they had been born and raised in Athens."[18] Petrarch maintained a correspondence with the king, the archbishop, and the court scholar John of Neumarkt. The poet even wrote to Anna of Świdnica, Charles's third wife, following the birth of her daughter Elisabeth. Petrarch comforted Anna for not producing a male heir and provided her with a list of accomplished and famous women as role models for her daughter. He assured the queen that she would produce a "nobler and more desired child," a son, in the future. His prediction came true—in 1361, Anna gave birth to a boy they named Wenceslas, finally providing Charles with a male heir who would live to adulthood.

Charles's city grew larger and more beautiful throughout his reign. The most visible contribution to Prague's landscape was St. Vitus Cathedral, which soon dominated the castle hill overlooking the Vltava River and became a showpiece of innovative art and architecture. The cathedral's original designer, French architect Matthew of Arras, came to Prague from the papal court at Avignon. Matthew's traditional design followed the strict proportions of the French Gothic style, with a slender, vertical form, a triple nave, a decagonal apse, and numerous side chapels. Following Matthew's death in 1352, the St. Vitus chapter granted the building commission to twenty-three-year-old architect Peter Parler of Swabia. Hailing from a family of prominent sculptors, woodcarvers, and master builders, Parler introduced decorative adornments and experimental architectural features to St. Vitus. The choir featured double-ribbed vaults that crisscrossed the ceiling in a playful pattern, and bell-shaped columns introduced a classical element into the Gothic design. Fanciful carvings—a cat and dog fighting, the devil ripping out Judas's tongue, and a nude Adam and Eve grabbing for an apple—infused a symbolic language of sin and its consequences throughout the cathedral. Busts of Prague luminaries—including Charles, his wives and children, the Prague archbishops, the court chronicler Beneš Krabice of Weitmil, and the cathedral's architects—were added to the cathedral's triforium arch. These sculptures, placed high above the nave, could only be seen by a select few, but their presence represented the intersection of secular and sacred power in Prague's new landmark.

FIGURE 2.3 St. Vitus Cathedral at Prague Castle. Construction began in 1346, but the church was not completed until 1929. Anonymous photograph, late nineteenth century. Rijksmuseum. Public domain.

Richly decorated side chapels honored Charles's Přemyslid ancestors. The bodies of past dukes and kings were exhumed and transferred to the Chapel of St. John the Baptist, the Imperial Chapel, and the Chapel of the Relics. Parler adorned the royal sepulchers with the rulers' stone effigies, guarded by lions, the symbol of Bohemia. Mary Magdalene Chapel, decorated with frescoes of Jesus's female followers, housed relics from Arles. The cathedral architects Arras and Peter Parler were honored with burial sites in the magnificent chapel.

Parler's masterpiece, the Chapel of Saint Wenceslas, became the symbolic heart of the cathedral, as it housed the remains of the emperor's patron saint. Located along the cathedral's southern wall, the chapel incorporated parts of the Romanesque rotunda so that Wenceslas's relics could stay in their original resting place. The chapel walls were embedded with over a thousand large, irregularly shaped Bohemian gemstones lined in gold, while a graceful polychromatic statue of a contemplative Wenceslas, holding a pennon with a lion made of pearls, overlooked the altar. The golden herma of Wenceslas's head, which had held the Bohemian crown before Charles's coronation, stood guard at the tombstone of the saint.

Charles commissioned a magnificent mosaic of the Last Judgment for the cathedral's exterior wall. An image of Christ flanked by angels dominated the scene, which included six Bohemian saints, Charles, and his wife Elisabeth. The Italian painter Niccolò Semitecolo designed the mosaic, and Venetian artists came to Prague to train local craftsmen to install it. Situated above the South Gate, facing the town, the piece is widely considered the most important medieval mosaic north of the Alps. Over a million gilded glass pieces in thirty-one hues glowed in the southern light, leading Prague dwellers to call the cathedral entryway "the Golden Gate."

Thousands of men and women contributed to the cathedral project. Leading artists, architects, and engineers came from all over Europe, but many Czech-speaking artisans and laborers carried out the daily work. The guild system that had been developing through the fourteenth century organized highly skilled craftsmen into societies of stonemasons, goldsmiths, woodworkers, and painters. Masters owned their enterprises, which employed and regularly reviewed the work of journeymen and apprentices, the guilds' lower ranks. With limited available work, masters often protected their coveted positions, forcing qualified artisans to remain at the journeyman rank for their whole careers. The poorest sector, often new arrivals in Prague, worked as day laborers and carried out basic tasks such as cleaning, bringing bread and ale to the artisans, and caring for horses.

It would take centuries for Prague's leaders and workers to build the cathedral; the last addition was not completed until 1929, for the millennium of Saint Wenceslas's martyrdom. Still, the rising edifice swiftly became the focal point of the city's landscape. Overlooking the Vltava, the cathedral's silhouette cast no doubt as to where the locus of Prague and Bohemia's power resided. Charles's building projects not only created symbols of power for the new imperial capital but also forged an integrated city from Prague's independent towns. Each sector—Lesser Town, Castle Town, New Town, and Old Town with its autonomous Jewish quarter—had its own administration and walls. Yet Charles ordered that city walls be constructed to form a large perimeter that enveloped the towns. A new fortification in Lesser Town became known as the Hunger Wall or the Toothed Wall, as Charles allegedly had it built to provide work and food for Prague's poor. The thick limestone structure featured a sawtooth pattern, which, according to tradition, signified that Prague's workers would always have something to eat as long as Charles's construction projects persisted.

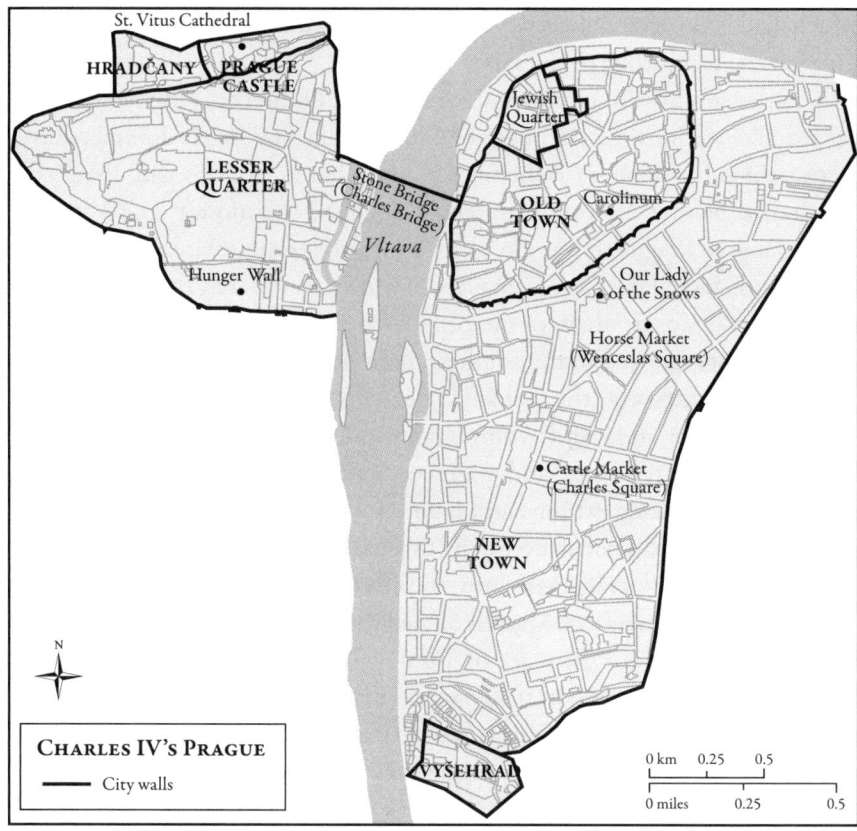

FIGURE 2.4 Map of Prague, second half of the fourteenth century. During the reign of Charles IV (1346–1378), Prague had four independent towns and two fortresses (Prague Castle and Vyšehrad). Charles founded the New Town and the sites marked on this map.

In Charles's era, a new stone bridge traversing the Vltava enjoined the towns on the left and right banks. In 1342, severe flooding had destroyed Vladislav II's Judith Bridge, but high costs delayed its replacement by fifteen years. Until then, temporary wooden structures and ferries offered passage across the river. Charles and his courtiers likely laid the foundation stone of the bridge on Saint Vitus's feast day, June 15, 1357. Yet a popular story claimed that the ceremony occurred on July 9, at 5:31 a.m., corresponding to a sequence of odd numbers: 1-3-5-7-9-7-5-3-1. A favorable conjunction of the sun and Saturn also fell on this date, and Charles often consulted court astrologers about the timing of his events.

Master Otto, an important Prague artisan, designed the bridge, and cathedral architect Peter Parler took over construction and likely designed the grand Old Town bridge tower. Built upon the foundations of the Judith

FIGURE 2.5 The Prague (Charles) Bridge as depicted in Wenceslaus Hollar, *Prague*, from "German Views," 1652–77, Metropolitan Museum of Art, New York.

Bridge, the new bridge's piers were reinforced with iron clips and molten lead. Whereas the Judith Bridge had thirteen arches, the Stone Bridge had sixteen and rose higher above the river. Its convex shape allowed rainwater to flow off the bridge. An unusually strong mortar—legend claims that its secret ingredient was eggs—attached the large sandstone blocks. While these design changes provided a sturdier structure, they also created more places for ice floes to get caught. Ten years into construction another flood ravaged the Vltava basin, followed by two more deluges in 1369 and 1370. Despite several floods and reconstruction projects over its six centuries, the Stone Bridge remains Prague's main pedestrian thoroughfare. Its massive size has accommodated jousting tournaments, music performances, and art kiosks. In 1870, Czech patriots renamed the landmark Charles Bridge after the visionary king.

The bridge tower doubled as a triumphal arch, through which the Bohemian kings rode to their coronations. The tower facade featured statues of Charles IV and his son and heir Wenceslas IV alongside likenesses of Saint Vitus, Saint Adalbert, and Saint Sigismund. At the very top of the bridge tower, artisans added small comical sculptures, including a man reaching under a woman's skirt and another fondling a woman's breast. Perhaps these figures warned Christians against lust, or artists and craftsmen may have hidden irreverent jokes among the royal and religious art that dominated their work.

As the cathedral and the city continued to grow, Charles envisioned Prague as a major pilgrimage destination for the Christian world. The young Charles adored the passion relics at Sainte-Chapelle in Paris and wanted Prague to have a relic collection second only to Rome's. Medieval Christians believed that holy relics mediated between the sacred and earthly realms, and rulers understood the holy objects as signifiers of spiritual and secular power.

Beneš Krabice wrote about Charles's profound experiences with holy relics:

> The lord Charles...came to the monastery of the nuns of Saint Clare at Saint Francis in the city of Prague and among other relics they brought to him the finger of Saint Nicholas, which the pope gave to Anežka...the founder of that monastery. And King Charles took a little knife and cut a bit from this finger, which he wanted to keep for himself because of his piousness. And when he looked at the little knife, he saw what seemed traces of fresh blood. He was frightened by this miracle because the finger was old and dried-up.

Prague's importance as a repository for precious objects dated back to the reign of Charles's patron Wenceslas, who brought Ludmila's body to Prague and acquired a shoulder bone of Saint Vitus. Charles honored Wenceslas's devotion by bringing Saint Vitus's full skeleton from Saxony to the eponymous Prague cathedral. At the time of Charles's coronation, Prague had seventy-seven relics, but by his death, he had over six hundred objects ranging from cloths that touched the foreheads of saints to full skeletons. Charles commissioned hundreds of reliquaries from Prague's guild of goldsmiths, and other objects were made of silver, amethysts, and precious stones. As Charles's collection grew, the cathedral and other churches began to issue pilgrimage medals to encourage foreigners to visit Prague.

The archbishop named January 2 a holy day to celebrate Prague's relic collection. The Prague archdiocese invited locals and pilgrims to share in the Eucharist and view the precious objects. Charles particularly esteemed saint-kings like Charlemagne and Louis. Following his 1365 coronation as king of Burgundy, Charles created a cult around the little-known Saint Sigismund, a sixth-century Burgundian king and martyr. He brought Sigismund's skull and half of his skeleton from Burgundy to Prague. A spectrum of Prague dwellers—including a beggar woman, a baker, a blacksmith, and the archbishop himself—attributed miracles to Sigismund's reliquary, and Charles and his fourth wife, Elisabeth of Pomerania, named their newborn son Sigismund in 1368. The Burgundian saint's image frequently joined the Bohemian saints in Bohemian devotional paintings.

The Prague "Imperial Style" adopted French, Italian, and German techniques to convey its subjects' personalities and emotions. Charles wanted Prague to rival Italy in religious objects and paintings, and his court attracted artists from many European cities. Devoted to Marian imagery, Charles donated the richly colored Zbraslav Madonna to the Cistercian monastery where his mother was buried. The tenderness between the Madonna and the infant Jesus perhaps touched the king, who lost his mother as a child. Charles understood the importance of his image as a man of faith and power. Fourteenth-century European rulers increasingly commissioned portraits that depicted them as individuals with recognizable traits and physical characteristics. A devotional altar made for Jan of Očko placed the king and the archbishop of Prague at Mary's heavenly coronation. (See Color Plate 4.)

Charles kept his most prized works of art at his private residence, Karlštejn Castle. Located less than twenty miles from Prague, Karlštejn was established in 1348 shortly after Charles ascended the Bohemian throne. In 1355, the king stayed there to oversee its construction and decoration. The Bohemian crown jewels and many of Charles's holy relics were stored in the heavily fortified castle. Karlštejn became Charles's retreat and a place of prayer and contemplation.

Karlštejn's main treasure is Charles's private Chapel of the Holy Rood, which was consecrated in 1365. Atop the castle tower, the chapel represented Charles's concept of paradise. Esteemed court painter Master Theodoric won the commission to design the chapel, which contains 129 portraits of saints.

FIGURE 2.6 Karlštejn Castle, founded by Charles IV in 1346. Photo by the author.

Masterpieces of medieval portraiture, the images have unique expressions, rich symbolism, reliquary niches, and gold, pearl, and jewel adornments. In Theodoric's portrait of Saint Matthew, considered one of his finest works, a small angel whispers into the evangelist's ear. Charles's beloved patron saint, Catherine, holds the wheel of her martyrdom, and Charlemagne has an imperial orb and shield. A mural in the Chapel of the Holy Rood, also by Theodoric, cast Charles IV as the third magi who visited the infant Jesus. *The Adoration of the Three Kings* is considered the first European royal crypto-portrait, an artwork that places a king's visage in a biblical scene. Theodoric's aesthetic became known as the soft style; smooth fabrics, silky hair, and blurred edges created an ethereal glow around his holy subjects. Theodoric was richly rewarded for his services. His house in the Castle District stood next to Peter Parler's home; he was appointed headmaster of the prestigious Old Town Painters Guild of St. Luke; and he received an untaxed estate outside the city. In return, he created a symbolic vocabulary that centered Charles's religious values and aesthetic tastes.

FIGURE 2.7 *Portrait of Saint Catherine*, one of 129 icon-like saintly portraits designed by Master Theodoric for Charles IV's Chapel of the Holy Rood, ca. 1355–1365. National Gallery, Prague, CC BY-SA 4.0 via Wikimedia Commons.

Charles died at Prague Castle on November 29, 1378. He was sixty-two years old and suffered from gout, pneumonia, and the long-term effects of his tournament injury. Following a failed mission with his son Wenceslas to reconcile the church's rival centers in Rome and Avignon, Charles came home exhausted and defeated. He died a few days later in the city of his birth.

Even in death, Charles exhibited grace and power. Attendants embalmed Charles's body and prepared for a funeral befitting the king of Bohemia, King of the Romans, and emperor of the Holy Roman Empire. For eleven days, Charles's body lay upon a bier at the royal palace. He was dressed in a purple cloak and covered with golden cloth. The crowns of Bohemia, Lombardy, and the Holy Roman Empire lay above his head, with his mace, orb, and sword at his side. Charles made his last journey through Prague in December 1378. The three-day funeral procession followed Charles's coronation route, from Vyšehrad through the New and Old Towns, across the Stone Bridge, and into Lesser Town. Thirty men and twelve knights carried Charles's cloth-covered bier, followed by Charles's widow, Empress Elisabeth of Pomerania. Noblewomen dressed in black filled forty black-draped carriages, and as many as seven thousand mourners walked in the procession. Every sector of Prague society participated, including representatives of the Bohemian nobility, Prague's Old and New Town councils, artisan guilds, professors, and students. At the end of the parade, a single knight in armor carried Charles's helmet and sword, pointed toward the earth.

Finally, on December 14, the procession journeyed to Charles's resting place at Prague Castle. At St. Vitus Cathedral, Charles's body, with the imperial crown on his head, lay in a pewter casket. Archbishop John Očko led the burial mass, and the Czech theologian Vojtěch Raňkův of Ježova eulogized Charles as the "Father of the country" (*Pater patriae*). Before his burial, attending monks replaced Charles's royal garments with a Franciscan habit, a symbol of his piety and humility. The emperor's sepulcher stands behind the altar of St. Vitus Cathedral to this day. The words engraved upon it remind visitors of Charles's power and piety:

> In the year one thousand three hundred and seventy-eight, November twenty-nine, I, Charles the Fourth, once the terror of the whole world, the emperor and invincible, by the death defeated, in this grave I am covered. Nurturing Lord, I beg, may my spirit reach the stars. Oh, let everyone pray for me, those whom I, dead, left and whom in life I cherished.
>
> And so let his soul rest in holy peace.[19]

The Caroline era marked the pinnacle of medieval Prague. Charles IV was the most powerful king in Bohemia's history, and Czechs today consistently choose him as their most beloved historical figure. He embraced his father's worldly outlook and his mother's Czech noble background to legitimize his authority in Bohemia and Central Europe. As Holy Roman emperor, he remade his birth city into a center of education, architectural innovation, popular religion, and political power. Prague's university, stone bridge, and largest square would all bear Charles's name.

3

Faith and Violence in Wenceslas IV's Prague

CHARLES IV HAD done everything possible to ensure an easy succession for his beloved son, Wenceslas IV. He had him crowned king of Bohemia at age two, and when Wenceslas turned fifteen, he asked the prince electors of the Holy Roman Empire to designate him as the future King of the Romans. However, the young Wenceslas—only seventeen when Charles died in 1378—lacked his father's abilities in statecraft. He ruled during a chaotic time and failed to resolve the manifold religious disputes, political rivalries, economic uncertainty, and spread of disease. The schism in the Catholic Church cast a long shadow over Wenceslas's reign. For four decades beginning in 1378, the church had two—and sometimes three—rival popes. Wenceslas was elected King of the Romans but did not seek a papal coronation as Holy Roman emperor, fearing it would stir up more tensions in a divided Europe. His decision weakened his symbolic power in the empire but perhaps protected his kingdom from further conflict.

Wenceslas had to contend with manifold rivalries in Prague. University professors quarreled over theology, while Czech and German burghers competed for linguistic and political prominence. Just over a year after Charles IV's death, the plague returned to Prague, much more devastating than the Black Death outbreak of 1348 to 1353. As much as 15 percent of the Bohemian population died, and Prague reportedly lost 30 percent of its Christian clergy. An economic downturn followed as silver mining and agricultural production declined precipitously throughout Bohemia.

In this tense environment, anti-Semitic rhetoric erupted in Prague. Some Christians blamed Jews for spreading the plague and causing economic decline. They began to call Wenceslas "the Jewish king," claiming he protected Jewish moneylenders while leaving the rest of the city to suffer. Since the church forbade usury—charging high interest on loans—many Christians relied on Jewish bankers. Few Prague Jews engaged in moneylending, but the stereotype persisted, especially during other economic crises. The church did not discourage the belief. In fact, in his Christmas sermon, Archbishop John of Jenstein warned Prague's Christians that Jewish wealth revealed the advent of the Antichrist:

> One key sign... is the prosperity of the Jews, who are multiplying and gathering everywhere, favored with such great immunity that we must greatly fear the wrath of the Lord, lest he permit the Antichrist to come.... The synagogue profits more than the church of Christ, and among princes, a single Jew can accomplish more than a nobleman or a prelate. Indeed, princes and magnates are impoverished by unheard-of interest rates (*usurias*), as if [the Jews] could enrich and assist their lord Antichrist with those treasures.[1]

The self-administered Jewish ghetto lay within the Old Town, and boundaries between Christian and Jewish spaces were often blurred, creating competition for living space. All houses in the Old Town were designated as Jewish or Christian, but Jews could petition to purchase a Christian house if they paid a tithe to the local parish. Christians often resented Jews' ability to buy so-called Christian property, and several lawsuits claimed that certain Jews had not paid the required tithes. The plague outbreak exacerbated these tensions. The fear of disease convinced several wealthy Old Town families to invest in rural estates and convert their townhomes into rental property, causing the area's economic stratification to increase. The area around Old Town Square and St. Gall's market remained affluent and German speaking, but poor Czech-speaking renters lived in the labyrinthine streets bordering the Jewish quarter.

The plague outbreak of 1380 also stifled the market for foreign luxury goods, threatening the incomes of many Old Town dwellers. The educated and prosperous elite associated with the university and archbishopric supported a market for luxury goods that surpassed other cities in the empire. Prague was a lucrative trade center for Flemish and Italian cloths and Eastern spices. A German chronicler of the era wrote, "In Bohemia, a pig eats more saffron in a year than a German in his whole life."[2] Yet, the plague hindered traders' travel abroad, and market stalls were shuttered. Jewish merchants and financiers again received blame for circumstances out of their control.

Although tensions had always existed, Prague's Christians and Jews usually coexisted with few disturbances. In 1389, a massacre of Prague Jews shattered that fragile peace. The event was the third anti-Jewish massacre in

Prague's recorded history and the first in over two centuries. Not since 1161, when eighty-five Jews were executed for allegedly poisoning a well near Vyšehrad, had Prague Jews experienced such large-scale anti-Semitic violence. Conflicts between European Christian and Jewish communities often peaked during the spring Easter and Passover celebrations. Holy Week passion plays accused the Jewish community of causing Jesus's death and mocked Jewish rituals and beliefs. Good Friday sermons rebuked the "perfidious Jews." Sometimes, Christians attempted to force conversion on Jews, as mobs confiscated Torah scrolls, religious texts, ritual objects, and personal property. However, the scale of the violence in 1389 was unprecedented in Prague.

At least twenty Christian texts—in Czech, German, and Latin—as well as a Hebrew lament (*selicha*) by Rabbi Avigdor Kara recorded the outbreak of violence. Kara witnessed the slaughter of his community when he was a boy, and years later, he described it in one of the most well-known Hebrew texts written in medieval Prague. While none of these sources represent a factual narrative of the massacre, the large number of writings and their emotional qualities testify to the significance of the massacre for Prague's Jews and Christians.

The Christian texts alleged that Jewish youngsters provoked the massacre by attacking a priest who was bringing communion to a parishioner living at the edge of the ghetto. This type of medieval narrative rationalized violence against Jews and taught Christians to fear the community. According to these accounts, local authorities apprehended and fined a few Jewish men for interfering with a Christian procession, but some members of the Old Town Christian community took matters into their own hands. On Easter Sunday, an angry mob gathered at the gate of the Jewish quarter, broke in, and set fire to the Old Synagogue.

Kara's Hebrew elegy, "All That Suffering," described a thong of Christians "with weapons in hand, bows and arrows, [and] axes." Kara recalled, "Blood touched blood in that Spring month on the last day of Passover, that feast of sweet salvation. And now a roasting fire has burnt me, has baked the Matzos." Kara mourned both the dead and the surviving community members who were "left without comfort" following the massacre. According to Kara, the victims included the community elders: "the rabbi, his pious brother, and his only son."[3] Up to one-half of the community—between four hundred and three thousand Jews—died that day. The survivors were blamed for the attack on their own town. The king's forces arrested the survivors and confiscated their property, worth, by some accounts, five barrels of silver. Kara's Hebrew account remained embedded in Prague culture. Each year on Yom Kippur, Prague's Jewish community gathered at the Old-New Synagogue to hear

Kara's lament. They remembered the desecration of the Jewish cemetery and the "sword of fire" that ravaged their synagogue. The practice continued in Prague until the Nazi occupation in 1939.

Religious strife was not limited to anti-Semitic attacks in Prague's residential neighborhoods. At Wenceslas IV's court, the monarch found himself at odds with church authorities led by John of Jenstein, the archbishop of Prague. A notorious dispute occurred in 1393 when the king and archbishop disagreed on whom to install as the new abbot in a wealthy Benedictine monastery. Investiture conflicts were common in the Middle Ages, as monarchs believed they should have input in the selection of church officials. Wenceslas wanted to place allies in key church institutions to counterbalance his numerous disputes with the secular nobility. Jenstein ignored the king's wishes and allowed the monks to choose an abbot from among their brotherhood. The archbishop's vicar general, the priest and canon scholar John of Nepomuk, followed Jenstein's orders and installed the new abbot in defiance of the king.

Furious, Wenceslas ordered Nepomuk's execution. Late at night on the spring equinox, Wenceslas's guards dragged the vicar general to the Vltava River, tied his limbs, and threw him into the cold waters. Residents of Prague reported that five stars rose from the Vltava's dark waters and considered the phenomenon Nepomuk's first miracle. Local church officials and noblemen venerated Nepomuk, and the archbishop referred to him as a saint and martyr.

A rumor spread in Prague that Wenceslas executed Nepomuk not for political reasons but because he would not reveal the queen's confessions. The story of Wenceslas IV as a jealous and vengeful husband resonated with those predisposed to dislike the king. Members of the Bohemian nobility formed an opposition group following Nepomuk's death and argued that Wenceslas IV was irrational and unjust. The Bohemian nobility had long prioritized their own interests over loyalty to the monarch. Since the advent of the "foreign" Luxembourg dynasty, Czech-speaking noblemen had championed their rights as native lords. In 1394, the opposition group captured and imprisoned Wenceslas, replacing him with his cousin Jošt, the Margrave of Moravia. In 1396, Wenceslas's half-brother Sigismund, the king of Hungary, helped negotiate a truce between the king and nobility. In return, the childless Wenceslas designated Sigismund as his heir. In 1405, Wenceslas agreed to fifteen demands, including reserving certain political offices, such as the Burgrave of Prague, for the native Czech nobility. The nobility won the right to approve Wenceslas's royal appointments and to challenge the king's promotion of burghers and gentry to state offices.

Wenceslas faced international challenges as well. He sought to end the Papal Schism and met with the French king, Charles VI, to strategize, but the two monarchs were unable to broker peace in Europe. Frustrated with Wenceslas's ineptitude, the Holy Roman Empire's prince electors deposed Wenceslas in 1400 and elected a new King of the Romans, Rupert of the Palatinate. In 1402, Wenceslas was temporarily imprisoned once more, this time by his half-brother Sigismund, who had his eye on the imperial title. Finally, in 1411, following Rupert's death, Wenceslas gave up all claims on the Roman crown in exchange for retaining the Kingdom of Bohemia. His young half-brother Sigismund ascended the imperial throne.

Prague's economy suffered from Wenceslas's political troubles, compounded by the post-plague recession. His loss of the imperial title in 1400 meant that Bohemia no longer had direct influence in the German regions, where Charles IV had conducted business and encouraged trade. Further, the Bohemian nobles had wrested considerable regional power from Wenceslas and supplemented their incomes by charging high tolls to traveling merchants. These fees and recessed textile prices discouraged German merchants from coming to Prague. A prominent textile merchant from Regensburg saw his profits from sales in Prague drop from 70 percent in 1383 to 13 percent in 1401 and closed his Prague business.

For ordinary workers, wages fell while unemployment and the cost of living increased. At the turn of the fifteenth century, an unskilled worker made a daily wage of a half groschen plus food or one groschen without food, whereas a skilled worker like a bricklayer could make about two to two and a half groschen per day, an adequate wage before the steep inflation took hold. In contrast, a priest who held an office at St. Vitus Cathedral earned over fifty groschen a day.[4] Food costs rose steeply when middlemen gathered at the Prague city gates to buy grain and other foodstuffs from the peasants coming into town. In turn, they greatly increased the prices at the Prague markets. The practice became so corrupt and costly that the Prague church synod in 1405 declared that "to buy the year's produce or wine at harvest or vintage, cheaper so that they can sell for a higher price later, such persons shall have sinned mortally."[5]

Under such a difficult economic situation, many Prague residents fell into serious debt. Homeowners took out mortgages on their houses and became beholden to the persons or institutions that lent them money. A debtor sometimes acquired cash by making a pious bequest to a priest or religious institution. The borrower agreed to pay a yearly sum "in rent" to pay back the loan, and the interest secured prayers for family members, a church altar, or food for the poor. In this way, the church circumvented the rules against usury, but the borrowers knew that these clergymen took advantage of the strained economy.

While many Prague citizens struggled to make ends meet, Wenceslas IV often retreated into his private world. He did not share Charles's political talents, but he did follow in his father's footsteps in his passion for the arts. Wenceslas IV became one of the foremost collectors of illuminated manuscripts and sponsored religious art in the International Gothic style—a fusion of influences from Italy, France, the German states, and Bohemia. Prague's manifestation of Gothic art became known as the Beautiful Style, which featured strong colors and stylized depictions of religious subjects. The Třeboň Altarpiece, rendered by a Prague court painter in the 1380s, set the standard for the Beautiful Style. The three surviving panels depict Jesus's night of prayer in the Garden of Gethsemane, his entombment, and his resurrection. The Beautiful Style's soft brushstrokes, strong colors, and authentic human emotions prefigured the Renaissance and Reformation discussions about individual piety.

Influenced by Archbishops Ernest of Pardubice and John Očko of Vlašim, Wenceslas IV favored illuminated manuscripts above other art forms. In addition to religious works, Wenceslas commissioned several secular manuscripts, including illuminated versions of his father's golden bull, a Bohemian mining law, collections of courtly poetry, and a Czech translation of the popular travelogue *The Travels of Sir John Mandeville*. The richly decorated *Viennese Astronomical Manuscript with the Alfonsine Star Tables* and the *Astrological Manuscript of Avenarre* shed light on late medieval scientific practices and contemporary tools for studying the heavens. Religious works in the king's collection included books of psalms, prayer books, and hymnals.

The Wenceslas Bible represented the pinnacle of Bohemian manuscripts. The Prague German burgher Martin Rothlöw, possibly the wealthiest man in the city, gifted the German-language Bible to the king and funded nine illuminators to work on it for over a decade. Written in a striking Gothic script, the Wenceslas Bible was one of the earliest German biblical translations of the Old Testament. The Bible's renowned depiction of the Tower of Babel elucidated medieval construction techniques and machinery. Members of the royal household are depicted throughout the manuscript's illustrations. Wenceslas IV watches an attack on Jezebel from above, and the king's and queen's portraits feature in several of the Bible's elaborate historiated initials. Recurrent popular motifs such as female bath attendants, love knots, kingfishers (Wenceslas IV's symbol), floral designs, and Bohemian coats of arms created continuity in the vast five-volume work. (See Color Plate 5.)

FIGURE 3.1 *Bifolium with Christ in Majesty in an Initial A, from an Antiphonary*, Prague, ca. 1410. Cloisters Collection, Metropolitan Museum of Art, New York.

Wenceslas had an extraordinary personal library with a strength in scientific topics. The manuscripts from Wenceslas's court gained international interest. When Wenceslas's sister Anne married Richard II of England, she brought a German, Czech, and Latin evangelistary, an illuminated collection of the Gospels. Some have suggested that Anne's literary influence on the English court impressed the writer Geoffrey Chaucer and may have inspired John Wyclif to embark on his English translation of the Bible.

Wenceslas also invested in Prague University, founded by his father. He purchased a building in the Old Town for the Carolinum (Caroline College) and founded another college across from it. These buildings created a campus for the university, enabling it to house students and professors, host lectures and seminars, and provide offices and meeting spaces to a growing administration. Wenceslas established scholarships for indigent students and bestowed gifts upon the various faculties. The Old Town became the intellectual center of Prague, where debates about religion, government, and philosophy abounded.

The Astronomical Clock (Orloj), installed in 1410 on the Old Town Hall tower, was a hallmark of early fifteenth-century Prague. Designed by imperial clockmaker Mikuláš of Kadań and Jan Šindel, a mathematics and astronomy professor at Prague University, the original clock had two working dials, one to tell the time and the other to show the solar astronomical sign. The remarkable clock conveyed an idealistic vision of Prague as a center for science and learning, public art, and broader political representation.

FIGURE 3.2 Astronomical Clock, Old Town Hall, 1410. Photograph ca. 1910. George Grantham Bain Collection, Library of Congress, LC-DIG-ggbain-27095.

The rise in education among the burgher class and noblewomen created an atmosphere in Prague ripe for intellectual exchange. By the late fourteenth century, the university had grown in size and reputation, and the movement of students and professors through Europe brought new ideas and debates to Prague. Even the church advocated for more religious education for laypeople and encouraged preaching on biblical texts and church teachings. Wenceslas's passion for illuminated books on religious and secular themes reflected a society more engaged with learning than ever before.

Among the educated, no topic was more important than church reform. The Papal Schism between Rome and Avignon had exacerbated tensions within the church, and both papal courts demanded financial support and declarations of loyalty from monarchs, archbishoprics, monastic communities, universities, and individuals. Prague's reformer priests became increasingly vocal, decrying corruption within the church hierarchy and monastic orders. In turn, church officials hurled accusations of heresy at those who dared to raise controversial issues.

In 1390, a young man from southern Bohemia entered this vibrant setting to enroll at Prague University. Little is known about Jan Hus's early life, but he likely grew up in a Czech-speaking peasant family and received an education at a grammar school or monastery. Hus must have shown great promise as a student since someone of his economic background rarely attended university. While in Prague, he struggled financially, supporting himself by singing in churches. Years later, he wrote about the pressure he felt to spend his last bit of money not on food but on an indulgence for the forgiveness of sins. This experience caused him to contemplate the unfair financial practices of the church.

While not an exceptionally strong scholar, Hus quickly established himself as a leader among his fellow students. Debates about church reform took place in university seminars and informal discussions among professors and students interested in theology. Hus soon became acquainted with the reformist teachings of the late Oxford scholar John Wyclif, who criticized excessive church wealth and corruption. Hus did not ascribe to all of Wyclif's teachings, but he found in the Oxford scholar a guide to think through the moral necessity of church reform.

Hus's 1396 master's degree from the Faculty of Philosophy compelled him to teach at Prague University for two years. He stayed in his post beyond this obligation, lecturing and continuing his studies in the Faculty of Theology. During this era, he was ordained into the priesthood and quickly rose through the university ranks. In 1401, Hus was named dean of the Faculty of

Philosophy. A year later, he was elected university rector, a rotating administrative post.

By the fourteenth century, popular preaching had become a phenomenon in Europe. Hus made a name for himself in Prague as a charismatic orator, and in 1402, Hus became the rector of the Bethlehem Chapel, the center of the Bohemian reform movement. The Prague burgher Jan Kříž and royal court member Hanuš of Mulheim founded the chapel in 1391 as a space where Prague residents could hear sermons in the Czech language. Kříž donated his large garden for the building, and Hanuš provided a cottage and cellar for the preacher and custodian. The founders had admired John Milič and hoped to reinstate inspiring vernacular preaching. As the largest indoor meeting space in Prague, Bethlehem Chapel could hold up to three thousand people. It soon became unofficially associated with Prague University and earned a reputation for challenging church practices. Reform-minded priests, university scholars, and ordinary Prague residents flocked to the chapel. Educated women attended services, as literacy among noble and burgher women had risen considerably during Charles's reign. Sources from the era suggest that even Queen Sophia, wife of Wenceslas IV, occasionally attended mass there. A group of noblewomen, some who had never married and some widows, bought several houses near the Bethlehem Chapel and formed a religious community similar to the Beguines of Western Europe. These women did not take holy orders but centered their lives on prayer, communal living, and listening to daily sermons.

The popularity of preaching in Prague meant that parish priests could not keep up with the demand for sermons. Some parishes had a special office (*benefice*) whose holder was responsible only for preaching, not pastoral care. In the early fifteenth century, at least fourteen Prague parish churches had special preaching posts, whereas Nuremberg, a city of similar size and wealth, had only two. Preachers like Hus prepared hundreds of sermons each year, usually one a day for most of the year and two during Lent and Advent. Hus preached to fellow priests, scholars, and students at the university in Latin, but his Czech sermons at Bethlehem were often extemporaneous exegeses on biblical passages. Hus emphasized God's divine power over the earthly power of the church hierarchy, and he criticized priests for claiming that they alone could perform the sacraments. He had his treatise "Six Errors," which described priestly abuses of power, inscribed on the walls of Bethlehem Chapel, and he would gesture toward them during his sermons.[6]

Popular medieval preachers like Hus used emotion and storytelling to challenge their congregations to live the message of the sermons. Hus called for an end to the extravagant lifestyles of the church hierarchy and monastic orders, and he wanted church leaders to acknowledge that Christ, not the pope or cardinals, was the true head of the church. Moral reform lay at the heart of Hus's message to his congregants. He advised his lay followers and fellow priests to focus on their personal faith, ethics, and responsibilities and quoted scriptures that warned against the sins of adultery, fornication, and drunkenness.

Around the time of Hus's Bethlehem appointment, his former student Jerome of Prague traveled to England, where he copied out several of Wyclif's writings and returned to Prague with the texts. Although many Wyclifite texts were already available in Prague, some university students traveled to England to meet his followers and search for more texts. Prague students and friends Mikuláš Faulfiš and Jiří z Kněhnic traveled to Oxford in 1406 and returned to Prague with a chip broken off Wyclif's tombstone, some texts that they had copied, and a document bearing the seal of Oxford University stating that Wyclif had never been condemned as a heretic. Despite the distance, many of Wyclif's supporters in England, known as Lollards, knew of the religious debates in Bohemia. The Oxford theologian Peter Payne met with Faulfiš and Kněhnic in England and eventually came to Prague. The Wyclifite priest Richard Wyche corresponded with Hus, acknowledging the persecution Wyclif's Bohemian admirers suffered. The journeys to England reinvigorated the university discussions of Wyclif but also engendered more conflict. In 1403, Prague University faculty met and voted to condemn a list of forty-five heretical statements attributed to Wyclif. Faculty voted within blocs, as represented by the four university nations: Bohemian, Bavarian, Polish, and Saxon. Only the Bohemian nation opposed the condemnation of Wyclif.

The conflicts among the faculty reflected the Czech-German tensions in Prague, which had steadily escalated since the reign of Přemysl Otakar II. Hus, like many in his era, perceived the local conflicts as rooted in linguistic identity. Anyone living in Prague in the early fifteenth century needed to be familiar with both German and Czech, but Hus lamented that Prague Czech had become tainted by German words and pronunciations. The story of the Tower of Babel was an instructive metaphor for Hus, who believed that God had created linguistic communities that should govern themselves. In a popular sermon, Hus drew parallels between Prague's Czech speakers and Nehemiah, the Hebrew prophet who must rebuild Jerusalem after the Babylonian captivity.

> Just as Nehemiah whipped and beat the Jewish children who could not speak Jewish but half Azotic, the people from Prague and the Czechs should be whipped who speak half Czech and half German and

say...*Handtuch* instead of *ubresec* (tablecloth)...*knedlík* instead of *šiška* (dumpling)...*mázhaus* instead of *svrchní sein* (measuring house).⁷

Hus argued that in Prague, "the Czech language has already been corrupted," such that "true Czechs" cannot understand it. Here, he shared the worries of the Czech nobility: Without cultivation, their culture could die out. Noble endowments provide evidence that Hus's wealthiest followers agreed. Lady Catherine of Vraba, a widowed noblewoman, provided a living for a priest at St. Vitus Cathedral whose main task would be preaching in Czech on each holy day and during Advent and Lent. She also funded a women's community in Prague, composed of twelve virgins and widows who had devoted their lives to God.⁸

Hus appealed to the Bohemian nobility's attachment to the Czech language. He wrote, "The princes should also take care that the Czech language does not die: if a Czech marries a German woman, the children shall learn Czech at once so that the language does not become confused. For the confusion of language is the beginning of envy, anger, conflict, and strife." Hus also claimed, "The Emperor Charles IV of holy memory has ordered the people of Prague to let their children learn Czech, and that in the town hall, which is called in German *rothaus*, they should speak and take actions in Czech."⁹ There exists no evidence that Charles IV commanded this, but Czech-speaking Prague embraced the deceased emperor's legacy of supporting Czech culture. Hus's early writings suggest the priest's frustration with German dominance at Prague University. A Latin manuscript that belonged to Hus included several anti-German jibes in the margins, including a famous yet ambiguous note: "Ha ha Germans! Out! Out!"

The international issues surrounding the Papal Schism created yet another conflict in Prague. In 1409, Wenceslas IV planned to end the schism once and for all by calling a council in Pisa that would select a single pope. However, neither Pope Gregory XII in Rome nor Pope Benedict XIII in Avignon would step down when the council selected Alexander V and then John XXIII following Alexander's untimely death. Constituencies throughout Europe declared their loyalty to one of the popes or remained neutral. Hoping that a third pope could be elected and the other two ousted, King Wenceslas IV asked the Prague University faculty to declare neutrality. Wenceslas had his own motivations for arranging the council. He hoped that a new pope would restore his title, King of the Romans, and anoint him as Holy Roman emperor. Wenceslas did not even have support in Prague for his scheme. The Prague archbishop, Zbyněk Zajíc of Hažmburk, remained loyal to Gregory XII, and the Bavarian, Saxon, and Polish nations at the university sided with him.

Only the Bohemian nation declared itself neutral. Frustrated by the lack of support from the university he helped fund, Wenceslas IV issued the Kutná Hora decrees of 1409, which gave the Bohemian nation three votes on university matters while the other three nations shared one vote. In protest, nearly one thousand faculty and students—mostly German speakers—disenrolled, many moving to the University of Heidelberg or the newly founded University of Leipzig, where they gossiped about the "Bohemian heresy." A 1410 papal bull prohibited preaching in private chapels like Bethlehem, but Hus continued to speak out against church corruption.

Hus found himself at odds with the archbishop of Prague. Barely educated, Zbyněk Zajíc of Hažmburk had served as a military commander under Wenceslas IV and then purchased the position of archbishop at age twenty-six. While he initially admired the erudite Hus, Zbyněk became wary of the preacher, whose criticism of church corruption, especially simony, implicated him. In 1410, Zbyněk ordered all books by John Wyclif to be confiscated and destroyed. On July 16, Prague residents gathered at the Archbishop's Palace courtyard to watch over two hundred books burn. Zbyněk then excommunicated Hus for failing to turn over his copies of Wyclif's writings. A mob of students and other Hus supporters taunted the archbishop at his palace gates, singing,

> Zbyněk, Bishop, A-B-C
> burned all the books
> never knowing what they say.[10]

Wenceslas understood Hus's tremendous popularity and ordered the archbishop to replace the books and reinstate Hus to the church. Zbyněk refused, but fearing for his life, he fled Prague. On his way to seek refuge in Hungary, Zbyněk fell ill and died. Rumors spread through the empire that the archbishop had been murdered.

Hus's excommunication was revoked, and he continued to preach against corruption and immorality. In 1412, the Pisan pope, John XXIII, turned to Wenceslas to help fund his crusade against the king of Naples by demanding the king pay indulgences on behalf of all Bohemian citizens. When Wenceslas agreed to the payments, Hus and his followers condemned the king. The radical priest Jakoubek of Stříbro declared the papacy a tool of the Antichrist, and

Hus accused the pope and king of simony. Encouraged by Hus's preaching, public demonstrations broke out in Prague. Three young men caused a commotion by decrying the king and pope during mass at Týn Church on Old Town Square. Hus tried to intervene on their behalf, but the authorities ordered them beheaded. Local Prague residents retrieved the victims' bodies and brought the corpses to the Bethlehem Chapel, singing and carrying a placard that read, "These men are martyrs." The following day, Hus celebrated a martyrs' mass instead of a traditional mass for the dead and permitted their burial at Bethlehem Chapel. In response, the Pisan pope excommunicated Hus and threatened to place the entire population of Prague under an interdict, meaning that no one in the city could receive the sacraments while Hus remained active.

Hus voluntarily left Prague to protect his followers there, and he preached in other parts of Bohemia for the next two years. He gained increased support from Czech noblemen who sympathized with Hus's critiques of King Wenceslas and the church hierarchy and shared his passion for maintaining the Czech language. While in self-imposed exile, Hus collected his ideas into a single text, *De ecclesia* (On the church).

Despite Hus's absence, the reform movement thrived in Prague. In 1414, Jakoubek of Stříbro introduced Utraquism (communion in both kinds) at the Old Town church St. Martin in the Wall. Utraquists advocated for lay worshipers to receive both bread and wine—body and blood—during the Eucharist. In the High Middle Ages, only clergy drank from the chalice. Priests at the Bethlehem Chapel, St. Adalbert's, and St. Michael's in Prague followed Jakoubek's example. Jakoubek also advocated frequent communion for the laity, whereas the church taught that lay Christians should only take communion once or twice a year. These practices symbolized the equality of lay Christians and the clergy.

Dissenters from throughout Europe journeyed to Prague to find like-minded Christians. Oxford theologian and accused heretic Peter Payne came to Prague in 1414. The Hussites held Payne in high esteem and nicknamed him "Master English." He befriended Jakoubek, supporting the lay chalice and other moderate Utraquist teachings. Payne became affiliated with Prague's Dresden school, a group of radical intellectuals who gathered at the House of the Black Rose in New Town to debate theological issues. The school's leaders also encouraged public demonstrations among Prague citizens.

In 1414, King Wenceslas's half-brother Sigismund, serving as King of the Romans and king of Hungary, called another church council, this time in

Constance. The conciliar movement emerged in the fourteenth century as church authorities questioned the singular authority of the pope. Reformers argued that the church comprised all Christian believers and that the pope should be beholden to a council of religious and secular leaders, including cardinals, archbishops, abbots, noblemen, and university professors with expertise in theology or law. Not only did Sigismund want to end the Papal Schism, but also he hoped the council would calm the chaos in Prague.

Sigismund invited Hus to speak to the council and promised him safe passage. Unlike in 1412, when Hus refused to appear in front of a church council, he agreed to Sigismund's offer. The council permitted Hus to travel with companions from the Bohemian nobility, and he spent a month in Constance before being arrested for violating the order against preaching. The council charged Hus with heresy and placed him in solitary confinement in a small, cold cell. Hus's supporters in Prague received reports throughout the trial of the emperor's stubbornness and arrogance, and even several church officials considered Sigismund difficult. When a cardinal corrected the emperor's Latin, Sigismund announced, "I am the emperor. I am above grammar."[11]

Hus endured a grueling prison stay, vomiting blood and suffering from the excruciating pain of kidney stones. During his incarceration, he wrote numerous letters to his followers, continuing to develop his philosophy and to critique church corruption. The most comprehensive record of Hus's trial comes from Peter of Mladoňovice, the secretary of Lord John of Chlum, a Bohemian nobleman who had protected Hus during his exile in southern Bohemia. Peter's account favored Hus and described a chaotic trial during which the bishops shouted over witnesses and contradicted one another. The council accused Hus of supporting Wyclif's arguments against transubstantiation, a claim that Hus denied until his death. While Hus stood trial, the council posthumously excommunicated Wyclif, making it easier to prove Hus's heresy. Hus felt especially betrayed by the Bohemian clerics who spoke against him, and he continued to maintain his innocence. In his last letter, dated June 26, 1415, he addressed his followers in Prague:

> I have determined to write that you may know that the Council, proud, avaricious, and defiled with every crime, hath condemned my Czech books, which it hath never either seen nor heard read, and if it had listened with all its power, would never have understood (for there were present at the Council Frenchmen, Italians, Britons, Spaniards, Germans, and other people of different nationalities).[12]

The trial lasted several months. In early July, the council gathered at the cathedral in Constance to read the guilty verdict and declare Hus a heretic. Hus had to stand upon a table at the front of the cathedral and dress as if preparing to say mass. In dramatic fashion, the bishops then defrocked the Prague priest, stripping him of his garments and cursing him, turn by turn. The eyewitness Peter of Mladoňovice reported, "First they took the cup from his hands, pronouncing this curse: 'O cursed Judas because you have abandoned the counsel of peace and have counseled with the Jews, we take away from you this cup of redemption.'" Next they removed the chasuble, the ornate outer vestment worn during mass, and then the liturgical stole that rested around his shoulders. Hus replied to each bishop's curse by repeating that he "gladly embraced the vilifications for the name of our Lord Jesus Christ" and reminding his inquisitors that Jesus, too, had been stripped and scorned.[13]

Once the garments had been removed, the bishops argued about whether to use a razor or scissors to destroy Hus's tonsure, the hairstyle worn by medieval priests and monks. According to Peter, Hus looked at Sigismund, who oversaw the proceedings, and called to him, "Look! These bishops so far do not know how to agree in this vilification!" Finally, they removed Hus's hair in four swift cuts. The bishops placed a paper crown upon Hus's head as they committed his soul to the devil. Hus responded, "And I commit it to the most merciful Lord Jesus Christ."

Having "deprived him of all ecclesiastical rights," the bishops turned Hus over to Constance's civil authorities, who burned him to death on July 6, 1415. Before his immolation, Hus again proclaimed his innocence of the charges against him. "For God is my witness that I neither preached, affirmed, nor defended [these teachings], though they say that I did." Peter of Mladoňovice and other witnesses attested that Hus sang as the executioners lit the pyre: "Christ, thou son of the living God, have mercy upon me." He chanted until the wind brought a flame to his face and extinguished his last breath. (See Color Plate 6.)

When news of Hus's death arrived in Prague, his followers condemned the execution and the betrayal by their city's religious leaders. Hus had informed them that "the Chapters of Prague and the Vyšehrad [heaped] insults upon God's truth and upon our fatherland, Bohemia." Bohemian noblemen gathered in Prague to issue a protest letter affixed with 452 individual seals, representing approximately one-third of the ninety noble families. Czech noblemen formed the Hussite League, a loose organization that declared its support for the beloved priest and his teachings.

On the first anniversary of Hus's death, followers gathered in the Old Town to commemorate him. The Hussite League kidnapped a bishop and forced him to ordain Utraquist priests and appoint them to posts in Prague churches. Even Queen Sophia, Wenceslas IV's second wife, supported the Hussite cause. Hus's followers at the university pledged to demonstrate Hus's belief that Bohemia "was a land of the purest faith."[14] The Utraquist priest and professor Jakoubek of Stříbro led the movement with the support of most university masters who had remained in Prague. In 1417, the Council of Constance banned giving the chalice to the laity, provoking another protest in Prague. The masters of Prague University issued a counter-decree, declaring Utraquism an orthodox practice.

Prague was the center of the Bohemian reform movement, but Hus had gained followers throughout the region. The fluidity between the countryside and Prague allowed news and ideas to travel efficiently. Noblemen invested in urban property, while wealthy burghers built second homes outside of the city. Noblemen with rural estates appointed priests willing to offer the chalice at mass, thus spreading Utraquist beliefs to peasants. Both in and out of Prague, Hussite priests were taking over pulpits.

In 1416, Prague residents learned that Hus's former student Jerome had also been convicted of heresy and burned to death in Constance. The following year, the Council of Constance finally ended the church schism, forcing the resignation of the three claimant popes and choosing Martin V, who, as Cardinal Otto of Colonna, had been particularly harsh during Hus's trial. Sigismund, in his role as King of the Romans and convener of the council, pledged allegiance to Martin in January 1418. The council issued twenty-four resolutions against the Hussites, and Sigismund directed an order to his half-brother King Wenceslas IV: "First and foremost, the king of Bohemia should swear to preserve the Roman Church and other churches under his jurisdiction in their liberties and should not impose the newly introduced ideas of Wyclif or Hus on either the secular or regular clergy."[15] Sigismund demanded that his brother set things right in Bohemia. Wenceslas, who had quietly tolerated Hus's movement in the past, acquiesced. He returned all Prague churches, save three, to non-Hussite priests, and he replaced several members of the Prague New Town council with anti-reformers. The Hussites on the Old Town and Lesser Town councils feared that they would be next to lose their positions.

Perhaps the Council of Constance believed that the Bohemian crisis ended with Hus's execution, but the people of Prague did not forget their spiritual leader so easily. For four years, protests broke out throughout

Bohemia, and more nobles, priests, peasants, burghers, and workers joined the Hussite cause. Each July, followers commemorated Hus's immolation with demonstrations in Prague, but tensions rose particularly high in 1419. Following King Wenceslas's anti-Hussite declarations, the New Town council imprisoned several men for supporting Utraquism and other heretical teachings. King Wenceslas IV banned public processions and singing as protesters demanded the prisoners' release.

The radical Hussite priest Jan Želivský emerged as a leader in Prague and referred to himself as "the preacher of poor, deprived, and oppressed people."[16] Želivský riled up his congregation with statements against the authorities: "To disobey an evil prince is to obey God," he proclaimed, and "There will be a harsh judgment on those who rule." In one sermon, he suggested that murder may occasionally be justified, as when Elijah had killed the idol-worshiping priests of Baal.

On July 30, 1419, Želivský preached a fiery sermon at Our Lady of the Snows. Earlier that month, upon King Wenceslas's orders, Želivský had been removed from his post at St. Stephen's of the Pond and transferred to one of the three remaining Utraquist churches. The gospel reading that day recounted the miracle of loaves and fishes, in which Jesus transformed seven baskets of bread and a few fish into a feast that fed four thousand followers. Želivský's sermon characterized members of the church hierarchy and monastic orders as selfish and lazy:

> Only those people who labor loyally deserve to be fed with the bread of Christ.... Only those who labor have the right to say, 'this is our daily bread.'... Without doubt, all those who work at useless endeavors eat their bread unworthily.[17]

The congregation of Prague residents and people from the surrounding countryside processed through New Town behind Želivský, who carried the Eucharist in a monstrance. Eyewitnesses reported that protesters carried clubs, swords, and pitchforks. They marched to the Basilica of St. Stephen of the Pond, Želivský's former New Town parish. The resident priest barred the doors, but Želivský's followers broke them down and took over the church. Želivský said mass and distributed communion in both forms to the entire congregation. The crowd then walked to the Gothic New Town Hall at the Cattle Market. The multipurpose building had spaces for local trials, town council meetings, prison cells, a treasury, and two apartments for the guards of the city gate. The crowd demanded freedom for the Hussite prisoners.

According to contemporary reports, someone threw a rock at the crowd from an upper window. Incensed, Hussites stormed the hall while Želivský stood on the square holding up his monstrance. Some accounts place the future Hussite general Jan Žižka at the helm of the crowd. Upon reaching the meeting room, members of the Hussite congregation seized the *burgermeister* and several council members and threw them from the meeting hall window. Some landed on the cobblestones, and others were impaled on iron spikes. All thirteen died of their injuries. Contemporary reports framed the event as a political act, contending that the Hussites did not loot the victims' bodies for their gold chains and coins.

Regional authorities arrived at New Town Square to gain control. John of Bechyně, the sub-chamberlain of Bohemia, arrived with three hundred mounted soldiers but withdrew his troops when he realized how much local support the Hussites had. The crowd had taken over the town hall and elected four military captains. As anti-Hussite residents of New Town fled the city, other Prague dwellers came with makeshift weapons to join the revolutionaries. Wenceslas IV was at Nový Hrad (New Castle), about a mile from New Town, when news of the violence reached him. Outraged, he swore revenge. Soon, though, he took the advice of his pro-Hussite councilors and members of the Old Town council to make peace with the Hussites who had swiftly taken control of New Town. Wenceslas confirmed a slate of pro-Hussite magistrates for the New Town council in exchange for a pledge of loyalty and an apology for the excesses of their demonstration.

This theatrical and deadly event became known as the First Defenestration of Prague and the first confrontation of the Hussite Wars. Scholars debate whether the attack at the town hall was spontaneous or premeditated. Želivský's congregants knew to bring weapons to Sunday mass, and many participants hailed from outside Prague. A week earlier, a Hussite assembly took place in southern Bohemia, where large outdoor ceremonies were common, and participants may have invited fellow believers to come to Prague the following week.[18] It is just as likely that Želivský planned to free the prisoners on a Sunday to avoid violence. The New Town meeting rooms were usually empty on Sunday mornings as councilmen attended mass with their families. Ironically, the town councilmen may have decided to meet on a Sunday because they had heard rumors of an impending revolt and believed the Hussites would avoid a confrontation on a Sunday.

Just over two weeks later, Wenceslas went hunting with his closest associates. As the king rode his horse into a nearby forest, he cried out in agony and collapsed. The king of Bohemia had died of a stroke, likely brought on by the strain of the recent chaos. The reign of Wenceslas, the favorite child of Emperor Charles IV, had come to an end, and his half-brother Sigismund ascended the Bohemian throne. The Hussites gained a foothold in Prague, but the Catholic Church and Holy Roman emperor responded by announcing a crusade to root out the Bohemian heresy. Two decades of warfare ensued.

4

Hussite Wars and New Dynasties

WENCESLAS HAD NOT been a reliable partner to the Hussites, but his untimely death created even more fear and uncertainty in Prague. To the consternation of Bohemia's Hussites, Wenceslas's half-brother Sigismund—the very man who had convened the Council of Constance—claimed the Bohemian throne. The contemporary chronicler Lawrence of Březová described the reaction in Prague: "The day after the death of King Wenceslas, some from among the common people gathered... [and] were running with utter temerity around the churches and were breaking, destroying, and violating organs and images, especially in those churches where people were not permitted to take Utraquist communion."[1]

The city was rent with violence. Radical Hussites attacked monasteries and desecrated churches, cemeteries, and chapels. They paraded monks over the Stone Bridge and to the Old Town Hall. The Bohemian nobility attempted to take control of the situation and demanded that Sigismund recognize Utraquism as the law of God and privilege the Czech language in government matters. Sigismund refused to negotiate until he was crowned king of Bohemia, while the nobility would not bestow the crown unless he negotiated.

Three factions dominated the political and religious landscape in Bohemia. The royalists, led by Wenceslas's widow Sophia, only favored reform within the bounds of the Roman Catholic Church. The Utraquists, also known as the Prague party, prioritized Eucharistic reform through communion in both forms (bread and wine for the laity). They viewed themselves as Jan Hus's true heirs and sought to end corrupt church practices like simony. The leaders of the Prague party included Jakoubek of Stříbro, Prague University masters, and Old Town burghers. Lawrence of Březová sympathized with the Utraquists and presented their moderate views in his chronicle of the Hussite era.

The radicals, known as the Taborites, campaigned for a complete overhaul of the social structure and believed that Christians should eschew wealth, live communally, and share property. The Taborites adopted a millenarian view and relinquished their possessions. They decried the veneration of relics and the religious art and architecture favored by Charles IV and Wenceslas IV. They likened popular depictions of the Virgin Mary, female saints, and angels to "whores" who aroused lust rather than piety. The radicals denounced attention to one's appearance as vanity and disapproved of clerical vestments still worn by Utraquist priests. While most fifteenth-century men were clean-shaven, the Taborites grew out their beards and hair. Women wore simple frocks. At their outdoor church services, the Taborites replaced ritual prayers with communal singing and emotional preaching. All worshipers, regardless of age, received the Eucharist in both kinds. In Prague, Taborites attacked moderates in the streets. Decrying vanity, they clipped off men's groomed mustaches and accosted women who wore stylish hats.

Religious dissidents from around Europe heard about the Bohemian reform movement and made their way to Prague. One group of French heretics proved too radical, even for the most extreme Hussites. They denied the virginity of Mary and the divinity of Jesus. Another dissenter, a French-speaking cloth cutter and Christian brother called Gilles Mersault, fled to Bohemia, where he embraced Hussite teachings. When he returned to Tournai in 1423, he tried to convince his fellow townsmen not to support the crusade against Bohemia. Mersault was burned at the stake.

Within months of the defenestration, Prague divided along religious lines. The royalists occupied the left bank, establishing strongholds at Prague Castle, Strahov Monastery, the Archbishop's Court, and St. Thomas Monastery. The Hussites controlled the Old and New Towns on the right bank. Violence peaked in early November 1419 when Utraquist and Taborite Hussites crossed the Stone Bridge and broke through the Lesser Town walls. The victorious Hussites rang the church bells of the Old and New Towns all night, and skirmishes continued for over a week. Queen Sophia negotiated a ceasefire with the moderate Utraquists, and the Taborites agreed to retreat from Prague.

Sigismund refused to accept the truce, and in March 1420, he convinced Pope Martin V to issue a crusading bull against the Hussites. The imperial army recruited mercenaries with the promise that those who died would earn "the fullness of eternal life."[2] The following month, leaders of the Hussite factions pledged to fight together to defend Bohemia. Despite theological differences, the leaders adopted the Four Articles of Prague, a platform of church reform that endorsed Utraquism, free preaching, abandonment of worldly riches, and loyalty to the country. "We stand...for the cleansing of the Bohemian realm and nation from false and evil slander."[3]

During the spring of 1420, over sixty thousand imperial troops from Meissen, Thuringia, Saxony, Silesia, and Hungary arrived in Prague. Lawrence described the tense atmosphere. Crusaders taunted Hussites "and howled like dogs across the river to the city: 'Ha, Ha, Hus, Hus, Heretic, Heretic.' If perchance a Czech fell in their hands... that person was immediately burned as a heretic without mercy even if that person had never partaken in the communion of both kinds."

The Hussites constructed fortifications, dug moats, and erected palisades of sharp metal spikes in strategic Prague locations. Their commander, Jan Žižka, began to garrison his troops in New Town and on Vítkov, a steep hill on the eastern side of Prague, just outside the city walls. With Sigismund controlling the other two high points of the city, Prague Castle and Vyšehrad, the Hussites needed to control Vítkov.

The imperial armies launched an attack, but the heavily armed Saxon cavalry under the command of Henry of Isenburg could hardly traverse Vítkov's steep terrain. Hussite chroniclers described a David-and-Goliath encounter. When imperial soldiers finally made it to the narrow ridge and approached the Hussite fortifications, twenty-six soldiers, including two women and one girl, hurled stones and lances. The tiny group staved off the soldiers long enough for Žižka to lead reinforcements up the south side of the hill. Žižka surprised the imperial armies by attacking from the rear. At the top of the ridge, the Hussites issued their ominous war cry and sang battle anthems. The imperial army was thrown into disarray as spooked horses ran off the ridge toward the river, and men "fell from the high rocks and broke their necks." Imperial troops waiting below were crushed as men and horses careened into them from above. The battle lasted an hour and ended with the imperial troops rushing back to their garrisons. At least three hundred imperial soldiers, including the commander, Henry of Isenburg, died, and another two hundred sustained injuries.

The Battle of Vítkov shocked the imperial armies and even the Hussites themselves. The Hussites had at most three thousand warriors, whereas Sigismund had almost twenty times that number. Lawrence of Březová praised the women warriors: "And one of the two women, though she was without armor, surpassed in spirit all men, as she did not want to yield one step." The unnamed woman fought until her dying breath when she cried out, "No faithful Christian must retreat from Antichrist!" Hussite women also nursed the injured, dug moats, built defensive structures, and led attacks on Prague convents such as Saint Catherine's. Imperial sources corroborated Lawrence's description of the Hussite women. The Margrave of Meissen informed the Duke of Bavaria that among the Hussite ranks were "women who had fixed their hair like men and had girded themselves with swords, with stones in their hands, wearing boots. Among these were some high-born."[4]

The imperial soldiers and officers were demoralized following their defeat at Vítkov. Decomposing bodies of men and horses remained unburied in the summer heat, creating a stench and attracting insect swarms. At the crusaders' encampment, high winds spread a fire through the soldiers' tents, and tens of thousands of men suffered from disease. Hussites executed sixteen German speakers accused of committing atrocities against Czechs. Lawrence reported, "These prisoners, sixteen in all, were burned in barrels outside the town within eyesight of the Germans. Only one monk was spared since he promised to continue to give the communion of the body and blood of the Lord to the faithful people." Many of Prague's German speakers and Catholics fled.

The Hussites took their win as proof that God favored them. They dubbed Vítkov "Žižka's Mountain" and adopted the chalice as their symbol. The Hussite priest Jan Čapek wrote a song that children performed in Prague's towns:

> Children, let us praise the Lord,
> Honor Him in loud accord!
> For he frightened and confounded,
> Overwhelmed and sternly pounded
> All those thousands of Barbarians,
> Suabians, Misnians, Hungarians,
> Who have overrun our land.[5]

A few weeks later, Sigismund held a secret coronation at Prague Castle. He insisted that the reluctant archbishop of Prague, Conrad of Vechta, pronounce him king of Bohemia. The coronation afforded Sigismund little power, as his allies abandoned him. Within a year, Conrad formally sided with the Hussites, and Prague's episcopal see remained vacant for 140 years. Imperial soldiers retreated from Prague and accused Sigismund of letting the Hussites win. Lawrence reported: "On 30 July, the third day after Sigismund's coronation, the entire army burned their camps and left. They berated the king as a friend of heretics, saying he had betrayed everyone's trust."

Emboldened by their victory, the Hussite troops turned their attention to the royalist stronghold of Vyšehrad. Volunteers erected barricades and cut off supply lines to Vyšehrad. By October 1420, the royalist noblemen, military officers, and mercenary soldiers ensconced there only survived by killing their horses and eating the meat. When Sigismund heard about the deteriorating

FIGURE 4.1 Jan Žižka leads Hussite soldiers who carry banners emblazoned with the chalice. The image is from the fifteenth-century Jenský Codex, National Museum, Czech Republic. CC BY-NC-ND 4.0 https://www.esbirky.cz/predmet/180453.

conditions at the fortress, he mounted an attack from Karlštejn, the castle lovingly built by his father, Charles IV. Along the way, according to Lawrence, "He ordered the burning of many villages...as well as the wine presses in the vineyards. He did this so that the mercenaries in Vyšehrad, upon seeing the fire...would take heart in the imminent hope that they would soon be relieved." However, the officers at Vyšehrad decided to negotiate with the

Hussites: "Many of them were dying of hunger, others had died, and they did not have even horseflesh to eat any longer."

Lawrence of Březová provided a firsthand account of the negotiations. He waited with university students and masters while the Hussites and royalists met. "[We were] looking out over the Vltava River waiting for the result of the meeting...when a rainbow appeared in the sky...like we had never seen before. Its arc arose practically at our feet in the Vltava River and extended over the city." Lawrence interpreted the rainbow as a sign that "the Praguers would soon be in possession of Vyšehrad. This is exactly what occurred." The royalists agreed to turn over Vyšehrad if Sigismund did not arrive by nine on the morning of November 1, All Saints' Day. The king arrived characteristically late, and the officers sent word to Sigismund not to attack. "But the king said,... 'It is absolutely essential that I fight these peasants today.'"

Sigismund's hubris cost his army more than five hundred lives, including those of two key advisers, Jindřich of Plumlov and Lord Peter of Šternberk, as well as a Russian prince, Georgii, Duke of Smolensk. Lawrence reported, "The king...stood on the top of a hill during the battle. When he witnessed the pathetic destruction of his men he was struck with terror..., and he left in tears." Fearing further violence, the royalists turned Prague Castle over to the Hussites.

Hussite leaders issued a manifesto a few days later, hoping to persuade more Czech barons to join their cause. The document called Sigismund an unworthy heir to his Luxembourg and Přemyslid predecessors:

> We wonder whether he even deserves to be called king, this one who has forgotten his noble birth, abandoned the example of kindness and gracefulness of all his ancestors, and is committing unheard-of cruelties. He is perpetrating them in this Crown of the Czech kingdom by atrocious raping of girls and wives, by murdering adults and children.... He is cunningly attempting to eradicate the Czech language, which he has defamed all over the world...calling us heretics.[6]

Enraged by his losses at Vítkov and Vyšehrad, Sigismund refused to negotiate and implored the pope to declare a second crusade upon the Hussites. By late 1420, Žižka, who had not lost a battle, became the chief captain of the Tábor troops. The position gave him authority over the Taborite community as well as military operations. Frustrated with the lack of structure at Tábor, he instituted community rules and sanitation responsibilities. With aid from Prague University masters, who issued a statement on heresies within the

Hussite community, Žižka and fellow leaders eliminated a radical subset in Tábor known as the Adamites who had adopted public nudism. Žižka accused the group of sexual misdeeds, Satanic worship, and dissenting views on the Eucharist. Hundreds were expelled or slaughtered over the summer of 1421.

The next military phases of the Hussite Wars occurred mainly outside Prague, but Prague University remained the center of radical intellectual thought.[7] A popular anthem, sung by Žižka's troops, reminded the Hussites they fought for Prague, their capital and their new Jerusalem.

> Arise, arise, great city of Prague,
> all the empire faithfully toward the
> Bohemian land and all knights and all
> powers of the land, against that king of
> Babylon, who threatens the city of
> Jerusalem, Prague, and all faithful people.[8]

Undeterred by the widespread support of Hussitism in Bohemia and Moravia, Sigismund ordered the death of all heretics. He beseeched pious Christians to join the new crusade, while Žižka called for military conscription throughout the Bohemian crown lands. "Command your priests to stir up the people to take up arms against the forces of Antichrist," ordered Žižka. "We shall soon be coming to you. Therefore, prepare beer, bread, food for the horses, and all the weapons for war. It is the time to fight."[9]

Sigismund's superior forces were still no match for the tactics and devotion of the Hussite warriors. In August 1421, the imperial forces failed to take Žatec, a northern Bohemian town they had besieged. The imperial army called for a third crusade and took possession of the invaluable mining town of Kutná Hora. However, Žižka regained it at the battle of Německý Brod in January 1422. The Hussites' military abilities mesmerized observers from both sides of the conflict.

Žižka pioneered the use of mass-produced armored wagons, considered precursors of modern tanks. The wagons were equipped with cannons and muskets and could carry about twenty armed soldiers. Once in formation, the wagons' wheels were chained together, creating a defensive wall. Cannons were mounted on the wagons, and soldiers carried firearms. Legends emerged about the fighting techniques never seen before on European soil. In the seventeenth century, Prague historian Bohuslav Balbín colorfully described the wagon fortresses: "The drivers coordinated their movements against their enemies by a previously agreed upon system of figures or letters and thus formed passageways that the Taborites understood quite well but which to the enemy appeared as a hopeless labyrinth." Contemporary artists depicted the wagon fortress as a monster "with numerous arms which very quickly and without warning snatches its prey, crushes it to death and devours it in pieces."[10] By the time Žižka led these battles, he was a man in his sixties who had fought in brutal wars for his whole adult life. In June 1421 he "was struck with an arrow and lost the one eye with which he still saw the light of the skies." Lawrence of Březová remarked, "Notwithstanding this, he did not retire from his work as a conqueror of castles nor from directing military operations. Generations to come will be amazed by this tale and will not believe it." (See Color Plate 7.)

Not all Hussites favored warfare. Theologian Petr Chelčický was dismayed by the violence advocated by Želivský and Žižka and argued that the devil had deceived the Hussites. In his best-known work, "The Net of Faith," Chelčický likened the pope and the emperor to whales who tear delicate fishing nets and lead the faithful astray. Chelčický's work influenced future church reformers, especially the United Brethren, an independent Hussite church that formed in 1457. His prolific writings in the Czech language made him a spiritual leader in his day as well as an important contributor to Czech vernacular literature.

Victory against the crusaders did not protect the Hussites from internal conflicts. Disagreements between the Prague party and the Taborites continued, and Prague was deeply divided between moderates and radicals. Želivský led the New Town radicals, while successful burghers and university masters held primacy in the Old Town. Želivský fashioned himself the spokesman of Prague's poor, but his detractors accused him of creating a dictatorship where he held all the power. On March 9, 1422, the Old Town Council summoned Želivský to the town hall, where he was sentenced to death and beheaded. According to his friend and confessor, Priest Vilém, blood spilled onto the courtyard and mixed with water running from the gutters. Želivský's supporters spotted the grisly sight and stormed Old Town Hall. A radical Hussite priest placed Želivský's head on a platter and processed it through Prague streets. An observer remarked, "When the people saw the head of Priest Jan they set up such a clamor and great outcry and such uproar the like of which I do not know if anyone could truly describe it adequately.... [There was] a great cry and the wringing of hands by women and children together with a great shout by the men.... [A] good many of them fainted because of their great grief."[11] Fighting in the streets with crossbows and makeshift weapons ensued, and Želivský's supporters captured and executed seven Old Town officials.

In October 1424, Žižka died of the plague, which delivered a severe blow to the Hussite cause. According to contemporary legends, Žižka asked his followers to flay his body and turn it into a warrior's drum. "With this drum in the lead, they should go to war. The enemies would turn to flight as soon as they heard its sound."[12] Indeed, even after Žižka's death, the Hussites continued to amass victories. Their battle song, "You Who Are God's Warriors," became a patriotic rallying cry for Czech patriots into the twentieth century.

> You who are God's warriors
> and follow His law,
> pray to God for help
> and have faith in Him,
> that finally with Him
> you will be victorious.[13]

Following Žižka's death, the Taborites were ably commanded by Prokop Holý, who led "glorious rides" in which soldiers invaded and looted German territories to dissuade participation in the crusades. The empire did not lack volunteers committed to eradicating the Bohemian heresy. Two more crusades, the fourth and fifth, were called in 1427 and 1431. Again, the Hussites defeated the superior imperial forces, with key battles near the Catholic-held city of city of Pilsen (Plzeň). Hatred toward the Hussites had spread through Europe. Even Joan of Arc addressed a letter to the Hussites in 1430, threatening to launch her own crusade against them:

> You corrupt the sacraments of the Church, you mutilate the articles of the Faith, you destroy churches, you break and burn statues...you massacre Christians unless they adopt your beliefs.... If I wasn't busy with the English wars I would have come to see you long before now; but if I don't find out that you have reformed yourselves I might leave the English behind and go against you.[14]

Finally, in 1431, the church convened the Council of Basel to end the Bohemian wars. The council allowed the lay chalice in Bohemia and Moravia but limited "free preaching" to ordained priests and deacons. The Compacta of Prague of November 1433 revoked the excommunication of Bohemia. However, the various Hussite factions could not agree on whether to accept the church's terms. The tensions within the Hussite movement came to a head in 1434 when Catholic and Utraquist noblemen united to defeat the radical Taborites at the Battle of Lipany, a site twenty-five miles east of Prague. Prokop Holý and other important Taborite commanders lost their lives, and the political and social community at Tábor never regained its strength. Upon hearing that the radical Taborites had finally been defeated, Sigismund allegedly remarked, "Only Bohemians could defeat the Bohemians."

———— ✦ ————

Prague needed to recover from nearly two decades of warfare. The Bohemian nobility agreed to accept Emperor Sigismund as their king, but the last Luxembourg did not enjoy his position for long. He died in 1437 at age sixty-nine. Without a son, he had designated his son-in-law Albrecht of Habsburg as his heir. When Albrecht died suddenly in 1439, the future of Bohemia remained unclear. The Bohemian nobility refused to acknowledge Albrecht's son, Ladislav Posthumous, who was born four months after the king's death. The Bohemian nobility ruled without a monarch for another thirteen years.

In this era, the Catholic nobility, led by the powerful Rožmberk (Rosenberg) family, moved to dominate politics in Prague, attempting to displace the power of the Utraquist nobles and the urban middle class. The nobleman and leader of the Utraquist party, George of Poděbrady, invaded Prague in 1448 to oust the Catholic nobility. Hussites in Prague supported George and forced the Catholic troops to retreat from the city. The Utraquist nobility recognized Ladislav Posthumous as king and named George his regent. When Ladislav died a decade later, the Bohemian nobility—both Utraquists and Catholics—chose George of Poděbrady as their king. He was the first—and only—Hussite king of Bohemia. An anonymous Utraquist chronicler described George's election in Prague's Old Town Hall on March 2, 1458. The Czech-speaking noblemen "rejoiced that they no longer had a German king.... And many of them wept for joy that the dear God had delivered them out of the power of German kings, who thought to do evil to the Czech people, and especially to those who hold to the Holy Scriptures."[15]

During his reign, George oversaw efforts to rebuild fortifications, churches, and monasteries destroyed during the Hussite Wars. A second tower was finally added to the Church of Our Lady Before Týn, the center of Utraquism in Prague. George placed a statue of himself holding a chalice inside Týn, where Hus's predecessors Conrad Waldhauser and Jan Milíč had first advocated church reform. Unlike Taborite services, the Utraquist liturgy closely followed the Catholic rite. The notable difference was the presence of the lay chalice. Most Utraquist parishes incorporated Latin and Czech segments into the liturgy, but some churches retained the full Latin mass, while others translated the entire service into Czech. The Utraquists declared Jan Hus a saint and added July 6, the day of his martyrdom, to the liturgical calendar.

George desired peace for his beloved Bohemia. A committed Utraquist, he tolerated Catholicism and attempted to forge a league of Christian nations to defend against Turkish influence in Central Europe. The popular monarch earned the monikers "the king of two peoples" and "the king of peace," but ongoing disputes between Bohemia and Rome marred George's reign. In 1466, the pope rescinded the Compacts of Prague and excommunicated the Bohemian king. Another civil war broke out when Bohemian Catholic noblemen attempted to replace George with the Hungarian king, Matthias Corvinus. Although George's army prevailed, his power had been considerably weakened.

King George's poor health prevented him from achieving many of his political and economic goals for the revitalization of Bohemia. Suffering from obesity, edema, and liver disease, George died suddenly in Prague in 1471, aged fifty-one. His sarcophagus was placed at St. Vitus Cathedral, where he could be laid to rest among his fellow Bohemian monarchs, but his heart and other internal organs were interred at the Utraquist Our Lady Before Týn. With George's death, the Bohemian crown passed to the Jagiellonian dynasty of Poland-Lithuania, never to be worn again by a native of Bohemia.

Vladislav Jagiellon was only fifteen years old in 1471 when he ascended the Bohemian throne. George of Poděbrady had promised that, after his death, the Bohemian crown would pass to the Jagiellonians. Vladislav pledged to honor the Compacts of Basel that permitted Utraquism in the Bohemian lands, even though his promise alienated his Catholic allies. The Bohemian nobility accepted Vladislav as king, but noblemen from Moravia and Silesia, where Catholicism remained strong, preferred Matthias Corvinus. Following a series of battles, an awkward arrangement divided the Bohemian crown lands between Vladislav and Matthias Corvinus. The region was unstable until Matthias died in 1490 without an heir. Vladislav took possession of the Hungarian throne and reunited the Bohemian lands.

Although Vladislav tolerated Utraquism, he remained a faithful Catholic and appointed several Bohemian Catholics to government positions in Prague. Utraquist officials in the Old, New, and Lesser Towns responded by murdering and defenestrating several Catholic officials in 1483, sixty-four years after the first defenestration of Prague launched the Hussite Wars. Vladislav had little interest in provoking the Prague leadership and preferred

FIGURE 4.2 Jan Vilímik, *Portrait of George of Poděbrady*, ca. 1890s. Public domain, via Wikimedia Commons.

to pacify the Utraquists. The Bohemian nobility made enormous gains during the Jagiellonian reign and called Vladislav "Král Dobře" (King "That's Fine") because he approved all the Bohemian Diet's requests.

During Vladislav's reign, tensions rose among Prague's Czech, German, and Jewish communities. Czech leaders attacked Jewish and German residents and attempted to have Jews expelled from the city. Violence in the Old Town necessitated Vladislav's decision to relocate his household and court to Prague Castle, which had not been occupied for several decades. The castle needed considerable repairs following the devastating Hussite Wars. Determined to restore Charles IV's seat to its former glory, Vladislav sponsored several renovation projects, including the completion of the Chapel of St. Wenceslas in St. Vitus Cathedral.

The king commissioned Vladislav Hall at Prague Castle, the largest secular gathering place in Bohemia. The Saxon architect Benedikt Reid designed the addition in a new Renaissance style. Its high ceiling featured interlacing stone ribs that did not require Gothic flying buttresses, and the windows were rectangular and symmetrical. The room's classical columns and a frieze carved

FIGURE 4.3 Aegidius Sadeler, *Vladislav Hall During the Annual Fair.* 1607. Print. Metropolitan Museum of Art, New York.

with the words "Hungary-Bohemia-1493" reflected the popular Italian Renaissance style. The multifunctional room, with its exceptionally wide staircase, could accommodate knights on horseback, jousting tournaments, duels, musical performances, balls, and banquets. Vladislav placed his eponymous hall adjacent to the Bohemian Diet's meeting room, symbolically acknowledging the nobility's power at the castle.

During Vladislav's reign, Benedikt Ried also designed Daliborka, a prison tower near the castle's Deer Moat. A pulley system carried prisoners to cells buried deep within the vaulted basement. Completed in 1498, the tower was given the name of its first prisoner, the knight Dalibor of Konojezdy, who had supported a rebellion of serfs from a nearby estate. Prague legends claim that Dalibor ceaselessly played his violin while he awaited execution, and for centuries, locals claimed to hear Dalibor's haunting tunes emanating from the tower.

Prague became an important printing center during Vladislav's reign. Prague's first books, printed in 1487 and 1488, were Czech translations of the *Chronicle of Troy*, the book of Psalms, and the Holy Bible. Books were printed in several languages, including Latin, Czech, and German. Texts using Cyrillic and Hebrew appeared several years later. The growing popularity of humanist thought led Prague intellectuals to study and translate classical literary, scientific, and medical texts. Prague University remained an intellectual center, but its international reputation had waned during the Hussite Wars. Wealthy Bohemian nobles and German-speaking burghers tended to send their children to universities abroad. As Prague University attracted more local students, Czech literature flourished.

Regional wars and rivalries threatened the stability that Jagiellonian rule brought to Prague. Vladislav and his brother, the king of Poland and Grand Duke of Lithuania, negotiated with the Habsburg Holy Roman emperor, Maximilian I. A peace agreement, signed in 1515 at the First Congress of Vienna, arranged a double wedding to link the two dynasties and forged a Jagiellonian-Habsburg succession treaty. At the time, it was unclear which family benefited more from the arrangement, but ultimately the marriages advanced Habsburg claims on the Bohemian and Hungarian thrones. Vladislav died a year later, and the crowns of Bohemia and Hungary passed to his ten-year-old son, Louis II. Nicknamed "the Child," Louis had to walk a fine line between his father's promises to the Utraquist nobility in Bohemia and the Jagiellonian-Catholic alliances across Europe.

In August 1526, Louis II led Hungarian troops against Ottoman invaders at the Battle of Mohács. As the Hungarian army suffered an overwhelming defeat, Louis led a retreat across the marshy terrain. The king fell off his horse into the wetlands, and the weight of his armor pinned him beneath the water. The nineteen-year-old monarch died without a legitimate heir, and the Bohemian crown passed to Ferdinand of Habsburg. Louis's untimely death and Ferdinand's installation as king marked a new era in Prague's history. Acquiring the Bohemian lands and the unconquered northern Hungarian territories made the Habsburgs the most powerful ruling family in Europe. The dynasty ruled Prague and the Bohemian crown lands from 1526 until the monarchy's fall in 1918.

Ferdinand acquiesced to the Bohemian Diet's many demands and agreed to reside in Prague. Though he regularly visited his family in Vienna and Linz, he invested substantial resources in Prague and the Castle District. Like his predecessors, the monarch was at frequent odds with Bohemia's powerful nobility, which viewed itself as the preeminent authority in the kingdom. Noblemen demanded local jurisdiction in civil and criminal law, and the

Bohemian Diet exercised considerable power over the economy and courts. The Diet administered the property rolls, land ordinances, and royal city charters, and it approved and levied taxes. The landed nobility took advantage of the change in leadership to increase rental fees and labor services. The Bohemian peasantry strained under the weight of this "second serfdom," an economic system that developed in sixteenth- and seventeenth-century Bohemia and lasted until the emancipation of serfs in 1781.

Like other Renaissance-era monarchs, Ferdinand favored centralized rule. A shrewd politician, Ferdinand appeased the nobility by regularly calling the Bohemian Diet to Prague while creating centralized institutions that circumvented its authority. He employed numerous scribes to codify his policies and insisted on printed documents over oral agreements. Through his political acumen, Ferdinand created the framework for the formidable Habsburg bureaucracy.

Ferdinand inherited the thorny religious problems that had persisted in Prague for generations. The German Reformation emboldened some Bohemian reformers to adopt Lutheranism, while a small but influential group joined the United Brethren, the heirs to the radical Taborites. Most Utraquists remained within the Catholic Church as long as they could receive communion in both forms. Martin Luther became fascinated with Hussite history and corresponded with Bohemian Utraquists and United Brethren. In a letter to Saxon humanist Georg Spalatin, Luther acknowledged the similarities between his and Hus's ideas, writing, "I have hitherto taught and held all the opinions of Huss unawares.... In short, we are all of us Hussites without knowing it.... I do not know what to think for astonishment."[16] Several years later, in his introduction to the German edition of Jan Hus's *Letters*, Luther remarked, "Observe...how firmly [Hus] clung in his writings and words to the doctrines of Christ; with what courage he struggled against the agonies of death; with what patience and humility he suffered every indignity, and with what greatness of soul he at last confronted a cruel death in defense of the truth."[17]

Within this complicated milieu, Ferdinand remained resolutely Catholic. Born in Alcalá, Spain, he was the grandson of Ferdinand and Isabella, who had united Christian Spain. Ferdinand embraced a humanist Catholicism inspired by the writings of Erasmus, the renowned Dutch philosopher and theologian. Ferdinand tolerated Bohemian Protestantism and brokered the Peace of Augsburg, which permitted Lutheranism in parts of the Holy Roman Empire. Yet, he also invited the Jesuits to Prague to create a Catholic educational structure for Bohemia, thus laying the foundation for a Counter-Reformation that would alter the city's spiritual and physical landscape for centuries to come.

A large Jewish migration contributed to Bohemia's complex religious landscape. European Jews' status had shifted substantially over the late fifteenth and sixteenth centuries. The church had lifted its strict prohibition on Christian moneylending, leaving Jews in German towns in a difficult situation. They could no longer thrive as financiers but were still forbidden to compete with Christians in trade and crafts. In response, West European Jews began to migrate toward Poland, which offered more favorable economic opportunities for Jewish craftsmen and merchants. Some eastbound migrants stopped and settled in Prague. A small community of Sephardic Jews resided in Lesser Town after the 1492 expulsions in Spain and Portugal but soon assimilated into Prague's Ashkenazi community.

In contrast to the experience of Jews in western German towns, the wealthiest Prague Jews retained their positions as Bohemia's most prominent financiers. The Hussite Wars' damage to the economy prevented many Christian burghers from having the means for large-scale finance, and the capital controlled by the main Jewish families easily competed with Christian bankers. Still, only a small percentage of Prague Jews made their living in finance; most worked as craftsmen, small-scale traders, or pawnbrokers. Some Prague Jews traded in silver, even though exporting precious metals was illegal and carried heavy penalties. Jewish merchants imported leather, furs, and Italian textiles and became known as skilled tailors and furriers. Throughout this period, some Prague burghers and noblemen called for the expulsion of Jews, citing economic inequities. As historian Jan Heřman explained, "A permanent feeling of insecurity accompanied the Prague Jew from the cradle to the grave."[18]

Despite anti-Semitic rumors of vast Jewish wealth, most Prague Jews were quite poor. An analysis from 1540 determined that nearly half of Prague Jews did not own property, and only 15 percent had wealth valued over one thousand Rhenish gulden (roughly $60,000 today). Recent immigrants often had more means than long-settled Prague Jews, leading to tensions and a wealth gap within the community. The Old Town's Jewish quarter could not accommodate the growing population; Jews temporarily settled in the New Town and Lesser Town but moved to the ghetto when more Jews left Prague for Poland.

Rumors of discord in the Jewish community reached rabbinical authorities as far away as western Germany and Italy. Some Prague Jews accused the wealthy Horowitz family of abusing royal privileges obtained by their ancestors. The

Horowitzes demanded two permanent seats on Prague's council of community elders and a guaranteed rabbinical appointment from within their family. In 1534, Josel of Rosheim, a prominent Alsatian Jew and legal scholar, came to Prague to assess tensions in the community. Widely known in Central Europe, Josel traveled through Europe to defend Jews against anti-Semitic persecution and to settle disputes among Jews. Josel heard the complaints in Prague and ruled against the Horowitzes, revoking their family privileges. With help from the chairman of the Jewish court, Abraham ben Abigdor, Josel drew up new community statutes that distributed power more equally. The Horowitzes had their loyal supporters, however, and a violent uprising broke out on the ghetto streets, forcing Josel to flee Prague.

The Horowitz family maintained its prominence through the sixteenth century and left a lasting mark on Prague's Jewish quarter. In 1535, a year after Josel's ruling, they opened the Pinkas Synagogue adjacent to the Horowitz family burial ground. Originally a private house of prayer, Pinkas Synagogue later installed a women's gallery and offered worship services for the entire community. Pinkas's interior had a late Gothic design featuring vaulted ceilings, but its facade incorporated Renaissance elements, including stone carvings and a portal adorned with classical columns.

As the growing Jewish population contended with overcrowding and poverty, the monarchy poured money into modernizing Prague Castle. Having promised Bohemia's leading nobles that he would remain in Prague during his reign, Ferdinand I sought to transform the Castle District into a residence that reflected his Renaissance ideals. While medieval castles were heavily fortified, with many homes and buildings crowded within the walls, the ideal Renaissance castle linked indoor and outdoor spaces, facilitated leisure activities, and conveyed openness. In 1534, Ferdinand connected his castle residence to the new Renaissance gardens by commissioning a covered wooden bridge across the deep Deer Moat. Master gardeners from Italy, France, and Spain cultivated apricot, peach, cherry, and almond trees. Southern European grapevines grew alongside medicinal and ornamental plants from Asia and Africa. An orangery protected the imported citrus trees, and a separate fig-tree atrium, equipped with heat and a removable roof, created ideal conditions for growing exotic fruit. The Italian botanist and physician Pietro Andrea Mattioli conducted studies at the royal gardens, culminating in his widely read botanical guide, *The Herbal*. Mattioli's work was richly illustrated by woodcuts and translated into dozens of languages. Prominent Prague astronomer and physician Tadeáš Hájek translated the book into Czech.

Ferdinand's early building projects suffered a major setback in June 1541 when a fire broke out in Lesser Town. Gusts of winds blew smoke and cinders uphill, igniting the Prague Castle complex. St. Vitus Cathedral's roof caved in, and the Bohemian Diet's meeting room, adjacent to Vladislav Hall, sustained significant damage. The new wooden bridge over the Deer Moat burned, and the stone paths leading to the royal gardens turned red and cracked. In Lesser Town, St. Thomas Monastery, All Saints Chapel, and over one hundred homes of rich and poor families alike succumbed to the great fire. Prague's left bank lay in ruins.

Some blamed the fire on a reconstruction project underway on the Lesser Town Square, although its rapid spread made it difficult to know if the conflagration began at the construction site, a private kitchen, or an artisan shop. While almost certainly an accident, the fire gave Prague burghers and nobles an excuse to redouble their anti-Semitic campaigns. A small band of Czech citizens kidnapped several Prague Jews, torturing them until they falsely confessed that they had hired shepherds to set the fire. The Prague Jewish community was one of the only European centers of Jewish life that had not experienced an expulsion before 1500, but in 1541, Ferdinand reluctantly agreed to sign such a decree. The eviction was never fully carried out, as Habsburg family members and even the pope intervened on the Jews' behalf. Still, several hundred Jews left Prague in fear for their safety, reducing the community from about thirteen hundred to under one thousand.

Despite the extensive damage at Prague Castle, Ferdinand I would not allow the fire to deter his renovation plans. At the end of 1541, he called the Bohemian Diet to Prague to demonstrate that the castle remained functional. Yet the destruction and subsequent remodeling project prevented him from living on the castle hill, so he spent more time in Vienna or Hungary. After a few years' hiatus, construction restarted on the Belvedere, a summer palace dedicated to Ferdinand's beloved wife, Anne. Designed by the renowned Lugano architect Paolo della Stella, who came to Prague in 1538, the summer palace represented the purest example of Italian Renaissance architecture north of the Alps. Italian builders and stonemasons created an exterior arched arcade held up by thirty-six pillars and decorated with a frieze of 114 carved reliefs. The intricate carvings depicted feats of the Greek hero Perseus and Ferdinand himself, hunting or on horseback. The most moving image showed a somber Ferdinand and Anne holding a fig blossom. Their arranged marriage had been a loving one, and Ferdinand mourned the queen's death in childbirth in 1547. Anne never saw her palace completed.

Following Paolo della Stella's death in 1552, Boniface Wohlmut became Prague Castle's chief architect. Influenced by the Italian architectural theorist Andrea Palladio, Wohlmut embraced Renaissance neoclassicism and decorated the Royal Garden's new ballgame halls with Italian sgraffito designs: black-and-white decorations scratched into plaster facades. Ferdinand commissioned a spectacular fountain—a collaboration by an Italian sculptor, a Moravian gunsmith, and a woodworker from Nuremberg—for the entrance to Anne's Summer Palace. Visitors from throughout Europe described Prague's remarkable "singing fountain." In 1603, the French diplomat and traveler Pierre Bergeron wrote that the fountain "plays like bagpipes, the water issuing from its top falls into the basin so gracefully that it emits a harmonious sound like the voice of that instrument."[19]

Another Renaissance masterpiece, the Star Summer Palace (Letohrádek Hvězda, Stern Schloss), stood on White Mountain, a low hillock west of Prague Castle, and served as the centerpiece of the royal game reserve established by Ferdinand I in 1534. The king's younger son Ferdinand of Tyrol, who served as governor of Bohemia between 1547 and 1567, helped design the building. Constructed by Italian master builders between 1555 and 1556, the palace had a unique six-pointed star floor plan and elaborate stucco designs on the interior vaults. Ferdinand of Tyrol viewed the Star Summer Palace as a place where the local nobility could mingle with the Habsburg Austrian-Spanish aristocracy. He hosted balls and diplomatic meetings, hoping to ease the friction between the Bohemian estates and the Crown.

In the Old Town, burghers and wealthy noblemen added Renaissance elements to their buildings. The Týn School on Old Town Square acquired an ornate Renaissance facade inspired by St. Mark's Square in Venice. The addition obfuscated the entry to Týn, creating an illusion that the Gothic church spires floated above the square. The Italian sgraffito technique used in the Prague Castle renovations was adopted throughout the city. Dům Minuty on Old Town Square featured elaborate sgraffito portraits of Habsburg leaders interspersed with images from biblical stories and Greek mythology. In Lesser Town, the municipal hall and other nearby buildings featured Palladian design elements—external arcades, pillars, and large rectangular windows. Wealthy burghers renovated their Gothic homes with Renaissance portals and carved emblems, giving them fanciful names like At the Two Bears and At the Donkey in the Cradle. The decorative feather merchant Jan Fuchs remodeled his aptly named Lesser Town home, At the Three Ostriches. He installed Renaissance ceiling beams and commissioned a fanciful facade with hand-painted exotic birds and the words "feather decorator" in Czech and German.

FIGURE 4.4 Queen Anne's Summer Palace and Singing Fountain at Prague Castle, completed 1560. Photo by the author.

FIGURE 4.5 The Star Summer Palace, completed 1556. Photo by the author.

Wealthy noble families took advantage of space made by the 1541 fire and commissioned palaces near the castle grounds and in Lesser Town. Since the late Přemyslid dynasty, Bohemian noblemen from rural areas sought homes in Prague, where they could conduct business and influence politics. Catholic families like the Rožmberks of southern Bohemia and Pernštejns of Moravia built stately residences that incorporated masonry from buildings destroyed in the fire. The Italian architect Giovanni Ventura replaced the Prague burgrave's residence, another casualty of the fire, with a Renaissance palace just outside the castle fortification wall. Noble families adopted Prague's art-collecting culture, purchasing paintings, sculptures, jewelry, and furniture from local artisans. Not since Charles IV's reign had such a diverse group of artists assembled in Prague's Castle District.

Ferdinand succeeded in reinvigorating learning and culture in Renaissance Prague, but he could not maintain a cordial relationship with the native nobility. In 1547, soon after the queen died in childbirth, the Utraquist-dominated Bohemian Diet refused to support a war against the Lutheran Schmalkaldic League. The Diet threatened to oust Ferdinand and presented him with a petition of fifty-seven articles that affirmed the local nobility's authority to elect the king and to appoint officials. Prague commoners joined the estates in protesting the king's war against the empire's Protestants, and Ferdinand responded to their brazenness by besieging Prague in June 1547. He subdued the revolt and ordered the execution of four rebel noblemen. The uprising was the final straw for Ferdinand. He centralized government institutions and inserted new levels of bureaucracy that weakened the power of towns and estates. The Crown confiscated land and mines owned by disloyal noblemen and imposed a strict tax system. Ferdinand focused his wrath on Prague, viewing its representatives as instigators in the uprising. The king levied heavy fines, disarmed Bohemia, and appointed royal governors for the four Prague towns. He established an appeals court at Prague Castle that superseded the towns' local jurisdiction and created a powerful administrative position, the viceroy of Bohemia. In October, he installed his younger son in this office, ordering him to make decisions without input from the Bohemian estates.

Although Ferdinand began spending less time in Prague, his power was still felt there. In 1556, following his brother Charles V's abdication, Ferdinand became the Holy Roman emperor. Charles divided the vast Habsburg lands between his son Phillip II of Spain and Ferdinand. With his increased power, Ferdinand supported a re-Catholicization campaign in Bohemia and reinstated his order to expel Prague's Jews. He invited the Jesuit order to Prague, instructing them to reinforce Catholic teachings among the rebellious Bohemians. The Jesuits moved into a former Dominican monastery in Old Town and established the Clementinum to rival Prague University, which the Utraquists dominated.

In 1562, two years before he died, Ferdinand transferred the Bohemian crown to his older son, Maximilian II. Well educated, intrigued by humanist philosophy, and sympathetic to Protestant ideas, Maximilian rescinded his father's anti-Jewish expulsions in 1567. The Jewish population grew as exiled families returned to Prague, and the Jewish community founded three new synagogues in the late sixteenth century. An anonymous Jewish chronicler fondly recalled a snowy day in February 1571 when "Emperor Maximilian and his wife, the empress, Madam Maria, paraded down the *Judenstrasse* (Jewish Street) accompanied by all the royal dignitaries" riding on sleds and "going from gate to gate in the twenty-second hour."[20] Although Maximilian preferred Vienna to Prague, he did not abandon his father's building projects there.

When Maximilian died in 1576 in Regensburg, he refused last rites. Nonetheless, his son and heir Rudolph brought his father's body to Prague for an elaborate Catholic funeral and burial at St. Vitus Cathedral. An anonymous Hebrew chronicler reported that the emperor "was buried with great pomp. There were lords, dukes, envoys, monks, and archbishops from all the lands. Preceding the coffin, twenty-one flags bearing the seals of the lands under his dominion were carried, followed by twenty-one horses with fancy trappings that had been ridden by [the emperor]."

The Jewish writer compared Maximilian's funeral to Charles IV's final procession through Prague two centuries earlier. "Such glory and might had not been seen or heard since the days of Emperor Charles, of blessed memory." The chronicler who had happily witnessed Maximilian's visit five years earlier described the city's somber mood: "There was great disorder in Prague when they bore the emperor, of blessed memory, to the castle, and no man had any spirit left." With each leadership change, Prague's Jews feared their fate under a new ruler. As the chronicler explained, after Maximillian's death, "great fear fell upon the Jews, and God, Blessed be He, delivered them from evil at their hands."

5
Rudolphine Prague

RUDOLPH OF HABSBURG first came to Prague as a ten-year-old boy to participate in his father's coronation, and the city's imposing panorama and warm welcome made a strong impression on the young prince. Years later, in 1583, Holy Roman emperor Rudolph II moved the imperial court to Prague, the first monarch to choose this capital since Charles IV.

Several factors influenced Rudolph's decision to relocate the imperial court. Rudolph and his brother Ernest were raised in their uncle Philip II's Madrid court. When Rudolph returned to Vienna after eight years abroad, he had become reticent and stiffly formal, leading Habsburg courtiers to call him haughty and arrogant. In turn, Rudolph detested Vienna's provincialism and its gossipy court. Prague's economic development, dense population, and wealth attracted Rudolph. With a population of around 70,000, Prague was considerably larger and more diverse than Vienna. Prague gave the introverted Rudolph the freedom to shape his imperial capital as a center of art and learning with artists and intellectuals from across Europe. Prague was also safer than Vienna, which stood only one hundred miles from Turkish garrisons. Bohemia's distance and mountainous border protected the region from the Ottoman wars.

No Bohemian monarch since Charles IV devoted so many resources to Prague. While the Viennese criticized Rudolph's aloofness, visitors to the Prague court found his personality appealing. One contemporary traveler remarked, "He was rather a small figure, quite pleasantly tall and comparatively quick in his movements. His pale face, nobly formed brow, gently wavy hair and beard, and his large eyes, which looked around with some placidity, made a great impression on all who met him." Another observer discounted the accusation of arrogance and instead commented on the emperor's reserve: "There was nothing haughty about his behavior; he was rather restrained and somewhat shy; he shunned everything boisterous and took no part in the usual amusements; he did not like jokes and was rarely heard to laugh."[1]

Rudolph's introversion inhibited his ability to choose a wife. His uncle, Philip II, expected him to marry his cousin, the Infanta Isabella of Spain, but Rudolph hesitated and lost the offer. Other diplomatic efforts to secure a marital union failed. Rudolph did father several illegitimate children with Katharina Strada, his longtime lover and the granddaughter of a famous antiquarian and art dealer. Rumors of numerous love affairs abounded, but Rudolph never married or produced a legitimate heir.

Under Rudolph, Prague reclaimed its reputation as a cosmopolitan city. The Peace of Augsburg declared that citizens of a particular polity must follow their ruler's faith, but the tolerant Rudolph did not hold his Bohemian subjects to this requirement. While Roman Catholics and Utraquists in communion with the church were the only legal confessions in Bohemia, Prague continued to welcome various Protestant groups and individuals. St. Nicholas Church in Lesser Town, which offered Utraquist masses, allowed Lutheran émigrés to use the space for worship services. Later, the Lutheran community obtained permission to build its own house of worship, the Church of the Holy Trinity, located beneath Petřín Gardens adjacent to Prague Castle in Lesser Town.

Several new Roman Catholic edifices were built in Rudolph's Prague. The Augustinian Church of St. Thomas, destroyed in the 1541 fire, was rebuilt, and the Jesuit order founded several churches and schools. The Capuchin order established a monastery and church in the Lobkowicz family gardens of the Castle District. Although Rudolph tolerated Protestants in his city and court, he remained a committed Catholic.

Rudolphine Prague was a diverse and cosmopolitan city. Fifty years after the great fire, Lesser Town had become one of Prague's most prosperous sections, with noble families and wealthy burghers building palaces around the main town square. An influx of Italian immigrants—mainly merchants and court employees—built a small chapel, a hospital, a pub, and a meeting place in Lesser Town, and German Lutherans formed a community near their new church. Old Town regained its German character as merchants and craftsmen immigrated to Prague. New Town remained almost entirely Hussite and Czech speaking, but new arrivals from the Low Countries, Spain, Poland, Croatia, Hungary, and Austria also settled there. The district surrounding the castle was declared a royal borough in 1592 and had a sizable German-speaking population.

Despite Rudolph's reputation for reclusiveness, he made Prague Castle a welcoming site for visitors. As the imperial capital, Prague Castle regularly received foreign delegations and ambassadors, who participated in tournaments, banquets, and hunts organized by Rudolph's court. A delegation from Persia in 1603 captured the attention of Prague residents, who vied to glimpse the richly dressed dignitaries. The Persian ambassador commemorated the visit with a portrait by court artist Aegidius Sadeler, who posed the dignitary with his pet falcon. Tourism was becoming a popular leisure activity for wealthy Europeans, and Bohemians were also encouraged to visit Prague Castle. Guests could climb Bonifaz Wohlmut's new tower on St. Vitus Cathedral, and the magnificent Vladislav Hall opened to visitors. Merchants set up stands along the room's perimeter to sell their wares. Sadeler had a stall there and captured the bustling scene in a 1607 print. Merchants also lined the castle steps, and travelers could enjoy the exotic plant and animal collections at the royal botanical and zoological gardens. A lion enclosure held large cats, the deer park provided ample hunting grounds for courtiers and their guests, and Rudolph's Spanish Riding Stables housed his exquisite, rare horses. The French diplomat Pierre Bergeron commented in 1603, "Within the castle are stables, some of the best looked after in Europe; there are nearly always three hundred horses there, originating from every possible country, and they are the most beautiful in the world."[2]

Rudolph made his residence in the recently completed New Palace. The new Long Building housed the famed Kunstkammer (Art Chamber), a fifty-meter-long corridor adorned with the emperor's art collections. Although the castle grounds were open to the public, Rudolph allowed only his most trusted courtiers to view the artworks. Rudolph sustained his father's and grandfather's interest in collecting, but he took the passion further, determined to own at least one example of every object made by humans or nature. His curiosities were kept in cabinets decorated with paintings and embroideries. Mechanical objects such as clocks and music boxes lined the tables, and unique musical instruments included a glass spinet. Goldsmiths, gem cutters, and textile artists came from across Europe to contribute their skills to Rudolph's court. The creative atmosphere inspired collaborations like the 1606 *A View of the City of Prague*, designed by Dutch embroiderer Philippe van der Bossche and etched by German artist Johannes Wechter onto nine separate plates. Sadeler printed the nearly four-foot-long panorama, which became the most well-known view of the Renaissance city.

Like Charles IV, Rudolph was passionate about gemstones. Early in his reign, he sent Bohemian stones to Florentine workshops for art commissions, but by the century's end, a royal lapidary was established at Bubeneč Mill, north of the castle. Rudolph employed Italian gem cutters from the Florentine

FIGURE 5.1 Johannes Wechter, Philippe van der Bossche, and Aegidius Sadeler, *View of the City of Prague*. 1606. Print. Metropolitan Museum of Art, New York.

Castrucci family, which also served the Medici court. Ottavio Miseroni from Milan, who was said to carve stone as if it were wax, designed Rudolph's new crown and precious objects, such as the fanciful *Bowl of Heliotrope with a Young Bacchus*. Under Miseroni's and the Castruccis' direction, Rudolph's collection included remarkable mosaics, intricate vessels, and inlaid cabinet door panels and tabletops. Early in the seventeenth century, gem engraver Caspar Lehman moved to Prague and received a license for etching on glass. He perfected the new technique in pieces such as the Lehman Beaker, whose allegorical design was taken from an image by the famed Flemish printmaker Jan Sadeler.

Rudolph was one of the greatest patrons of northern Renaissance art, and the room above the Kunstkammer housed more than three thousand paintings. In 1595, he granted the Prague Painters Guild of Old Town and Lesser Town an imperial privilege. While primarily symbolic, the gesture recognized painters as artists rather than craftsmen and confirmed painting as an intellectual activity that shaped imperial and urban culture. Rudolph acquired Renaissance masterpieces from Italy and Northern Europe, including a large assembly of Albrecht Dürer's works; Leonardo da Vinci's *Lady with an Ermine*;

and paintings by Titian, Veronese, Tintoretto, and Caravaggio. Rudolph likewise championed the Dutch masters Hieronymus Bosch and Pieter Bruegel the Elder. Court artist and renowned mannerist Giuseppe Arcimboldo depicted Rudolph as Vertumnus, god of the four seasons. He represented the emperor's features with fruit, vegetable, and flower imagery that symbolized Rudolph's gifts of prosperity and peace. Arcimboldo's late-career masterpiece became a symbol of Rudolphine Prague. (See Color Plate 8.)

Prague became the center of Northern Mannerism, a style whose dark palette presented mythological subjects with elongated physical features and complex poses. Flemish painter Bartholomäus Spranger decorated the ceiling of the Hall of the New Land Rolls with classical allegories depicting Hermes and Athena as patrons of the arts and sciences, while Hans von Aachen's *Allegory of Peace and the Arts* reflected Rudolph's taste for erotic subjects. Adriaen de Vries led the Prague Castle foundry, which cast sculptures for Rudolph's Spanish Hall and New Spanish Hall. Court artists idealized Rudolph in manifold portraits that depicted him as a military leader, a Renaissance scholar, or a patron of the arts.

FIGURE 5.2 Aegidius Sadeler, *Portrait of Emperor Rudolph II on Horseback*, ca. 1586–1629. Metropolitan Museum of Art, New York.

As a small town unto itself, the castle grounds housed poor residents as well as wealthy courtiers. Rudolph invited his marksmen to tear down dilapidated hovels on Golden Lane, a narrow street that led from St. George's Convent to Daliborka prison tower. Despite popular belief, the street's name originated not from court alchemists but from goldsmiths who lived there in earlier centuries. The marksmen occupied the twenty-four tiny houses and supplemented their paltry incomes with day labor and craftwork. Since the town guilds had no jurisdiction at the castle, the guards worked without supervision and determined their own prices. Golden Lane became known as a place of carousing and occasional violence, and the nuns of the neighboring St. George Convent made frequent complaints about noise and public drunkenness. (See Color Plate 9.)

The other Prague towns housed a mix of poor and wealthy citizens. In 1591, English lawyer Fynes Moryson complained about the city's stench, which he claimed could drive away the Ottoman Turks if they dared to invade. He wrote, "The streets are filthy...the building of some houses is of free stone, but the most part are of timber and clay, and are built with little beauty or art, the walls being all of whole trees, as they come out of the wood."[3] Moryson did find the food and drink satisfying but was stunned that the Czech "men drink (if it be possible) more than the Germans...and the women swill Wine and Beere daily." On the other hand, diplomat Pierre Bergeron enjoyed court banquets and visits to the salons of wealthy ladies. "While riding through the streets of the town, we admired many lovely ladies in carriages which were all drawn by six horses."[4] Indeed, social class segregated the Prague streets. Obora, the Lesser Town neighborhood known in Charles IV's time for prostitution and gambling, had retained its rough character, as had the outskirts of New Town, where migrants from the countryside or abroad settled upon entering the city.

During Rudolph's reign, efforts were made to solve Prague's water supply issues. In 1577, a Renaissance-style water tower was built for the Old Town, and a marble fountain, where residents could gather daily supplies, adorned Old Town Square. Bergeron described the impressive engineering of the "very high tower by a bridge in which there are two pumps raising the water upwards, which is then distributed all over Prague. One of them works with the help of an iron chain with many stoppers to hold in the water, which continuously rises and falls in two great hollowed-out tree trunks."[5] Public baths lined the Vltava riverbanks. Rudolph also had water diverted through a tunnel from the Vltava to the Royal Deer Park to supply his fishponds and his animals' drinking sources. An aqueduct fitted with high-fired clay pipes led to the Castle District to provide potable water for the residents.

As the imperial court increased trade and industry, the standard of living for Prague's middle classes rose. Burghers and wealthy artisans expanded their New Town homes to accommodate their families and servants. Most residents used public baths, but private tubs and separate rooms for ablutions became fashionable in this era. Middle-class families accumulated more luxury items, including dinnerware, paintings, religious objects, books, and nonessential furniture like desks and display cabinets. The collecting culture that occupied Rudolph's energies spread to other social classes as well.

Rudolph supported intellectual pursuits and scientific research. He amassed thousands of maps and books, including ethnographies, histories, and classical literature. He envisioned Prague Castle as a center for scientific experimentation, and he invited learned men from throughout Europe to join his court. Rudolph developed an interest in the dark arts, including alchemy and astrology. Renaissance scholars considered alchemy an integral part of scientific thought and practice. The study of matter and precious metals intersected with the work of metallurgists, dye-makers, pharmacists, distillers, and scientists. Even at Prague University, scholars reconciled their Catholic faith with new theories of matter. The renowned intellectual, physician, and scientist J. Marcus Marci, who served as dean of medicine and rector of Prague University, applied alchemical theories to his pathbreaking studies of light and color.

In November 1577, Europeans encountered a great comet that appeared close to Earth. Several Renaissance astronomers, who would later work in Rudolph's court, recalled the event as a turning point in their lives. Danish scientist Tycho Brahe produced numerous sketches and calculations, and six-year-old Johannes Kepler and his mother viewed the comet near their home in the Black Forest. Lutherans claimed that the comet signified God's approval of the Reformation, while others thought it portended doom. Czech artist and writer Jiří Dačický created a celebrated print of the comet over Prague. In his work, several men and women stand on a hilltop above the city and stare at the sweep of light above their heads. Others watch the artist furiously sketch the night sky filled with five zodiac signs, a crescent moon, and the planet Saturn. The work revealed the broad interest in scientific phenomena in this Renaissance city.

Rudolph, too, was fascinated by the heavens, and the emperor employed several renowned European astronomers at his court. In 1599, on the suggestion of Prague scientist Tadeáš Hájek, Rudolph invited Tycho Brahe to

FIGURE 5.3 Jiří Jakubuv Dačický, *The Great Comet of 1577 Above Prague*, Zentralbibliothek Zürich. Public domain, via Wikimedia Commons.

Prague as his royal astronomer. Brahe had fallen out with the new Danish king, Christian IV, and was living in exile in Germany. Brahe received a castle in Benátky nad Jizerou, thirty miles from Prague, where he built an observatory and used Anne's Summer Palace for astronomical experiments. Brahe was quite happy in Prague. He felt isolated and scorned in his native Denmark, but in Prague, he and his wife and children were esteemed members of Rudolph's court.

The young German astronomer Johannes Kepler and the self-taught mathematician and inventor Jost Bürgi assisted Brahe at his observatories. Brahe was the last important astronomer to work without a telescope, and he continually labored to make more accurate instruments, perfecting the sextant and inventing a large quadrant. Brahe welcomed interested scientists to his observatories. The Prague Jewish scholar David Gans, who believed that the sciences and mathematics could become a common language for Jews and Christians, recalled,

> I sat with [the astronomers] in their observation rooms, and I saw what was done, not just with the planets … but also most of the stars. Their names were called when each star reached the meridian [and] it was

measured by three types of instruments. At each instrument sat two scholars, and all was immediately recorded in a book, the time that each star reached the meridian, the hour and minute and second, for which there was a wonderful innovative clock.[6]

Like many in Rudolph's court, Brahe was a colorful character. As a young man, he lost his nose in a duel and wore a brass prosthetic held on by paste and glue. On special occasions, he changed to a silver or gold nose covering. He quickly befriended local noblemen and partook in banquets and festivities. At a feast hosted by the nobleman Vilém Rožmberk, Brahe became delirious, shouting in pain and begging that his life work not be in vain. Brahe died the following morning. Some suggested the cause of his death was mercury poisoning, while others claimed that his bladder burst because, in an abundance of manners, he did not excuse himself from his host's table. An autopsy in the twentieth century determined that Brahe died of uremia, an excess of uric acid in the bloodstream, which may have been exacerbated by his failure to relieve himself. The exhumation revealed considerable amounts of gold particles in his remains. Brahe shared an interest in alchemy with his fellow court intellectuals and may have ingested gold in a quest for eternal life.

Prague's elite gathered at Týn Church on Old Town Square to mourn Brahe. Twelve imperial guards and two horses led the funeral procession, and pallbearers carried the coffin covered in black velvet and emblazoned with Brahe's coat of arms. Jan Jesenský (Jesenius), who had recently gained fame by performing the first public autopsy in Prague, gave the eulogy. Humanist poet Jan Campanus composed an ode to the scholar:

> Also there lived Tycho de Brahe, the pride of our age,
> This famous scholar is buried in the soil of Prague.
> It did not help him that he took pride in the titles of his ancestors,
> And that he subdued with his rare spirit the empire of the stars.
> He became a new Hercules, who could in these times
> Bear on his shoulders the enormous weight of heaven.[7]

After Brahe's death, the ground floor of Anne's Summer Palace became an astronomy museum. Pierre Bergeron noted in his travel account, "On the arcaded galleries...one sees countless spheres, globes, astrolabes, quadrants, and a thousand other mathematical instruments, all of bronze and pewter and astonishingly large."[8]

Kepler completed Brahe's *Rudolphine Tables*, which was finally printed in 1627 following long disputes with Brahe's heirs. He became the court's royal mathematician, a position he held through the subsequent reigns of Matthias and Ferdinand II. A devout Lutheran, Kepler believed that astronomical calculations offered a way to understand God's grand vision for the universe. His heliocentric model reinforced the concept of the Holy Trinity, with God the Father as the sun and center. These theories did not fare well in Europe's Catholic regions, and Kepler acknowledged the advantages of living in a tolerant city.

While the astronomers looked to the sky, the era's alchemists searched for secret knowledge within the smallest of substances. Alchemists sought to manipulate matter and turn base metals into gold. Believing that gold had magical powers, wealthy hosts sometimes sprinkled gold flakes in their guests' wine chalices and wove gold into their hair or garments. Most Prague alchemists were reputable scientists and medical doctors, like Prague University professor Adam Huber and the emperor's physician, Michael Maier. Metallurgists, including some prominent Jewish goldsmiths, had positions in royal workshops. The court alchemist Michael Sendivogius, a Polish philosopher and engineer, spent more time designing mines and developing metal foundries than experimenting with alchemy.

Two infamous alchemists in Prague were Englishmen John Dee and Edward Kelley, who arrived in 1583 hoping to earn the emperor's patronage. Dee, an Oxford-trained mathematician, was an adviser to Elizabeth I and the proprietor of England's largest scientific library. In contrast, Kelley was younger, flamboyant, and mendacious. He wore his hair long to obscure his missing ears, which had been cut off as punishment for fraud. The unlikely pair joined forces to experiment in the dark arts, and they traveled through Europe to meet with scholars and seek noble patrons. During Dee's six-year stay in Prague, he had only one audience with the emperor, but other intellectuals, including the nobleman Vilém Rožmberk, attended his séances and offered financial support. Dee's diaries provide a detailed account of his time in Prague and describe a visit by the archangel Uriel, who gave him thirty-eight books of supernatural wisdom. When Dee returned to England, the charismatic Kelley enjoyed a brief period of fame in Prague. He received a knighthood from Rudolph, earned Bohemian citizenship, and purchased a house on New Town Square, later called Faust's House because of its association with alchemy.

Kelley's fortunes changed in 1597 when he allegedly killed a soldier and died attempting to escape prison. He left behind a wife and stepdaughter, the

Englishwoman Elizabeth Jane Weston. She soon emerged as an unlikely leader of Prague literary circles. Weston had benefited from Kelley's belief that girls should be educated like boys, and she received tutoring in Latin, French, German, and Czech. She attended university lectures in Prague and mingled with poets, artists, and musicians whom Kelley befriended. The teenager composed neo-Latin poetry, an important Renaissance genre that revived classical verse and explored themes of nature and love. When Kelley died, Weston and her mother faced destitution. She used her poetic talent to seek wealthy patrons and addressed poems to Rudolph describing her family's precarious situation: "I groan at my mother's poverty, she laments her daughter's sad fate. Bitter grief grows on both sides." She pleaded with Rudolph to release her family from its misery:

> For if Kelley offended you formerly,
> He suffered a great punishment for a modest offense.
> He paid the penalty of death; will his death appease your wrath?[9]

Weston's tactics paid off. She received commissions from wealthy patrons and was the first female poet laureate in the Holy Roman Empire. By the mid-1590s, Weston's neo-Latin poetry had a following throughout Europe. Known as Virgo Anglia (the English Maiden) or Westonia, she published two volumes of poetry. One poem described Prague's disastrous 1596 flood with sensuous images:

> The sky's inclemency stirs up the angry winds;
>   the watery clouds are soaking with ceaseless rain.
> The turbulent Vltava, swollen with rainy waves,
>   bursting, impetuous, breaks through its river-banks.

Weston interrogated the nature of art and humanity. In another poem, a dove suffering from heat and thirst espies a painting "on which a water-pot had been painted with vivid color, and liquid with cheating appearance, a visual fraud." Believing she found an oasis, "The poor creature lunged toward the desired water. And gliding hastily against the painted tablet, she perished in the collision, her gullet crushed." Westonia's poem reflected on the distinction between humans and animals, a common Renaissance theme. While humans can distinguish art from reality, the ignorant bird loses her life in a quest for water. Westonia's career was cut short by marriage and motherhood; she died in her early thirties while giving birth to her seventh child. Her body of literature remains a window into Rudolph's court, where the arts, the sciences, and the occult mingled as never before.

While Rudolph's court promoted innovation in art and literature, Prague's Jewish quarter flourished as a center for Hebrew and Yiddish scholarship and printing. Prague's first Hebrew manuscript to be produced on a movable-type printing press appeared in 1512. While scholarly works were written in Hebrew, literature and personal prayer books began to appear in Yiddish. Prague's earliest printed Jewish books came from Christian workshops that leased the machines to Jews. Over time, Jewish printers established businesses and took over the production of their texts. The Katz family dominated Prague's Jewish printing industry. In 1526, Gershom Katz produced the famed Prague Haggadah, a Passover seder text illustrated by Hayyim Schwarz. The elaborate woodcuts depicted contemporary Jewish fashion and the Ashkenazi practices of gathering traces of leaven with a feather and small bowl or leaving a door ajar for Elijah's visit. The book's ornamental borders and ornate initials at the beginning of sections reveal the influence of Christian printing techniques on Jewish manuscripts.

In the late sixteenth century, Jewish leaders encouraged personal piety; individuals and small groups gathered to pray in family homes. Women used *Tkhines*, prayer books that contained supplications on female concerns, including infertility, miscarriage, pregnancy, and birth. The earliest known *Tkhine* was produced in Prague in 1590 and included five prayers rendered in both Hebrew and Yiddish. Each prayer was introduced with a short verse from the *siddur* (liturgy) or the Hebrew Bible. These books functioned as sacred objects but also commodities. The first Prague *Tkhine* included a rhymed advertisement that encouraged faithful Jewish women to buy it, promising: "Everyone who says this *Tkhine* every day, I promise him that he will earn the world-to-come."[10] Most *Tkhines* were anonymous, but scholars believe that women composed some of the prayers, while rabbis wrote others on their behalf.

This intellectual environment attracted Jewish scholars to Prague. In 1573, the eminent rabbi Judah ben Loew founded the Klaus (Kloyyz) Yeshiva in Prague, which became a center of Renaissance Jewish thought. The rabbi was known by the acronym Maharal, which stood for "Moreinu Ha-Rav Loew" ("Our Teacher, Rabbi Loew"). He was a prolific writer and an esteemed community leader. Loew moved several times during his career, serving as the chief rabbi in Poznań and Moravia before returning to Prague to lead the community. Rudolph II admired Prague's erudite rabbi who taught in the city's yeshivas. On February 16, 1592, Rabbi Loew had an audience with Rudolph II, though little is known about their discussion. David Gans, Loew's student, recorded the event in his chronicle, expressing that Rudolph II talked to the Maharal "as to a friend." While some assumed that the two discussed the Jewish mysticism of Kabbalah, Gans admitted that the contents of the conversation were "mysterious, sealed, and hidden."[11] Loew was interested in the mathematical underpinnings of Hebrew texts, but he was not a magician or wizard, as later legends would claim. In the nineteenth century, Loew became associated with the story of Prague's Golem. Czech and German folktales credited Loew with bringing the monstrous creature to life by inserting the secret name of God into a clay man's mouth. However, such stories would have been considered sacrilegious in Loew's day.

Loew's genuine accomplishments included authoring fifteen books in the fields of education and theology. Loew displayed a keen understanding of children's psychology and decried the contemporary method of teaching Hebrew through rote memorization rather than grammar and context. He criticized teaching methods that did not align with children's natural intellectual development. Loew advocated a holistic approach to Torah study for adults. In his era, many rabbinical circles practiced *pilpul*, an analytical strategy for debating esoteric topics and searching for contradictions within Torah commentaries. Loew believed this trend circumvented the true purpose of studying scripture and advocated focusing on the original text over complex interpretations. Loew explained:

> Do not think that if a person has a passage from the Mishnah or the Gemara and is able to split hairs and debate and raise problems and uproot mountains that such a person is indeed worthy of being called a Torah scholar. It is not clear that he possesses true Torah learning, only that he has mastered the knowledge of how to split hairs.[12]

After Rabbi Loew died, he was buried in Prague's Jewish Cemetery. A Renaissance-style *tumba* (small house) served as his memorial stone. This new, elaborate style of grave marker became popular with wealthy and prominent individuals whose many accomplishments were carved into the stone. Symbols on the *tumba* reflected the deceased's family lineage, occupation, or personal attributes. The engraving of a lion represented the rabbi's family name, and the bunches of grapes celebrated a good and prosperous life. Loew's wife Pearl, with whom he had seven children, was buried next to her husband. The gravesite became a gathering place for faithful Jews to leave prayers and petitions, a practice that continues to this day.

FIGURE 5.4 Ephraim Moses Lilien, *Tombstone of the Maharal, Prague Cemetery*, early twentieth century. Jewish Cemetery, Prague/בית עלמין בפראג. William A. Rosenthall Judaica Collection—Postcards, College of Charleston Libraries, Charleston, SC, USA. Courtesy of Special Collections, College of Charleston Library.

While Loew served as the community's intellectual leader, Mordechai Maisel—likely the richest man in late sixteenth-century Prague, contributed to the institutional wealth of the Jewish community. A financier, economic adviser to the king, and Jewish community patron, Maisel left an indelible mark on his city. In 1568, he and his first wife Eva founded the Jewish quarter's High Synagogue and town hall, where Maisel served as mayor. Two decades later, he and his second wife, Frummet, received a royal charter to build the Maisel Synagogue, designed by the Jewish architect Judah de Herz. A Renaissance building with Gothic elements, the three-nave structure was the largest Jewish synagogue in Prague. In addition, Maisel funded poor women's dowries, almshouses, a ritual bath, and pavement stones for the Jewish quarter's streets. He donated ritual objects—such as Torah scrolls, gold and silver vessels, and candelabra—to his Prague community and distant congregations in Poland, Turkey, and Jerusalem. The Jewish scientist and historian David Gans closed his *Jewish Chronicle* with a tribute to Maisel and enumerated his good deeds: "Was there ever found a man like this, such a princely and liberal giver? Will not his righteousness exist forever?"[13]

Although he had no sons, Maisel received a written document from Rudolph II, promising that his nephews could inherit his enormous wealth. However, when the philanthropist died in 1601, the Crown claimed and seized his property. As was reported in a contemporary newsletter:

> Notwithstanding that he left his imperial Majesty [Rudolph II] ten thousand forints and much cash to the hospital for poor Christians and Jews, his imperial Majesty on the following Saturday, viz. the Sabbath of the Jews, ordered Herr von Sternberg, at that time President of the Bohemian Chamber, to enter the Jew's house forcibly and to seize everything there was.[14]

Maisel's widow watched as her home was emptied of her precious possessions and discovered that her husband's status prevailed only when he was useful to the court. Although the authorities took forty-five thousand florins in cash as well as silver objects, artwork, jewels, and clothes from the home, they believed the widow had hidden more family assets. A few nights later, men from the royal court broke into the house and arrested Maisel's nephew, torturing him until he revealed the whereabouts of the remaining family wealth. Coins from Salzburg, England, Portugal, and other regions, totaling over five hundred thousand florins, were handed over to the authorities. The Jewish community collected funds to help Maisel's widow and to construct a gravesite *tumba* befitting Mordechai's stature and contributions.

The second half of the sixteenth century has been called the golden age of Prague Jewry, but the community occupied a precarious position. Men like Maisel received privileges only when their work served the court. Christians interacted with Jewish merchants and pawnbrokers but often resented their dependence on cash loans or credit. Prague's burghers complained about Jews' supposed economic advantages and royal protections. Yet the court often turned its back on the community, withheld privileges, and even seized Jews' assets. Elizabeth Weston reflected her society's prejudiced views in a poem that called Jews "gold diggers and faithless bandits."[15] Renaissance Jews succeeded in Prague despite ubiquitous anti-Semitism and arduous, overcrowded living conditions.

While culture flourished under Rudolph, the king had less interest and skill in statecraft. Early in his reign, he was praised for not taking sides in various conflicts, especially the rivalries between Catholics and Protestants. He sought to find common ground among his subjects, but this strategy did not last indefinitely. Rudolph's frail mental health weakened his position during the last decade of his reign. Contemporaries referred to the emperor as either melancholy or obsessed with a particular idea; the symptoms suggest a struggle with depression or bipolar disorder. Never one to enjoy large social gatherings, Rudolph retreated further into the private world of his collections and made rash decisions that threatened the empire. His ongoing conflict with the Ottoman Empire, known as the Long Turkish War, took resources away from the court. Closer to home, Catholic leaders sought to take advantage of Rudolph's weakness by attempting to push Protestants and Utraquists out of powerful positions. In turn, the Bohemian nobility demanded protection from their king. In 1609, Rudolph gave into political pressure and issued a *Letter of Majesty*, which guaranteed "the free practice of the Christian religion in both Kinds permitted without let or hindrance, and sufficient assurances be given to the Estates by Us."[16]

The letter was the most liberal toleration edict in European history, but it brought tensions within the Habsburg family to a head. Rudolph's only living brother, Matthias, had been negotiating with Rudolph to be named his successor, but Rudolph refused to anoint the brother he despised. In February 1611, during the annual carnival, the armies of Passau, Germany, entered Prague, ostensibly to aid Rudolph in his fraternal conflicts. Protestant townspeople reacted to the invasion by defending their homes, attacking Catholic churches and monasteries, and injuring or killing clergy members. It was the most serious anti-Catholic violence in Prague since the Hussite Wars.

The chaos in Prague allowed Matthias and his supporters to enter the city in July 1611 and overthrow Rudolph. The deposed emperor became a prisoner in his chambers and died nine months later. Matthias assumed the throne and moved the imperial capital back to Vienna, leaving the Bohemian court in the hands of hard-line Catholic officers known as the Spanish Party. Although Matthias affirmed the freedom of religion promised in the *Letter of Majesty*, the conservative Bohemian court blocked appointments of Protestant noblemen to political offices and sought to reclaim Catholic lands.

Matthias accomplished little after he took power. He soon withdrew from public life and refused to intervene in Bohemia's religious disputes. At the time of his death in March 1619, his only lasting mark on Prague was the eponymous Matthias Gate, erected in 1614 at the walled entrance to

FIGURE 5.5 Matthias Gate at Prague Castle, 1614. Photo by the author.

Prague Castle. Rudolph had commissioned the gate from the Italian sculptor and architect Giovanni Maria Filippi. Still, by bearing his brother's name, it symbolized Rudolph's stolen legacy and the end of Prague's golden era. Prague would never again serve as the imperial capital or rise to the prominence it held in the Caroline and Rudolphine eras.

6

Revolt and Defeat in Habsburg Prague

ON THE MORNING of May 23, 1618, a group of Bohemian noblemen gathered at Prague Castle. Armed and angry, they burst into the royal offices to confront the king's leading officials. The noblemen demanded the freedom to worship according to their consciences and insisted that the king honor the long-standing division of powers between the monarch and the estates. Count Jindřich Matyáš Thurn, a wealthy Protestant who had ably served the empire in the Turkish wars, presided over an impromptu trial. Finding the kings' representatives guilty of violating Rudolph's *Letter of Majesty*, which Matthias had also signed, the Bohemian noblemen grabbed three royal officials and threw them out of a third-story window. To the astonishment of all, the three men survived the defenestration with only minor injuries. Even so, the assault set in motion a series of events that brought war to much of Europe. The shocking event became known as the Second Defenestration of Prague and the spark that set off the Thirty Years War.

A new policy on church building was the immediate cause of the confrontation. In 1618, the Bohemian court's conservative Catholics overturned plans to build several Lutheran churches in Bohemia. Catholic religious orders and bishops, backed by the court, reclaimed property that had been seized during the Hussite Wars and ordered the destruction of Protestant churches on these lands. The Czech nobility, over 90 percent Utraquist or Protestant, considered the 1618 ruling a suppression of their religious and political rights and a challenge to the Bohemian tradition of shared governance. Protestant members of the estates met at Prague University to discuss the crisis. The king's representatives declared the meeting illegal, thus threatening the Bohemian estates' right to assemble. These encroachments into Bohemian sovereignty led the Protestant and Utraquist noblemen to take action at Prague Castle.

The 1618 defenestration symbolically connected the Bohemian rebellion to the Czech Hussites and Protestants, who carried out similar attacks in 1419 and 1483. A statement by the rebels confirmed that the confrontation at Prague Castle was planned "in accordance with the old custom." Supporters of the Protestant nobility took to the streets of the Old Town and Lesser Town and attacked churches and other Catholic property. Protestants and Utraquists controlled the Old, New, and Lesser Town Councils, which maintained their own militias and weapons stores. Many residents stepped forward to defend their city against royal troops.

Catholics also responded to the crisis. The victims of the attack were the imperial regents, Jaroslav Bořita of Martinice and Vilém Slavata, and their secretary, Philip Fabricius. In his account of the event, Bořita recalled being shoved out the window "bare headed" as his hat, with a "beautiful braid decorated with gold and precious stones, had been ripped from his head." As he fell toward the castle moat, "which was perhaps thirty cubits [seventy feet] down and rocky," Bořita called out to Jesus and Mary. He later recounted the miracle that saved him: "The most holy and praiseworthy Virgin Mary… slowed him in his fall with her outstretched coat placed beneath him, such that he might fall to the earth much more softly."[1] Catholic leaders lauded the Virgin for saving Bořita, Slavata, and Fabricus, but Protestants claimed that the officials landed on a dung heap, which broke their fall.

The rebellious noblemen justified the defenestration on behalf of "all three estates of the commendable kingdom of Bohemia who receive the body

FIGURE 6.1 Matthäus Merian, "The Second Defenestration of Prague in 1618," copper engraving from the book *Theatrum Europaeum*, 1662. Universitätsbibliothek Augsburg. Public domain, via Wikimedia Commons.

and blood of the Lord Christ in both kinds." The document censured the Jesuits, who "once again began to issue a variety of abuse, slander, and denunciations against Protestants...that we were heretics." They decried the appointment of Catholic magistrates to oversee Protestant churches and the replacement of Protestant government ministers with Catholics. The noblemen blamed the royal representatives for not upholding the king's promises, calling them "the enemies of the king, the land, and the common peace [who] turned back to their accustomed tricks."[2]

While the rebellious noblemen had the support of the majority-Protestant population, Prague Jews worried that they would lose royal protections if the rebels took power. The writer of a contemporary Hebrew narrative showed little sympathy for the rebel estates: "While the emperor traveled from the capital city of Prague to the city of Vienna, some of the noblemen of Bohemia formed a conspiracy. They went up to the castle here in Prague, to the chamber of the imperial councilors.... And they took three of them and threw them out of the window into the moat. And they shot arrows after them, but they escaped."[3]

Multidenominational Bohemia was again at the center of heated religious and political strife. The kingdom represented a microcosm of the Holy Roman Empire at the beginning of the seventeenth century. Long a patchwork of self-ruling principalities and free cities, the empire had been a cohesive force when it united Central European territories within a Roman Catholic framework. Since the Reformation, the loose confederation made less political sense. In 1608 and 1609, the empire's princes formed competing alliances, the Protestant Union and the Catholic League. Bohemia was not a member of either union, but the Bohemian estates expected the Protestant Union to back them in conflicts with the empire.

Emperor Matthias died in March 1619, and the Bohemian estates deposed his successor, Ferdinand II. A new constitution created a government of thirty directors and affirmed freedom of religion. The Bohemian Diet sought a new king and looked to Protestant leaders, including the Duke of Savoy and the Elector of Saxony. Finally, the members agreed on Frederick V of the Palatine, whose father had founded the Protestant Union in 1608.

Frederick and his wife Elizabeth arrived in Prague in October 1619. Their unorthodox coronation, conducted by the leader of the Utraquists rather than the archbishop of Prague, took place at St. Vitus Cathedral the following month. A long procession featured nearly four thousand participants in Hussite regalia, carrying banners featuring the Utraquist chalice. The coronation medal presented to Frederick asserted the estates' authority in Bohemia: "King by the Grace of God and the Estates."[4]

Bohemian Protestants and Utraquists hoped that Frederick would unite Central European Christendom in a way the Roman church had ultimately failed to do. Jacob Boehme, the famed Lutheran mystic, witnessed Frederick's coronation in Prague but had little faith that the young king could make meaningful changes in the empire. "Before anything of the sort could come to pass," he wrote to a friend, "devastating war would take place, laying waste to the lands and the Holy Roman Empire."[5]

Boehme's prediction proved to be accurate. At age twenty-three, Frederick had excellent credentials: He was an imperial elector, a devout Protestant, the son-in-law of England's James I, and the son of the Protestant Union's founder. Yet he had little political and no military experience, and as a Calvinist, he did not enjoy support from the empire's Lutherans. The alliances Frederick counted on swiftly dissolved. James I refused to intervene in Habsburg territory, and the Protestant Union signed the Treaty of Ulm in 1620, promising neutrality in conflicts between Frederick and the Catholic League.

Furthermore, Frederick and Elizabeth did little to earn popularity in Prague. They showed no interest in learning Czech, and Elizabeth did not even know German. The couple conversed publicly in French and appeared to care more for fashion and festivities than the Bohemian crisis. Frederick's Calvinist advisers had little patience for Bohemian Protestantism and considered the Utraquists crypto-Catholics, whose rituals and icons differed little from their Roman Catholic counterparts. Palatine Calvinists who had arrived in Prague with Frederick attacked St. Vitus Cathedral on Christmas 1619; the mob tore down the main altar's crucifix, desecrated tombs, and destroyed precious medieval art. Frederick failed to quell the unrest. His detractors began to call him "the Winter King," suggesting he would not be on the throne come spring.

The first phase of the Thirty Years War, known as the Bohemian revolt, pitted the estates against the Habsburgs' imperial forces. The Bohemian estates built an army with mercenaries but had little success in gaining European allies. England, the Netherlands, and even the German Protestant leaders remained neutral. The army of the estates failed twice in a mission to occupy Vienna. The troops' movements through southern Bohemia cost them the support of many peasants and poor town dwellers, who resented the violence and pillaging. Military commander Ladislav Velen Žerotín urged his troops to fight in the spirit of Jan Žižka and Prokop the Bald, but the sentiment failed to resonate.

The new Holy Roman emperor, Ferdinand II, sought to reunify the Holy Roman Empire under Catholicism, recapture Bohemia, and punish the recalcitrant rebels. His field marshal, Johann Tserclaes, Count of Tilly, commanded an army of twenty-five thousand men, including mercenaries and professional soldiers. Albrecht von Wallenstein, a military man who served as a royal chamberlain in Emperor Ferdinand II's household, also lent his military prowess to the Catholic League troops. Frederick commissioned a fellow Calvinist, Prince Christian of Anhalt, to lead the Bohemian army of over thirty thousand men.

The Catholic League conquered most of western Bohemia in the summer and fall of 1620 and prepared to march on Prague. Ferdinand's armies, partially funded by Spain and other Catholic allies, invaded Bohemia from the south with aid from Bavarian forces. The Saxon army took advantage of the unrest and invaded Bohemia from the north. Although Lutheran, Saxony refused to aid the rebels and sought to take advantage of Bohemia's weakness to secure power in Lusatia. Anhalt advised Frederick not to engage with the formidable forces moving toward Prague, but the king rejected his counsel. Frederick ordered Anhalt to mount a defense on a small plateau called White Mountain, near the Star Chateau and royal hunting ground. The Bohemian troops began to erect defensive structures. However, neither time nor weather was on their side. An unusually cold November left the encamped soldiers hungry, and several died from exposure to the elements. The demoralized mercenaries had not received pay in several months. Close to half of the army deserted.

Tilly's imperial troops arrived at White Mountain on November 8, and a small reconnaissance unit investigated the opponent's defenses. Upon seeing the imperial troops, most of the Bohemian foot soldiers retreated. Tilly sent in reinforcements, and the Bohemian line crumbled. Anhalt countered by sending in the calvary, led by his son Christian II. The armies engaged in close combat and sustained significant casualties on both sides. In the end, Tilly's men prevailed. They surrounded the Bohemian cavalry and drove them into the middle of the battlefield. As other Bohemian units retreated, the imperial troops pushed their opponents back to the Star Chateau, which created a dramatic backdrop for the ill-fated battle. The Bohemian forces surrendered less than two hours after the fighting began. Upon hearing of his army's devastating loss, King Frederick fled the city, accompanied by several rebel leaders. Although Frederick had occupied the throne for a full year, the name Winter King stuck. Cartoons lampooned the young king, depicting him hiding in a beer barrel or running off with his trousers around his ankles.

The imperial victory at White Mountain enabled Ferdinand II to retake the Bohemian throne. In the months following the surrender, imperial authorities arrested hundreds of accused rebels, seized the property of noble landowners and town burghers, and resold land and dwellings to Habsburg loyalists. Ferdinand II's representative in Prague, Karl of Liechtenstein, oversaw the trial and sentencing of forty-one rebels, twenty-seven of whom received death sentences. A public execution was planned for the longest day of the year, June 21, 1621.

In the days leading up to the summer solstice, royal authorities transformed Old Town Square into an execution site. The square represented the spiritual center of the Bohemian opposition. The Utraquist Church of Our Lady Before Týn faced the Old Town Hall, a symbol of the secular power of the towns and their burghers. Between these sites, carpenters constructed a wooden platform draped in black cloth and placed a large crucifix near a chopping block and gallows. The execution methods reflected the rebels' social status and roles. Noblemen were to be beheaded, while town burghers would be hanged.

The day of the public execution began at five o'clock on Monday morning when the condemned entered the square from their prison cells in the Old Town Hall. Catholic priests stood on the execution scaffolding to hear confessions or elicit conversions, but at the last minute, Ferdinand II allowed Protestant clergymen to accompany the prisoners. While local spectators crowded into the square, military bands and drum corps drowned out any speeches the rebels tried to make. The executioner, Jan Mydlář, worked swiftly. In four hours, he beheaded fifteen prisoners, using four sharp swords that he

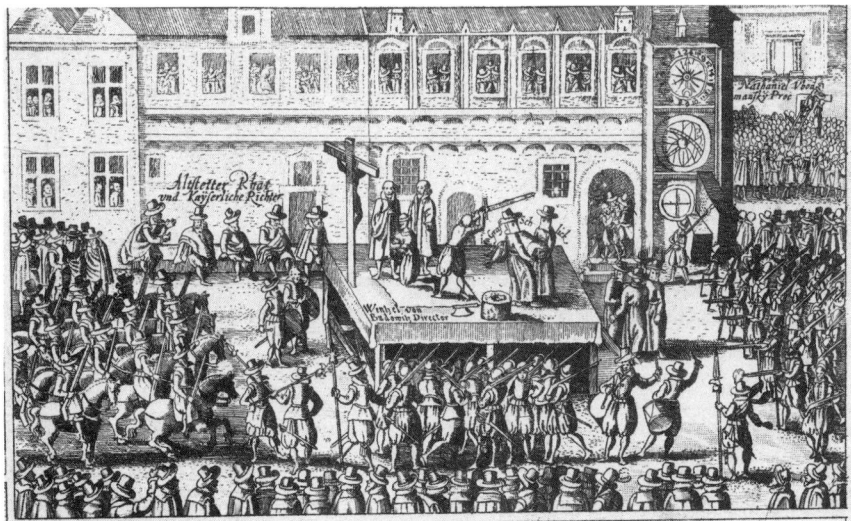

FIGURE 6.2 Frans Hogenberg (Workshop), *Execution of Twenty-Seven Bohemian Rebels on Old Town Square, June 1621*. Rijksmuseum, Amsterdam. Public domain.

exchanged when each became dull. The remaining twelve traitors were hanged at the gallows or from windows of the Old Town Hall.

The public execution of twenty-seven rebels was a disturbing spectacle. Joachim Andreas von Schlick, a wealthy Lutheran and German-speaking nobleman, climbed up on the scaffolding first. The outspoken proponent of religious freedom had his right hand cut off before his beheading. The eighty-year-old knight Kašpar Kaplíř had to be helped up the scaffolding steps. Jan Jesenský, the Lutheran rector at Prague University, received the most brutal sentence because he had spoken at Frederick's coronation and published the treatise *In Favor of Legitimate Intervention Against Tyrants*. The sentencing committee in Vienna declared, "*Ex gratia imperialia*, his tongue will be cut out alive, then he will be beheaded and quadrisected and hung at a crossroads close to the scaffold; his head with his tongue will be placed at the bridge."[6] The royal government displayed twelve heads in iron cages on the Old Town Bridge Tower, and an anonymous Catholic poet wrote, "All the world should recognize who sinned against the King." Except for one victim, whose wife successfully petitioned to have his head returned for proper burial, the skulls remained on the bridge tower for ten years. The skulls were finally removed in 1631, during the brief Saxon occupation of Prague, and interred in the Týn Church, steps away from the site where the rebels had met their fate.

As always, Prague's Jews had to negotiate their position in a political and religious landscape that both excluded and threatened them. In 1620, Jews breathed sighs of relief when the imperial troops avoided the Jewish quarter. According to an anonymous Hebrew narrative, "On that night, the imperial army entered the castle.... And on Monday, the thirteenth of Heshvan...and the next day, Tuesday...the Old City, where we live, did not surrender; nor did the New City surrender. And we were in great danger until in the evening they surrendered."[7] The Hebrew account praised the Habsburg emperor and his military for protecting Jews and quoted from the book of Esther: "God caused the generals of the army to be gracious and merciful towards us, and they set guards over our streets. For His Majesty, the Emperor—may God reward him—had ordered his generals not to touch any Jew, [and to take] neither his life nor his property, but to guard them carefully." The chief rabbi of Prague, Isaiah Horowitz, ordered his followers to fast from dawn to dusk on each anniversary of White Mountain to thank God for protecting the community. Rabbi Yom-Tov Lippmann Heller praised God in his poems about the defenestration and the Battle of White Mountain:

> My voice cried out to God, for I was sunk in the abyss of despair
> He opened for me the strait, He was gracious to me,
> He gave me joy when I heard the news spoken
> That army officers had come to our streets to guard them, lest they be touched…
> Upon my walls, He placed watchmen all the night and the day,
> "And we are left as a remnant to this day" (Ezra 9: 15).

Jewish liturgical poetry rarely mentioned secular events, but Jewish leaders needed to assert their loyalty to the victorious Habsburgs, who could expel the entire community at will. In 1623, when Ferdinand II visited Prague, the Jewish community arranged a celebration in their neighborhood and invited local Christians to participate. The Catholic priest and historian Jan František Beckovský described the event: "First there were three small girls. One was playing a small violin, the other a lute, and the third a zither; they were followed by Jews in equal groups, dressed as for the sabbath; behind them were groups of Jewish butchers in their white robes, carrying two banners; on each of them stood two small boys; behind the banner there walked the Jewish rabbi."[8] In return, Ferdinand II bestowed privileges on the Jewish community, including the right to display a new banner and use an official seal.

Despite these achievements, the Jewish community faced a resurgence of vitriolic anti-Semitism during the Thirty Years War. Jewish bankers, such as Jacob Bassevi, became scapegoats for the rampant inflation that followed the Bohemian revolt. Bassevi had advised Emperor Ferdinand II to seize Bohemian silver mines and debase the currency to fund the ongoing war, and he partnered with military commander Albrecht Wallenstein to mint coins. Bassevi expanded the Jewish quarter by purchasing property from Old Town's struggling residents. Angry Prague residents accused Bassevi of war profiteering. As in times past, the actions of one Jewish person reflected on the entire community.

Prague's chief rabbi, Yom-Tov Lippmann Heller, was charged with blasphemy in 1629. The Viennese court alleged that Heller called trinitarian Christianity a polytheistic faith. Heller denied the charge and received a relatively short prison sentence and a fine. When he returned to Prague, he fell ill and remained bedridden for three months while friends and family gathered money to pay Heller's fine. He and his wife sold their possessions and their seats in the Prague synagogues and journeyed east, spending the rest of their lives in Russia, Lithuania, and Poland. Heller remained loyal to the Habsburg monarchy and never blamed the emperor or his advisers for his misfortunes.

Still, his arrest occurred within a context of increased anti-Semitism in the Holy Roman Empire and the papacy. The authorities confiscated and burned Jewish books and forced Jews to attend Christian sermons. Attempts to convert Prague Jews to Catholicism became a hallmark of the era.

Jews were not the only religious group to suffer increased persecution. Roman Catholicism became the only religion permitted in Bohemia and Moravia. The royal court forbade Utraquism and expelled non-adherent priests from royal towns. Lutherans, Calvinists, and Brethren had to convert or leave the country. A new constitution annulled the Bohemian estates' right to elect their monarch and confirmed Habsburg hereditary rights through the male and female lines. The state seized the property of the native nobility and resold their estates and palaces to aristocrats from other parts of Europe. In 1622, the Jesuit order, which already controlled the Roman Catholic Clementinum University, took over the Protestant Academy (formerly the Carolinum's Faculty of Arts). The Jesuits dominated intellectual life in Prague and sought to convert the Bohemian heretics.

Catholic orders and noble families commissioned art and building projects throughout the city. The popular Baroque style conveyed church and state power and encouraged individual piety. Taken from a Portuguese word meaning "irregular," the term "Baroque" designated art that diverged from Renaissance order and static geometry. Paintings, sculptures, and ornate architecture glorified God and emphasized penitence, the sacraments, and Christian duty. As Catholic culture permeated Prague society, noble and burgher families incorporated Baroque objects into their home décor. Middle-class women displayed their piety and growing wealth by collecting holy objects, such as rosaries and jewelry.

In 1624, Ferdinand II gave the Lutheran Church of the Holy Trinity to the Carmelite nuns. Built in 1611 by Lutheran settlers in Lesser Town, the church was reconsecrated as Our Lady Victorious to commemorate the Catholic victory against the Bohemian rebellion. The church's entrance was moved away from Petřín Hill, and Baroque statues by esteemed sculptor Jan Jiří Bendl occupied the reconstructed nave. A center of Marian devotion in Prague, Our Lady Victorious's most important treasure was the Infant of Prague, a wax statue of the child Jesus wearing elaborate robes and a crown. The piece had important connections to the Pernštejn, Rožmberk, and Lobkowicz families, Bohemia's most important Catholic noble clans. Maria Maxmiliana Manriquez de Lara, the Spanish bride of Vratislav of Pernštejn, brought the statue to Prague in the mid-sixteenth century. Her daughter Polyxena married into the Rožmberk and Lobkowicz families and was one of the most politically active Bohemian noblewomen of her era. In 1618, the three victims of the defenestration were brought to the nearby Lobkowicz palace, and Polyxena protected them in her home. Ten years later, she donated the statue to the Carmelite order. Stories about the statue's healing properties spread throughout Europe, and Catholic pilgrims, especially Spanish and Italian women, flocked to Prague to visit it. The Carmelites cared for the statue and dressed it in garments appropriate to the liturgical season, such as white at Easter and purple at Advent.

The pilgrimage site Loreto (Loreta Praha), founded by the Lobkowicz family in the Castle District, also attracted believers to Prague. The shrine included a replica of the Holy House in Loreto, Italy, which many Catholics considered the place where the archangel Gabriel announced Jesus's conception to Mary. Legends claimed that angels carried the shrine from Palestine to Italy during the Crusades. Prague's Loreto expanded to include churches, libraries, a carillon, and a treasury featuring the Prague Sun, a gold monstrance encrusted with 6,222 diamonds. Like the Infant of Prague, Mary's home attracted female believers. The Counter-Reformation church sought to win back believers by offering women a faith connected to motherhood and individual piety. Noblewomen and cloistered nuns led efforts to mold a faith that reflected their values. Furthermore, after two centuries of religious strife, Prague had revived Charles IV's vision of Prague as a holy city, a place of pilgrimage.

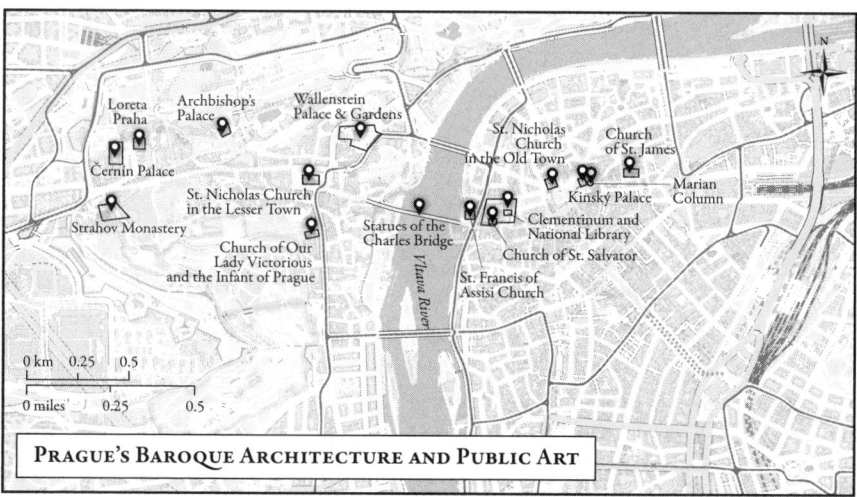

FIGURE 6.3 Map of modern-day Prague showing the locations of Baroque architecture and public art built during the seventeenth and eighteenth centuries.

Baroque architecture was not limited to religious building projects. The palace of imperial military commander Albrecht von Wallenstein transformed the Lesser Town. Wallenstein was born to a poor family in northern Bohemia, and his background reflected Bohemia's complexities. His father was a German-speaking Lutheran, and his mother preferred the Czech language and Utraquism. After being orphaned, Wallenstein converted to the United Brethren (Unitas Fratrum), the church of his uncle and guardian. As a student in Protestant academies, Wallenstein became known for his intelligence, ambition, ruthless careerism, and violent temper. He frequently joined pub brawls and duels and was once arrested and fined for severely beating his servant.

Wallenstein later studied in Bologna and Padua, where he became fluent in Italian, and then attended the Jesuit college in the Moravian city of Olomouc. He converted to Roman Catholicism in 1606, possibly because he recognized that Protestants were no longer granted political appointments in Rudolph's court. Through two lucrative marriages and his keen political and economic acumen, Wallenstein became one of the wealthiest men in Bohemia.

Following White Mountain, Wallenstein was awarded lands from exiled Protestant noblemen, and he used his new fortunes to buy property in Prague. In 1624, he began the construction of a palace below Prague Castle. To the dismay of Lesser Town residents, Wallenstein destroyed twenty-six houses, six gardens, and the Pisek Gate, a thirteenth-century Gothic edifice. Wallenstein's palace design mixed Renaissance, mannerist, and Baroque elements that conveyed domination and power rather than aesthetic continuity.

Wallenstein employed myriad court artists who had remained in Prague after the Matthias court moved to Vienna. The demanding and irascible patron frightened some artists, like the young Florentine painter Baccio de Bianco, who fled Prague before finishing his commission. Wallenstein's massive outdoor garden featured Renaissance arcades, loggia, an artificial grotto, pools, and caves. Court sculptor Adriaen de Vries designed the garden's statuary, including a dramatic rendering of Hercules fighting off a dragon. Wallenstein made specific suggestions to the artists: "As regards the loggia in the Prague garden, we believe that it would not be a bad idea to paint some parts of it. Write to tell them not to take down the scaffolding to leave it for the painters who will do this next spring."[9]

Whether because of his taste or the availability of former court artists, Wallenstein's collection mimicked Rudolph's aesthetic rather than the Baroque favored by the new regime. Belgian tapestries, Venetian calf leather, and murals by Florentine painter Domenico Pugliani covered the interior

FIGURE 6.4 Wallenstein Palace and Gardens in Prague's Lesser Town, 1623–1630. Photo by the author.

walls. The Mythological Corridor featured scenes from Ovid's *Metamorphosis*, and the Astrological Corridor was designed by a pupil of Galileo. St. Wenceslas Chapel, Wallenstein's personal prayer room, embraced the Prague Baroque style.

Wallenstein continued to amass victories over Protestant forces, but his fate changed in 1631 when the Swedish and Saxon armies beat the Catholic Alliance at the Battle of Breitenfeld. The emperor lost faith in Wallenstein and offered a reward for his capture, dead or alive. In February 1634, Irish and Scottish assassins murdered Wallenstein at Eger Castle.

The following year, peace negotiations took place in Prague Castle, at the very site of the defenestration. The Peace of Prague ended the Saxon involvement in the Thirty Years War and secured Lutheran rights in certain parts of the empire. Fighting would continue in Europe for another fourteen years during the war's French phase. The war no longer mirrored religious differences in Europe as Catholic France allied with Protestant Sweden and the Dutch Republic against the Habsburgs. Bohemia was spared most of the fighting.

The peace treaty encouraged Prague-born artist Wenceslas Hollar to visit his birthplace in 1636. While there, Hollar made a series of etchings that captured the architecture and everyday life. His *Great View of Prague* depicted the city panorama stretching from Prague Castle to Vyšehrad, and his

FIGURE 6.5 Wenceslaus Hollar, *Woman from Prague*, 1643. Art Institute of Chicago CC0.

portraits of Prague women showcased the elaborate fashions of the merchant and burgher classes: ruff collars, broad-brimmed hats, and tall wool caps. Although the city had suffered during the war, members of the upper class displayed their wealth by investing in home furnishings and trendy fashions.

As the war finally neared an end, the Swedish army launched an attack on Prague in July 1648. Dissatisfied with the ongoing peace negotiations in Westphalia, Swedish leaders believed they could push for indemnity by threatening one of the richest Habsburg cities. A handful of Czech Protestant emigres had joined the Swedish forces and provided insight into weaknesses in Prague's defense system. The Swedish army traversed the battlefield at White Mountain and entered Prague on the night of July 24. The surprise attack enabled them to capture the castle and Lesser Town, where soldiers looted the palaces of the new nobility. The Swedes could not penetrate beyond the left bank. Unlike in 1618, when Prague residents took to the streets against the imperial forces, the urban dwellers of 1648 sided with the Habsburgs. The Counter-Reformation efforts of the Jesuits and the centralized Austrian bureaucracy had influenced a whole generation. Prague residents defended their homes and workplaces, and university students set up movable barricades on the Stone Bridge. Two more Swedish armies attempted to enter Prague from the north and east, but Old and New Town residents fiercely defended their neighborhoods. Imperial troops, burghers' militias, and university students led by the Jesuit priest Jiří Plachý repelled the invaders. Jewish quarter residents demonstrated their loyalty to Austria by setting up hospitals and charities behind the ghetto walls.

FIGURE 6.6 Johann Georg Schleder, Carl Henric de Osten, and Johan Merck, "Siege of Prague (1648)," in *Theatri Europæi*, 1663. Skokloster Castle, Sweden, Public domain, via Wikimedia Commons.

When news came on November 5 that the Peace of Westphalia had been signed, the Swedes waited five days to honor the ceasefire. As they retreated, their soldiers ransacked Prague Castle and dismantled Wallenstein's garden and palace. Hundreds of priceless objects, including Wenceslas IV's illuminated manuscripts and Wallenstein's Adriaen de Vries sculptures, were loaded onto barges, sent up the Vltava and Elbe Rivers, and taken across the North Sea. They remain in Sweden to this day.

The Habsburgs celebrated their victory over the Swedes by erecting a Baroque Marian column in Old Town Square in 1650. Prague sculptor Jan Jiří Bendl created a sensuous Virgin Mary crowned as Maria Regina, standing atop a sixteen-meter pillar. The pedestal's four warrior angels, representing the cardinal virtues of bravery, wisdom, righteousness, and gentleness, slayed devils, a lion, and a dragon. Christian and Jewish Prague residents held festivals to mark the anniversary of the siege. Yehuda Leb ben Yoshua Porit Porges, a Jewish observer, recalled, "Young and old men...walked to and fro, from gateway to gateway, along the Jewish street, in orderly groups.... Two banners which had been given to us Jews by previous emperors for glory and decoration and as a sign of freedom towards all nations, were carried through the streets of the town, and between the banners there was a canopy and a Torah across."[10]

The Peace of Westphalia mandated toleration for Lutheranism and Calvinism in parts of the empire, but that did not extend to Bohemia or the Austrian hereditary lands. Bohemians who did not convert to Catholicism fled into exile. Prague had become a loyal Habsburg city. In years to come, Czech speakers would consider the Marian Column a stinging reminder of their lost sovereignty.

Jesuit historian Bohuslav Balbín led efforts among Catholic intellectuals to make the church more appealing to Prague's Christians. A native Czech speaker, Balbín wrote the anonymous and influential Latin text *An Apology for the Slavic and Especially the Bohemian Tongue*. Although the work was censored, it circulated in Prague in self-published formats. Balbín edited and republished the tenth-century Latin hagiography *The Lives of Saints Wenceslas and Ludmila*, which helped boost the popularity of Bohemia's patron saints. In 1680, an equestrian statue of Saint Wenceslas by the Baroque master Jan Jiří Bendl was placed atop the Horse Market, a significant reminder of the relationship between Czech statehood and the Roman church.

Balbín wrote several texts about the relevance of Mary in Bohemian culture, and in 1670, he published a Latin hagiography of John of Nepomuk, the priest murdered by Wenceslas IV's officers in 1383 on the order of the king.

While Nepomuk attracted a following soon after his death, the Hussite movement eclipsed Nepomuk's popularity. During the Counter-Reformation, the Jesuits revived the memory of Nepomuk to create a foil for Hus. When Calvinist supporters of Frederick, the Winter King, attacked St. Vitus Cathedral and desecrated Nepomuk's tomb, the Prague archbishop declared John of Nepomuk his patron and submitted his name for beatification. Balbín's hagiography promoted the story that Wenceslas IV had ordered Nepomuk to reveal the queen's confession: "Do you hear, priest, he said, you must die if you do not immediately reveal to me the confessions of my wife." When Nepomuk refused, "He was thrown from the bridge and drowned on May 16 in the year 1383." Balbín's description of a miraculous phenomenon supported the case for Nepomuk's canonization:

> The death which Wenceslas wanted to keep secret was immediately revealed by a celestial miracle. The same fiery flame that had appeared at John's birth illuminated him in death as he was ascending to heaven, so that the whole Vltava reddened. You could see countless numbers of bright lights [that] surrounded the martyr on the water.[11]

In 1683, a statue of John of Nepomuk was installed on the Stone Bridge. Designed by Jan Brokoff, the monument included bronze plaques depicting scenes from Nepomuk's life. Balbín's scholarship and Brokoff's statue popularized the medieval figure, who was beatified in 1721 and canonized in 1729. Nepomuk's remains were interred in a silver sarcophagus placed in St. Vitus Cathedral. The Baroque sculptor Johann Bernhard Fischer von Erlach designed the elaborate tomb, which is decorated with angels, cherubs, and a silver statue of Nepomuk holding a crucifix.

The Thirty Years War cost Prague its status in the empire. At the beginning of the seventeenth century, the city ranked among the most populous in Europe, with between fifty thousand and seventy thousand residents. The population shrunk to thirty thousand by the war's end, the result of the Protestant exile, war-related disease and hunger, and the relocation of the imperial court to Vienna.[12] Prague's population began to climb again by 1700 but did not reach prewar numbers. As mortality outstripped the birth rate, the population could only recover through immigration. The expansion of artisan guilds, the favorable conditions for Catholic nobility, and a relatively safe location for Jews made Prague an attractive destination. Wealthy burghers, noble families, and church leaders sponsored educational institutions, charities, and Baroque buildings. Yet, Prague would never regain its

FIGURE 6.7 Jeremias Jakob Sedelmayr, *Baroque Silver Tomb of St. John Nepomuk by Fischer von Erlach*, 1729. Metropolitan Museum of Art, New York.

former prestige and could no longer compete with the urban centers of London, Paris, Rome, Antwerp, and Amsterdam.

After the Peace of Westphalia, Bohemian and foreign Catholic noble families erected new homes throughout the city. By 1700, Prague boasted more than two hundred Baroque palaces. The emboldened Catholic orders and their noble patrons invested in church architecture, building new structures and renovating Gothic edifices to suit the Counter-Reformation era. The Catholic leadership created a sacred landscape where the "true faith" saturated everyday life. Statues of saints, plague columns, and crucifixes adorned roads and public squares. Church towers, frescoes of the heavens, and stirring organ music emphasized religious ecstasy. Roadside shrines, religious statues on the Stone Bridge, and the pilgrimage churches attracted a new generation of believers who were educated in Jesuit schools and had no memory of Hussite traditions.

Northern Italian, German, and French artists made their way to Prague after the war and accepted both secular and religious commissions. Carlo Lurago, a plasterer from Como, Italy, redesigned the facades of the Jesuit

Church of the Holy Savior and the Clementinum university buildings. Giovanni Battista Orsi designed the Theological Hall at Strahov Monastery, which featured elaborate stucco designs and carved wooden cartouches. Troja Chateau, by French architect Jean Baptiste Mathey, featured a two-winged monumental staircase, a classical French garden, and trompe l'oeil murals by Flemish masters Abraham and Isaac Godijin. Viennese court architect J. B. Fischer von Erlach designed Old Town's Clam-Gallas Palace, whose portico featured imposing Baroque statues of giants. Karel Škréta, a Czech-speaking and Protestant portrait painter, converted to Catholicism and returned from his exile in Saxony. His church paintings, including the *Madonna Blessing the Maltese Knights at the Battle of Lepanto* and the *Beheading of St. Barbara*, became hallmarks of the Prague Baroque.

The father-son duo Christoph and Kilian Ignaz Dientzenhofer led a second wave of Baroque architectural activity in Prague. Born in Bavaria to a family of architects and master builders, Christoph Dientzenhofer came to Prague with his brothers in 1676, and his son Kilian was born in Prague in 1689. The Dientzenhofers used rhythmic repetition of motifs and patterns, curved structures, sculptural exteriors, and contrasting textures, colors, and materials. Christoph designed the elaborate Baroque Church of St. Margaret for Břevnov, the oldest monastery in Prague, and together, the father and son added the Baroque facade and central belfry to the Loreto pilgrimage site near Prague Castle.

The striking copper dome and tower of the Dientzenhofers' St. Nicholas Church in Lesser Town transformed the Prague landscape. Two churches and over twenty residences were demolished to accommodate the massive structure. A marvel of engineering, the church had a complex geometric design of interlocking cylinders and embedded pillars that supported curved walls and a monumental dome. Karel Škréta decorated the interior with a passion cycle and celestial frescoes. (See Color Plate 10.) Kilian Dientzenhofer designed a second St. Nicholas Church for the Old Town Square near his Goll-Kinský Palace, which featured a stucco rococo facade with contrasting pink tones and plaster adornments. The Dientzenhofers experimented with unique forms in their two churches dedicated to the recently canonized John of Nepomuk. The Castle District church had an octagonal nave that created arching vaults for Wenzel Lorenz Reiner's frescoes, and St. John of Nepomuk on the Rock in New Town was embedded into a steep vineyard near Charles Square to create the illusion of height.

Between 1706 and 1714, two dozen Baroque sculptures joined Jan Brokoff's 1683 Nepomuk statue on the Stone Bridge. The works conveyed personal piety and strong emotions to speak to a new generation of believers. Exotic elements emphasized missionary work and conversions of Turks, Arabs, and Jews. Christian saints expelled demons and shoved away devils. The statue of Frances Xavier by Ferdinand Brokoff depicted the saint baptizing Japanese and Indian men and women while a group of admirers—including the sculptor himself—look on. Prague's Baroque landscape contained manifold reminders that faith was an active undertaking.

The Catholic Church's efforts to revive Roman Catholicism stirred up anti-Semitism in Prague society. Vandalism and harassment of Jews became more frequent. Christian youth taunted Jewish merchants at the Tandlmarkt and stole small items like buttons and ribbons. New decrees censored blasphemous books, including the Talmud, and required rabbis to submit their sermons for pre-approval by Jesuit University professors who read Hebrew.

When a plague broke out in 1679, Old Town burghers established a Jewish Reduction Commission, which required the Jewish elders to submit a list of at least one thousand residents to expel from Prague. Christian Europeans frequently blamed the crowded and unsanitary conditions of the Jewish quarters for plague outbreaks. As a sixteenth-century English traveler Fynes Moryson reported, "At Prage many Familyes of Jewes lived packed together in one little house, which makes not only their howses but their streetes to be very filthy, and theire City to be like a Dunghill."[13] Of course, these living conditions resulted from the severe residential restrictions placed on Jewish communities. In the spring of 1680, Prague's surgeon general ordered the ghetto to be sealed and left without medical assistance. As 2,616 Jewish residents died in those months, the Reduction Commission abandoned its plan to expel part of the population.

A decade later, the Jewish population had recovered to its pre-plague numbers. But, on June 21, 1689, an arson attack by French soldiers passing through Prague destroyed most of the Jewish quarter. Old Town burghers demanded a complete expulsion of Prague Jews. The Holy Roman emperor, Leopold I, immediately agreed and issued an order, but Bohemian financial authorities and leaders of the New Town and Lesser Town municipalities protested, citing their fiscal needs. The fire displaced thousands of Jewish families, who needed to find accommodations while their homes were rebuilt. The archbishop of Prague tried to prevent Jews from renting in buildings where Christians lived. He issued orders forbidding priests from visiting private chapels or delivering last rites in buildings that housed Jews. The ultimatum was so outrageous that the Bohemian vice regent asked the emperor to reverse the archbishop's position. The emperor, not normally known for his tolerance, chastised the archbishop for abandoning Christian charity.

FIGURE 6.8 Prague's Old Jewish Cemetery in use between 1439 and 1787, with a view of Klausen Synagogue. Photo by the author.

Following the 1689 fire, municipal fire authorities issued rebuilding permits only for six synagogues to reduce access to Jewish services. A cluster of three sixteenth-century buildings, including a Yeshiva and synagogue, was replaced by a single Baroque structure known as the Klausen Synagogue. The largest structure in the Jewish quarter, Klausen overlooked the Jewish cemetery and became the meeting and prayer space for the Jewish Burial Society. The building opened in 1694, and two years later, the community unveiled a monumental three-tiered Torah Ark. The Viennese court adviser Samuel Oppenheimer provided funds for Klausen and other rebuilding projects in the ghetto.

Although some Catholic authorities decried Jews living among Christians, the Jesuits saw an opportunity to convert young Jews by introducing them to opulent Baroque art and emotional rituals. In 1693, Simon Abeles, a Jewish youth and alleged convert to Catholicism, was brutally murdered, and his father, Lazar Abeles, was accused of the crime. Lazar was a successful merchant whose own father had served as mayor of the Jewish community. According to contemporary narratives, Simon ran away from home at age twelve and expressed interest in baptism. When Lazar learned that his son was studying as a catechumen, he found him and brought him home. A few months later, Simon was murdered. Witness testimony described a family altercation in which Lazar Abeles's cousin Löbl Kurtzhandl hit the boy for not eating his dinner. Simon fell against a chair and broke his neck, and Lazar hastily buried his son. When the body was discovered, Jesuit missionaries who remembered the boy insisted that the court bring charges of first-degree murder for hatred for the faith (*ex odio fidei*). Lazar hanged himself in prison, and Kurtzhandl suffered excruciating torture. Meanwhile, Catholic leaders exhumed Abeles's body and buried him at Our Lady Before Týn. The inscription on his tombstone celebrated him as a "martyr for the faith" and falsely accused Simon's family of whipping, starving, and imprisoning him. Artists depicted Simon holding a small crucifix surrounded by a wreath of flowers, lying in a glass coffin on a bed of roses, or being greeted by cherubs as he rose to heaven on a bed of clouds.[14]

A few decades later, another sensational court case cast aspersions on the Jewish community. One of eighteenth-century Prague's most colorful characters, Giorgio Dio-Dato, brought a lawsuit against Prague's chief rabbi, David Oppenheim, accusing him of treason. Dio-Dato was a Syriac Christian from Damascus who converted to Roman Catholicism. He established Prague's first coffeehouse at the House of the Three Ostriches in Lesser Town, where he sold the fashionable "black soup" and delicacies such as spices, lemons, liquors, and chocolate. Travelers to Prague commented on the aroma of roasted coffee beans rising from his shop, which became a center of conviviality for Prague residents and visitors.[15]

A Jewish patron from Smyrna told Dio-Dato that Rabbi Oppenheim owed him money. Dio-Dato befriended him and convinced him to convert to Catholicism. An anti-Semite, Dio-Dato likely saw an opportunity to shame the prominent Jewish scholar and renowned book collector. Dio-Dato filed a lawsuit, claiming that Oppenheim was a traitor who paid tributes to the Ottoman sultan and used the honorary title of "Prince in the Land of Israel." The protracted court case culminated in Oppenheim's exoneration, but the rabbi had to revoke his honorary titles and abandon his charitable organization.

False accusations against Jews marked the end of Prague's seventeenth century. In 1696, a Jewish community leader, Elias Backoffen, faced charges of blasphemy for dishonoring *Calvary*, the crucifixion statue on Prague's Stone Bridge. As punishment, Backoffen had to fund a gold-plated Hebrew epigraph on the Stone Bridge's imposing crucifix. The words *Kadosh, Kadosh, Kadosh, Adoshem Zavaosh* (Holy, Holy, Holy, the Lord of Hosts) created a banner of Hebrew letters stretching across Christ's cross. This punishment forced Prague Jews to read a declaration of Jesus's divinity in their sacred language, the ultimate humiliation.

FIGURE 6.9 Charles Bridge crucifix with inscription in Hebrew: "Holy, Holy, Holy is Lord of Hosts." In 1696, a Jewish man was forced to pay for the lettering following an accusation of blasphemy. Prague's Jewish community bore the shame as the Hebrew epigraph contradicted their beliefs. Photo by the author.

Despite the anti-Semitism that marked Counter-Reformation Prague, the Jewish community thrived. In 1702, Prague's Jewish elders conducted a census that recorded 11,517 residents of the Prague ghetto, making it the largest Jewish community in all of Europe. As in earlier eras, eighteenth-century Jews found themselves caught between town authorities who sought to reduce the Jewish population and royal authorities who relied on Jewish bankers and high tax revenue. Jews paid extra excise taxes on beer, wine, meat, honey, and flour and were required to provide "gifts" to soldiers and officials. Without Jewish contributions, Prague's economy might not have rebounded following the war.

The Jesuits' promotion of intellectual and artistic pursuits influenced lay culture as well. By the early eighteenth century, Prague patrons could experience contemporary secular music and theater. Prague's first public theater opened in 1724. Its founder, Count Anton Sporck, was born into a peasant family but amassed a fortune during his military service. He championed Italian operas and commissioned works from the renowned Italian composer Antonio Vivaldi, whose *Argippo* premiered in Prague in 1730. Sporck broadened the Prague sound, traditionally heavy on woodwinds, when he introduced the French horn to local musicians. Sporck's contributions to Prague culture won him few friends among the Habsburg and church authorities. The Jesuits pointed to Sporck's foundation of Prague's first Masonic Lodge as evidence of anti-church beliefs. In 1729, Charles VI ordered local authorities to confiscate Sporck's library of over thirty thousand volumes, close his printing press, and censor his writings. Although cleared of all charges in 1734, Sporck was bankrupt and despondent. He closed down his bankrupt theater in 1735 and spent his last years as a recluse, humiliated by his treatment and mourning his beloved wife. The count died in 1738, two years before Maria Theresa's long reign began. Prague was not long without a public theater. In 1739, the Kotzen Theater opened in the Old Town and presented operas, ballets, and plays. It employed a series of Italian impresarios to bring a European repertoire to the city.

The era of the Thirty Years War and Counter-Reformation was one of the most contentious in the history of Prague, marking the end of Bohemian autonomy and independent religious thought. Bohemia no longer survived as a Protestant island within the Catholic Habsburg lands. Foreign aristocrats, all Roman Catholic and loyal to the Habsburgs, replaced the native nobility, and Prague became a center for Catholic education and culture in the monarchy. The Jesuits stood determined to rid the city of its heretical past by rooting out crypto-Protestants and encouraging the conversion of Jews. Future generations of Czech nationalists named this era *Temno*, the Czech word for darkness. Yet the Baroque building projects transformed Prague's landscape into the city we know today. Imposing domes joined the city's Gothic spires, and stone saints were positioned to guard the bridges and portals of Prague. Intellectual movements began to expand beyond the religious realm, bringing new opportunities to Prague's citizens.

7

Enlightened Prague

ON NOVEMBER 25, 1741, a French military corps led by Maurice de Saxe advanced on Prague. De Saxe detected several defensive weaknesses and directed Colonel François de Chevert to invade the city under the cover of darkness. The French soldiers stealthily climbed ladders to a parapet atop the city walls and descended into the town. They used bayonets rather than muskets to dispatch the guards on duty so as not to alert the Habsburg soldiers garrisoned inside. Once the French soldiers opened the city gates, de Saxe rode in triumphantly with his full cavalry following. Surprised and overwhelmed, the Austrian troops immediately surrendered. According to an account by Voltaire, "The town of Prague...had been taken in a half-an-hour."[1]

The French capture of Prague represented a major loss for the Habsburg monarchy in the Wars of Austrian Succession, which preoccupied Europe from 1740 to 1748. When Holy Roman emperor Charles VI died in 1740, he left his territorial possessions to his twenty-three-year-old daughter, Maria Theresa. Charles, who lacked a male heir, had issued the Pragmatic Sanction in 1713, which allowed the crown to pass to a female descendant. Yet, as a woman, Maria Theresa could not hold the title of Holy Roman emperor, which the Habsburgs had controlled since 1440. The imperial crown symbolically unified the varied Habsburg territories; without it, Maria Theresa remained vulnerable to the claims of other European powers. Although the German states initially accepted the Pragmatic Sanction, Bavaria and Saxony challenged the young queen's tenuous position. Backed by France, Bavaria attacked the Austrian hereditary lands and Bohemia, while the Prussian king, Frederick II, occupied Silesia, which had been a part of the Bohemian crown lands since the reign of John of Luxembourg.

The prince elector of Bavaria, Charles Albert, claimed the Bohemian throne. Believing that Maria Theresa could not prevail against Prussia and its allies, the Bohemian estates swore their allegiance to Charles Albert. On December 19, 1741, the archbishop of Prague installed Charles Albert as king of Bohemia at St. Vitus Cathedral but could not bestow on him the Crown of

Saint Wenceslas since the Bohemian crown jewels were in Vienna. A month after his Prague coronation, the imperial electors declared Charles Albert the Holy Roman emperor, Charles VII, the first non-Habsburg to hold the title in over three centuries.

Maria Theresa remained determined to retake Prague and remove Charles Albert. She negotiated a separate peace with Prussia, ceding most of Silesia to Frederick in return for his neutrality in the ongoing conflict with Bavaria and France. In June 1742, Hungarian armies loyal to Maria Theresa besieged Prague and starved out the French occupiers. The French Enlightenment philosopher Voltaire described the misery of the French troops in Prague: "When we ... see the extremities to which they were reduced, the loud and incessant complaints among the troops, the series of disappointments, their want, and the accumulated miseries whereby they were discouraged, it is astonishing to think where this general could draw his resources." At least twenty French soldiers died daily from disease and malnutrition.

In September, a French relief column forced the Habsburg military to lift the blockade, but by November the Austrians had reestablished the siege. The French military commander Marshal Charles Fouquet du Belle-Isle quietly evacuated fourteen thousand French troops on December 16, 1742. Charles Albert fled Munich for Frankfurt and earned the moniker "both Emperor and nothing," meaning he wore the imperial crown but controlled no territory.

With Prague secured, Maria Theresa planned her coronation as king of Bohemia. She used the title *rex femina* (female king) and not *regina* (queen) to demonstrate her sovereignty in Bohemia. Although she believed that the Bohemian nobles had betrayed her by swearing fealty to Charles Albert, Maria Theresa treated them leniently, unable to afford discord in the monarchy. While there were several arrests of Bohemians who had supported Charles Albert's coronation, no one was executed. This was a great departure from the punishment meted out on disloyal nobles a century earlier when twenty-seven Bohemian nobles were executed on Old Town Square. Maria Theresa's May 1743 coronation was a lavish affair. The archbishop of Olomouc presided over the ceremony at St. Vitus Cathedral because the archbishop of Prague was under house arrest for installing Charles Albert as king. Operas, banquets, and dances entertained Prague residents for weeks. The city had suffered heavy damage during the occupation and blockade, so ruined buildings served as a backdrop to the royal celebrations.

Maria Theresa inaugurated the era of Enlightened Despotism in Prague. The Enlightenment reforms of Maria and her son Joseph II would transform Prague into a modern imperial city with free public education, a

FIGURE 7.1 Philipp Andreas Kilian (after Martin van Meytens), *Kaiserin Maria Theresia*, ca. 1750. In this image, Maria Theresa is depicted as the queen of Bohemia and the queen of Hungary. She gestures toward the Bohemian Crown of Saint Wenceslas and the Hungarian Crown of Saint Stephen to demonstrate her sovereignty. Public domain, via Wikimedia Commons.

centralized state bureaucracy, and streamlined economic, religious, and legal institutions. Under Maria Theresa and her son, Prague residents were increasingly well educated. The German language dominated all aspects of life, and the influence of the Czech language and culture significantly waned in the city.

Just over a year after Maria Teresa's coronation, in August 1744, the Prussian king Frederick the Great mounted an offensive campaign into Bohemia, leading seventy thousand men in three columns toward Prague. In September, the Prussian army bombarded Prague with heavy artillery for more than a week, forcing the city to surrender. Frederick left a garrison stationed in Prague and amassed more victories throughout Bohemia. The occupation of Prague was short-lived, though, as Austrian troops surrounded the city and cut the Prussian supply lines. Frederick ordered a retreat from Prague in November. In the peace agreements, Maria Theresa agreed to hand over Upper Silesia to Prussia, and in turn Frederick supported the election of her husband, Francis I of Lorraine, as Holy Roman emperor. Francis became Maria Theresa's co-regent, but she remained head of state. A remarkable leader, Maria Theresa gave birth to sixteen children, ten of whom lived into adulthood, but she remained involved in all aspects of statecraft.

Under Maria Theresa, Prague became a provincial capital with few autonomous powers. Like her contemporary Enlightenment rulers, Maria Theresa sought to create an organized, centralized state bureaucracy, but she did not embrace the intellectual liberalism of her era. Instead, she maintained a conservative Catholic agenda and implemented anti-Jewish and anti-Protestant policies throughout her forty-year reign. Maria Theresa's relationship with Prague was complex. She never fully trusted the Bohemian nobility or the city burghers, who had acquiesced to the French occupation and supported Charles Albert's coronation. Yet she relied on the region's manufacturing income, so she treated her Bohemian subjects with a cool fairness. She saved her wrath for Prague's Jewish community, accusing them of siding with Bavaria and Prussia in the Wars of Austrian Succession.

Maria Theresa's anti-Semitism mirrored her father's. In 1726 and 1727, Charles VI had issued the Familiants Laws (Familiantengesetze) to curtail the Jewish population in the Bohemian crown lands. The laws restricted the number of Jewish families permitted in Bohemia, Moravia, and Silesia and allowed only first-born Jewish males to marry. While some Habsburg predecessors believed they should protect their Jewish subjects, Charles VI and Maria Theresa sought to sever Jewish ties to their lands. According to an English ambassador in Prague, Maria Theresa ordered "that no Jew should presume to enter into the precinct of the Prague Palace during her residence there." On December 18, 1744, she issued a Jewish expulsion order to be concluded by January 1745: "After Mature deliberation We have been induced by many weighty Reasons and Considerations to resolve and Determine that no JEW shall hereafter be Suffered or permitted to dwell in our Hereditary

Kingdom of Bohemia."[2] Prague Jews pled with other European Jewish communities to put political and financial pressure on Maria Theresa so she would reconsider her order:

> What shall we poor souls do?...The children, women, infirm and aged, are not in a condition to walk, especially at this juncture, being cold and frosty weather, besides in the condition we are at present in, for they stripped many hundreds quite to their shirts.... Brethren, we humbly beg, you would commiserate our condition, considering the imminent danger many thousand souls are in by this decree, and not delay interceding for recommendations from all courts, that we may have time allowed us for a commission of enquiry.[3]

Maria Theresa reversed the expulsion order three years later. She faced pressure from some foreign emissaries but especially Bohemian and Moravian Christians, who claimed that the cost of living had risen exponentially since the expulsions. In 1748, 301 Jewish families were permitted to return to Bohemia for a period of ten years, provided they pay an exorbitant "toleration tax." The ten-year rule and quotas were largely ignored, and Jews reestablished their religious and political lives in Prague.

Three wars with Prussia between 1740 and 1763 occupied the first two decades of Maria Theresa's reign. In May 1757, Prussia invaded Bohemia from four directions. The Austrian commander, Prince Charles of Lorraine, surrendered and retreated, but Prussia's win was a Pyrrhic victory. Frederick the Great lost fourteen thousand men, including two generals, and lacked the strength to breach Prague's city walls. Instead, the Prussian forces surrounded the city, trapping forty thousand Austrian troops inside for nearly two months. The empress was determined to hold onto the economically important Silesian territory, but armed conflict continued until 1763, when Austria finally capitulated and ceded Silesia to Prussia.

Although the confrontation held little military significance, the Battle of Prague became a compelling subject in eighteenth-century Germanic literature. Renowned playwright Friedrich Schiller based his play *The Robbers* on the adventures of Christian Andreas Käsebier, a notorious criminal whom Frederick freed in exchange for intelligence on the Austrian garrisons in Prague. Käsebier smuggled himself in and out of Prague three times to spy for Prussia, but he disappeared on his fourth mission, likely captured and executed. Poet Gottfried August Bürger also found inspiration in the Austrian-Prussian confrontation. His popular ballad "Lenore" told the story of a distraught woman who longs for her betrothed to return from the Battle of Prague:

> Up rose Lenore as the red morn wore
> From weary visions starting;
> "Art faithless, William, or, William, art dead?
> 'Tis long since thy departing."
> For he, with Frederick's men of might,
> In fair Prague waged the uncertain fight.[4]

Lenore wanders each night searching for her love, until they finally reunite at a macabre cemetery wedding. Bürger's work contributed to the development of horror writing, an important genre within Prague's German-language literature. Wealthy Prague aristocrats embraced a cosmopolitan, secular culture centered around German literature and French Enlightenment philosophy. They preferred a rational approach to Christianity that emphasized personal morality over the Jesuits' metaphysical and hierarchical schema. Prague's Jewish scholars also embraced modern philosophy by studying the Haskalah, a Jewish Enlightenment movement that originated in Berlin.

Although Maria Theresa seldom resided in Prague, she invested considerable funds to restore and modernize Prague Castle, her seat of power in the Bohemian lands. The castle had been neglected since Matthias moved the court back to Vienna a century earlier, and the French and Saxon occupations had taken an enormous toll on the city. The Saxons stationed their soldiers in the Castle District, bombarded the city walls and castle buildings, and even hit St. Vitus during an artillery attack. Soon after, lightning struck the cathedral, causing more damage. Maria Theresa envisioned a more modern look for the sprawling grounds and brought the royal architect Nicolo Pacassi to Prague. Pacassi had redesigned Vienna's Schönbrunn Palace according to the empress's wishes, and she entrusted her Prague renovations to him and Anselmo Lurago, the protégé of Kilian Dientzenhofer.

Maria Theresa's architects added rococo elements to classical forms and transformed Prague Castle from a medieval fortress to a residential chateau. Pacassi also implemented a uniform style with coordinating facades and a consistent color scheme in shades of Maria Theresa's favorite yellow. The outer buildings formed an architectural shell that protected the diverse historical styles within the castle's interior. While some contemporary artists decried the lifelessness of Maria Theresa's renovation, other Prague leaders praised its unity and symmetry.

Enlightened Prague 151

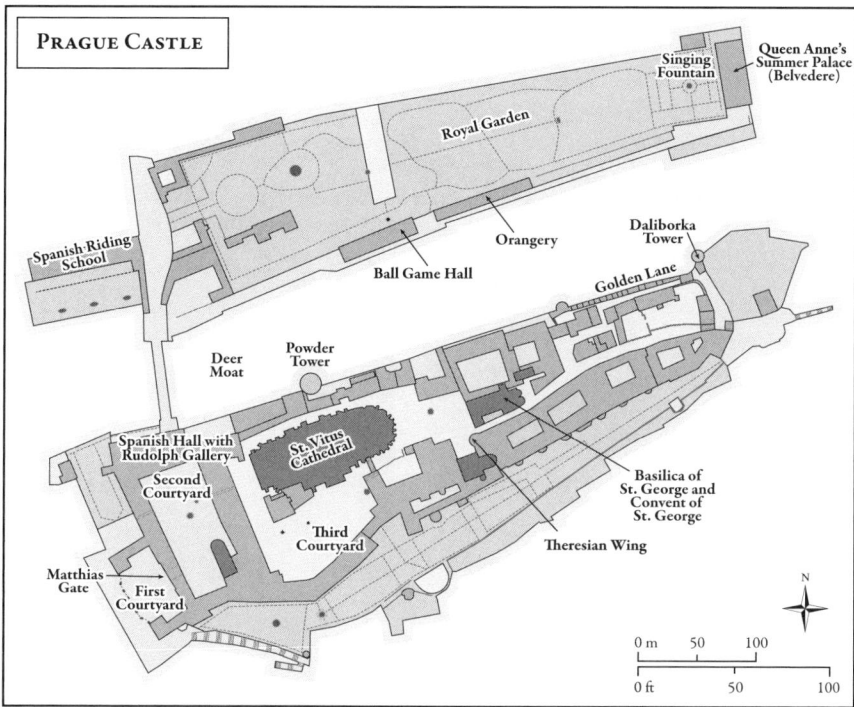

FIGURE 7.2 Map of Prague Castle following reconstruction in the mid-eighteenth century.

Pacassi designed the castle's First Courtyard, a new entry to the castle grounds. A rococo filigree arch connected two stone parapets held by Ignaz Platzer's monumental statues, *The Fighting Giants*. (See Color Plate 11.) The Renaissance-Baroque Matthias Gate, commissioned by Rudolph II at the end of his reign, became the entrance to the second courtyard. The new Theresian wing connected the Royal Palace to the Rosenberg (Rožmberk) Palace, which the Habsburg family had purchased in 1600. There the empress founded the Institute for Gentlewomen, a secular convent for thirty impoverished aristocratic ladies. The women did not take vows of chastity and could leave to get married. The abbess always hailed from the Habsburg family and had the great privilege of crowning the Bohemian queens. The entrance to the new wing, known as the Maria Theresa entrance, featured a domed portico covered with a copper dome held up by two stone Ionic columns. Above the dome two stone griffins protected a royal shield and crown. The Latin inscription on the dome's perimeter, *Maria Theresia Pia Felix Augusta*, reminded visitors of the empress's piety, contentment, and power.

Jews who had returned to the city following the expulsions invested their resources in new architecture and institutions. Following a ghetto fire in 1754,

FIGURE 7.3 Neoclassical portal dedicated to Maria Theresa at the entrance to the Institute for Gentlewomen at Prague Castle, ca. 1755. Photo by the author.

they built a hospital, treasury, rabbi's house, fountain, and gate. The community also commissioned a new rococo facade for the Jewish Town Hall and hired the royal clockmaker Sebastian Landesberger to design the tower. When the clock was unveiled in 1763, the community discovered that Landesberger had created two clocks, one with Roman numerals and the other with Hebrew numbers. The hands on the Hebrew clock moved counterclockwise because the clockmaker wanted to mimic the way Hebrew texts are read. Of course, Jews did not tell time this way, and the clock became a daily reminder of Christians' misunderstanding of Jewish culture.

Enlightenment philosophy informed Maria Theresa's rational approach to statehood. She curtailed the power of the estates and centralized government institutions, continuing the work that Ferdinand I began two hundred years earlier. A three-tier administrative structure formed a hierarchy among local, regional, and imperial authorities, with the lower levels taking direction from Vienna. The state abolished tax exemptions for the nobility and church and limited the peasantry's labor obligations to landlords. Maria Theresa believed in the contemporary theory of physiocracy, which argued that ameliorating

FIGURE 7.4 The Jewish Town Hall's lower clock features Hebrew numbers and a mechanism that moves counterclockwise. William A. Rosenthall Judaica Collection—Postcards, College of Charleston Libraries, Charleston, SC, USA. Courtesy of Special Collections, College of Charleston Library.

the peasants' condition would stimulate population growth and bolster the Austrian economy and military. Over the course of Maria Theresa's reign, an independent Bohemian state virtually disappeared. Maria Theresa's advisers modernized the civil service and reformed the military, enabling educated middle-class professionals to replace aristocratic functionaries. They abolished internal tariffs to create a uniform imperial economy and began to restructure the imperial education system.

Maria Theresa's forward-thinking son Joseph II became his mother's co-regent and the Holy Roman emperor in 1765, upon the death of his father, Francis. In 1774, Maria Theresa introduced compulsory schooling for children of all social classes, both boys and girls. Some Bohemian aristocrats ignored the mandate to provide education on their estates, but by the end of the century, Prague and its surrounding region had one of the empire's highest literacy rates. The state also took control of education after the pope disbanded the Jesuit order in 1773. The Clementinum was renamed Prague University, and the state took control of the curriculum, facilities, library, and observatory.

◆

When Maria Theresa died in 1780, Joseph II inherited his mother's titles and holdings. Joseph did little to win over his Bohemian subjects. Disdainful of pomp and ceremony, he refused to hold a coronation in Prague and took the title of king of Bohemia without receiving the Crown of Saint Wenceslas. Joseph considered the state the center of society, and his reforms were intended to increase state power and boost the imperial economy. Joseph's *Klostersturm* (storming of the cloisters) dissolved hundreds of monasteries and convents, targeting those that did not engage in education or charity work. The decree disproportionately affected female mendicant orders in Prague. St. George's convent at Prague Castle, founded in the tenth century by the Přemysl princess Maria, shut its doors, and the pilgrimage church of Our Lady Victorious, home to the Carmelite nuns who cared for the Infant of Prague, was subsumed into an existing parish. The influential convent of Princess Anežka, founded in the thirteenth century, was converted into one of the city's first textile factories.

The order also shuttered some of Prague's oldest and most important monasteries for men: Břevnov, founded by St. Adalbert in 990, and Zbraslav, where Charles IV's mother took refuge following her separation from John of Luxembourg. Monks could become so-called secular priests, serving parishes, but had to renounce their monastic orders. In Prague, a single state-sponsored archiepiscopal seminary replaced the multiple religious training institutions. With funds from the sale of monastic property, Joseph established a religious fund to pay priests, whom the emperor regarded as civil servants in black cassocks.

Although he never wavered from Roman Catholicism, Joseph II believed that religion was a personal matter. Religious intolerance, he believed, had negative economic ramifications. Thousands of Protestants had emigrated during the Jesuit era. In 1781, Joseph legalized Lutheranism, Calvinism, and Eastern Orthodox Christianity, allowing followers to worship privately in buildings that did not resemble churches. The native church, the United Brethren, was still not recognized. In 1782, Joseph's Edict of Tolerance emancipated Jews, allowing them to learn trades, attend university, and live in unsegregated neighborhoods. The decree opened unprecedented economic and educational opportunities but also harmed Jewish culture and independence. Jews could not print books in Hebrew or Yiddish and had to establish German-language schools or attend Christian schools. The Jewish community also lost its autonomy over its legal affairs. Jewish families had to register new Germanic surnames, and men could be conscripted into the Habsburg military.

Joseph II's 1781 Patent on Serfdom began a process that would bring enormous changes to Prague. Seeking to increase tax revenue from the peasantry and create more economic mobility throughout the empire, Joseph granted peasants civil liberties, including the right to choose marriage partners, pursue education and trades, and move between estates. The Bohemian aristocracy refused to adhere to aspects of the law but could not disregard the peasants' new legal status. The increased freedom within the labor market encouraged Czech-speaking peasants to seek new opportunities in Prague, significantly altering the demographics and linguistic makeup of the city.

The emperor took little interest in Prague's rich architectural heritage. Not only did he allow former monasteries to become industrial establishments, but also he gave the military several important Prague buildings. The Summer Palace at Prague Castle, heavily damaged during his mother's wars with Prussia, became an artillery laboratory. The Renaissance Ball Games Halls were converted into military storage facilities. The state seminary took over the Carmelite nuns' orchards and gardens and the neoclassical Jesuit chapel on Petřín Hill. Joseph II ordered an auction of Rudolph II's unsurpassed art collection, already considerably thinned by the Swedish pillage of 1648. Priceless objects were relocated to Vienna or sold to the Dresden court.

While Maria Theresa viewed Prague as a necessary investment, her son sought to reduce it to a peripheral city in a centralized empire. In 1784, the four independent towns of Prague—Old Town, New Town, Lesser Town, and Hradčany (Castle Town)—were united into a single administrative unit known as the Royal City of Prague. Prague's city government adopted Old Town's crest: a knight's arm brandishing a sword and emerging from a three-towered city gate.

Joseph II's benign neglect of Prague allowed the arts to flourish in ways not possible in conservative Vienna. The liberal aristocrat Count Franz Anton Nostitz-Rieneck won permission to open a public theater on his own Old Town property. The owner of the nearby Kotzen Theater protested that Prague could not sustain two major theaters, and the university masters at the adjacent Prague University argued that the noise and crowds would disturb scholars and students. Nonetheless, workers broke ground in June 1781 and unearthed a small container of silver coins. The city's theater lovers hailed the discovery as an auspicious sign.

The Nostitz National Theater was designed by architect Anton Haffenecker and featured a neoclassicist design. Four Corinthian columns supported a triangular gable engraved with the words *Patriae et Musis* (To the Country and the Muses). The first production debuted in 1783, the same year the Kotzen Theater closed for safety reasons. Gotthold Ephraim Lessing's Enlightenment play *Emilia Galotti* critiqued the aristocracy's abuse of power, a literary theme gaining currency throughout Europe.

While German served as the lingua franca of education, civil service, the law, and commerce, the Nostitz Theater was a bilingual space offering German

FIGURE 7.5 Vincenc Morstadt, *Estates Theater*, 1835. In this image, porters carry props and scenery for an upcoming performance. CC BY-NC-SA 4.0: ©KHM-Museumsverband.

plays, Czech translations of German and French plays, and original Czech-language works. Actor and playwright Jan Šimon Václav Thám penned fifty Czech plays, including the historical dramas *Břetislav and Jitka* and *The Swedish Army in Bohemia, or The Bravery of Prague Students*. He also translated German plays and encouraged bilingual members of the Prague theater community to create original Czech works. The talented conductor Johann Joseph Strobach elevated the level of musicality on the Prague stage. His extensive contacts helped attract strong musicians and brought the latest composition trends to Prague.

In late 1783, Wolfgang Amadeus Mozart's lighthearted *Singspiel* (operetta) *The Abduction from the Seraglio* delighted Prague audiences. Mozart's friend and biographer Franz Xaver Niemetschek performed in the orchestra and recalled the excitement that surrounded Mozart's operetta. "I was witness to the enthusiasm that its performance in Prague created.... Everyone was enchanted—everyone amazed at the novel harmonies and the original, previously unheard passages for wind instruments."[5] Prague audiences sought out performances of Mozart's music in symphony halls, churches, and private salons.

Mozart wrote that January 19, 1787, was "one of the happiest of [his] life." It was the composer's first visit to the Bohemian capital, and his Symphony no. 38 in D Major K. 504—soon called the Prague Symphony—premiered at

Count Nostitz's National Theatre in the Old Town. Mozart and his wife Constanze found the city bursting with his music. Franz Xaver Niemetschek confirmed that "Figaro's tunes echoed through the streets and the parks; even the harpist on the alehouse bench had to play *Non più andrai* if he wanted to attract any attention at all." Mozart expressed similar delight when writing to a musician friend in Vienna. "All these people flew about in sheer delight to the music of my 'Figaro' arranged for contrivances and German dances. For here they talk about nothing but Figaro. Nothing is played, sung, or whistled but Figaro. No opera is drawing like Figaro!" In his memoir, Mozart's collaborator Lorenzo Da Ponte confirmed Mozart's remark: "It is not easy to convey…the enthusiasm [Prague's citizens had] for Mozart's music. The pieces which were admired least of all in other countries were regarded by [Prague's citizens] as things divine; and, more wonderful still, the great beauties which other nations discovered in the music of that rare genius only after many, many performances, were perfectly appreciated by the [people of Prague] on the very first evening."[6]

Mozart's Prague hosts kept him on a relentless schedule. He and Constanze stayed at the Lesser Town villa of Count Thun-Hohenstein, where his host feted him with dinners, balls, and performances of his works by local musicians. He toured churches and palaces and used the Clementinum's remarkable library collection to research new composition ideas. He was invigorated yet exhausted. Mozart and his small entourage returned home in February with substantial earnings and a commission from the Prague impresario Pasquale Bondini, who implored him to collaborate with his librettist Da Ponte on an opera to premiere in Prague later that year.

Mozart returned to Prague in the autumn of 1787 to prepare *Don Giovanni* for the stage. During this visit, Mozart spent time with his hosts Franz Xaver and Josefa Duschek, a noted soprano, at their Villa Bertramka in Smíchov, a district just south of the Lesser Town. On October 29, 1787, Mozart conducted the premiere of his magnum opus. Contemporary accounts indicate that Mozart worked up to the last minute and only finished the overture the night before the opening, forcing the orchestra to sight-read. A cross section of Prague society attended the performance. Aristocratic women arrived in their carriages but had to step down "into a sea of mud." In the upper galleries, the lower classes stood, some leaning precariously over the rail. They ordered sausages and beers from vendors, whereas the genteel crowd below drank lemonade and almond milk. The singer Joseph Meissner later wrote that when Mozart stepped onto the stage, a hush descended, and "one thousand hands lifted up to greet him." At the end of the premiere, the audience burst into "boundless applause," and Mozart supposedly uttered the now-famous phrase, "My Praguers understand me."

Mozart's last stay in the city was in 1791, when he was commissioned to write an opera for the Prague coronation of Leopold II. Joseph II had died in February 1790, a broken man, as uprisings against his reforms sprung up in parts of the empire. Unlike Joseph, who had eschewed pomp and circumstances during his reign, Leopold II wanted to use his coronation to demonstrate his new power. Mozart began work on *La Clemenza di Tito*, which retold the familiar story of the ancient Roman emperor Titus.

Following Leopold's coronation on September 6, 1791, Mozart conducted the world premiere of *La Clemenza di Tito*. The new opera did not stir his audience; Empress Maria Louisa wrote that she was unimpressed with the music, and many guests fell asleep. Three days later, the opera did not attract a full audience. His friend Niemetchek later reflected, "While he was in Prague, Mozart became ill and was continually seeing doctors. His complexion was pale, and his expression was sad, although he often demonstrated his lively humor in the company of his friends with merry jokes. While saying farewell to his circle of friends, he became so melancholy that he shed tears." Mozart's last major instrumental composition, the Clarinet Concerto in A Major, debuted in Prague with his friend Anton Stadler performing, but the composer was too ill to return to Prague. Less than two months later, the beloved maestro died in Vienna at age thirty-five.

On December 14, just over a week after Mozart's death, St. Nicholas Church in Lesser Town hosted a requiem mass with performances from his friend Josefa Duschek and the 120-member Prague Orchestra. In January, Prague musicians donated their services at a gala to raise funds for Mozart's widow and children. Prague newspapers contrasted their city's commemorations with those in Vienna, where few residents attended Mozart's funeral. Deeply in debt, the composer was buried in a paupers' mass grave.

Scholars and music lovers have long asked why Prague society embraced Mozart. For one, Prague's musical community had a rich tradition of reed and woodwind virtuosity, and Mozart expanded the repertoire for the clarinet and basset horn. Prague citizens also appreciated Mozart's celebrity status. His extravagant fashions and quirky mannerisms charmed theatergoers of all social classes. Mozart's visits brought the spotlight to the former imperial capital. After Mozart's death, the Austrian composer Joseph Haydn famously criticized Prague's musical leaders for not doing more to employ the impoverished composer, but Mozart had resisted spending more time in Prague. No city could compete with Vienna's wealth, resources, and musical talent. In

1837, Prague opened Europe's first Mozarteum, a library collection at the Prague Clementinum devoted to the composer's works. His bust was installed in the Clementinum's Mirror Chapel, where Mozart had played the organ. The Prague cultural elite believed they shared a special affinity with the musical genius.

———— ✦ ————

Prague intellectuals and noblemen continued to discuss their city's position in an increasingly centralized empire. Their patriotism for Bohemia—and its capital Prague—was based on geography, not language. There was no question that German was the language of government, trade, and education, but Prague's cultural leaders shared a curiosity about the Czech tongue. Bohemian patriots believed that the mixture of German and Slavic cultures made Prague unique. Intellectuals sought to reinvigorate Czech as a language of literature, journalism, and academic research. Count Nostitz-Rieneck and Count Franz Sternberg employed Czech scholars to tutor their children, sponsored research projects on Bohemian history and languages, and held salons to discuss Bohemia's hybrid culture.

In 1782, the *Prague Postal News* (*Pražské poštovské noviny*) announced it had resumed publication: "St. Wenceslas's language, which was nearing its fall, [will] once more begin to flourish and renew itself, and our patriots can read the news in it."[7] Prague's first Czech-language newspaper had appeared in 1719 and had ceased publication in 1772. For ten years there was no Czech-language newspaper in the city. With the financial backing of the German-speaking publishing magnate Johann Ferdinand von Schönfeld and the talent of the journalist Václav Matěj Kramerius, Czech-language publications began to flourish in Prague. Kramerius founded a second Czech-language newspaper, a Czech publishing house, and a bookstore, Česká expedice (The Czech Expedition). He wrote more than eighty Czech-language books, including a highly successful series of farmers' almanacs, and published works by fledgling Czech writers.

Joseph II's educational reforms and the spread of Enlightenment ideas sparked research on topics ranging from Bohemia's natural history to its linguistic cultures. Prague cultural leaders founded the Bohemian Academy of Sciences in 1784. František Martin Pelcl, the Nostitz and Sternberg family librarian, published the first modern academic project in Czech in 1792. *Nová kronika česká* (A new Bohemian chronicle) used medieval sources to create a Czech-language history of the region. Pelcl's student and friend Josef Dobrovský, a linguist and historian, wrote the first scholarly treatise on

Czech literature and a comprehensive Czech grammar, and Josef Jungmann, the son of a German-speaking cobbler and a Czech mother, published a five-volume Czech-German dictionary. In their attempts to develop a modern literary Czech, linguists like Jungmann and Dobrovský turned to sixteenth-century texts, because they considered writings from the Protestant Reformation, such as the *Bible králická* (Bible of Kralice), the apex of Czech literature. Rather than codifying the contemporary spoken language of the Bohemian countryside, intellectuals created a written language based on older formal texts.

The development of Czech-language scholarship emerged alongside radical changes in European politics and culture. The French Revolution led to a decade of wars between France and Austria from 1792 to 1802, followed by the European-wide Napoleonic Wars that began a year later. Napoleon's 1806 victory at Austerlitz, a town in Moravia, forced Holy Roman emperor Francis I to abdicate his title and dissolve the empire in 1806. Francis declared himself emperor of Austria, the ruler of the Habsburg hereditary lands, the Bohemian crown lands, and the Kingdom of Hungary. Napoleon consolidated the remaining German states into the Confederation of the Rhine, a vassal state of France.

Napoleon's fortunes eventually changed. He surrendered to Russia, Prussia, and Austria in 1814 and suffered a final defeat at the Battle of Waterloo in 1815. The peace talks at the Congress of Vienna resulted in a reorganized Central Europe that replaced the defunct Holy Roman Empire with a loose alliance of the Austrian lands and the German states, banded together for mutual defense. The ascension of Prince Klemens von Metternich as Austrian foreign minister in 1809 and chancellor of state in 1821 led to the suppression of liberal and nationalist ideologies through increased censorship and police surveillance. Political oppression could not erase the Napoleonic Wars' deep influence; the concept of a political state based on rights, common citizenship, and the rule of law had taken hold. Among Prague's rising middle classes—both Czech and German speaking—liberalism dominated.

Enlightenment reforms and the Habsburg loss of Silesia helped spur Prague's proto-industrial revolution in the 1740s. By the late eighteenth century, Bohemia had become the manufacturing center of the empire as Prague aristocrats and burghers sought new sources of income. Prague's most important industries—food production, textiles, and chemicals—relied on close relations between the city and the countryside. Noble family estates provided raw materials for large-scale production in urban areas. Within a few decades, Prague was a major manufacturing center specializing in food production, papermaking, textiles, and processed chemicals. New factories expanded the reach of more traditional crafts, particularly luxury goods like alcoholic beverages, perfumes, watches, and hats.

The first factories were built in the Old Town and along the Vltava River. A cotton manufacturer opened in the House of the White Deer on Old Town Square in 1766. Within two decades, Prague was home to eleven cotton-printing factories. The Hergot and Berger calico firms had fifty employees on site and commissioned home-based piecework, engaging thousands of female cotton spinners and male weavers. Following the Patent of Serfdom, Czech-speaking peasants had more freedom of movement, and many sought their fortunes in urban areas. Prague's growing population expanded the workforce and the consumer base for basic commodities such as food, clothing, and housing materials.

In 1781, Franz Anton Leonard Herget, who taught engineering at the Estates Technical College, built a brickworks on the bank of the Vltava River, near the Stone Bridge. The brickworks provided materials for new factories and homes. Engineers encouraged builders to replace wood frames with sturdy brickwork. In 1787, Herget sold the enterprise to the Prague court architect Josef Zobel, who expanded the complex and renovated several important city buildings in the Empire style made popular by Napoleon. A physical representation of Enlightenment principles, the Empire style combined neoclassical symmetry and rigid lines with elaborate ornamental motifs. While the earliest factories occupied renovated Gothic houses, mass-produced bricks enabled architects to design new industrial buildings.

Joseph II's Edict of Tolerance enabled Jews to establish industries for the first time. In 1801, the Epstein brothers applied to build a cotton-printing factory in Prague, and by 1805, they already had forty-eight printing tables and employed ninety-six workers. As the business expanded, the Epsteins purchased a neighboring factory and more land along the Vltava. The Porges family started as lower-class rosewater manufacturers in the Jewish quarter and became one of the most successful textile-printing families in the empire.

Innovators pooled resources and research with other business founders and scientists. Prague chemical enterprises invented new color-fast dyes for the textile industry and made improvements to beet sugar processing. Francis Xavier Brosche, who arrived in Prague at age nineteen as a poor, German-speaking merchant in 1805, emerged as one of the city's most influential industrialists. By 1815, he had established a chemical factory, which distilled coal into hydrochloric acid, nitrates, and salts used in food preservation. The firm expanded to liquor production, using wastewater from sugar-processing plants to create an array of alcoholic beverages. By 1820, he was exporting his products throughout Europe. Beer production also took off in this era. Prague's oldest large-scale brewery, Zámecký pivovar, mechanized production and produced seventeen hundred liters of beer annually. Bavarian imports introduced Prague to bottom-fermenting beers, whose crisp, hoppy flavor became more popular than sweeter, top-fermenting ales. Prague breweries perfected the process and became renowned for their local lagers.

By 1800, the Prague city government had ceased issuing manufacturing permits for the city center to manage crowding, noise, and pollution in residential areas. Villages surrounding the city, such as Smíchov, Žižkov, and Holešovice, rapidly industrialized and became Prague suburbs. Prague's population grew from forty thousand in 1705 to more than eighty thousand by 1771. Fifty years later, the number of residents had nearly doubled again. Despite this unprecedented development, Bohemia and Moravia remained a predominantly rural region; just over 3 percent of the overall population lived in Prague at the beginning of the nineteenth century. A symbiotic relationship developed between city dwellers and the rural population. Prague was the hub of an expanding network of industrial entrepreneurs and workers that relied on the country for materials and sustenance.

An unintended consequence of Joseph's Enlightenment reforms was a shift in Prague's linguistic demographics. The emperor had codified German as the state language, and it served as the language of Austrian bureaucracy, commerce, and education. Yet Joseph's economic reforms, particularly the abolishment of serfdom, meant that the Czech of the countryside was increasingly spoken on Prague's streets. Prague's elite, made up of aristocrats, state officials, army officers, wealthier businessmen and industrialists, and higher clergymen, was still German speaking, but even they began to learn enough Czech to converse with their customers, clients, and workers. By the end of the nineteenth century, the Czech tongue would dominate Prague culture once more.

8

Creating a Czech City

IN 1823, A young man named František Palacký came to Prague. A half-century later, Czech patriots would call him the "father of the nation," but when he arrived, he had just begun his lifelong journey to understand and help define what it meant to be Czech. Palacký grew up in Moravia, the son of a schoolteacher. His ancestors belonged to the United Brethren Church, a descendant of the Hussite movement, and secretly adhered to this faith after White Mountain. Following Joseph II's 1781 Patent of Tolerance, the family joined the legalized Lutheran church, and in 1812, Palacký enrolled at the Evangelical Lutheran Academy in Pressburg, the northern Hungarian city also known as Pozsony and, later, the Slovak capital of Bratislava.

In multilingual Pressburg, Palacký explored Slavic linguistics and history. He read Josef Jungmann's essays on Czech grammar in 1819 and remarked in his diary, "I was fired by sincere patriotic fervor which, still continuing unabated will, I hope, never abate."[1] His evangelical roots propelled him to explore Hussite history, and after several years of private teaching, he decided to go to Prague. He planned to consult original historical documents to better understand the Hussite era, which he considered the apogee of Bohemian history.

Palacký quickly became part of the vibrant salon culture that emerged in Prague during the Enlightenment. Prague lawyer Jan Měchura welcomed the young Palacký to gatherings at his home, a rococo palace in New Town. There Palacký met Měchura's daughter Theresa, and they married in 1827. Palacký also befriended the linguist Joseph Dobrovský and the wealthy noblemen Anton and Francis Sternberg. Palacký's newfound intellectual community helped him to rethink the concept of the nation and to contemplate Bohemia's place in a reorganized Europe. Many Prague intellectuals embraced Bohemism, a regional patriotism rooted in Enlightenment philosophy. Bohemists embraced the region's multilinguistic culture and sought a scientific approach to understanding their identity. In 1818, Count Casper Sternberg-Mandershied helped establish the Bohemian Museum, which focused on natural history, botany, and mineralogy.

Meanwhile, other intellectuals in the city gravitated toward a Romantic nationalism rooted in language. The German philosopher and theologian Johann Gottfried Herder inspired Europe's Slavs to identify their unique cultural and linguistic *Volksgeist* (spirit of the people). Herder believed that the Slavic peoples would play an increasingly prominent role in Europe and admonished them: "You, once diligent and happy peoples who have sunk so low, will at last awaken from your long and heavy slumber, will be freed from your enslaving chains."[2] Herder's work inspired students and scholars to delve into the Bohemian past.

Czech-speaking intellectuals in Prague strove to assert their nation's legitimacy. In 1817, the Prague-based poet and linguist Václav Hanka announced his discovery of the *Zelená hora* and *Královský dvůr* manuscripts, which he dated to the ninth and fourteenth centuries. The documents, written in Old Czech, chronicled early Bohemian history and emphasized a proto-democratic past when Libuše ruled harmoniously alongside an elected assembly of elders. Hanka claimed the documents provided evidence of a sophisticated Old Czech literary language as early as the ninth century, and the discovery fed the Romanticists' passion for linguistic identity. However, many intellectuals raised doubts about the chronicles' authenticity. Prague's most prominent Czech linguist, Josef Dobrovský, dismissed them as a hoax, but Palacký, Hanka's colleague at the Bohemian Museum, defended the manuscripts' authenticity and regularly consulted them. In 1824, the Slovak Lutheran minister Jan Kollár published an epic poem in the Czech language. *Slávy dcera* (The daughter of Sláva) juxtaposed love of country with amorous passion.

Palacký believed that historical research was essential to national development. His first academic project in Prague focused on Bohemia's chroniclers, from Cosmas to Hájek. In 1825, he became the founding editor of the Bohemian Museum journal and encouraged the directors to expand their studies to human history. He successfully advocated for German and Czech versions of the museum journal to make scholarship more accessible. In 1831, Palacký founded the Matice česká, a cultural and educational society and press devoted to publishing Czech-language scholarship. In 1833, Slovak scholar Pavel Josef Šafařík, who had befriended Palacký in Pressburg, moved to Prague and began to write exclusively in Czech. His pan-Slavic opus *Slavonic Antiquities* traced the origin of all Slav tribes and was translated into Russian, Polish, and German. The new academic field of Slavistics, a comparative approach to Slavic history, linguistics, and literature, grew from Šafařík's influential work.

The Prague-based Bohemian estates commissioned Palacký to write a comprehensive history of the region. Palacký's influential first volume appeared in 1836 in German, still the main language of academics, but he interpreted Bohemian history through a Czech national lens. He viewed the region's history as a dialectic between the Czech and German cultures in the historical Bohemian kingdom. Palacký explained, "The main content and essential drive of all Czech-Moravian history…is enduring the meeting and struggle of Slav, Roman, and German cultures." Since Roman Christianity came to Bohemia through the German bishops, Palacký further argued, "We may say also that Czech history is based actually on their struggle with Germanic culture, the acceptance or refusal of German manners and habits by the Czechs."[3] Palacký's conceptualization of Bohemian history became a cornerstone of Czech political culture for the next century.

Czech linguistic culture blossomed in Prague as peasants poured into the city. Cultural leaders considered themselves national awakeners who would impart Czech values to their fellow Bohemians. Some German-speaking intellectuals, like Karel Vladislav Zap, switched linguistic allegiances and began to consider themselves Czech. Zap became entranced with Czech language and history while a student at Prague University. He changed his name from Zapp to Zap and began conversing and writing in Czech. In 1835, he published the first Czech-language guidebook to Prague, *A Description of the Royal City of Prague for Foreigners and Locals*, and a decade later, he wrote *A Guide to Prague: A Necessary and Useful Book for Everyone Who Wants to Become Familiar with the Memorabilities of the Bohemian Capital City*.[4]

Like Zap, other patriots turned to Prague for inspiration. Antonín Langweil, a bilingual clerk at the Bohemian Museum's library, spent the last decade of his life creating a 1:480-scale paper replica of Prague that included remarkable details like house numbers, lampposts, frescoes, and sundials. In 1833, Langweil displayed his models of Old Town, the Jewish quarter, Lesser Town, and the castle at an industrial exhibition held in honor of Emperor Francis's visit to Prague. However, he never realized his plans to construct Petřín Hill, Strahov Monastery, and the New Town. The artist searched in vain for patrons to support his work and died at age forty-five, deep in debt. Years later, his widow donated the model to the Bohemian Museum, where it became a renowned Prague treasure.

The Czech language was increasingly heard in Prague's public spaces and theatrical stages. Civic institutions sponsored debates and dances where attendees had to speak Czech. In 1826, the first Czech-language opera, František Škroup's *Dráteník* (The tinker), premiered at the Royal Estates

Theater, the former Nostitz National Theater. German dramas, German operettas called *Singspiele*, and Italian operas dominated the event calendar, but Czech performances took place on Sundays and holidays. In 1828, Josef Kajatán Tyl, the director of Czech-language productions at the Estates Theater and founder of the annual Czech ball, premiered his play *Fidlovačka*. Its song "Kde domov můj?" (Where is my home?) became popular among Prague's Czech speakers. The melancholy yet hopeful tune inspired Czech patriots to conceive of Bohemia as a land they had lost. Eventually, "Kde domov můj" became the Czech national anthem.

> Where is my home? Where is my home?
> If, in the heavenly land, you have met
> tender souls in agile frames,
> of clear mind, vigorous and prospering,
> and with a strength that frustrates all defiance,
> that is the glorious race of Czechs,
> Among the Czechs, my home!
> Among the Czechs, my home![5]

―――― ✦ ――――

By the 1830s, Prague had recovered from an economic depression that followed the Napoleonic Wars. Breakthroughs in steam power, shipping and navigation, road networks, and communication fueled a new phase in the industrial revolution. The Prague municipal government updated infrastructure, paved roads within the city walls, and connected the old city to the new suburbs. The city also began to demolish the medieval city walls, which hindered modern transportation. In 1847, the first Bohemian gasworks was built in Karlín, and on September 14 of that year, Prague's streets and squares were gaslit for the first time. Horse-drawn omnibuses that could carry up to twenty passengers linked neighborhoods, and the municipal postal service rapidly expanded. The Austrian state poured resources into steam-engine railroads, and by mid-century, Prague was connected to Vienna and dozens of other cities. The first Prague railway station opened in 1845. Early trains were used primarily for freight, but passengers soon took advantage of opportunities to travel for leisure and work.

While members of Prague's elite expanded industries and debated political culture, most residents focused on adequate housing and feeding their families. The mechanization of industry disrupted the livelihoods of many working-class residents. Tensions came to a head in the 1840s when Prague's largest textile factories installed French *perrotines*, printing machines that could produce as much printed cloth in twenty-four hours as twelve hand-block printers and painters made in a week. Industrialists could replace forty to fifty workers with a single machine. Hundreds of skilled workers across Prague's fifteen textile enterprises lost their jobs and were forced to resort to badly paid day labor. In 1844, the Porges textile factory in Prague's Smíchov district lowered workers' wages by one-third. In response, employees stormed the factory and smashed machines. Cotton printers and workers from other industries joined the Porges workers in the largest workers' strike in Austria to date. On June 24, 1844, a week into the protests, Bohemia's military governor, General Alfred I, Prince of Windischgrätz, sent troops from the nearby Habsburg military garrison to subdue the protests. The soldiers encircled the protesters at a workers' lodging house and arrested five hundred strikers.

Although Prague's textile factories employed both men and women, the protests were organized by the all-male workers' brotherhoods from Prague's industrial neighborhoods. After the mass arrests, Prague's working-class women hurled rocks through factory windows. A new popular song cast these women not as fellow workers but as aggrieved wives and mothers.

> And when women saw
> The men were arrested,
> They wailed.
> Took their children.
> Picked up stones.[6]

Although the strikes ultimately failed, the solidarity and strength of 1844 contributed to a growing sense of working-class camaraderie in Prague.

Meanwhile, the potato blight that devastated Ireland in the late 1840s also wreaked havoc on Northern and Central European agriculture. Rye remained the most common source of starch in the Prague diet, followed closely by potatoes. In 1847, the Bohemian potato crop fell to between 50 and 75 percent of its normal level, causing urban and rural death rates to skyrocket. Unusual weather patterns, torrential rains, thunderstorms, and hailstorms destroyed other crops that July, and Bohemia and Moravia experienced at least one hundred thousand excess deaths that year. Frustrated by inflation and job insecurity, Prague workers demonstrated against Jewish businesses and attacked bakeries to demand lower bread prices. Violence spilled into Prague's Jewish quarter as rioters scapegoated Jews for their suffering.

A nascent Czech-Jewish literary movement in Prague met resistance from some Czech intellectuals. Nationalist leader, poet, and journalist Karel Havlíček Borovský decried the publication of a Czech poetry collection by a Prague Jewish writer, Sigfried Kapper. Havlíček wrote, "It is impossible to belong simultaneously to two fatherlands and two nations, or to serve two masters. Therefore, anyone who wants to be a Czech must cease to be a Jew."[7] While some Jewish intellectuals were attracted to a Czech liberal discourse in the 1840s, they were quickly put off by Czech-speaking workers' anti-Semitic attacks and violent strikes.

By the 1840s, Czech political thought had divided into two camps. The moderate liberals, led by František Palacký, favored negotiation and compromise with Austria. They envisioned the empire as a federal state organized by historical territories rather than language groups. The moderates petitioned the emperor to expand the role of the Bohemian Diet. The Czech radicals defined themselves through an ethnolinguistic lens and agitated for immediate change. They founded secret societies such as the Repeal Club, modeled on Irish nationalist organizations, and met in Prague pubs to discuss impending revolution. Student and workers' groups prepared for potential armed conflicts by organizing a Czech national guard (*Svornost*) and a students' legion. Inspired by their patriotic fervor, twenty-four-year-old musician and composer Bedřich Smetana, who would later be called the father of Czech music, composed two marches dedicated to the new militias.

Prague's German-speaking burghers embraced liberalism but had to contend with challenges from conservative clerical politicians. Czech and German liberals shared an interest in open elections and free speech and briefly joined forces. Yet liberal organizations soon split along linguistic lines, as rising nationalism made working together impossible. Prague radicalized as revolutions raged across Europe. In February 1848, the French overthrew Louis Phillipe's constitutional monarchy and elected Louis Napoleon Bonaparte as president. During this "Springtime of the Nations," European citizens from Sicily to Central Europe demanded reforms, constitutions, and civil rights. Uprisings in Vienna forced Metternich to resign his dual roles of foreign minister and Austrian chancellor on March 13. Two days later, Emperor Ferdinand I issued a preliminary constitution that guaranteed an elected legislature and the abolition of peasants' obligatory labor services.

With the promise of constitutional reform, Czech political leaders sought their place in a reformed empire. Prague's Czech activists rallied to support their fellow liberals in Vienna. Students organized public demonstrations and assembled for a mass at the Church of Our Lady Before Týn in Old Town

Square to honor the fallen Viennese revolutionaries. In late March, German liberals convened a pre-parliament in Frankfurt to organize elections and to discuss the German states' future. Liberal nationalists debated between creating a *Kleindeutsch* (small German) state or a *Grossdeutsch* (large German) state that incorporated the Austrian Empire into a unified Germany.

Czech nationalists feared their irrelevance in a large German state and instead pushed for autonomy within an Austrian federation. In 1846, journalist Havlíček Borovský wrote, "We are Czech by nationality... but politically we form together with the other nations of the Austrian Empire. About a German Empire we know nothing and wish to hear nothing."[8] In 1848, Czechs boycotted the German elections, and Palacký refused the invitation to attend the Frankfurt parliament. In a letter published in numerous Czech and German newspapers, Palacký contended that he honored Germans' aspirations for unity but saw no place for his people in such a configuration. Palacký declared, "For I am a Bohemian belonging to the Slav group of nations."[9]

To counter the Frankfurt meeting, Palacký and moderate Czech nationalists organized a Pan-Slav Congress held in Prague from June 3 to 14, 1848. The leaders sought more autonomy for Austro-Slavs but favored maintaining the imperial framework. The conference was organized into three sections, representing the main Slavic groups in Austria: the South Slavs (Croatians, Slovenes, and Serbs), the Polish-Ukrainian sector, and the Czech-Slovak wing. The majority of delegates were Czech-speaking middle-class men, and Czech and Slovak scholars led the proceedings. The complexity of political boundaries presented numerous challenges. Galician Poles were welcomed as fellow Habsburg subjects and congress delegates, but Poles from the Prussian and Russian partitions could only attend as guests. The Slovak scholar of pan-Slavism, Jan Kollár, had his travel permit revoked by Hungarian authorities who feared the growing activism of Slavs in their territories. The anarchist Mikhail Bakunin arrived at the congress and declared himself the lone representative of the Russian Empire. He challenged Palacký's moderate stance and called for revolution in Russia and the destruction of the Austrian Empire. Although the theme of unity pervaded the congress, language barriers and political rivalries kept the various Slavic groups separated.

Austrian authorities allowed the congress to proceed but stepped up the military presence in Prague. General Windischgrätz, the commander of forces in Bohemia since 1840, staged a military parade on June 7 to coincide with the Pan-Slav Congress. In response, student groups placarded Prague with red-printed posters demanding the general surrender weapons and artillery units stationed in the city. On June 12, Pentecost Monday, Czech patriots organized an outdoor Catholic mass at Prague's Horse Market. Father Jan Arnold, brother of the radical Czech politician Emmanuel Arnold, celebrated the mass for twenty-five hundred men, women, and children from all social classes. At the end of the ceremony, students began to chant, "Let's march past Windischgrätz," and processed through the streets of Prague. The protestors encountered Austrian troops on Celetná Street, which connected the New and Old Towns. Students taunted the soldiers and demanded they leave Prague, and the Austrian troops opened fire. On the first day of fighting, Prince Windischgrätz's wife was killed by a stray bullet while watching the fighting from an open window.

The violence lasted for six days. Student leader Josef Václav Frič commanded the rebel troops. Prague youth, including the young musician Bedřich Smetana, built and manned barricades in various parts of the city. Town burghers supplied the rebels with food, and young women tended to the wounded. Street fighting pitted students and young workers against the military. Although some German liberals joined the fighting in support of an autonomous Bohemia, most combatants came from Czech student and workers' groups. Windischgrätz stationed troops from the nearby garrison on Prague's left bank and shelled the Old and New Towns from across the river. The bombardment forced the insurgents to surrender on June 17. The Czech rebels had lost forty-three men, and an additional sixty-three suffered injuries. About twenty thousand residents fled Prague in fear of reprisals. Most did not return until after October when Windischgrätz left to quell uprisings in Vienna. The imperial government cracked down on Czech political organizing. It abolished the National Committee and the Czech militia and stationed soldiers at factories to prevent workers' uprisings.

Despite the defeat, Czech patriots viewed 1848 as a symbolic turning point in their national struggle. The early nineteenth-century Czech scholarly movement had broadened into a diverse nationalist community of students, workers, middle-class burghers, and intellectuals. Czechs on Prague's city council fought to rename sites that reflected Slavic history. The Horse Market became St. Wenceslas Square (Václavské náměstí, Wenzelplatz). A popular legend spread that Wenceslas and his knights slumbered within Mount Blaník, ready to emerge when the nation needed them most.

The Austrian state convened the imperial diet in Vienna in July 1848, promising to consider the constitutional aims of its citizens. The assembly moved to Kroměříž (Kremsier), Moravia, in October after uprisings in Vienna interfered with the proceedings. Palacký and František Rieger led the Czech

FIGURE 8.1 František Palacký and František Rieger ca. 1870, Angerer, L.&V., Atelier. Public domain, via Wikimedia Commons.

delegation, and Rieger distinguished himself as an orator and political strategist. The assembly drafted a liberal constitution that created a federal state and included a bill of rights. Palacký and Rieger became close friends and political allies, and in 1853, Rieger married Palacký's daughter. Marie Palacká-Reigerová became a leader in women's rights, advocating for girls' education and nurseries for Prague's working mothers.

In December 1848, Emperor Ferdinand I abdicated in favor of his young nephew, Francis Joseph. Czech activists celebrated the selection of a more liberal monarch. The new emperor's priority was to end the war with Hungary. Of all the uprisings in the empire, the Hungarians' was the most successful and had been raging since April. With support from Russia, Austria finally defeated the Hungarian rebels, and Windischgrätz occupied Budapest in January 1849.

Hungary's defeat had repercussions throughout the empire, as the imperial state cracked down on all suspicious activity. The minister of the interior, Alexander von Bach, became more conservative once in office, and Emperor Francis Joseph advocated a strong centralized state. He nullified the Kroměříž draft constitution, restricted freedom of the press, and canceled public trials. Prague was placed under martial law until 1853, and the Catholic Church regained its grasp on education and family policy. Conservative German speakers, led by publisher and property owner Andreas von Haase, took the helm of Prague's city government. It appeared that Czech political life had come to a standstill.

Fortunes began to change for Czech patriots at the end of the decade. On June 24, 1859, Emperor Francis Joseph was commanding his armies at Solferino in Lombardy, a province then controlled by Austria. The inexperienced twenty-nine-year-old emperor suffered a devastating loss to the allied armies of France and Piedmont-Sardinia, commanded by Napoleon III and Victor Emmanuel II. Over two thousand Austrian soldiers, including ninety-four officers, died in just a few hours. The loss, coming on top of a major financial crisis within the Austrian government, led to Alexander von Bach's dismissal. Bach was blamed for failing to modernize the Habsburg military and enabling the Italian states to move closer to national unification.

For political activists in Prague, Solferino had a positive outcome. Francis Joseph loosened Bach's censorship and surveillance activities, which enabled the development of Czech cultural life and civil society. Czechs founded voluntary associations and aid societies for Czech traders and craftsmen. Urban and rural Czech speakers forged alliances, especially since the abolition of serfdom had yielded a prosperous community of Czech-speaking farmers. Rural Czechs migrated into Prague in large numbers and brought a modern vernacular to the city that differed from the erudite and outdated Czech language of scholars. The Czech newspaper *Národní listy* began publication in 1861, and each year, more patriotic Czech newspapers and journals appeared.

Prague Germans also took advantage of the more liberal atmosphere to found political and voluntary organizations for their compatriots. The German Casino, established in the early 1860s, became the center of German liberal society in Prague. The founding members were the city's German elite—wealthy manufacturers, lawyers, and university professors—but the organization broadened to include German speakers from all walks of life. Their headquarters occupied a New Town palace on Am Graben / Na Přikopě, a commercial avenue at the bottom of Wenceslas Square. The casino sponsored lectures, a reading room, a game room, a restaurant, and a garden. Over the next few decades, Germans and Czechs created parallel civil societies. Each linguistic community founded separate professional associations, chambers of commerce, charity organizations, and Protestant churches. Cultural organizations that had Czech and German members before the 1848 uprisings split into separate groups. Germans seceded from the Magic Flute, a singing club that performed German-language music but also had Czech members. The Germans called their new club simply Flute.

In 1861, Prague German speakers, who had long shared a sports hall with Czech athletes, established a new gymnastics club for Germans only. In response, two Czech patriots, Miroslav Tyrš and his father-in-law, Jindřich Fügner, founded the Prague Sokol, a gymnastics organization for Czech-speaking men. Within a few years, the organization spread throughout Bohemia and into Moravia. Tyrš and Fügner grew up in German-speaking households but adopted the Czech language as a political statement. Tyrš envisioned the Sokol organization as a training ground for full national realization: "We do not train only for ourselves, for a true Sokol, in the full and noble meaning of the word, does not indulge in such fantasies.... Not for ourselves—rather we dedicate our fervent struggle to our homeland and nation, and because of this, the people welcome us and cheer our parades." Writer Karolina Světlá designed the Sokol flag, and artist Josef Mánes created its costumes. One early Sokol member recalled, "Of course, we had other national clubs, such as the *Matice*, Museum Society, etc., but they were only scholarly and not understood by the majority of people.... The Sokol concept, accessible and comprehensible to the masses, fell like a spark into a slumbering Czech society."[10]

In 1866, an Austrian military defeat altered the trajectory of Czech nationalist politics once more. Prussia's victory over Austria at the Battle of Königgrätz (Hradec Králové) in Bohemia forced the Habsburgs out of the German Confederation. Prussian foreign minister Otto von Bismarck favored a *Kleindeutsch* (small Germany) solution to German unification and paved the way for Prussian domination in Central Europe. From Solferino to Königgrätz, the Habsburg monarchy had lost both significant territory to Italy and primacy in German politics.

Austria's weakened position in Central Europe enabled Hungarian nationalists to relaunch their campaign for autonomy within the empire. Boycotts of taxes and government institutions forced Austria to the negotiating table, and in 1867, an *Ausgleich* (agreement) split the empire into a dual monarchy with two capital cities, Vienna and Budapest. Austria and Hungary—united in the person of Francis Joseph—shared a common military, foreign policy, and economy. Hungary had autonomy in all other matters within its historical kingdom. Bohemia was part of the Austrian half of the empire, known as Cisleithania. Virulent protests broke out in Prague when Czech nationalists received news of the *Ausgleich*. In turn, the Austrian authorities declared a state of emergency and forbade political demonstrations. Czech politicians demanded Bohemian autonomy within a federalized Austrian state, but the Hungarians vehemently opposed this plan.

The *Ausgleich* crisis exposed fissures in the Czech nationalist bloc. Palacký and Rieger led the conservatives, who called for Czech politicians to boycott Austrian political institutions. Progressives believed that this type of passive resistance equaled political suicide and advocated for radical actions. In 1874, Czech activists Karel Sladkovský and Vincenc Vávra founded the Young Czech Party, which called for universal manhood suffrage, Bohemian autonomy, and an end to the influence of the Catholic Church in imperial politics. Palacký, who had serious misgivings about universal suffrage and other radical ideas, led the political bloc known as the Old Czechs. The two wings of the national movement maintained separate associations and publications from then on.

Until the *Ausgleich*, it was not a foregone conclusion that Prague politics and culture would bifurcate along national lines. Most residents of Prague spoke at least some Czech and German. While the Austrian bureaucracy, commerce, and education used German, Czech was commonly spoken on the streets of Prague. Prague's German-speaking elite, comprising aristocrats, state officials, army officers, wealthy businessmen, industrialists, and higher clergymen, learned enough Czech to converse with their customers, clients, and workers. The Habsburg compromise with Hungary pushed Czech politicians to emphasize language rights and national identity as the basis of politics. As in 1848, these nationalists sought to mark Prague as a Czech place. Civic leaders renamed the Stone Bridge for Charles IV in 1870.

The emergent Czech-speaking middle class dominated Prague's municipal politics in the decades following the *Ausgleich*. The Prague Board of Aldermen required that all municipal services be offered in Czech and German. Czech became the primary language of instruction in elementary schools, except in neighborhoods with a clear German-speaking majority. The Czech nationalist grip on Prague politics was so profound that the German parties eventually ceased putting candidates forward in municipal elections. Only one German speaker was elected in 1883, and five years later, the term of Dr. Ludwig Bendiener, a German-Jewish community leader, ended. From 1888, Prague's Board of Aldermen was entirely Czech speaking. The university was renamed the Royal Imperial Charles-Ferdinand University and divided into German and Czech institutions in 1882. Although the two segments shared medical and scientific facilities, a library, a botanical garden, and the school insignia, the German and Czech faculties maintained complete autonomy.

Not everyone agreed with the nationalist impetus to divide all forms of social and cultural life. The historian Anton Gindely was born in Prague to a Hungarian father and a Czech mother and was educated in German. Even though his mother tongue was Czech, his acclaimed German-language scholarship on the Bohemian Reformation earned him a position on the German faculty of Charles-Ferdinand University. Gindely remained skeptical of the strict divisions developing in Prague society. He feared a day when Prague residents would have to choose whether to breathe German or Czech air.[11]

◆

Czech literature blossomed in the decades following the 1848 uprising and reached a pinnacle after the *Ausgleich*. Patriotic Czech writers made it their mission to bolster the nation's cultural realm and to support fellow artists. Prague writers often found inspiration in Bohemia's natural landscape and the rural culture of their forebearers rather than in their urban homes.

The literary journal *Máj* (May) first appeared in 1858, published by a patriotic cultural society of the same name. *Máj* was named for Karel Hynek Mácha's 1836 epic love poem, praised for its lyrical Slavic poetics. Prague writers romanticized the poet's working-class background and his early death at age twenty-six. The poem's opening lines—"It was late evening—first of May—was evening May—the time for love"—created a Prague tradition. On the first of May each year, young lovers meet on Petřín Hill to pledge themselves to one another. Mácha's poem expressed his love for Bohemia:

> Oh, lovely earth, beloved earth,
> my cradle and my grave, my mother,
> my only homeland, my given inheritance,
> this vast earth, this one and only![12]

Urban intellectuals from Prague journeyed to the countryside to collect Czech folk stories, songs, and customs, which they published in ethnographic studies. Máj circle member Karel Jaromír Erben, who worked with František Palacký at the National Museum, published a collection of Czech folk songs before the 1848 uprising, and in 1853 he released *A Bouquet of Slavic Folk Legends*. Erben popularized the folk character Vodník, or Water Goblin, a character in Antonín Dvořák's 1901 opera *Rusalka*. Visual arts also embraced the rural aesthetic. The patriotic painter Josef Mánes decorated the Old Town Hall Astronomical Clock with romanticized images of Czech peasants carrying out agricultural duties. His illustrations of Bohemian sites like Říp Mountain and the Troský Castle ruins encouraged Prague families to venture outside the city. Local tourism increased, and urban Czechs shared artists' nostalgia for the villages their families had left only a generation or two earlier.

Patriotic women emphasized their central role as mothers and teachers of future Czech generations. Several female writers rose to prominence during the Czech national awakening. In 1855, Božena Němcová published the popular novel *The Grandmother* (*Babička*), which told the story of a village elder who keeps Czech traditions alive despite the Germanization of the region. Němcová's success did not prevent her from falling into poverty. Němcová's husband, a civil servant for the Austrian government, was transferred to a Slavic-speaking region of northern Hungary, but Němcová could not bring herself to leave the Prague Czech community. Wives of civil servants were not allowed to seek paid employment, and Němcová, a mother of four, was destitute while her husband worked abroad. She died in 1862, only forty-two years old, and was buried at Vyšehrad, where patriots began constructing a national cemetery to honor Czech cultural figures. In 1867, Karolina Světlá, a friend and protégé of Nemcova, published *A Village Novel* (*Vesnický román*). The author grew up in a wealthy German household, but she adopted the Czech language and pen name after her music teacher and future husband, Petr Mužák, introduced her to Czech culture. In turn, Světlá mentored Eliška Krásnohorská, who founded Prague's first Czech women's newspaper and first girls' gymnasium, a university preparatory high school. A poet and essayist, Krásnohorská also penned four librettos for Smetana operas.

Jan Neruda, the de facto leader of the Máj circle, departed from his contemporaries' fascination with the countryside and focused on urban stories. Neruda published popular newspaper columns that recounted vignettes from his life in Lesser Town. With skill and humor, Neruda captured daily life in a rapidly changing Prague. Neruda recounted his solitary walks through the city, commenting on the quality of the butter, eggs, hares, and chickens for sale at the Peasant Market. He crossed the Charles Bridge each Thursday to visit the booksellers' stands on Old Town Square. His senses delighted in the sound of nightingales and the scent of lilacs on Petřín Hill, and he marveled at Saint John of Nepomuk's silver tomb in St. Vitus Cathedral. In the comical story "What Shall We Do with It?" Neruda described his painstaking efforts to discard old mattress stuffing. He and his maid secretly placed small bunches of straw in various receptacles around Lesser Town so as not to exceed the strict refuse limits. Neruda despaired that it would take "six months of strolls"

PLATE 1 Prague Castle and St. Vitus Cathedral stand above the Lesser Town on the Vltava River's left bank. Photo by the author.

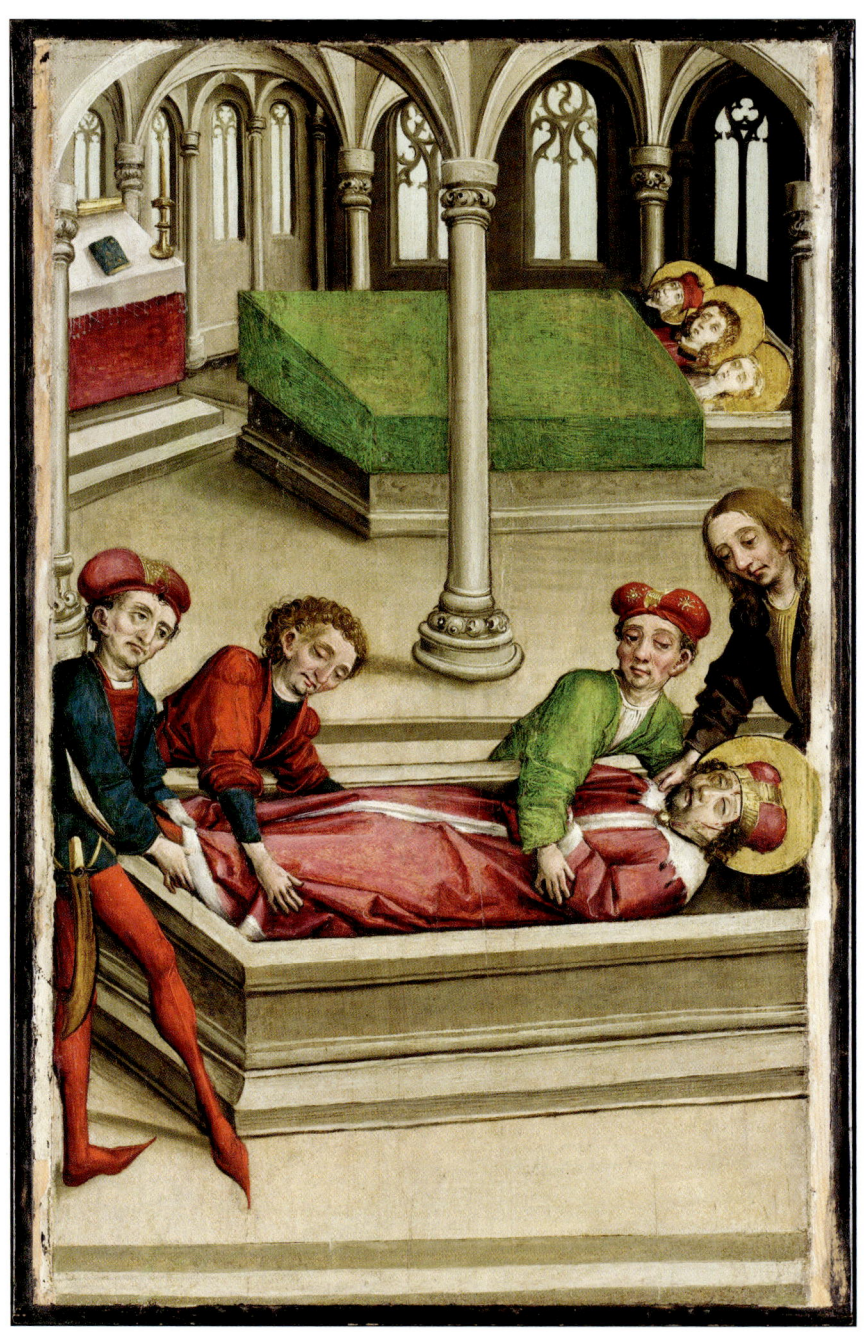

PLATE 2   Master of Eggenburg, *The Burial of Saint Wenceslas*, ca. 1490–1500. Cloisters Collection, Metropolitan Museum of Art, New York.

PLATE 3 *Saints Procopius and Adalbert*, ca. 1340–1350. Cloisters Collection, Metropolitan Museum of Art, New York.

PLATE 4   Emperor Charles IV and his son King Wenceslas IV kneel before the Virgin Mary and child Jesus. *Votive Panel of John Očko of Vlašim*, ca. 1370. National Gallery Prague, Circle of Theodoric of Prague. Public domain, via Wikimedia Commons.

PLATE 5 "Tower of Babel" from the *Wenceslas Bible* ca. 1390–1400. Austrian National Library Digital Edition. Public domain, via Wikimedia Commons.

plate 6 Jan Hus at the Stake from the Jenský Codex, late fifteenth century. National Museum, Czech Republic. Public domain. CC BY-NC-ND 4.0, https://www.esbirky.cz/predmet/180453.

PLATE 7 Contemporary drawing depicting Jan Žižka's famous war machine. Johannes Wienner, *Manuscript on the Art of War*, ca. 1400–1460. Austrian National Library Digital Edition. Public domain, via Wikimedia Commons.

PLATE 8 Giuseppe Arcimboldo, *Vertumnus* (Portrait of Rudolph II as the Roman god of seasons and plant growth), 1590–1591. Skokloster Castle, Sweden. Public domain, via Wikimedia Commons.

PLATE 9 Golden Lane at Prague Castle. Photo by the author.

PLATE 10 Dome of St. Nicholas Church in Lesser Town, 1737–1752, designed by Kilian Ignaz Dientzenhofer. Photo by the author.

PLATE 11 Eduard Gurk, *At the Castle District in Prague*, ca. 1838. Gurk's view of the entrance to Prague Castle features Maria Theresa's renovations and the creation of the First Courtyard. Albertina Museum Wien. Public domain, via Wikimedia Commons.

PLATE 12 The National Theater on the Vltava River Embankment, ca. 1905. Library of Congress Prints & Photographs Division, LC-DIG-ppmsc-09302.

PLATE 13 Poster advertising the Prague Ethnographic Exhibition of 1895. The Miriam and Ira D. Wallach Division of Art, Prints and Photographs: Art & Architecture Collection, New York Public Library.

PLATE 14 Živnoteská Bank, Fifth War-Bond Campaign Poster, 1916. Library of Congress Prints & Photographs Division, LC-USZC4-12050.

PLATE 15 Alphonse Mucha, poster for the Slav Epic Exhibition in Prague, 1928. Public domain, via Wikiart.

PLATE 16 Adolf Hoffmeister, *Wanted in Prague*. The Czechoslovak writer and artist Hoffmeister designed this poster during his wartime exile in New York City. It was shown in the exhibition *War Caricatures* at the Museum of Modern Art in May and June 1943. Illinois State University. Public domain, via Wikimedia Commons.

PLATE 17 Republic Square, Kotva Department Store. The rooftop sign reads, "Hail to the KSČ" (Communist Party of Czechoslovakia), 1974. Mezey András for Fortepan/CC BY-SA 3.0 via Wikimedia Commons.

PLATE 18   Kurt Gebauer, *A Heart for Václav Havel*, 2016. The memorial to Havel stands near the National Theater in Prague. Photo by the author.

FIGURE 8.2 Samuel Prout, *St. Nicholas, Prague, from facsimiles of sketches made in Flanders and Germany*, 1833. CCO Public domain designation, Art Institute of Chicago.

to discard all his mattress stuffing, but at least his covert walks enabled him to observe the daily lives of his friends and neighbors.[13]

While known for its self-deprecating humor, Neruda's work had a dark side. A virulent anti-Semitism emerged in a series of front-page articles he published in *Národní listy* in 1869. "For Fear of the Jews" was written with Neruda's characteristic humor but revealed the author's negative views on Jewish assimilation. Like many nationalists, Neruda believed that Jews represented a distinct ethnic and linguistic group that could never truly be part of the Czech nation. He wrote, "Deep down, none of them adhere to a foreign nationality, even if they don't know a word of their own national language."[14]

Neruda's writings reflected a growing anti-Semitism in Prague, but political opportunities did exist for both German- and Czech-speaking Jews. Middle-class Prague Jews tended to identify with German liberal culture, especially after the 1867 constitution granted Austrian citizens equality under the law. Prominent Prague Jews joined the German Casino in large numbers, and in 1879, they made up 38 percent of the membership. For nearly three decades, the Jewish lawyer and politician Ludwig Bendiener led the casino's political wing. Some Jews identified with the Czech movement. Bohumil Bondy, who transformed a family metals business into a thriving factory, served as a Czech representative in the Prague chamber of commerce. His advocacy for expanded voting rights helped secure Czech supremacy in city politics. In the second half of the nineteenth century, no one in Prague—Christian or Jew—could remain neutral on the nationality question, even when many residents spoke both languages.

Patriotic composers longed to capture the essence of Czech music. Bedřich Smetana left Prague for Sweden in 1856 and returned to Prague five years later to discover a transformed atmosphere. With Alexander Bach's regime behind them, artists faced less censorship, and Czech audiences were hungry for national music. In 1861, the emperor approved plans for a Czech National Theater. A year later, Smetana became the first director of the Provisional Theater, which provided a space for Czech music until the permanent Czech National Theater was completed. Count Jan Harrach's competition for a Czech-language opera reinvigorated Smetana's compositional career. He sought inspiration from local music, rural dance styles, and national legends but resisted direct quotations from folk songs. Smetana chastised his contemporaries for their unimaginative ethnographic style and instead took inspiration from German composer Richard Wagner. In the 1860s, the Czech and German Prague press featured polemical articles in music criticism, a growing field at universities and conservatories. Czech aesthetician and musical critic Oskar Hostinský championed Smetana's work, but mainstream audiences did not immediately warm to Smetana's experimental style. In 1866, Smetana's first two operas—both with Czech librettos—premiered in Prague. *The Brandenburgers of Bohemia* (*Braniboři v Čechách*), set in the thirteenth century following Přemysl Otakar II's death, featured Czech peasants who drove German occupiers from Prague. Cleverly, Smetana's opera centered on a Czech-German conflict—a theme that Czech nationalists would find appealing—but did not provoke the Austrian authorities. The Brandenburger antagonists were Prussians, Austria's main rival. A few months later, in May, Smetana debuted his comic opera *The Bartered Bride* (*Prodaná nevěsta*). Like the Prague writers Erben, Němcová, and Světlá, Smetana embraced the "village mode," setting the story in rural Bohemia and including both spoken dialogue and song.[15] The opera received mixed reviews and closed after only two performances. The Provisional Theater closed its doors as impending war between Austria and Prussia threatened the region.

Frustrated by the reviews and the theater's shutdown, Smetana immediately began to rework the opera. Three years later, the new *Bartered Bride* enhanced the picture of a joyful Czech rural culture, where peasants wore national costumes, danced polkas, and sang rousing choral pieces like "Let Us Drink and Be Merry" and "To Beer!" *The Bartered Bride* eventually became the most beloved Czech national opera in Prague, but Smetana was never satisfied with it. He felt pressured into creating a light, comical piece to combat the criticism that his work was too heavy and Wagnerian. Smetana returned to serious, quasi-historical themes with his work on *Libuše*, the story of the soothsayer who founded Prague. The first libretto, in German, was prepared for Francis Joseph's Bohemian coronation, but the emperor never followed through on a Prague ceremony. Smetana commissioned a Czech translation and decided to save the opera's premiere for the National Theater's opening.

Toward the end of his life, between 1874 and 1880, Smetana found inspiration in Bohemia's geography. His magnum opus *Má vlast* (My Country) comprised six symphonic poems, each celebrating a historical or natural site. The first two movements feature Prague locales. "Vyšehrad" begins with an unaccompanied harp melody, representing the mythical bard Lumír, and transitions into a lively military march. The segment ends with descending arpeggios that signal the castle's fall and hint at Czech subjugation. The stirring second movement, "The Vltava" (Der Moldau), conveys the river's journey through Bohemia. The composer explained that his most famous melody mimicked the region's geography: "The Vltava swirls into the St. John's Rapids; then it widens and flows toward Prague, past the Vyšehrad, and then majestically vanishes into the distance, ending at the Elbe River."[16] While Smetana labored to write *Má vlast*, he became deaf and suffered from the effects of syphilis and other ailments. He told his friends that only his fervent patriotism kept him alive to complete the work. The father of Czech music died in 1884.

During this era, another Czech composer gained recognition in Prague and beyond. Antonín Dvořák came to Prague to study music in 1857 when he was sixteen years old. Unlike Smetana, who grew up speaking German,

Dvořák came from a Czech-speaking household in Nelahozeves, a small town twenty miles north of Prague. His father worked as an innkeeper and butcher but was also an accomplished zither player who regularly performed Czech folk music. In 1858, Dvořák joined the orchestra of the popular Prague bandleader Karel Komzák, who performed in Prague's Czech restaurants and patriotic balls. Komzák's group caught the attention of Jan Nepomuk Máyr, who invited the musicians to join the orchestra of the Provisional Theater.

In 1866, Smetana took control of the Provisional Theater, and Dvořák admired his director's commitment to a Czech national idiom. Like Smetana, Dvořák studied and performed the music of Richard Wagner and yearned to do for Czech culture what Wagner achieved for Germany. He left the Provisional Orchestra in 1871 to pursue composition. After entering the Austrian Prize competition for several years, Dvořák finally won in both 1876 and 1877. German composer Johannes Brahms and esteemed music critic Eduard Hanslick served on the prize committee and encouraged Dvořák to make his music known outside of his Bohemian homeland. In December 1877, Dvořák dedicated his String Quartet No. 9 to Brahms, whose composition of Hungarian dances had inspired Dvořák to write sixteen Slavonic dances, full-length orchestral works inspired by the polka, *skočna*, and *furient*. Dvořák also experimented with symphonic tone poems based on the Czech legends of Karel Jaromir Erben.

The composer spent three years teaching and composing in the United States, and his music became popular in Britain and Germany. Yet, he reported feeling ostracized whenever in Vienna, where audiences resented his unabashed Czech style. He gradually moved away from his early interest in Wagner, confessing to fellow Czech composer Bohumil Fidler, "Despite the fact that I have moved considerably in great music circles, I still remain what I have always been—a simple Czech musician."[17]

Czech speakers in Prague celebrated the opening of a new theater devoted to their national culture. The community began planning a national theater in 1845 when František Palacký petitioned the Bohemian Assembly for "the privilege of constructing, furnishing, maintaining and managing an independent Czech theater." The National Theater Society purchased twenty-eight acres on the right bank of the Vltava River, but political upheavals prevented the project from getting underway until 1868. On May 16, Bohemian and Moravian representatives in traditional costumes laid twenty-six foundation stones emblazoned with the names of the towns that contributed to the building fund. Smetana spoke at the ceremony and proclaimed, "In music is the life of the Czechs."[18]

Architect Josef Zítek, a professor at the Prague Polytechnic University, combined various architectural traditions in his design for the National Theater. A neoclassical exterior loggia featured Corinthian columns and two impressive statues of the goddess Victory riding a three-horse chariot, while the mansard roof with golden parapet nodded to Prague Baroque. The facade facing the river shared the clean geometric lines of the nineteenth-century Renaissance revival. On June 11, 1881, the theater opened with the premiere of Smetana's opera *Libuše* in a performance dedicated to the Habsburg heir apparent, Crown Prince Rudolph.

Following the triumphant opening night, the theater temporarily closed to complete construction. In August 1881, tragedy struck. Workmen accidentally started a fire that destroyed the brand-new theater's copper roof, auditorium, and stage. Prague's Czech press declared the fire a national catastrophe and immediately advertised a fundraising campaign. Within forty days, Czech volunteers raised over one million Austro-Hungarian guldens. The Austrian state and the Habsburg family also contributed funds. The renovation involved replacing the original gas lighting with electricity and rebuilding the stage with steel. The auditorium accommodated more patrons at different price levels. Czech artists Mikoláš Aleš and František Ženíšek redecorated the building's interior with scenes from Slavic legends and Old Czech chronicles. The words *Národ sobě* (The nation for itself) were inscribed above the presidium arch, reflecting the Czech national philosophy of self-sufficiency.

The National Theater reopened on November 18, 1883, with another performance of Smetana's *Libuše*. František Rieger, the Old Czech politician and head of the theater committee, declared, "We may say that our National Theater, as it now stands, is the most democratic theater in the world. Nowhere else may people in the least expensive seats obtain such a good view of the stage." German-language newspapers in Prague and Vienna complimented the opening as celebratory but not overtly nationalist. Prague's new landmark, whose gold crown twinkled in the sunlight, became known as the Golden Chapel or the Cathedral of the Revival. (See Color Plate 12.)

Two additional theaters opened in Prague during this decade. Prague Germans called for a large modern theater focused on producing German works, as the Estates Theater could no longer meet the demand for live music. German cultural leaders founded the *Deutscher Theaterverein* (German Theater Society) to raise funds, and the Viennese architects Ferdinand Fellner and Hermann Helmer designed a neo-Renaissance building with Prague's largest stage and seating capacity. The German Theater opened on January 5, 1888, with a production of Wagner's *Die Meistersinger von Nürnberg*, a piece that asserted German cultural patriotism.

Prague's third new theater did not align with a national-linguistic community but instead embraced Bohemism or regional patriotism. The Bohemian Savings Bank (Die Böhmische Sparkasse) celebrated its fiftieth anniversary by donating the House of the Artists—a multi-use space with a theater, a gallery, classrooms, and studio space. The architects of the Czech National Theater, Josef Zítek and Josef Schulz, also designed this neo-Renaissance edifice, which faced Prague Castle from the Vltava's right bank. Locals began to call the building the Rudolfinum to honor the building's patron, Crown Prince Rudolph, as well as the sixteenth-century emperor Rudolph, who ruled during the apotheosis of Prague's creative history.

The February 1885 grand opening was a great success even though illness prevented Crown Prince Rudolph from attending. The gala concert featured works by Ludwig van Beethoven, and the National Picture Gallery offered a beautiful exhibition space. Despite the theater's national neutrality, the Czech press complained that the new House of the Artists "felt too German." Indeed, in its first decade, the Rudolfinum featured few Czech artists and composers, but by the end of the nineteenth century, it had become a Czech-oriented space. The newly founded Czech Philharmonic Orchestra held its first performance at the Rudolfinum on January 4, 1896. Dvořák conducted his Slavonic Rhapsody No. 3 in A-flat major, the world premiere of his *Biblical Songs* Nos. 1–5, and the Ninth Symphony ("From the New World"). The Czech press declared, "The flowering of domestic art is a sacred thing."[19]

German and Czech cultures became increasingly polarized in Prague. Years after German-speaking Jewish writer Egon Erwin Kisch left Prague, he declared, "No Czech citizen attended the German Theater at that time and vice versa."[20] Yet patronage was not as bifurcated as Kisch and others suggested. The most vehement nationalists would not step across the threshold of the rival theater, but other Prague residents attended the venue where their favorite music played.

Investment in patriotic cultural institutions continued into the 1890s. In mid-May 1891, two important buildings opened in Prague: the National Museum on Wenceslas Square and the Industrial Palace in Bubeneč-Holešovice, a working-class suburb of Prague. The National Museum's collections had been scattered among various Prague palaces, but the treasures were brought together in one neo-Renaissance home. While the permanent exhibits focused on the region's natural history, the grand entry lobby celebrated the national past. Beneath the dome, the architect Josef Schulz created a

FIGURE 8.3 The National Museum on Wenceslas Square, 1891. Photochrom Print Collection. Public domain, via Wikimedia Commons.

pantheon featuring busts of prominent Bohemians. The grand staircase honored the sixteen Bohemian noblemen who had established the museum. Artists František Ženíšek and Václav Brožík contributed large-scale paintings of key moments in Slavic intellectual history, including Prague University's founding and Saint Methodius completing his Slavonic Bible. Patriots called the National Museum a secular cathedral.

The Industrial Palace's inaugural event commemorated the centennial of the first Bohemian Industrial Exhibit. The jubilee was an undertaking of both Prague Czechs and Germans, but several disagreements about the event convinced the German representatives to announce a boycott. The German withdrawal enabled the Czech organizers to emphasize nationalist themes. Bedřich Münzberger's Industrial Palace housed displays of Bohemian accomplishments in various fields. The exhibition space itself was an art nouveau masterpiece of steel and glass, featuring a fifty-one-meter-high clock tower from which visitors could capture a view of Troja Chateau across the river. Other pavilions displayed large machinery and information about the sugar industry, paper manufacturing, banking, and engineering. Inventor František Křižík, who electrified the Czech National Theater, designed an illuminated fountain with twenty-six arc lamps, fifty water jets, and rotating disks that created colorful patterns in the spurting water. Exhibition organizers visited the Paris World's Fair in 1889 and commissioned a smaller Eiffel Tower replica for Petřín Hill. Tragedy almost struck on June 16, 1891, when a hot air balloon demonstration crash landed into a Prague foundry. All three on board survived, but the event cast a shadow on the joyful celebrations. Nonetheless, a review of the jubilee in the Czech press celebrated it as a national accomplishment:

> The exhibition opened for the first time the eyes of the nation... [to] its strength and power, its genius and hard work, its indefatigable and indomitable persistence. The exhibition placed the Czech nation among the most advanced and best educated nations in Europe. We had lacked this consciousness of our strength and our significance in the hierarchy of nations; in this realization lies the great moral meaning of the exhibit.[21]

While the themes of progress and industry dominated the Jubilee Exhibition, the Czech folk art exhibit, housed in a traditional Bohemian

FIGURE 8.4 Jaroslav Kronbauer, from *Our Jubilee Exhibition*, 1892. National Library of the Czech Republic, CC BY-SA 4.0.

cottage, drew large crowds. The numerous agricultural exhibits on machinery, animal husbandry, fishing, and gardening reflected Prague Czechs' nostalgia for rural culture. The successful Bohemian cottage exhibit inspired the 1895 Prague Ethnographic Exhibition held at the old Royal Hunting Grounds at Stromovka Park. Record numbers of patrons attended the celebrations of Bohemian and Moravian Slavic cultures. The Jubilee and Ethnographic Exhibitions asserted Prague as the Czech regional capital. (See Color Plate 13.)

Although the Czech nationalist community had much to celebrate, many Prague Czechs remained frustrated by their limited political influence. In early 1891, the Young Czech Party triumphed over the Old Czechs in the elections to the Austrian parliament by appealing to a broader constituency and calling for the extension of voting rights to the lower curia. Suffrage remained limited to male property owners and city residents who paid a minimum of ten guilders in taxes per year. The Young Czechs launched a campaign called *svůj k svému* (each to his own), which encouraged their constituents to patronize only Czech businesses. German and Jewish businesses suffered in the boycotts, as did many lower-class Czech speakers who faced inflated prices. Disenfranchised citizens took to Prague's streets to demand the vote.

Fearing the growing power of the urban working class, the Bohemian governor, Count Franz Thun-Hohenstein, declared martial law in Prague. The university professor Tomáš Garrigue Masaryk, who represented the Young Czechs in parliament, resigned his seat in condemnation of Thun's actions. In 1893, a public alliance of students and workers, many associated with the radical *Omladina* (Youth) movement, led another round of protests. In one provocative action, *Omladina* members tied a noose around a statue of Emperor Francis I. Hundreds were arrested and given prison sentences.

Emperor Francis Joseph responded to the unrest in Bohemia by asking Minister-President Count Kasimir Badeni to implement suffrage reform in Austria. To win support from the Young Czech voting bloc in parliament, Badeni acceded to demands that he address the language question in Bohemia and Moravia. In April 1897, Badeni's language ordinance declared that "Czech and German should be the languages of the 'inner service' throughout Bohemia." Civil servants had to prove fluency in both Czech and German, a requirement that favored Czechs, who learned standard German in school. Badeni also granted amnesty to *Omladina* defendants still serving prison terms.

The Young Czechs' victories proved short-lived. In November, German-speaking members of parliament protested the ordinances so vehemently that they forced Badeni to resign and dissolve his government. In response, Czech nationalists unleashed a violent campaign aimed at Jewish and German businesses and cultural institutions in Prague. In the worst violence in three decades, Czech mobs smashed every window in the New German Theater and vandalized synagogues in Žižkov and Smíchov.

As the end of the century approached, several new political parties emerged in Prague and spread their influence among Bohemian and Moravian Czech speakers. The Young Czech Party could no longer hold together a unified national movement. In 1897, Václav Klofáč founded the National Socialist Party that fused non-Marxist socialism and Czech patriotism.[22] Three years later, Masaryk, the former Young Czech parliamentarian, founded the Realists to counter the jingoism of other Czech parties. Masaryk fused patriotism with a rational, scientific approach to politics and scholarship. Masaryk and the philosopher-linguist Jan Gebauer exposed the Old Czech manuscripts *Zelená hora* and *Královský dvůr*—which Václav Hanka claimed to have discovered in the early nineteenth century—as forgeries. This did not make him popular with nationalists who cherished the romantic old legends.

Masaryk also decried growing anti-Semitism in Bohemia. In 1899, a sensational crime exposed divisions within Czech society on the so-called Jewish question. Anežka Hružová, a young Czech seamstress, was found brutally murdered in the small town of Polna, about thirty-five miles from Prague. The authorities arrested Leopold Hilsner, an unemployed Jewish glove maker in his early twenties. The press and trial lawyers spread rumors that Hružová had been sacrificed in a Jewish blood ritual. Masaryk responded with a series of newspaper columns that railed against the superstitions that fueled such cases and declared that anti-Semitism was un-Christian. Masaryk's vocal condemnation of the case resulted in a reduced sentence for Hilsner and illuminated Czech nationalism's propensity toward anti-Semitism. Masaryk's stance in the Hilsner case earned him few friends. For several years, extreme nationalists heckled and protested when Masaryk gave public speeches in Prague and other Bohemian towns.

Prague's political landscape and social demographics had changed significantly between 1848 and the end of the century. Municipal power belonged to the Czech-speaking majority, but new political parties advocated for their social classes and philosophies of governing. Even though "states' rights" remained at the forefront of political discourse, Czech leaders did not advocate independence from Austria. Czech liberals, progressives, and socialists all believed that their nation should remain within the framework of the Habsburg monarchy. While most Czech politicians advocated increased autonomy and language rights, they understood that only a large empire could protect their small nation from outside threats.

9

Prague in a New Century

AS A NEW century dawned, Prague had expanded well beyond its historical boundaries. The greater city's population more than doubled during this era, from 204,488 residents in 1869 to 442,017 in 1910. Over this period, Prague shifted from a city where German was the language of public affairs to a predominantly Czech-speaking city in both the private and public realms. In 1880, only 15 percent of Prague residents declared their everyday language as German, and that number further decreased to 7 percent in 1910. Although the German-speaking population was relatively small, it was concentrated in the city center and maintained a strong cultural presence. Much of the city's educated and affluent elite belonged to the German community. Because many Prague citizens understood both Czech and German, ethnic identity was fluid; residents who wanted to join the increasingly influential Czech community could assimilate within a few years. Most Prague residents were Roman Catholic. Only a handful of Protestants lived in the city, but Prague's Hussite legacy remained popular with Czech nationalists. Five percent of the city's population was Jewish.

Innovation in the arts, urban renewal, and increased political activism marked the fin de siècle, the period roughly spanning 1890 to 1914. Prague artists and writers, intrigued by the symbolism of a new century, confronted the meaning of modernity and progress. A sense of alienation pervaded Europe's urban centers, even as society embraced rapidly changing technology, transportation, and lifestyle. Prague's decadent literary movement explored macabre themes and human psychology. In 1900, writer Jiří Karásek za Lvovic published *The Gothic Soul*, whose main character wanders Prague's dark, dilapidated streets, longing for spiritual connection. "He did not speak a word to a living creature for months. He spoke with only dead things in churches, chapels, crypts, and cloisters. He felt that his soul had suddenly found their magic circle." On the verge of madness, the protagonist realizes that modern Prague has lost its soul and exclaims, "The Middle Ages are dead!"[1]

While writers focused on the intangible essence of the city, the working class demanded more influence in politics and economic life. Manual laborers represented the largest sector of Prague's population, and most lived in impoverished and overcrowded neighborhoods. In this era, the city dismantled 95 percent of Prague's defensive walls, thus integrating the old city with the new suburbs. In 1875, the city council divided the former site of Charles IV's vineyards into two sections: fashionable, upper-class Vinohrady and working-class Žižkov. Josef Mocker designed a neo-Renaissance church for each neighborhood, and St. Procopius in Žižkov acquired Karel Skřeta's priceless seventeenth-century Baroque painting of St. Wenceslas.

Žižkov received an independent town charter in 1881, but it was well integrated into Prague's railroad network. Named for the fifteenth-century Hussite general, Žižkov developed into a working-class community known for radical politics and rousing pubs. Large apartment buildings occupied streets named to honor fifteenth-century Hussite heroes. Two large cemeteries dominated Žižkov's southeast corner. Olšany, a Christian burial ground, was founded in 1680 when a plague ravaged Prague, while the New Jewish Cemetery opened in 1890. Earlier in the century, the area that became Žižkov had 169 inhabitants, but in 1900, it had 42,000 residents living in 750 buildings. Most working-class apartments were very small and lacked private kitchens and toilets. One of the largest employers in Žižkov was a match factory built by French entrepreneurs atop Parukářka hill, and dozens of new factories and workshops sprung up in the bustling neighborhood. Many Prague artists moved to Žižkov, attracted by the hilly streets, views of Old Prague, colorful building exteriors, and affordable rents.

Žižkov surpassed the population of Smíchov, but that older industrial suburb also experienced unprecedented growth. The center of the calico printing industry, beer production, and machine and wagon production, Smíchov had about thirty-two thousand residents by the century's end. The railroad and an expansive waterworks project made Smíchov more inhabitable, but the district had an odd mixture of old estates and cheap new housing. The noble Kinský family lands dominated the district, which included an English-style park and classical villa. Little by little, though, the family sold its land to various organizations, such as the Institute for the Deaf and Mute, which opened a school beneath Petřín hill, and the city of Prague, which converted the villa into an Ethnographic Museum that housed the exhibits from the 1891 jubilee.

These juxtapositions inspired the young writer Rainer Maria Rilke. Hans Trausil, who wrote the introduction to Rilke's 1918 poetry collection, mused, "Prague, the city in which Rilke was born in 1875, with its sinister palaces and crumbling towers that rose in the early Middle Ages.... This Prague of mingled grotesqueness and beauty gave to the young boy his first impressions."[2] A German-speaking Catholic whose prosperous family lived in New Town, Rilke found himself sympathetic to the Czech national cause and to the plight of the city's working families. Rilke attended a military academy in lower Austria from ages eleven to fifteen, but he briefly returned to Prague to study literature at Charles-Ferdinand University. His book, *Two Stories of Prague*, published in 1899 when Rilke was twenty-four, contemplated the class and linguistic differences that shaped his home city. The poem "Out of Smichov," written while Rilke was still a teenager, casts a romantic yet sympathetic eye on Prague's industrial workers:

> Homewards, through hot evening reds:
> factory-men and whores
> with distress written in sweat and grime
> on their low, dull foreheads.
> You could break an eye on their slumped
> demeanor. Heavy slam their bootsoles
> on the road, stirring the dust
> which howls after them like Fate.[3]

Prague's city council and various voluntary associations attempted to ameliorate the living conditions of the working class and improve their health. Physical education campaigns were introduced in schools, and the Sokol began to train children and teenagers in gymnastics. Nonetheless, Prague had one of the highest infant mortality rates in Europe: 50 percent of children born in Prague in the mid-nineteenth century would not live to their first birthdays. In 1875, Prague's first maternity hospital opened, and in 1887, the Circle of Prague Ladies founded a canteen to provide lunches for industrial workers. Within a decade, there were eleven such establishments throughout the city. Still, the gap between Prague's rich and poor remained profound. Public health officials admonished mothers to improve family hygiene, but socialist activists like Karla Machová blamed the factory system.

> Men profit by underpaying women.... Women are ruining themselves physically, especially mothers deprived of the necessities of life.... It is not woman herself who destroys family life; it is society; it is the employer's unscrupulous thirst for gain; this is the scourge that drives woman from the home out into the battle of life.[4]

While Vinohrady families enjoyed wide boulevards and homes equipped with toilets and kitchens, the working poor of Žižkov, Smíchov, and similar working-class neighborhoods spent over 80 percent of their income on substandard housing and low-nutrition food.

Public health experts pointed to overcrowded urban neighborhoods as vectors of disease. A campaign to stem the spread of tuberculosis warned Prague citizens: "Do not raise dust. Do not linger in dust.... Air apartments.... Do not live in dark, damp apartments.... Move around often in open healthy air!"[5] The Prague city council sponsored studies of several residential areas and in 1893 enacted slum clearance legislation, which designated 380,000 square meters to be redeveloped. City planners determined principles for healthy, modern living conditions. Housing should be out of factories' prevailing wind paths, and courtyards should provide fresh air. Building height should be proportional to street width. The city council worked to expand Prague's electric network, public transportation, street lighting, and potable water sources.

Seeking to thrust the city into a sleek modern era, Prague embarked on another major urban renewal project. Civic leaders proposed razing overcrowded and unhealthy sections of Prague and focused their attention on Old Town's old Jewish ghetto. By the time of the so-called sanitation project, the ghetto no longer housed a Jewish majority. In the late nineteenth century, most residents of the Jewish ghetto were impoverished Czech Christians. After Joseph II's 1782 Edict of Tolerance granted property rights to Jews, many families moved away. Yet, some Orthodox and poorer Jews still resided there, and several Jewish businesses and religious institutions remained in the district. Between 1896 and 1920, eighteen thousand residents of the old Jewish quarter were displaced. One-quarter of the buildings that were razed during Prague's sanitation campaign were in the tiny Jewish ghetto.

The sanitation plan threatened to destroy eight centuries of Jewish history. Medieval synagogues, the Old Jewish Cemetery, educational institutions, shops, and homes were slated for clearance. Some politicians employed anti-Semitic rhetoric to gain support for the slum clearance plan. City officials described the Jewish quarter as "our Orient here at home" and a "repulsive labyrinth of twisting, narrow streets filled with devilish odors...and animated figures and scenes, which looked as if they were carried to Prague straight from...somewhere in Baghdad."[6] Anti-Semitism had risen among Czech nationalists, who associated Jews with German language and culture. More Prague Jews began to embrace the Czech language and culture toward the end of the century and founded groups such as the National Union of

Czech Jews in Prague. Yet widespread mistrust and prejudice persisted in most Gentile quarters.

Prague artists and intellectuals who opposed the ghetto clearance focused on the neighborhood's architectural uniqueness rather than its historical significance to Jews. A group of Czech historical preservations, architects, and scholars founded the Club on Behalf of Old Prague to protect landmarks and historic architecture. The club argued that the unique mix of Gothic, Renaissance, and Baroque styles distinguished Prague from other European cities and contributed to the Czech national identity. Several prominent Czech artists and writers protested the "uncultured ignorance" of the demolition and petitioned the city to "preserve the antique character of Prague."[7] Illustrator Zdenka Braunerová and writer Vilém Mrštík published a small book, *Bestia triumphans* (The triumphant beast), which decried the demolition.

Despite these efforts, the forces of modernization won out, and a complex urban renovation plan was approved. On the eve of its destruction, the ghetto became a tourist destination for Prague's residents and visitors. In December 1896, guides took over two thousand people on candlelight tours of the ghetto. Stories of a magical and haunted neighborhood drew onlookers determined to visit before the twisted, narrow streets disappeared forever. In 1906, the remnants of the ghetto became part of the Jewish Museum in Prague, one of the first such institutions in Europe. The leader of the Czech-Jewish movement, city council member August Stein, worked with the Jewish historian Salomon Hugo Lieben to collect and display the sacred items from the synagogues demolished during the slum clearance. When the project ended in the 1920s, only a few landmarks remained: six historic synagogues, the Jewish Town Hall, the old Jewish Cemetery, and the roads that had served as the ghetto border. A wide boulevard sliced through the former ghetto, joining Old Town Square to the Vltava River embankment. Inspired by Baron Georges-Eugène von Hausmann's renovation of Paris, the Prague architects lined the street with posh apartment buildings and upscale shops.

Years later, the Jewish writer Franz Kafka discussed the ghetto clearance project with his friend Gustav Janouch: "We walk through the broad streets of the newly built town. But our steps and our glances are uncertain. Inside we tremble just as before in the ancient streets of our misery."[8] If the ghetto clearance project stemmed partly from an anti-Semitic desire to rid Old Town of its Jewish remnants, that portion of the plan failed. The Jewish population of Old Town increased after the clearance; several Jewish families moved back after the renovation, taking advantage of the beautiful new apartments along Paris Avenue and its side streets.

FIGURE 9.1 *Onlookers gather in front of a metal-goods shop in Prague's Jewish Quarter, late nineteenth century.* William A. Rosenthall Judaica Collection—Postcards, College of Charleston Libraries, Charleston, SC, USA. Courtesy of Special Collections, College of Charleston Library.

Prague artists and writers sought to capture the ghetto's singular atmosphere before it disappeared from living memory. Following the 1893 sanitation laws, the city set up a monuments commission and hired artists to create a visual inventory of the ghetto in photographs, oil paintings, and watercolors. Amateur photographers Zikmund Reach and Karel Ferdinand Bellmann chronicled the destruction and sold prints and postcards in local shops. Folk tale collections by German, Czech, and Jewish writers featured tales of the Prague ghetto. The legend of the Golem, a creature brought to life by Jewish mystics, had long circulated throughout Europe, but in the nineteenth century, the story's setting crystallized as Prague. Leopold Wiesel, who moved there in the 1830s to study medicine, devoted himself to preserving Bohemian Jewish folklore. Wiesel was among the first to center the Golem legend in Prague, and his German-language stories credited Rabbi Judah Loew with giving life to the creature.

Czech readers became acquainted with Loew and the Prague ghetto through the patriotic writer Alois Jirásek. In his 1894 collection *Old Bohemian Tales*, Jirásek described Loew's miracles. The rabbi conjures visions of the prophets to entertain Rudolph II's court, and he expands his cramped ghetto house to produce a banquet for the emperor. Jirásek adapted his Golem tale from Wiesel. One Friday before sundown, the rabbi forgot to remove the plug that contained the secret name of God from the Golem's head. While the community prayed in the synagogue, Golem ran rampant through the ghetto, killing any creature that got in his way. Jirásek explained how Loew restored order: "The rabbi stretched forth his arms, and walked right up to him, staring him fixedly in the face. Golem gave a start, and stood still, staring at his master. The rabbi reached into Golem's mouth, and with a single twist took out the magic plug. Golem toppled over, as though felled, and lay there powerless, as inert as a clay puppet."[9] Loew brought the clay man to the attic of the Old-New Synagogue, where he remains to this day. Jirásek's chapter on Jewish legends celebrated Prague's modernization campaign. "Complete segregation was done away with, the gates were removed, the streets, the houses, the inhabitants themselves were altered. Only the synagogue and the cemetery remained as they had always been." Thanks to multiple renditions of Golem lore, Loew became a popular figure, even within Czech Christian communities. In 1912, the patriotic sculptor Ladislav Šaloun created an art nouveau statue of Loew for a prominent corner niche on the new Old Town Hall.

Twenty years after Jirásek's collection appeared, the German-language writer Gustav Meyrink published his horror novel *The Golem*. Meyrink lived in Prague from 1883 to 1904 and witnessed the destruction of the Jewish quarter. The illegitimate son of a German count, Meyrink relocated to Prague with his mother, an itinerant actress. Meyrink was not Jewish but became interested in all forms of mysticism after contemplating suicide as a young man. Sitting in his Prague flat with a loaded gun, Meyrink noticed a brochure that had been slipped under his door. The pamphlet introduced Meyrink to spiritualism and promised a world beyond the realm of the everyday. Taking this as a sign, Meyrink abandoned his self-destructive plan and threw himself into studies of the Kabbalah, mysticism, and the occult.

Several European newspapers serialized Meyrink's novel between 1907 and 1914. By this time, the author lived in Bavaria and worked as a translator of Charles Dickens, Rudyard Kipling, and other British writers. Meyrink confessed Prague's hold on him, even years after he left: "I lived in Prague, the city with the secret heartbeat. It has never entirely left me, even today it comes over me when I think back to Prague or dream of it at night.... [If] I summon up Prague, it appears more clearly than anything else."[10]

In Meyrink's dark novel, the Golem appears corporally every thirty years, but its omnipresent spirit exists as the collective consciousness of the ghetto. When the unnamed narrator accidentally exchanges hats with a stranger in a café, he finds himself thrust thirty years into the past, shortly before the ghetto's demolition. He has occupied the body of Athanasius Pernath, a somnambulist, occultist, and likely criminal. As Meyrink's narrator attempts to solve the mystery of his new identity, he experiences the alienation and despair of the modern city. "You know yourself how little sunshine reaches Prague's dark streets and alleys." The narrator describes the dark labyrinth that was the ghetto: "At last the ground became level. From the dull crunching sound of my footsteps, I guessed I was walking on dry sand. It could only be one of those countless passages that run, without rhyme or reason, from the Ghetto down to the river. I was not in the least surprised; half the town had been built over this network of tunnels and since time immemorial the inhabitants of Prague had had good reason to shun the light of day."

French poet Guillaume Apollinaire, who visited Prague in 1902, similarly reflected upon the ghetto's mystical atmosphere. One of his poems described the ghetto's odd landmark, the Jewish Town Hall clock with Hebrew numbers:

> The hands of the clock in the Jewish quarter turn the wrong way
> And you too move back slowly through your life going
> Up to Hradčany and through the evening listening
> To them singing Czech songs in the taverns.[11]

The Jewish Town Hall was among the few ghetto buildings to avoid destruction in the slum clearance. Apollinaire understood that no modernization campaign could destroy the historic essence of Prague.

Franz Kafka also felt Prague's transcendent power. In a 1902 letter to his friend Oskar Pollak, Kafka proclaimed, "Prague won't let go. This old crone has claws. One has to yield it, or else. We would have to set fire to it on two sides, at Vyšehrad and at the Castle Hill, then it would be possible for us to get away."[12] In his diaries and letters, Kafka expressed his desire to leave Prague yet his inability to live anywhere else. Kafka rarely set his fiction in Prague, instead creating anonymous, alienating modern spaces. Yet even Kafka's unnamed settings reveal Prague's hold on the author.

Kafka was born in Old Town in 1883, just outside the borders of the Jewish quarter. His parents, Hermann and Julia (née Löwy) Kafka, owned a successful haberdashery in the Kinský Palace on Old Town Square. Their son's schooling reflected the city's complex demographics and nationalist politics. Families had to decide whether to send their children to German or Czech schools. Though Kafka attended the German Boys' Elementary School in

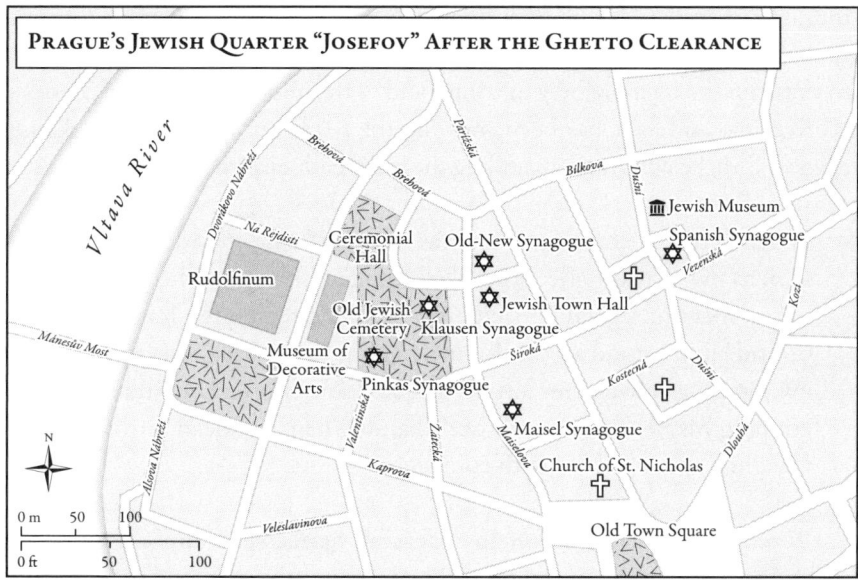

FIGURE 9.2 Map of Prague's Jewish Quarter (Josefov/Josefstadt) after the ghetto clearance.

Old Town, he diligently studied the Czech language there. For his secondary schooling, Kafka enrolled at German State High School in Old Town Square's Goltz-Kinský Palace, the building that also housed his father's shop. Kafka then studied at the Prague German University, the German section of Charles-Ferdinand University. He began in chemistry, switched to German language and literature, and finally settled on a pragmatic choice, law. During his fourteen-year career at the Workers' Accident Insurance Institute for the Kingdom of Bohemia, Kafka used both German and Czech. Even in this era of divisive nationalism, Prague remained a dual-lingual space.

The Jewish ghetto destruction began the year young Franz prepared for his bar mitzvah at the Old-New Synagogue. Kafka recalled weaving through construction zones on his way to school. Later in life, he told a friend, "In us all [the ghetto] still lives—the dark corners, the secret alleys, shuttered windows, squalid courtyards, rowdy pubs, and sinister inns."[13] For most of his life Kafka resided in the Old Town, but he spent a year at his sister's claustrophobic cottage on Golden Lane, the Castle's legendary center of alchemy.

Prague appears explicitly only in Kafka's early short story "A Description of a Struggle," in which a young man journeys through the icy streets of a wintry Prague. Simultaneously exhilarated and afraid, the narrator cannot resist jumping on the back of his mysterious acquaintance and riding him like a horse through a popular Prague park known as Laurenziberg to Prague's German speakers and Petřín Hill to the Czechs. The protagonist thinks, "It's ridiculous to climb up the Laurenziberg in winter and in the middle of the night. Besides, it's freezing, and as it has been snowing the roads out there are like skating rinks."[14] Still, he continues ascending the steep path near the castle:

> The road on which I was riding was stony and rose considerably.... As soon as my acquaintance stumbled, I pulled him up by the collar and the moment he sighed I boxed his head. In doing so I felt how healthy this ride in the good air was for me.... Now I even began to exaggerate my jumping movements on my acquaintance's broad shoulders and gripping his neck tight with both hands I bent my head far back.... I laughed and trembled with courage.

When Kafka's narrator becomes fearful, he reassures himself by taking note of the familiar Prague scenery. "I had to run away; it would be quite easy. At the turning to the left onto the Charles Bridge I could jump to the right into Charles Alley. It was winding, there were dark doorways, and taverns still open; I didn't need to despair."

Kafka maintained a friendship with a small group of German-speaking Jews he met at university. Max Brod, Felix Weltsch, Oscar Baum, and other friends frequently met Kafka at the Café Arco in New Town. Brod, a critic and writer, convinced Kafka to publish "Description of a Struggle" and to devote more time to his creative endeavors. Excerpts appeared in the German literary magazine *Hyperion* in 1908 and 1909, but Kafka never considered it a complete work. Although Kafka struggled with anxiety and feelings of isolation, his friends recalled him as funny and considerate. He often read his work aloud to his circle and sometimes laughed so hard at his own prose that he could not continue. Although their numbers had dwindled in the last century, German speakers, both Jewish and Gentile, made up a sizable portion of Prague's intellectual and artistic community. Kafka's group often intersected with a wider circle of local and foreign writers and scholars, including writer Franz Werfel and physicist Albert Einstein, who taught for a time at the German division of Charles-Ferdinand University. The young men, whom Max Brod later dubbed "The Prague Circle," discussed literature and debated philosophical and political movements, including Zionism. As Kafka's friend Felix Weltsch reminisced, "It was certainly an idyllic time— for the Jews and also for the world in general—those years at the turn of the century. But they were also years marked by a strange aloofness from reality, by a surprising lack of consciousness of the past, and of history, especially among the Jews."[15]

A turning point for Kafka occurred in 1911 when a Polish-Yiddish theater group toured Prague. Kafka befriended the group's leader, Jizchak Löwy, and became enthralled with Yiddish culture. For the first time in his life, he felt connected to a Jewish faith and community. In his famous essay "Letter to His Father," Kafka had complained about the perfunctory Judaism he practiced as a boy, visiting the synagogue only four times a year. The Yiddish theater allowed the writer to connect to the faith through literature and language. Kafka remained a secular Jew, but his interaction with Löwy's troupe profoundly affected him. The Yiddish plays he attended likely inspired some of Kafka's fiction. Löwy performed in *The Wild Man*, which displayed the protagonist's devolution into a beast reduced to crawling on the ground. In Kafka's 1915 novella *The Metamorphosis*, Gregor Samsa wakes up one morning transformed into a primitive insect. In "Report to the Academy," an ape named Red Peter explains his journey in discovering how to live like a man. Yet the more human Peter becomes, the more his teachers display ape-like behavior. Red Peter explains, "My ape nature fled out of me, head over heels and away, so that my first teacher was almost himself turned into an ape by it and was taken away to a mental hospital." Kafka's surreal tales also alluded to the pervading anti-Semitism that considered Jews less than human.

Kafka dreamed of a life devoted to writing, but he knew he could not live without a steady income. At the Workers' Accident Insurance Institute for the Kingdom of Bohemia, he investigated industrial workers' injury claims and even invented some safety equipment for workers. He wrote to his friend Max Brod that his responsibilities felt never-ending, yet he managed to insert his grim humor: "People fall off the scaffolds as if they were drunk, or fall into the machines, all the beams topple, all embankments give way.... And I have a headache from all these girls in porcelain factories who incessantly throw themselves down the stairs with mounds of dishware."[16] Indeed, injuries were commonplace in Prague's factories, and workers used strike tactics to push for safer conditions. The frequent work stoppages created tensions both within and between social classes. Factory workers pushed to have nonunionized workers dismissed, and violence sometimes broke out between factory workers and strikebreaking agents who tried to recruit workers. While Kafka's professional life intersected with manual laborers, his fiction primarily focused on the pressures facing the educated middle class. The authorities in Kafka's fiction manipulate and control society through an invisible and impenetrable modern bureaucracy. In *The Metamorphosis*, Samsa's sales manager comes to his apartment to chastise him for missing work. In *The Trial*, bank clerk Josef K is accused of a crime, but no one will reveal the charges.

Most of Kafka's major work was published posthumously by Max Brod after the writer's death from tuberculosis in 1924. Brod ignored Kafka's request to burn his writings and published the novels *The Trial*, *The Castle*, and *Amerika* in the 1920s. In subsequent decades, Brod released edited collections of Kafka's letters and diaries as well as his own biography of his friend. When

FIGURE 9.3 Franz Kafka at Oppelt house on Old Town Square, 1922. Public domain, via Wikimedia Commons.

Brod emigrated to Palestine in 1939, he brought Kafka's manuscripts, likely saving them from destruction. Within a few years of publication, critics worldwide recognized Kafka's unique voice, which captured the surreal elements of modern urban life.

In this atmosphere of profound change, a prominent group of Prague artists declared a new direction for Czech art. In 1887, a coalition founded the progressive Mánes Union of Fine Artists, named for the mid-century patriotic painter Josef Mánes, who had died in 1871. While artists explored modern themes of alienation and decadence, Prague's middle- and upper-class patrons continued to promote nationalist and romantic art. The Mánes Union journal *Volné směry* (Free directions) explained that these approaches need not be mutually exclusive: "On one side, there is historicism; on the other, its negation... which is modernism. And between the two there is this kind of happy medium that some people have found to safeguard patriotism in art."[17]

The sculptor Stanislav Sucharda advocated for a Czech national art that embraced international trends. The Mánes Union organized the Prague exhibition of Auguste Rodin's sculpture. The 1902 exhibit required an enormous space, given the magnitude of Rodin's pieces like the *Burghers of Calais*, *The Kiss*, and *Balzac*. The innovative architect Jan Kotěra designed an open, well-lit space for the Kinský Gardens in Smíchov. More than thirteen thousand visitors viewed the Prague exhibit between May and August 1902. Rodin himself came to Prague to see the exhibition and tour Moravia. Enthusiastic crowds greeted the famed artist at the Prague Main Train Station.

Although neo-historical architecture remained popular, many Prague architects embraced French art nouveau and the Viennese secessionist movement. The luxurious Hotel Paris opened in 1904, and the Grand Hotel Europa on Wenceslas Square was rebuilt between 1903 and 1905. A year later, Prague's Jewish community opened the Jerusalem Synagogue in New Town, which combined Moorish-revival architecture with art nouveau decorations. Wealthy Prague homeowners adorned their homes' facades with modern sculptures and designs.

The Municipal House (Obecní Dům), designed by the architects Osvald Polívka and Antonín Balšánek, was the jewel of Prague's art nouveau movement. The Czech city government intended the building to showcase the accomplishments of Czech society and culture. The Municipal House opened in 1912 and housed a concert hall, meeting spaces, a café, several restaurants, and the fashionable American Bar. The building's magnificent entrance

FIGURE 9.4 The Municipal House under construction near Prague's Powder Tower, ca. 1905. Photo by Frigyes Schoch for Fortepan. Public domain, via Wikimedia Commons.

featured Karel Špillar's mosaic, *The Allegory of Prague*, and Ladislav Šaloun's contrasting sculptural groups, *The Nation's Humiliation* and *The Revival of the Nation*. The patriotic Czech poet Svatopluk Čech added an inscription: "Hail to you, Prague! Resist time and anger in the same way you have resisted all storms!" Alphonse Mucha contributed art nouveau paintings to the mayor's reception rooms. The commercial artist had recently returned from Paris and turned to patriotic art. Mucha's *Slavic Concord* adorned the circular ceiling, and his three wall panels portrayed Slavic youth swearing allegiance to the mother nation.

Czech nationalists founded a national cemetery at Vyšehrad, and its artistic development coincided with the era's rapidly shifting architectural tastes. A neo-Gothic Catholic church dedicated to Saints Peter and Paul was built between 1887 and 1903. Designed by Josef Mocker, the church features art nouveau frescoes telling the history of Christianity among the Slavs. Architect Antonin Wiehl redesigned the church's small burial ground in 1881. Along the perimeter, neo-Renaissance arcades sheltered elaborate tombs of wealthy patrons and famed artists such as Antonín Dvořák. A simple churchyard housed the remains of other important figures, such as the writers Božena

FIGURE 9.5 Josef Mauder's sculpture atop the *Slavín* Mausoleum at Vyšehrad National Cemetery, 1889–1892. Photo by the author.

Němcová and Jan Neruda. Wiehl also designed Slavín, a monumental tomb for the nation's leading cultural figures, at the eastern end of the cemetery. In 1904, the sculptor Josef Mauder added allegorical statues called *Nation in Mourning*, *Nation in Victory*, and *Genius of the Country*, a winged female figure atop the monument who embodies Slavín's inscription: "Though dead, they still speak."

As Czech patriots continued to remake their city, tensions between Czechs and Germans were running high. During the summer of 1908, sixty years after the 1848 Pan-Slav Congress coincided with the outbreak of the Prague uprising, Czech patriots hosted a Neo-Slav Congress in Prague. However, political rivalries weakened the effectiveness of the 1908 meetings as the National Socialist and Young Czech parties held competing events. Prague's German-speaking press accused the delegates of hypocrisy for toasting the emperor while advocating a radical program of "Freedom, Equality, and Brotherhood."

As politicians prepared for the Bohemian Diet's opening meetings in September 1908, violence between Czechs and Germans broke out on the streets. Conflicts mounted the following month when Emperor Francis Joseph announced the annexation of Bosnia-Herzegovina, a region on the Balkan peninsula that the empire had occupied since 1878. The independent state of Serbia believed that the predominantly Slavic province rightfully belonged to it, and many Czech nationalists sympathized with Serbia's position. Several Czech political leaders opposed the increased militarism of the empire and claimed an affinity with their fellow Slavs in Serbia. Czech political parties differed on the tactics for expressing their discontent. The Young Czechs, Czech Social Democrats, and Agrarians believed that their security lay in loyalty to the Habsburg monarchy and sided with Austria on foreign policy. The confrontational National Socialist Party advocated oppositional politics and called for public demonstrations against Austria's increasing militarism. Fistfights broke out in the Bohemian Diet, which was disbanded on October 15, 1908.

On November 8, 1908, amid the violent clashes between German students and radical Czech nationalists, the National Socialist Party organized a *tábor lidu* (gathering of the people) in Prague to commemorate the 288th anniversary of the Battle of White Mountain. Participants sang patriotic songs and Hussite hymns and carried Slavic tricolor flags and banners emblazoned with chalices. More than ten thousand Czech patriots marched from Prague Castle to White Mountain. Violence peaked in Prague on December 1, 1908, the sixtieth jubilee of Francis Joseph's ascension to the throne. Twenty thousand protestors filled Old Town Square and hurled cobblestones at Austrian soldiers, who responded by attacking the crowd with bayonets. One person died, and scores were injured in the melee. The bloody confrontation ended only when the army declared martial law.

◆

Prague's municipal leaders continued to mark their city as historically and culturally Czech. In 1911, a new statue of Saint Wenceslas replaced the Baroque equestrian statue that had stood on Wenceslas Square from 1678 to 1879 when severe weather damage forced its removal. Jan Jiří Bendl's original statue reflected the Jesuits' goal to beautify Prague with Catholic art, but the new statue was a secular enterprise supported by Prague businesses, banks, schools, clubs, and the city council. Advocates for a new Wenceslas statue argued that the duke's legacy was "not only a regional question, or solely a religious question, or purely a question of patriotism, or only Czech." The statue would speak to "the entire Prague community."

J.V. Myslbek, a Czech patriot and professor at the Prague School of Applied Arts, won the commission and followed the long tradition of depicting the duke

FIGURE 9.6 Josef Václav Myslbek, "Equestrian statue of St. Wenceslas," 1911, from *Modern and Contemporary Czech Art*, by Antonín Matějček and Zdeněk Wirth (1924). Public domain, via Wikimedia Commons.

as a warrior on horseback rather than a pious medieval saint. Wenceslas wears full armor and raises a banner in his right hand. Four Bohemian saints occupy the corners of the large pedestal, and the inscription quotes the medieval Saint Wenceslas Chorale: "May we and our descendants not perish." By the time his Wenceslas was unveiled in June 1912, fellow artists—many who had been Myslbek's students—considered the equestrian statue outmoded and mundane. The public loved it, though, and it soon became a symbol for Prague itself.

The following year, the city unveiled Stanislav Sucharda's memorial to František Palacký. Located on the Vltava River's right embankment, the monument juxtaposed traditional and modern styles, as allegorical human forms surround a realistic seated statue of Palacký. The unveiling took place during the 1912 Sokol Slet, an international gymnastics festival. Sucharda, dressed in top hat and tails, presented his monument to delegates and journalists from across Europe and the United States. The Slet celebrated progressive and inclusive values, as female gymnasts from around the world displayed patriotism and athleticism.

FIGURE 9.7 Chicago girls perform at the Prague Sokol Slet in 1912. Library of Congress Prints & Photographs Division. Bain News Service, George Grantham Bain Collection, LC-DIG-ggbain-11567.

Modernist architecture developed alongside the decorative and allegorical art nouveau and the popular neo-historicist styles. Jan Kotěra, a professor at the Prague Academy of Fine Arts, insisted that buildings reflect their function, and he encouraged architects to focus on the purpose of interior spaces rather than a decorative facade. Kotěra embraced the modern style of his Viennese teacher Otto Wagner and studied the work of Americans Frank Lloyd Wright and Louis Sullivan, but he also looked to folk architecture of the countryside, which he regarded as "truthful" designs that did not stray from a building's purpose.

Inspired by the paintings of Pablo Picasso and other artists, the Prague cubists sought to play with space in a new way. Broken lines and planes enabled viewers to experience a static structure from multiple angles, allowing shifts in perspective and meaning. Prague architects wondered if they could translate Picasso's approach to buildings. Josef Gočár, a student of Kotěra, designed The House at the Black Madonna, the first recognized cubist building in the world. The department store and café—built in 1911 and 1912—acquired its name from a rescued Baroque statue that Gočár placed in the modern building's niche. Its double roof and window place-

FIGURE 9.8 Josef Gočár, "Cubist House of the Black Madonna on Celetná Street," 1911. Photograph from *Umělecký Měsíčník*, 1912. General Research Division, New York Public Library Digital Collections. https://digitalcollections.nypl.org/items/510d47e3-bb0c-a3d9-e040-e00a18064a99.

ment complemented the surrounding Baroque architecture. Located in the Old Town, near the Powder Tower, the Black Madonna occupied an important place along Prague's Royal Route.

A generation of avant-garde architects created innovative styles in conversation with Prague's historical idiom. Emil Králíček designed the Adam's Pharmacy building on Wenceslas Square and the whimsical cubist lampposts on nearby Jungmann Square. Králíček's Diamant Building in New Town created a cubist archway that formed a roof over a 1717 Baroque statue of Saint Jan of Nepomuk. Private entrepreneurs and wealthy families embraced cubist architecture. Josef Chochol designed three cubist villas near the Vyšehrad park grounds, and Jan Kotěra located his own modernist home there.

The two decades that straddled the turn of the century brought Prague further into the modern era. The ghetto clearance transformed parts of Old Town into an affluent center with wide boulevards and architectural innovation. The suburbs grew, and each area developed a strong individual character based on social class and local history. Writers and artists embraced the creative spirit of the fin de siècle, and innovations in these fields brought attention to the relatively small Central European city. Although tensions between Czech and German speakers continued to cause strife, international rather than local conflicts would plunge Prague into a new, violent era.

10

Prague During the Great War

ON JUNE 28, 1914, citizens of the monarchy heard shocking news. The heir to the Habsburg throne, Archduke Francis Ferdinand and his wife Sophie, née Chotek, were assassinated in Sarajevo, the capital of Bosnia-Herzegovina. Francis Joseph's annexation of Bosnia-Herzegovina in 1908 had put Austria-Hungary in a vulnerable position as independent Serbia made claims on the neighboring territory. Nationalists in Serbia and Bosnia viewed Francis Ferdinand's 1914 visit to Sarajevo as a provocation, and the terrorist organization the Black Hand plotted an attack on the archduke. A young Bosnian Serb, nineteen-year-old Gavrilo Princip, received weapons and training from the Serbian military and snuck into Sarajevo days before the archduke's visit. During a military parade in Sarajevo, the archduke's car stopped unexpectedly, and Princip fired, killing the Habsburg heir and his wife. A month after the assassination, on July 28, 1914, Austria declared war on Serbia and began mobilizing troops. Princip was arrested and imprisoned at Theresienstadt fortress, located forty miles north of Prague, where he died of illness in 1918. By August, the Central Powers—Austria-Hungary, Germany, and the Ottoman Empire—stood against the Entente countries—Russia, Serbia, Britain, and France—in Europe's deadliest armed conflict to date. The powder keg of European alliances had exploded.

The late archduke and his wife had a special connection to Prague. Sophie hailed from the prominent Bohemian aristocratic Chotek family, ardent Roman Catholics with strong ties to the Habsburg monarchy. The couple likely met at a Prague ball in 1894 when Francis Ferdinand was stationed at a nearby military garrison. By this time, Francis Ferdinand was the presumed heir to the throne following the 1889 suicide of the emperor's son, Crown Prince Rudolph. Francis Joseph opposed his nephew's relationship with Sophie Chotek, as she did not come from a European ruling family. The emperor finally permitted the marriage, but Francis Ferdinand had to agree that his children could not inherit the throne. The archduke and his family spent much of their time at Konopiště, a Bohemian chateau with a famous rose garden and hunting grounds, twenty-five miles south of Prague. The German emperor, Wilhelm II, and Austria-Hungary's foreign minister visited the archduke there only two weeks before the assassination to discuss the situation in the Balkans. The archduke favored a peaceful solution in Bosnia but agreed to visit Sarajevo to "show our colors" and demonstrate imperial power.[1] That decision cost him his life and threw Europe into a brutal war.

After the war, Prague writer Jaroslav Hašek published a multivolume satirical novel, *The Good Soldier Švejk and His Fateful Adventures in the Great War*. In his opening lines, he played on Francis Ferdinand's connection to Prague:

"And so they've killed our Ferdinand," said the charwoman for Mr. Švejk.

"Which Ferdinand, Mrs. Müller?" asked Švejk. "I know two Ferdinands. One is a messenger at Průša's, the chemist's, and once by mistake he drank a bottle of hair oil there. And the other is Ferdinand Kokoška who collects dog manure. Neither of them is an*y loss*."

"It's His Imperial Highness, the Archduke Ferdinand, the one from Konopiště, the fat churchy one."[2]

Following this conversation, Švejk heads to a bar where a plainclothes policeman arrests him for high treason. The bar's owner, Palivec, is also taken into custody when he admits that he had removed a portrait of Francis Joseph from behind the bar: "Flies used to shit on it, so I put it away in the attic."

Hašek's absurd account reflected a culture of mistrust between Austrian authorities and their Czech subjects. So, unsurprisingly, Austrian authorities worried about Czech loyalty as the empire readied for war. In late July 1914, Prague became a center of Austrian mobilization efforts. Robert Seton-Watson, a British historian and associate of Tomáš G. Masaryk, would later comment that, unlike in Vienna and Budapest, "in Prague there was not a trace of warlike enthusiasm."[3] This was an exaggeration, to be sure. Men reported for duty throughout the summer, and conscription notifications covered walls and kiosks around the city. Recruits from the surrounding region poured into Prague to register for military action or employment in war-related industries. Prague residents characterized the city as "paralyzed" by the influx of citizens during the first months of the war.[4]

Much to the surprise of the military leadership, who feared riots similar to those in 1908, the mobilization of troops from Prague went smoothly. In public celebrations similar to those seen in cities throughout Europe, women and children cheered for the recruits. Soldiers paraded down Wenceslas Square, wearing the Slavic tricolors on their Austrian uniforms. On the eve of the war, it was not considered a contradiction to exhibit Czech pride and loyalty to the Habsburg monarchy.[5] Newly formed regiments were often associated with particular Prague neighborhoods. Coworkers and friends became soldiers-in-arms and posed for formal pictures in Prague photography studios.

Several centers of power coexisted in wartime Prague: the Czech-controlled municipal government, the Habsburg-loyalist Bohemian government, and the Austro-Hungarian military, which maintained a police apparatus. The military kept a strong presence on Prague's streets, and its headquarters on Lesser Town Square became a site of pro-war events. In the war's early months, men gathered at the Field Marshal Radetzky memorial and sang songs supporting Austria. Citizens also expressed their loyalty with financial contributions to the war effort. Prague's Živnostenská Bank—established in 1868 as the empire's first Czech-financed bank—advertised war bonds on colorful posters placed around the city. (See Color Plate 14.)

Prague's Czech political parties retained a conciliatory stance toward Austria in the early months of the war. The Young Czech Party leader and pan-Slav sympathizer Karel Kramář condemned the assassination of the archduke. The Social Democratic Party reaffirmed its commitment to Austria, and the Agrarian Party press proclaimed the war "right and just."[6] The Czech Catholic parties, longtime imperial allies, remained loyal to Vienna. Even the more radical Czech parties, the National Socialists and States Rights' Progressives, reserved judgment on the mobilization efforts. Despite the subdued and cooperative mood in Prague, the military authorities feared subversive politics and shut down several Czech nationalist newspapers. Censorship reached levels not seen since the repressive Bach regime of the 1850s. In September 1914, Austrian authorities arrested National Socialist Party leader Václav Klofáč "as a preventative measure" and sent him to a military prison in Vienna.

While Czech politicians scrambled to realign their tactics with the wartime atmosphere, ordinary citizens faced new economic realities and demographic shifts. In August 1914, the Russian army invaded Austrian Galicia, the predominantly Polish territory on the eastern edge of the monarchy. The violence sent citizens fleeing to other parts of the empire, and by the end of 1918, close to eighteen thousand refugees—many of them Jewish—had arrived in Prague. The civilian government of Bohemia, under the direction of the governor, Count Franz Thun-Hohenstein, regarded the refugees as war victims who deserved support. Voluntary associations served refreshments to refugees arriving at Prague train stations, and the Jewish community supported Galician Jews. Schools provided primary students with lessons in Polish and Ukrainian. Refugee women and children found work in war industries, such as sewing uniforms for the Austrian military.

With men leaving for battle, women filled traditionally male roles: driving tramcars, serving as conductors, and working in factories. Middle-class women continued their prewar trajectory toward higher education and new professions. In 1915, the first two women earned doctorates at Charles-Ferdinand University in Prague, and fifty-one women graduated with bachelor degrees. The following year, fifteen women matriculated at the Prague Technical Academy. This was a hard-won achievement for women, who had been considered incapable of understanding science and engineering coursework. Before 1916, female students could only attend the Technical Academy as "listeners."

Women staffed hospitals throughout Prague. The Sokol trained women as nurses and partnered with the Red Cross to fund these efforts. The military collaborated with voluntary organizations to set up makeshift hospitals and clinics for soldiers. Existing health facilities became centers for treating ailing and wounded soldiers. A Red Cross infirmary at the Žižkov Sokol gymnasium housed war amputees, and a psychiatric hospital founded by Joseph II in the eighteenth century provided treatment for soldiers experiencing post-traumatic stress. The military requisitioned school buildings, chapels, and club headquarters to house the half million soldiers who received care in Prague during the war. Women also worked at public kitchens and canteens that provided food for poor citizens and refugees who could not source enough food. By 1916, the middle class began to patronize the network of cafeterias. A charity shop opened in the Wallenstein Gardens, and Red Cross donation boxes appeared on street corners. Long lines for bread, flour, and beer became the norm of daily life in wartime Prague.

The city's appearance changed in subtle ways during the war. The Austrian authorities measured loyalty by visual patriotic displays. Yellow-and-black Austrian flags, emblazoned with the Habsburg double-headed eagle, hung on Prague businesses, schools, and family homes. A handful of streets and squares were renamed for members of the Habsburg family, including Francis Joseph and the new heir to the throne, Charles, who was elevated after the death of Francis Ferdinand. The Czech Commission for Child Protection and Youth Welfare named its new hospital in honor of the future empress Zita, following the lead of a similar institution in Vienna.[7] In 1915, the public came together for patriotic celebrations of the Austrian victory at Lemberg (today, Lviv, Ukraine) and Francis Joseph's eighty-fifth birthday.

Czech nationalism was not dead, though. Prague's Czech civic leaders planned to mark the five hundredth anniversary of Jan Hus's martyrdom on July 6, 1915, by unveiling a memorial across from the Marian Column on Old Town Square. Prague's Catholic leaders opposed commemorating a convicted heretic and issued a statement earlier in the century: "This statue will stand as a disgrace and insult to the Catholic Church and its people, humiliating this Catholic city."[8] The tensions on the Prague home front convinced the city council to cancel the public celebration of Hus's anniversary. Instead, workers unveiled Ladislav Šaloun's art nouveau Hus Memorial in the dark of night. The headline in a Czech-language newspaper read, "Silent Day for the Great Jubilee." Voluntary associations and individual citizens visited the memorial and laid red and white flowers and wreaths "in quiet respect."[9] Evidence of the Czech nationalist cause was subdued, even on this sacred anniversary.

News of battlefield defeats and high casualty rates tempered Prague citizens' initial enthusiasm for the war. Food shortages, rationing, and rampant inflation likewise increased despair and anger on the home front. A wave of anti-Semitic demonstrations targeted Jewish Galician refugees for straining the dwindling food supplies. Some politicians rekindled Pan-Slavic sentiment and questioned the morality of fighting against their Slavic brothers, the Serbs and the Russians. Leaders of several Czech political parties and organizations formed a loose coalition known as the Czech Maffia, which secretly communicated with Czech politicians abroad.

FIGURE 10.1 Visitors bring wreaths to the Jan Hus Memorial, which was unveiled on Old Town Square on July 6, 1915. Postcard from the author's collection.

Tomáš G. Masaryk had fled Prague early in the war and traveled in Western Europe and North America to rally support for Czech and Slovak autonomy. Masaryk worked closely with two politicians who were in exile in Paris: the Czech activist and sociologist Edvard Beneš and the Slovak scientist and diplomat Milan Štefánik. As leaders of the "struggle abroad," the three men sought support from Western European and American politicians. As the war progressed, Masaryk's political rhetoric shifted from autonomy within Austria to independence. On July 6, 1915, Masaryk marked the anniversary of Hus's execution with a speech in Geneva's Hall of the Reformation: "In the spirit of our Hussite ancestors, we are fighting for a moral as well as for a political purpose.... Every Czech must decide to be for reformation or against reformation; for the Czech model or for the Austrian model, an organ of European Counter Reformation and reaction." The Vienna-based *Neue Freie Presse* called Masaryk's address "the first Czech declaration of war against Austria."[10]

Signs of unrest in Prague led the Austrian military to arrest some of the most vocal Czech nationalists of the prewar era, including Karel Kramář, Alois Rašín, and Josef Scheiner, the head of the Sokol. Rumors spread that Czech nationalists planned to convert the Sokol gymnastics organization into an independent national guard, and the Austrian military banned Sokol events. Other high-profile arrests included Masaryk's daughter, Alice Masaryková, and Beneš's wife, Hana Benešová, who were accused of treason for allegedly safeguarding Masaryk's papers. They were sent to Vienna's K.K. Landesgericht Prison, where Masaryková served eight months and Benešová stayed for four. Alice later wrote that she feared for her life since several women on her floor had been executed for lesser crimes. While in prison, she learned of the death of her brother Herbert from typhoid, which he contracted caring for Galician war refugees. Alice recorded her experiences in letters to her mother, Charlotte Garrigue Masaryková: "I have had a nervous breakdown. Every night I have waked and not known where I am." Her mother attempted to comfort her daughter by reminding her of Prague's beauty and the wonderful walks Alice and her sister Olga took in the Royal Gardens at Prague Castle: "Wherever you look—there is beauty.... The deer moat...the Daliborka Tower, the Golden Lane with its miniature houses all the way up to the St. Vitus Cathedral, and then the view of Prague below and the Žižkov hill on the blue horizon across the river."[11]

The mood in Prague grew increasingly somber. On September 27, 1916, the eve of St. Wenceslas's feast day, Prague's Roman Catholic churches rang their bells in unison for the last time. The Austro-Hungarian military faced metal shortages and requisitioned church bells throughout the empire. The German daily newspaper *Praguer Tageblatt* mourned their absence from the urban soundscape: "Bells belong to the city, and it is as if a part of the city has been sacrificed."[12] In November 1916, two deaths rocked Prague. On the first of the month, Governor Thun-Hohenstein died. He had been an important leader in Prague politics for decades and favored compromise with Czech nationalist politicians. Three weeks later, on November 21, Emperor Francis Joseph I drew his last breath. His successor, Charles I, declared himself the supreme commander of the military and ordered all soldiers to swear an oath of loyalty. The Prague regiment assembled on Karlín's main square, and the sick and wounded pledged their "faith and obedience" from hospital beds. Charles did not announce plans for a coronation in Prague but confirmed a ceremony for Hungary. Many Czechs interpreted this decision as the new emperor's slight to their nation.

In 1917, Charles issued an amnesty of political prisoners, saving Czech politicians Kramář and Klofáč from execution. The economic situation in Prague was dire. Women sold clothes, shoes, and even their hair in exchange for a sack of potatoes. Industrial workers organized strikes to protest the deteriorating conditions in factories. Major General Eduard Zanantoni, the station commander of Prague, wrote in his diary, "From 31 May [1917] onwards...[s]trikes followed each other in quick succession, in particular among the metalworkers, who were primarily tasked with producing the ammunition. On repeated occasions, all the factories in Prague stood empty and it was only through the use of force that the workers could be made to resume their work." Zanantoni empathized with the employees, writing that he could "well understand how [a worker] must feel when he had to work and neither he nor his family had any proper food to eat."[13] Factories were militarized in July 1917, and thousands of workers were hauled from their homes to their workplaces.

As the war persisted, the Austrian state imposed stricter rations on Prague residents. The Austrian government determined the caloric needs of laborers in various war-related industries, but workers retorted that the amounts were insufficient to carry out the back-breaking tasks. By 1917, each Prague resident was entitled to only half a loaf of bread weekly. In working-class Žižkov, food riots became weekly occurrences, as hungry families plundered shops, demanded lower prices, and accused merchants of war profiteering. With supply routes cut across the continent, the Austrian state could do little to ameliorate these conditions. Instead, they cracked down on residents who were breaking rationing laws. In Prague, one could not buy, sell, or consume meat on Mondays, Wednesdays, and Fridays. Authorities broke into the villa of the textile factory owner Ludvík Jelínek and fined him five hundred crowns because his maid was cooking two goose thighs for his lunch. Working-class mothers were hauled off to jail for adding small amounts of beef or horsemeat to their families' meals.[14] Austria's harsh treatment of its hungry citizens exacerbated tensions between Prague and the monarchy.

Private organizations strove to provide food for the empire's children. In 1917, Prague doctors, social workers, and volunteers established the Czech Heart (České srdce) to aid orphans and hungry children throughout Austria. In addition to charity work in Prague, the organization raised funds for Viennese children suffering from food and clothing shortages. Vienna was hit particularly hard by the Entente's embargo and the disruption of domestic agricultural and nonmilitary industrial production. The patriotic artist Alfons Mucha contributed an image of a suffering mother and child to help raise support for the Czech Heart, whose publications announced that "the Czech Heart lived in Vienna," a bold statement for Czech volunteers, who rarely collaborated with their German-speaking counterparts before the war.

FIGURE 10.2 A municipal shop in a girls' school in Prague's New Town, where residents could purchase rationed flour and bread, c. 1915. Archiv ZŠ Brána jazyků (Praha 1), Eva Špačková, Roman Elner, foto Kříženecký. Public domain, via Wikimedia Commons.

By the beginning of 1918, most Austrian citizens had lost faith in the monarchy. In mid-January, the Austrian state halved flour rations, a move that convinced over seven hundred thousand workers in the monarchy to strike. In Prague, thirty thousand workers participated in the campaign. On January 22, between fifty thousand and seventy thousand citizens assembled in Old Town Square for a peaceful protest against the food rations and the ongoing war, and isolated riots broke out in Prague neighborhoods and suburbs. Throughout the spring, groups of women petitioned the Bohemian governor to demand food, coal, and gas. On July 31, the astronomical clock on Old Town Square stopped working, leading residents to joke that even the rotating apostles had gone on strike.[15]

The Central Powers' defeat was imminent. The Entente launched an offensive against Germany in September 1918, while the Austro-Hungarian army faced devastation on the Italian front. Soldiers, reeling from hunger, lack of supplies, and exhaustion, deserted in large numbers. In Prague, news from the battlefield inspired a new wave of protests. Major General Eduard Zanantoni reported to his superiors in Vienna that by mid-September, the situation in Prague had become chaotic: "Thousands of people, Sokols in their uniforms and ladies in national costume, thronged day and night through the streets of the city.... [They] no longer sang the national anthem, but only the Czech anthem and the rousing song 'Hey, Slavs.'"[16] Czechs defied the censorship laws, publishing anti-Austrian leaflets and staging patriotic plays at the National Theater. Soldiers stationed in Prague were placed on high alert, and military leaves were canceled.

On October 14, Count Coudenhove demanded that Zanantoni "do everything to prevent the proclamation of the republic at least in Prague, the regional capital," but authorities in Vienna amended the order: "Avoid any bloodshed, do not make a scandal and arrange a peaceful transition to a nation state."[17] Zanantoni's priority was public safety. He stationed all the troops at his disposal—between forty thousand and sixty thousand men—throughout the city, thwarting a plan by members of the National Socialist Party to occupy Old Town Square. Two days later, on October 16, Emperor Charles I made a final attempt to save the empire by signing the Völkermanifest (People's Manifesto), which created a federation of autonomous national states. However, by that time, the goal of most Czech politicians had changed; they sought sovereignty, not autonomy. Politicians from various parliamentary parties formed a National Committee in Prague.

During the autumn of 1918, Masaryk was in the United States, where he had prominent friends and associates. His wife, Charlotte Garrigue, was

American, and his daughter Alice had studied in Chicago. Masaryk first met Woodrow Wilson in 1902, and in 1918, he presented the US president with the Declaration of Independence of the Czechoslovak Nation. Slavic immigrants in American cities such as Pittsburgh and Chicago rallied behind Masaryk. The Declaration, signed in Philadelphia, claimed that a Czech state had existed since the seventh century, and it accused the Habsburgs of illegally usurping Bohemian sovereignty. A Paris newspaper published the declaration on October 18, 1918, and other international newspapers followed:

> We, the Czechoslovak National Council...realizing that federalization, and, still more, autonomy mean nothing under a Habsburg dynasty, do hereby make and declare this our Declaration of Independence. We do this because of our belief that no people should be forced to live under a sovereignty which they do not recognize, and because of our knowledge and firm conviction that our nation cannot freely develop in a Habsburg mock-federation, which is only a new form of the denationalizing oppression under which we have suffered for the past three hundred years.[18]

Ten days later, on October 28, 1918, Czech leaders in Prague took power. The change in sovereignty did not unfold in an organized manner. With Austria-Hungary in free fall, National Committee leaders negotiated with Austrian generals to divide military buildings and provisions and to allow individual soldiers to choose which army to serve. Czech politicians at home were unsure if they should form an autonomous state within a federalized Austria or hold out for a republic as outlined in Masaryk's Declaration of Independence.

On October 28, Governor Coudenhove was in Vienna, seeking advice on how to handle the situation in Prague. That morning, the agricultural council, acting in the name of the National Committee, took over the Grain Office on Wenceslas Square to prevent more food from leaving Bohemia for the front lines. Politicians, the civil service, and the general public began peaceful takeovers of various offices and buildings throughout the city. Sokol members formed small militias and discouraged their fellow citizens from destroying private property. Public squares filled with demonstrators who called for the formation of a republic and a complete break with Austria.

That day, rumors reached Prague that Emperor Charles had accepted Woodrow Wilson's terms for an armistice. Czech patriots gathered in Wenceslas Square, where overenthusiastic Czech politicians Isidor Zahradník and Jiří Stříbrný announced the formation of a Czechoslovak state.

Meanwhile, National Committee leaders meeting at the Municipal House scrambled to gain control of the situation. They stepped onto a balcony overlooking Francis Joseph Square and declared independence. They kept the statement vague, as they did not want to undermine the efforts of their colleagues abroad. To maintain order, the National Committee announced that Austrian law was still in effect.

The atmosphere in Prague was chaotic, with citizens celebrating in the streets for days. On Sunday, November 3, 1918, Austria-Hungary formally surrendered to the Entente. Czech nationalists and socialists celebrated the news on White Mountain, where the Bohemian nobility met defeat three centuries earlier. Singing patriotic songs and Hussite hymns, the revelers marched to Old Town Square, where they met a rambunctious group of patriots from Žižkov. The citizens formed a ring around the Baroque Marian Column that had stood on the square since 1650. Speakers told the crowd that the column symbolized Catholic and Austrian supremacy and no longer belonged in Prague. Moderate politicians from the National Committee pleaded with the rioters not to vandalize their new capital city. Prague anarchist František Sauer disagreed and exclaimed, "You are the National Committee. We are the Nation!" Firemen, who had attached ropes and pulleys, began to tug at the column. Minutes later, onlookers heard a loud crack and watched the Marian Column tumble onto the square, where it broke into three large chunks. The delicate statue of the Virgin Mary shattered on the cobblestones.

Prague's Czech patriots favored "de-Austrianizing" Prague. The National Council worried about Prague's anticlerical atmosphere and asked residents to show more tolerance for their religious compatriots. "The principle of freedom excludes every violent act, especially during this era of developing relations with Slovakia, when we are developing a way for the whole nation to be happy."[19] The city government proposed new names for various streets, squares, and buildings. Francis Joseph I Main Train Station now bore the name of President Woodrow Wilson. The area in front of the Rudolfinum concert hall became Smetana Square, and Archduke Francis Ferdinand Bridge was renamed for nineteenth-century Czech painter Josef Mánes. Francis Joseph Square, the pedestrian area in front of the Municipal House, was dubbed Republic Square to commemorate the announcement of the Czechoslovak state.

The celebrations and demonstrations in the autumn of 1918 had an unintended consequence: spreading the deadly Spanish influenza epidemic through the city. In September 1918, the Prague press reported that Egon M. Prorok, a twenty-five-year-old lawyer, was the city's first confirmed

FIGURE 10.3 The Baroque Marian Column in front of Our Lady Before Týn Church in Old Town Square, ca. 1890–1906. Library of Congress Prints & Photographs Division, LC-DIG-ppmsca-52237.

victim of the influenza outbreak. In November, the Prague art community mourned the art critic and cubist innovator Bohumil Kubišta, who succumbed to the disease. Prague's daily newspapers published suggestions for hygienic practices and self-isolation. As infection numbers rose over the autumn, Prague hospitals banned visitors and admitted only severe cases. The high number of deaths meant that cemeteries and mortuaries were at capacity. Dead bodies often remained on the streets for several days before health

FIGURE 10.4 Prague residents pose by the demolished Marian Column on Old Town Square, November 3, 1918. Photograph from the author's collection.

workers could clear them away. Mortality rates were highest in working-class neighborhoods, likely because of crowded living conditions. The municipal government called on the fledgling state to increase funds for supplies and health workers. Many Prague women heeded the call to train as nurses or enter other health professions.[20]

The provisional National Committee hastened to transform Prague from a revolutionary city into the capital of an independent state. The wealthiest and most cosmopolitan city in the new country, Prague had a long political history, having served as the seat of the medieval Kingdom of Bohemia and the provincial capital of Austrian Bohemia. Not all citizens agreed, though. Prague represented the center of a nationalist movement that had pitted Czechs against Germans, and Slovak citizens had few ties to the Czech capital.

Masaryk claimed that the Czechs and Slovaks represented a single nation, and he advocated for statehood using the principle of national self-determination. However, the situation was more complex. Fifty percent of Czechoslovakia's citizens spoke Czech, while 15 percent spoke Slovak. The languages were mutually understandable, but the two groups did not share a political history. Bohemia, Moravia, and Austrian Silesia belonged to the lands of the Bohemian Crown, while Slovakia was a Slavic-speaking region in northern Hungary. Masaryk insisted that the state retain the historic borders

FIGURE 10.5 Tomáš G. Masaryk, flanked by Czechoslovak Legionnaires, rides in an open car to Wenceslas Square following his arrival in Prague on December 22, 1918. Photo by Heinrich Guttmann. Public domain, via Wikimedia Commons.

of the Bohemian kingdom, which meant incorporating about three million German speakers into Czechoslovakia. Just under a quarter of the population was German, and the remaining 10 percent included Hungarians, Poles, Ukrainians, Roma, and self-described ethnic Jews. Borders with Poland and Hungary remained disputed and would not be secured for several years.

During the country's first few months, life in the capital was precarious. The international influenza pandemic raged, and soldiers—many injured and traumatized—were returning home from the front in need of care. Food shortages continued throughout Central Europe. The Czech and Slovak leaders who had the backing of the allied nations were still abroad. The National Committee convened a Constitutional Congress, which elected Masaryk president in absentia. Masaryk sailed from New York City to England and made his way across the continent, finally reaching Prague on December 21. Cheering crowds greeted Masaryk at the Main Train Station and accompanied him to Wenceslas Square. The president-elect rode in an open motorcar flanked by members of the Czechoslovak Legionnaires, a paramilitary organization whose soldiers fought alongside Entente troops in Russia, Italy, and France. The following day, Masaryk addressed the Czechoslovak National Assembly, once again proclaiming Czechoslovak independence and quoting the words of the seventeenth-century Protestant theologian Jan Komenský (Comenius): "The government of your affairs returns to you, [the] people."[21]

II

Capital of the Republic

PRAGUE HAD MANY functions in the new Czechoslovak state: the national capital of a multiparty democracy; a center of culture, education, manufacturing, and commerce; the historical birthplace of a medieval Czech state; and the country's largest city. Prague hosted a bicameral legislature, the executive branch of government, a judiciary, and foreign embassies. Masaryk and other leaders of the First Republic sought to make the capital city—and, by extension, the country—a showplace of twentieth-century modernity while preserving its historic architecture and rich traditions. The city's identity wavered between a vibrant, progressive urban space and a site of linguistic and class divisions.

The Greater Prague Act of 1921 incorporated thirty-seven neighboring municipalities, including Žižkov and Vinohrady, tripling the city's population to 676,700. These suburbs were mostly Czech speaking, and the expansion shifted the city's linguistic demographics even further in favor of Czechs. Only 6 percent of Prague's population reported German as their primary language. There were sharp class divisions as well. Only 10 percent of center-city residents described themselves as manual laborers. In contrast, the working class made up nearly half of Prague's outer-ring population. The foundation of the Czechoslovak state did not signal a clean break from the past. Street violence continued for the first several years of the republic, and Prague inherited problems caused by the war: food shortages, disabled veterans, orphans, and refugees. International aid organizations set up soup kitchens, clinics, and shelters for the many Prague residents who continued to suffer in the aftermath of the war. The city remained dark at night into 1920, as coal shortages prevented the city from providing public lighting.

Pent-up anger toward Austria persisted as well. Despite warnings by the new government, attacks on Catholic and Habsburg symbols continued during the first few years of the republic. After toppling the Marian Column, a group of men attempted to destroy the John of Nepomuk statue on Charles Bridge. Patriots decapitated another statue of Nepomuk, which stood in

FIGURE 11.1 Children and adults wait for soup in Prague, 1919. Photo by US Sgt. Sheridan McAuley, Signa Corps. National Archives photo no. 313154601.

front of the law faculty. Several parish churches reported raids by nationalist groups, and a priest was assaulted while celebrating Nepomuk's feast day at Our Lady Before Týn on Old Town Square. Catholic Party leader Mořic Hruban remarked, "In Prague, one observed the appearance of two main trends of thought: the social revolutionary and the anti-Catholic. The casual observer could not recognize the real situation because everything around was hidden under flags and flowers and covered by a mood of rejoicing for the newly won state and national independence."[1]

While municipal and national authorities encouraged order and nonviolence, the rhetoric of "de-Austrianizing" the capital city encouraged enthusiastic citizens to remove symbols of Austrian rule. People tore down signs in German and removed the once-ubiquitous Habsburg double-headed eagle from city buildings. In 1919, the city government removed the statue of Austrian Field Marshal Joseph Radetzky from Lesser Town Square and the equestrian figure of Emperor Francis I from the Vltava embankment. Ruth Crawford, an American social worker who came to Prague in 1919 to oversee a health survey, characterized the capital as "ecstatically Czech." She reported that German signs had been removed, and "the consciousness of the German-speaking minority was still wavering between post-revolution antagonism and acceptance of the government's stated policy of recognizing minority groups."[2]

FIGURE 11.2 Josef and Emmanuel Max's Field Marshal Joseph Radetzky Memorial was removed from Lesser Town Square in 1919. Library of Congress Prints & Photographs Division, LC-DIG-ppmsc-09303.

Prague also witnessed instances of anti-Semitic violence following the declaration of the new state. Nationalists associated Prague Jews with the German language and culture and blamed them for high postwar inflation. In May 1919, uniformed Czechoslovak Legionnaires oversaw public looting of Jewish and German businesses, and Galician Jews, who had taken refuge in Prague during the war, faced various forms of prejudice, including eviction from their homes.³ In November 1920, a mob broke into the Jewish Town Hall to harass Jewish refugees. Jewish organizations demanded recognition of their minority status in the new state, and Kafka's friend Max Brod advocated Jewish rights in Czechoslovakia.

Minority issues remained the most contentious issue in the state. All citizens had the right to suffrage and proportional representation, but many resented Czech dominance in national affairs. In May 1919, Slovak citizens lost their most influential representative when Masaryk's wartime ally, Milan Štefánik, died in a plane crash. Some German speakers in the borderlands hoped to unite with the new Austrian republic. The Czechoslovak state placed restrictions on nomadic Roma and Sinti citizens, referred to as "wandering gypsies." These individuals had to carry identity cards, submit to fingerprinting, and seek permission to enter certain locations, including Prague and Brno. A branch of the Ministry of the Interior opened in Prague to spearhead the efforts, and sixty-five hundred "gypsy" identity cards were issued during the First Republic.

President Masaryk came to embody the successes and contradictions of First Republic Prague. He was celebrated worldwide as a stalwart democrat but had significant blind spots. He believed that Czechoslovaks were the national people and regarded the Germans and other minority groups as guests with citizenship rights. While charismatic, Masaryk could also appear arrogant. Frequent press releases and public appearances advanced Masaryk to celebrity status in the new state. His official photographers depicted him as a wise father figure, an ascetic intellectual, or a military leader on horseback. Masaryk resembled Emperor Franz Joseph, tall and lean with a long mustache and clipped beard, and his detractors claimed the country retained Austria's imperious atmosphere. His supporters, however, embraced him as the "President Liberator."

While some Czechoslovak politicians advocated a weak, symbolic presidency, Masaryk preferred an American-style executive branch. Upon his return to Prague in December 1918, Masaryk formed a chancellery and cabinet that guided state policy on all aspects of domestic and foreign policy. Citizens referred to the national government as the *Hrad* because of its location at Prague Castle. Pro-*Hrad* politicians, financial leaders, and cultural representatives enjoyed unique access to Masaryk and his chief ally, the foreign minister, Edvard Beneš. Masaryk received information on his political opponents from a state intelligence service, which stepped up its activities following the 1923 assassination of Minister of Finance Alois Rašín by an anarcho-Communist. The two leaders had ties to several newspapers, publishing houses, and voluntary organizations at home and abroad. Masaryk's unofficial forms of power led to tensions with parliamentary leaders who favored legislative authority. Czechoslovak democracy depended upon a rich civil society, coalition governments, and cooperation among political parties. An extralegal parliamentary committee, known as the *pětka* (the five), included leaders of the five coalition parties who pushed through a legislative agenda to combat stalemate. Those outside the coalition accused the *pětka* of silencing dissent and predetermining political outcomes. Compared to its neighbors, Czechoslovakia had a robust, functioning democracy, but not all citizens could access the informal channels of power.

The state's progressive attitude toward women became a pillar of Prague's modernity. The Czechoslovak Declaration of Independence averred, "Our democracy shall rest on universal suffrage. Women shall be placed on equal footing with men, politically, socially, and culturally." In his first address to the National Assembly, President Masaryk declared, "I am happy to see women in this assembly. I believe that women should devote themselves to public life just as men [do]."[4] Masaryk's daughter, Alice Garrigue Masaryková,

FIGURE 11.3 President Tomáš Garrigue Masaryk, 1919. Library of Congress Prints & Photographs Division, American National Red Cross Collection, LC-DIG-anrc-03759.

a prominent figure in interwar Prague, served as first lady after her mother Charlotte died in 1923. She also led the Czechoslovak Red Cross for nearly two decades. Trained as a social worker at Jane Addams's Hull House in Chicago, Masaryková launched a social survey of Prague. A team of Czech and American social workers concluded that the new state occupied "a high rank among the nations. Social insurance providing for sickness, maternity, accident, unemployment, old age, and invalidity; regulation of hours, child welfare, safety, sanitation and health, and minimum wage had been subject to new legislation."[5]

The survey highlighted the significant class divisions in the Greater Prague region. The Red Cross and other voluntary organizations provided services to poor women, offered mothering classes, and set up day camps for children, but this could not resolve significant economic challenges. Many working-class women lost their jobs when men returned from the war, and they struggled to maintain the hygienic standards that medical professionals and social workers advised. Contemporary health publications portrayed rural women as backward and superstitious, but the urban population relied on the surrounding countryside for its sustenance. Prague's middle-class and rural women interacted at farmers' markets throughout the city.

FIGURE 11.4 Market Scene in Prague, 1919. Library of Congress Prints & Photographs Division, American National Red Cross Collection, LC-DIG-anrc-03931.

Postwar Prague's "new women" came from the middle classes and took advantage of the city's expanding educational and social opportunities. Teenage girls and young women attended training schools for secretaries, nurses, and social workers. Women pursued higher education at the Masaryk Academy of Labor, which the president founded in 1920 to educate a new generation of citizens in technical fields and engineering. Some Prague women achieved important recognition in Prague's male-dominated art community. Milada Marešová embraced the "New Objectivity" movement popularized in Berlin. Her portraits of the urban bourgeoisie hinted at the emptiness and isolation of modern life. In 1925, she and her friend and fellow painter Vlasta Vostřebalová-Fischerová had a two-woman exhibition in Prague, and in 1930, Marešová's first solo show debuted at the Aventinum Mansarda gallery. Marešová's work, such as her *Bride with a Cigarette*, ironically explored the psychological state of Europe's "new women."

As Prague's young women enjoyed increased freedom and some disposable income, many explored the capital's energetic nightlife. As in other parts of Europe, many Prague women cut their hair short, raised their hemlines, and wore androgynous clothes. Women frequented the shopping passages in complexes like Lucerna Palace on Wenceslas Square. The new women's magazines *Eva* (Eve) and *Moderní dívka* (Modern girl) catered to their interests, focusing on traditional feminine topics such as fashion and beauty while also supporting their career and social aspirations. Prague journalist Milena Jesenská published popular newspaper columns on women's issues. She encouraged women to wear trousers, especially while bicycling, and told her readers that the trench coat "belongs to you, just as the whole world belongs to you." Jesenská became known for her Czech translations of Kafka's work and her passionate correspondence with the author. When Kafka died in 1924, Jesenská wrote the writer's Czech-language obituary for *Národní listy,* declaring that her beloved friend had written the most important recent works in German literature. Over the interwar era, Jesenská's writing shifted from women's special interests to politics. She explored communist philosophy but eventually joined the staff of the liberal magazine *Přítomnost.* Like many Prague women of the 1920s and 1930s, Jesenská's attitude toward female roles evolved. Rather than emphasizing wifely and motherly duties, she asserted that modern women should seek equal partnerships with men. She told her readers that women were "independent, hard-working, tough and brave; who could be companions for men, friends and helpmates; who could take responsibility for themselves and support themselves by their own effort."[6]

FIGURE 11.5 The model Augusta Kurz at her Vinohrady apartment in 1931. Smoking a cigarette and wearing a pantsuit, Kurz represented the new woman of the interwar era. Fortepan under Creative Commons CC-BY-SA-3.0 license.

The Czechoslovak Women's National Council (ŽNR) was established in Prague in 1923. Its members lobbied the national government for paid maternity leave and equal access to divorce. They called to end the outdated practice of firing married women and mothers from teaching jobs. ŽNR founder Františka Plamínková, one of the first women in the National Assembly, remained frustrated that Czechoslovak culture still portrayed motherhood as women's primary duty. Czech women fought for access to education and professions well before the war, and their fights for rights did not end with suffrage in 1918.

◆

As Czechoslovakia's capital, Prague symbolized Bohemia's long political history and served as an emblem of modern democracy. Masaryk located his residence and presidential offices at Prague Castle, but he also envisioned the castle grounds as a functional public space. A writer for the Prague newspaper *České slovo* captured the castle's modern significance in a 1919 article:

The castle does not consist solely of the courtyards and surrounding district. It is not only the presidential seat.... It is a pleasure to look at the castle early in the morning, when it is rousing to life...and know that once again, inside, the feelings and fears of the people, their joys and concerns, are being considered, that work is being done, and that a democratic, governing care for the state and nation is flowing.[7]

Masaryk entrusted the castle renovation to Jože Plečnik, a Slovenian architect and professor at Prague's School of Decorative Arts. Nationalist newspapers decried the appointment of a Slovene architect, and a group of 245 Czech women petitioned the national government to replace Plečnik with a Czech architect. Masaryk remained loyal to Plečnik, telling him in a 1923 letter, "Something remarkable could be made of the castle and its surrounding, and I can see nobody else but You capable of carrying out this historic task."[8] The Prague public warmed to the pioneering designer as Plečnik's castle gardens and courtyards won numerous awards. The art journal *Volné směry* featured a twelve-page photographic essay that celebrated Plečnik's "remarkable comprehension of the people's soul and environment" combined with an "independence and freedom...that has given birth to powerful departures" from hackneyed interpretations.[9]

Plečnik embodied Czech national traditions more than many Czech architects who favored avant-garde modernism. He insisted on using local stone and wood and sought inspiration from Prague's diverse architectural styles. Plečnik's neoclassical columns and capitals tied Czechoslovakia to ancient Greek symbols of democracy. Majestic staircases welcomed visitors into the castle grounds, and three paved interior courtyards eased movement through the sprawling complex. The Bull Staircase, which connected the third courtyard to the Castle Rampart gardens, had a curved metal canopy held up by columns and sculptures of Minoan bulls. After Plečnik added an observation terrace in the sixteenth-century Paradise Gardens, Prague families and visitors congregated to view the spectacular City of One Hundred Spires.

Plečnik redesigned the castle's third courtyard, which was dominated by St. Vitus's Cathedral. He planned to erect a granite obelisk to mark Czechoslovakia's tenth anniversary and honor fallen soldiers. The monolith had a difficult journey to Prague Castle. The first stone, selected from a quarry in Moravia, fell and shattered during its transportation. Rumors spread that the driver, so ashamed of the accident, took his own life. Masaryk contributed personal funds to purchase and transport a second granite obelisk to the capital. In November 1928, the president telegrammed Plečnik to announce that the monument finally stood upright.

FIGURE 11.6 Victor Alfred Lundy, *Entrance Courtyard, Prague Castle, Prague, Czech Republic*. The sketch shows Jože Plečnik's obelisk and bull staircase. Library of Congress Prints & Photographs Division, LC-DIG-ppmsca-53493.

Masaryk shared deep personal connections with his trusted advisers. Just as Plečnik consulted on art and design, other professionals guided the president in their fields of expertise. An informal circle known as the Friday Men met weekly at the home of writer Karel Čapek to discuss politics, culture, and philosophy. These liberal intellectuals were Masaryk's close friends and political allies. Journalist Ferdinand Peroutka, who chronicled the republic's first years in his multivolume account *Budování státu* (The building of the state), advocated Masaryk's centrist positions in his Prague newspaper columns. These men helped shape state policies and priorities outside normal government channels.

Masaryk surrounded himself with people like him, and the state's identity reflected that. In 1895, he wrote *The Czech Question*, which argued, "All Czech history pointed to the great era of the Czech Reformation in the fourteenth century and thus to freedom of conscience."[10] The Czech nationalist affinity for Jan Hus carried into the new state, even though that history alienated religious Roman Catholics and did not resonate with Slovaks and Germans. The new state's motto, "The Truth Prevails," echoed Hus's admonition to "Seek the truth, hear the truth, learn the truth, love the truth, speak the truth, hold the truth and defend the truth until death."[11]

The anniversary of Hus's death, July 6, became a state holiday in 1925. At Prague Castle, the Hussite flag flew between the state and presidential flags for two days. Festivities in the capital city attracted large crowds of citizens. *Národní listy* reminded its readers, "Ten years ago this type of public declaration was forbidden."[12] The celebrations commenced on Old Town Square, where President Masaryk greeted citizens. Politicians watched from the town hall balcony as Sokol members and Czechoslovak Legionnaires stood on the Hus Memorial. Czechoslovak army riflemen encircled the memorial while a brass ensemble performed the Hussite battle hymn. The Hus celebrations represented a major tension of the interwar era. Prague held on to its nineteenth-century Czech revolutionary culture, while Czechoslovaks across the country wondered if the capital city represented their beliefs. Roman Catholics and church representatives decried the Hus festivities, and the papal nuncio left Prague "as a meaningful protest for this offense against…all Czechoslovak Catholics." Relations with the Vatican were not mended until 1928.

Prague's 1929 commemorations of the Wenceslas millennium appealed to a broader constituency. Masaryk underscored Wenceslas's political significance: "As Head of State, I am naturally anxious that the fact should be properly publicized that we had a well-organized state even in the late ninth and early tenth century."[13] In contrast, the church emphasized Wenceslas's martyrdom and sainthood. The millennium coincided with the official reopening of St. Vitus Cathedral after a major renovation project that began in 1844. The neo-Gothic addition included a new entrance, two towers, and a nave with side chapels. František Kysela's rose window depicted the biblical creation story, and Alfons Mucha's art nouveau stained-glass window conveyed Bohemia's early Christian history. The cathedral's two new towers transformed Prague Castle's imposing silhouette. (See Color Plate 1.)

Prague's artistic community thrived in the creative atmosphere of the fledgling republic. In 1919, Masaryk's friend Karel Čapek translated Apollinaire's *Zone*, a long free-verse reflection on the French poet's visit to Prague and other cities. Apollinaire's 1913 poem contrasted ordinary joys with the knowledge that death must come. The French poet's 1918 death from influenza made the stanza about Prague particularly poignant:

> You are in the garden at an inn outside of Prague
> You are completely happy a rose is on the table
> And instead of getting on with your short-story
> You watch the rosebug sleeping in the rose's heart
> Appalled you see yourself reproduced in the agates of Saint Vitus
> You were sad near to death to see yourself there
> You looked as bewildered as Lazarus.[14]

Years later, the Czech writer Milan Kundera credited Čapek's translation with transforming Czech literature for the rest of the twentieth century. Prague writers moved away from the formal verse of earlier eras, eschewed punctuation, and used contemporary Czech vernacular. Many Prague artists and writers embraced international movements: the French avant-garde, wartime Dada, the German Bauhaus, Russian constructivism, and American modernism. Čapek explored dystopian themes in his science fiction works. His 1920 play *RUR (Rossum's Universal Robots)* portrayed a single day in a factory where sentient automatons work. The play became an international sensation, and the word "robot" (from the Czech *robota*, a serf's service obligation) found its way into languages worldwide. Two years later, Čapek debuted *The Insect Play*, written with his brother Josef. The satirical work assigned human character traits to various insect communities and served as a warning against militarism and greed.

In December 1920, a group of Prague artists founded Devětsil, an avant-garde association of photographers, actors, dancers, jazz musicians, writers, and painters. In their manifesto, the founders rejected "staid, bourgeois art" and declared that their art would confront social and political issues in the new state.[15] Their journals and almanacs—including *ReD*, *Pásmo*, and *Život*—showcased members' work and introduced theoretical discussions of modernity and art. Devětsil represented Prague's intellectual left wing, and its members strove to give voice to the working classes. Jaroslav Seifert, a young poet from Žižkov, published his first collection in 1921. More than sixty years later, Seifert would become the only Czech to win the Nobel Prize in Literature. *The City in Tears* rejected the cliché of mysterious, magical Prague and focused on its workers' struggles:

> Although I look
> upon the glory of my city, my heart it cannot overpower;
> its majesty and greatness do not bewitch me;
> I shall return to the mysterious embrace
> of star, of wood, of brook, and field and flower
> but so long as one of my brothers
> is suffering, I cannot be happy
> and bitterly revolting against all
> injustice, I shall long
> continue, amid the suffocating smoke, to lean against
> a factory wall
> and sing my song.[16]

Devětsil's founders, Karel Teige and Vítěslav Nezval, articulated the concept of Poetism, a uniquely Czech movement they described as "the poetry of ordinary life," "art for the five senses," and "an art of living and enjoying."[17] Their art was accessible to a wide audience that needed no rarefied education to grasp and enjoy it: Circuses, jazz music, cinema, skyscrapers, airplanes, and gourmet food were all forms of poetry. In 1926, Teige and Nezval collaborated on *Abeceda* (Alphabet), a mixed-media book of Nezval's childlike poems and Teige's photomontages. The dancer and choreographer Milada Mayerová dressed in a gymnast's costume and swim cap and posed as each letter. The three artists also performed the work as a theatrical evening, demonstrating art's mutable forms.

New developments in music led to clashes between conservative supporters of the arts and Prague musicians and composers who embraced modernism. In an event that became known as the *Wozzeck* affair, a performance at the National Theater erupted into anti-Semitic and anti-leftist protests. In 1926, the National Theater's director, Otakar Ostrčil, announced the premiere of *Wozzeck*, a new opera by Austrian composer Alban Berg. Whereas Czech journalists often criticized German productions on nationalist grounds, this opera became controversial because of its untraditional music and the libretto's communist themes. A Czech Catholic newspaper misidentified Berg as a "Berlin Jew," and a critic for *Národní listy* wrote that the National Theater had "fallen prey to musical bolshevism."[18] Audience members and hired thugs disrupted a performance of the opera, whistling and stomping until the director cut the evening short. The provincial bureaucrats who had jurisdiction over the theater responded to the controversy by banning the opera. Prague artists and intellectuals published a statement entitled "For the Freedom of Artistic Expression" in several Czech and German newspapers. The conservative reaction to *Wozzeck* backfired. The province of Bohemia lost its jurisdiction over the National Theater, which became an independent body within the national government.

Younger musicians embraced international, avant-garde, and atonal compositions. Popular music, jazz, and cabaret captivated audiences, who attended live shows in record numbers. Czechoslovakia was the second country in Europe, after the United Kingdom, to have regular radio broadcasts. Beginning in 1923, Prague residents could listen to classical and jazz concerts, as well as the news in Czech, English, and Esperanto. Prague's Liberated Theater, affiliated with Devětsil, became one of the city's most popular venues. Its top-billed artists Jiří Voskovec and Jan Werich—also known as (v + w)—inaugurated their play *Vest Pocket Revue* in 1927. In collaboration with Czech jazz composer Jaroslav Ježek, they went on to write, direct, and star in numerous theater pieces and early Czech-language films. Combining clowning, satire, and song, the duo poked fun at the optimistic patriotism and bourgeois values of the new republic. Their comedy took a darker turn in 1932 with their play *Caesar*, a satirical critique of European fascism.

In central Prague, new shops, studios, cafes, restaurants, and apartments attracted the middle class. Modern urban "palaces" represented a democratic approach to luxury, catering to middle-class consumers rather than Old World aristocrats. Vácslav Havel—whose grandson Václav would become the president of Czechoslovakia in 1990—built the Lucerna Palace complex on Wenceslas Square, the first Prague building made from reinforced concrete. The art nouveau building, designed before the war and completed in 1921, featured Islamic architectural influences, a luxurious marble hall, and a grand staircase. The American stars Josephine Baker and Louis Armstrong performed at the Lucerna Music Bar, and Prague's first talking picture premiered at its cinema.

Pavel Janák's Adria Palace housed a gallery, theater, café, and insurance company, and Josef Gočár designed the Archa Palace as the headquarters of Legiobanka. Construction projects in New Town showcased rondocubism, a distinctly Czechoslovak interwar innovation that juxtaposed circular and oval elements with cubist design to evoke traditional Slavic styles. The facade featured high-relief sculptures of the Czechoslovak Legionnaires, who had become national heroes in the new state. These palaces of commerce spared no expense and incorporated marble walls and staircases, elaborate mosaic floors, and stained-glass windows. The ornate and busy rondocubist aesthetic met with sharp criticism from European modernists such as Le Corbusier, who visited Prague in 1928.

Other Prague architects were ready to embrace the streamlined and modern functionalist style. Architect and critic Oldřich Starý proclaimed: "The most important elements of modern architecture? Hygiene: air, light, cleansing, airing, heating, artificial lighting."[19] Prague architects became leading innovators in air circulation and capturing natural and artificial light. Josef Fuchs and Oldřich Tyl designed the Trade Fair Palace, which opened in 1928 to commemorate the tenth anniversary of the republic. The massive structure in Holešovice, considered the largest functionalist building in the world, incorporated long ribbons of windows that brought abundant light into the exhibition spaces.

The Baťa shoe store on Wenceslas Square featured a six-story glass facade, lit from within each night. The illuminated building functioned as a large-scale advertising campaign, which competed with the neon lights on nearby buildings. In 1930, the Mánes Union of Artists opened its new center, which housed

FIGURE 11.7 Josef Gočár, "Czechoslovak Legion's Bank," (Legiobanka), 1923, from *Modern and Contemporary Czech Art*, by Antonín Matějček and Zdeněk Wirth (1924). Public domain, via Wikimedia Commons.

a gallery, café, and meeting space on the Vltava riverbank. The architect Otakar Novotný juxtaposed a low, white-glazed building with large square windows against the tall fifteenth-century Šítkovský Mill and Renaissance water tower.

Left-leaning functionalist practitioners eschewed ornamentation in favor of sleek, utilitarian buildings, but most building projects served the middle

FIGURE 11.8 Advertisement for the International Autumn Festival and opening celebrations for the Trade Fair Palace, October 1928. *Pestrý Týden*. Public domain, via Wikimedia Commons.

and upper classes more than Prague workers. The city expanded into outer-ring suburbs like Dejvice and Strašnice, each with stylish apartment buildings and neighborhoods modeled on the British concept of garden cities. Families in these green suburbs enjoyed modest attached or semi-attached single-family homes with small yards where they planted fruit trees or vegetables. Wealthy patrons commissioned modernist homes. Austrian architect Adolf Loos, who

FIGURE 11.9 The Mánes Union of Fine Arts Building with Štítkovský Mill Water Tower, ca. 1930. Photo by the author.

moved to Prague and took Czechoslovak citizenship, designed the Villa Müller for construction magnate František Müller. Located in the suburb of Strešovice, the villa's austere white-cube structure enclosed a complex multilevel interior with smooth walls, small windows, a central staircase, and spatial illusions. The Dejvice municipal quarter north of Prague Castle showcased urban modernist design. Architect Antonín Engel devised an integrated community with wide boulevards converging radially into a massive central roundabout. Prominent Prague architects designed fashionable functionalist villas for the Hanspaulka and Baba colonies north of Prague Castle. Members of Devětsil embraced German Bauhaus architecture and furniture. Architect Jaromír Krejcar remodeled the home of art theoretician Karel Teige and designed a villa for avant-garde writer Vladislav Vančura. Krejcar also built a residence in New Town for himself and his wife, the journalist Milena Jesenská.

The Great Depression inspired some artists to reexamine the philosophical underpinnings of their work. Toyen, one of only three women in the Devětsil group of nearly one hundred artists, pushed the Czech avant-garde toward surrealism. Born Maria Čermínová, Toyen adopted a gender-neutral name, which derived from the French word for citizen (*citoyen*) but could also be interpreted as a play on the Czech phrase *To je on* (it is he). She often wore men's clothing and used male grammatical forms when speaking Czech. Toyen's drawings and paintings explored eroticism and sexuality. In 1931, Devětsil disbanded. Three years later, some former leaders established the Czech Surrealist Group. Founding members Teige, Styrský, Toyen, and Nezval exchanged ideas with the French surrealists André Breton and Paul Éluard. In 1936, Vitěslav Nezval published *Prague with Fingers of Rain*, a collection of surrealist poetry. Nezval's title poem juxtaposed the sacred and the profane and contrasted real Prague sites with abstract images:

> Prague of one-hundred towers
> With the fingers of all saints…
> With the intoxicating fingers of women lying on their backs
> With fingers touching the stars
> On the abacus of night…
> With the fingers of the rain, cut off, and the Týn cathedral
> on the glove of dawns.[20]

The artistic community embraced new technologies, and Prague became a European center of filmmaking. The sons of Lucerna founder Vácslav Havel followed in their father's footsteps and invested in urban development. In the late 1920s, Václav Maria Havel built Barrandov Terraces, a modernist housing settlement south of the city center, and his brother Miloš Havel founded the Barrandov film studios there in 1931. *A Murder on Ostrovní Street*, the first in the studio's long line of successful films, premiered in 1933. The renowned urban planner, architect, and film director Max Urban designed Terraces, a landmark entertainment center on Barrandov's rocky outcrop. Inspired by the Cliff House in San Francisco, Urban's functionalist building housed cafés, restaurants, and a ballroom with river views.

Several Prague architects earned commissions for new churches in the "City of One Hundred Spires." Gočár designed the functionalist Catholic Church of St. Wenceslas in the Vršovice section of Prague. Its tall, thin clock tower with a cross guided onlookers' eyes toward the heavens. Janák became fascinated with Russian constructivism, which emphasized large geometrical shapes created with industrial materials. His design for the Evangelical Hussite Church in Vinohrady featured a detached minimalist bell tower topped by a chalice. Plečnik designed the Church of the Most Sacred Heart for a Roman Catholic parish in Vinohrady. Its dark red brick exterior contrasted with white Doric columns, obelisks, and an enormous glass clock tower. President Masaryk, a convert to Protestantism, admired Plečnik's new approach to Roman Catholic architecture. He wrote to his friend, "How should a church with its internal arrangement express the main idea of religion?...I would picture the church as a space for the Sermon on the Mount.... Your church is spacious, airy, and I like that."[21]

On the tenth anniversary of the republic, October 28, 1928, Masaryk laid the foundation stone for a National Liberation Memorial on Vítkov Hill. Jan Zázvorka designed the white concrete behemoth to include a large hall with a pipe organ, small meeting rooms, a mausoleum, a military museum, an equestrian statue of Jan Žižka, and mosaics of the Legionnaires fighting at the 1917 Battle of Zborov. Art critic Karel Teige added the National Memorial to a list of "dada absurdities"—a functionalist building without a function.[22] Another contribution to the national celebrations of 1928 was the exhibition of Alphonse Mucha's *The Slav Epic*. Mucha's twenty monumental paintings depict Slavic history from its origins in the Carpathian basin. The final canvas, *Apotheosis of the Slavs*, celebrates the achievement of statehood in the twentieth century. Although Mucha presented his work as inclusive of all Slavic history, eleven canvases focused on Czech themes, particularly the Hussite era. Mucha's exhibition poster incorporated his familiar commercial design with the Slavic symbolism that obsessed the artist later in life. (See Color Plate 15.)

The pace of building in Prague slowed with the onset of the Great Depression in 1929. Art Deco enjoyed a brief window of popularity in the mid-1930s. Famous Prague cafés, including Slavia and Adria, were renovated with bold, black-and-white tiling and stylized lighting. These cafés catered to middle- and upper-class residents of central Prague. The working-class suburbs, however, still lacked affordable apartments with modern amenities. The national and municipal governments recognized that Prague workers suffered from inadequate housing and sponsored competitions to design new apartments for industrial laborers. In 1930, the Prague city government announced that it would initiate a housing project for ten thousand lower-income homes to be built within a few years. However, the ongoing international financial crisis prevented the project from getting off the ground.

Prague did not have as large a manufacturing base as cities like Pilsen and Brno. Only eleven factories in Prague employed more than five hundred workers. The Praga Car Factory, founded in 1907, became an international leader in transportation design. In 1927, Praga joined the ČKD (Českomoravská Kolben-Daněk) engineering firm, making it one of the largest producers in Czechoslovakia. The corporation expanded its footprint in the eastern suburb of Vysočany, adding homes for some workers and additional production and storage facilities. The architect Josef Kalous designed a new factory for ČKD. The innovative E-shaped building had large glass windowpanes, which allowed light to infiltrate from several angles. The company produced motorcycles and cars, including the sleek Praga Alfa convertible and the smaller, boxier, but more affordable Praga Piccolo. The Praga Lady model beckoned to a new generation of young, independent women.

The Great Depression ushered in a blow to Czechoslovakia, one of the ten most industrially developed countries in the world. The country's industries lost 40 percent of their value within a few years. The Great Depression put luxury goods and personal cars out of most people's reach. Praga diversified its production to include airplanes and military transportation. The company sold its new light tanks to the Czechoslovak army and exported them to other countries, including Sweden, Iran, Ethiopia, Switzerland, and Peru.

The economic crisis exacerbated tensions within the state. Heavy industry was concentrated in Czech-speaking regions, which fared better than the German-speaking borderlands and the rural eastern provinces of Slovakia and Ruthenia. The armament and transportation sectors outperformed traditional German exports such as glass, textiles, paper, and toys. As high unemployment rates strained daily life, citizens resented Prague and Bohemia's relative economic success.

The Prague government watched international issues with trepidation. In bordering Germany, Adolph Hitler took power in January 1933. German nationalism rose in Czechoslovakia's borderlands as well. Konrad Henlein, a German nationalist, war veteran, and gymnastics instructor, founded the Sudeten German Homefront (Heimatfront) in 1933. Henlein called for German autonomy in Czechoslovakia but worked within the democratic system in the party's early years. The renamed Sudeten German Party (SdP) triumphed in the 1935 parliamentary elections, winning forty-four seats and 15 percent of the national vote. Only the Agrarian Party had more at forty-five. Still, the SdP remained outside the governing coalition, which the Czech parties continued to dominate. As Nazi Germany radicalized, Henlein's rhetoric shifted toward extremism as well. Nationalist ideology also affected other state groups. Slovaks resented their absorption into a "Czechoslovak" identity, while Poles and Hungarians in border regions disliked the frequent reminders of their minority status.

The problems of Czechoslovakia's complex identity were far from settled when President Masaryk resigned from the office he had held since the birth of the republic. On December 14, 1935, the presidential standard was slowly lowered over Prague Castle. The octogenarian's health had declined, and Masaryk recommended that the parliament choose Foreign Minister Edvard Beneš as his successor. Following a short ceremony in which Masaryk affirmed his decision to step down, he reviewed his Guard of Honor for the last time. Contemporary newspapers reported that veterans of the Czechoslovak army wept as the president waved from the balcony following the national anthem. Masaryk left his beloved office at Prague Castle, having never wavered from his faith in democracy and fervent defense of universal suffrage for all citizens, including women. However, he stubbornly clung to his belief that Czechoslovakia was a singular nation-state with minorities he saw as "guests."

The President Liberator took his final journey through Prague on September 14, 1937. A week after Masaryk's death at Lány Chateau at age eighty-seven, over 750,000 Czechoslovak citizens queued to pay their final respects at Prague Castle. Thousands more lined the streets of the capital as Masaryk's funeral procession followed the royal route once used by Bohemian monarchs. There had not been such a public display of mourning in Prague since Emperor Charles IV died in 1378. President Beneš followed his mentor's coffin, walking just behind Masaryk's son and grandsons. Musicians performed the Saint Wenceslas Chorale and the Hussite battle hymn, and in his eulogy, Beneš promised that the nation would uphold Masaryk's legacy. Masaryk's remains were brought from Prague to the presidential retreat at Lány, his chosen burial place. Journalist Ferdinand Peroutka commented on the strength and unity of the citizenry during those sad days: "Those unforgettable multitudes that gathered in the space between Prague castle and White Mountain—That wasn't a crowd, it was a nation."[23]

12

Prague Under Nazi Rule

In one of the most famous speeches of the twentieth century, British Prime Minister Neville Chamberlain addressed a London crowd on September 30, 1938. He assured them that he held the guarantee of "Peace for our time." Believing he had staved off war with Germany, Chamberlain celebrated the "solution to the Czechoslovak problem." Yet the Munich accord was a key step in the Nazis' march to war. Hitler had given Chamberlain and French President Édouard Daladier the false promise that he would seek no further European territory once Germany had annexed the Sudetenland. This could not be further from the truth. Within six months, Nazi troops marched into Prague, which remained an occupied city until May 1945.

Following the annexation (*Anschluss*) of Austria in March 1938, Hitler turned his attention to the three million German speakers living in Czechoslovakia. The Sudeten German Party (SdP) espoused increasingly radical views, and the Anschluss inspired Henlein's irredentism. As the SdP stepped up protests and provoked confrontations in the borderlands, Henlein apprised Hitler of his fellow Germans' dissatisfaction with Czechoslovakia. Hitler used the demonstrations and work stoppages in the borderlands to show Britain and France that Wilson's policy of self-determination had failed his fellow Germans.

Hitler harbored a long-standing animosity toward the Czechs, blaming their disloyalty for the fall of the Austrian Empire. In September 1938, Hitler spoke in Berlin about Czech treachery: "Every Czech is a born nationalist, who subordinates to his interests all his other duties.... The Czech is the most dangerous of all Slavs, because he is diligent. He has discipline, order.... The Czech state had a long German educational example of purity."[1] Chamberlain met with Hitler in the Führer's Berchtesgaden Alpine retreat to negotiate the Sudetenland issue but reached no agreement. A few weeks later, on September 26, 1938, Hitler addressed a crowd in Berlin's Sportspalast and decried Czechoslovak President Beneš for standing in the way of peace. Claiming he had no designs on the neighboring state beyond the restitution of the German population, Hitler proclaimed, "When Czechoslovakia solves her problems, that means when the Czechs have come to terms with their other minorities, peaceably and not through oppression, then I have no further interest in the Czech state.... We want no Czechs! But... with regard to the problem of the Sudeten Germans my patience is now at an end."[2]

Three days after Hitler's Berlin speech, on September 29, 1938, Chamberlain, Daladier, Benito Mussolini, and Hitler met in Munich to discuss the Czechoslovak crisis. Beneš was not invited to negotiate the fate of his country. Spontaneous demonstrations broke out in Prague every day as Hitler amplified his nationalist and anti-Czech rhetoric. Citizens filled Wenceslas Square and other public spaces, shouting for the army to mobilize and singing the national anthem. Foreign newspapers reported that "Prague is furious" and described people weeping in the streets. Several hundred thousand individuals joined the rallies, demanding that their government refuse to capitulate to the German demands or British and French compromises.

The leaders of Great Britain, France, Italy, and Germany signed the Munich Agreement on September 30, 1938. The treaty not only allowed Germany to annex the Sudetenland but also ceded territory to Hungary and Poland. Slovakia gained autonomy within a federalized state, renamed Czecho-Slovakia. Chamberlain defended his actions, believing that he enabled Britain to "escape from this great peril of war." Although Czechoslovak troops were positioned at the German border, Beneš saw no choice but to accept the agreement. He ordered the army to stand down, knowing his small country could not win, but many citizens felt ashamed that their country did not put up an armed resistance.

Despite the uncertainty in the country, some Czechs projected optimism. František Halas, a lyrical poet, former member of Devětsil, and a contributor to communist newspapers, published *Fragments of Hope* in 1938. Within the collection, the patriotic poem "Prague" cast the statue of Saint Wenceslas as a symbol of resistance.

> Beyond our rivers' gates
> hard hooves do thunder
> Fear not the dark Fear not the dark
> The bronze horse of St Wenceslas
> did last night restless stir.[3]

Jaroslav Seifert, another Devětsil poet, did not share Halas's confidence. Humiliated that his country offered no armed resistance to Germany, Seifert penned *At the Tomb of Czech Kings* and admitted he carried "shame in [his] heart" that "the faithful sword whose resting place is near was not to hand!"⁴

With the annexation of the Sudetenland, the democratic experiment of the First Republic came to an end. The predominantly Czech leadership had never adequately addressed its minorities' concerns, and the fledgling state dissolved when an outside threat manifested. President Beneš resigned from the presidency under German pressure and left the country, accompanied by other government leaders. In Prague, conservative politicians formed the National Unity Party and dismantled democratic institutions. The Second Czechoslovak Republic was a one-party state under President Emil Hácha. A retired conservative judge and former head of the Czechoslovak Supreme Administrative Court, Hácha viewed himself as a mediator between Czechs and Germans, naively believing he could preserve the Czech character of the state while cooperating with Germany. As a devout Roman Catholic, he wanted to forge a new Czech nationalism devoid of the Hussite symbolism Masaryk had favored. Like Czech leaders before him, Hácha took advantage of Wenceslas's malleable symbolism. He urged his cabinet, "The Czechoslovak statesmen should take the national saint, Duke Wenceslas, as their model.... [He] fought for German-Czech understanding, although initially he did not find understanding with his own people."⁵

Czechoslovakia's Jews faced a precarious situation after the Munich Agreement. In 1938, approximately 118,000 people in Bohemia and Moravia identified as Jewish, and perhaps 14,000 more had Jewish parentage.⁶ Some 30,000 Jews left the Sudetenland in the chaotic weeks following Hitler's annexation, most heading to the capital. Prague's Jewish population swelled from about 35,000 to 56,000 Jews, who faced the anti-Semitism of the Second Republic government and many citizens. Some Prague professional organizations lobbied to reduce the number of Jewish members. Ironically, as German speakers, many Sudeten Jews were turned away from seeking sanctuary in Prague, even though these individuals had been Czechoslovak citizens only weeks earlier. In November 1938, the *New York Times* reported that the Prague government turned away Sudeten Jewish refugees whose homes and synagogues had been burned during the Kristallnacht pogroms. When Czech authorities discovered a group of Jewish families hiding in a ditch in wet, frigid weather, they allowed them across the border, only to return them to the annexed German territory forty-eight hours later. Those who made it to Prague feared registering with the authorities.

In Prague, assimilated Jewish families agonized over whether to emigrate or send their children abroad. Even before Munich, Jewish organizations in

Prague began to organize responses to potential refugee crises. Marie Schmolka and Hannah Steiner, leaders in the Prague Jewish community, worked with Martin Blake of the British Committee for Refugees from Czechoslovakia to plan evacuations of Jewish children. In December 1938, Blake sent a telegram to his friend Nicholas Winton, a British businessman of German-Jewish descent: "600 children in Prague and elsewhere in Czechoslovakia urgently require emigration to England."[7] Winton canceled a skiing trip in Switzerland to come to Prague, where he helped Schmolka and other Jewish leaders to organize a *Kindertransport* modeled on similar programs in Germany and Austria. Winton first ran the organization from his Prague hotel room, taking applications from Jewish parents who hoped to send their children to safety. He returned to London to raise funds for the emigrations, and the Jewish community in Prague partnered with four British women—Doreen Warriner, E. Rosalind Lee, Tessa Rowntree, and Beatrice Wellington—to identify families and provide papers. In the first half of 1939, seven *Kindertransports* took 669 Jewish children to Britain. The altruism of the program was complicated by the Christian mission of many volunteers, and some British rabbis objected to the policy of baptizing these young Jews and sending them to live with Christian families. Schmolka faced brutal interrogation by the Gestapo and went into exile in France and then Britain, where she died of a heart attack at age forty-six.

Many of Prague's Jewish intellectuals left the country in these early months, fearing domestic bigotry and Hitler's expansionist ambitions. Publisher and art critic Max Brod and his wife Elsa Taussig boarded a train leaving Prague for Kraków on March 14, 1939. Brod took little with him, but he did carry his late friend Franz Kafka's papers, which he continued to edit and promote until his death in Israel in 1968. Years later, Brod recalled his terror when he spotted Gestapo officers at a station near the Czech-Polish border. Brod's train also carried 160 Jewish families rushing to leave their homes before catastrophe struck. In August 1939, the head of Prague's Jewish community addressed Jewish leaders from throughout Bohemia and Moravia at the Jewish Town Hall. He reminded his colleagues that Maria Theresa had expelled twenty thousand Jews from Prague in the dead of winter. Still, he warned, "In the 1,000 years of Jewish history in Bohemia, there has never been such a grievous time as now."[8]

In the months after Munich, it became clear that Hitler's goals went beyond the annexed borderland territory. In addition to uniting Europe's Germans, Hitler coveted Czechoslovakia's strong manufacturing base—including the world's seventh-largest armament industry—and the significant gold reserves stored in Prague's banks. The country's proximity to Poland facilitated Hitler's long-term plans to conquer Eastern Europe. Hitler courted the pro-independence wing in Slovakia, including the Slovak fascist priest Josef Tiso, and he pressed Hungary for assurance that it would aid in the dismemberment of Czechoslovakia. On March 14, Slovakia seceded from Czechoslovakia to become a fascist client state. Hitler next ordered Hácha to Berlin and made him wait until after one in the morning on March 15 to begin the meeting. Hácha, ill, exhausted, and grieving his recently deceased wife, signed his country over to Hitler, who had threatened airstrikes on Prague. Hácha begged Hitler to maintain Czechoslovak independence, a domestic military, and a police force. He settled for assurance of a peaceful invasion provided the Czechoslovak army surrendered immediately. Hácha addressed the citizenry on the radio, asking them to remain calm and informing them that he had "confidently placed the fate of the Czech people and country in the hands of the Führer and German Reich."[9]

At 4:30 in the morning of March 15, the people of Prague first heard the news that the German army had invaded and was approaching the capital. Before dawn, Nazi banners had replaced Czechoslovak flags throughout the city. Bewildered Prague citizens milled around the old city squares, leaving flowers at the monuments to Jan Hus, Saint Wenceslas, and František Palacký. Groups of Czechs stood weeping at the Jan Hus Memorial, and young men called out "German Swine!" to Nazi soldiers. Later that day, members of the German Wehrmacht stood at attention in front of Prague Castle's Baroque gates. Adolf Hitler, flanked by guards and Nazi officers, reviewed the troops and entered the first castle courtyard. Later that day, German soldiers stood below the castle offices to salute the Führer with cries of "Heil Hitler."

Journalist Milena Jesenská described the surreal first hours of occupation. "The city under our windows looked the same as it had on every other night.... Only the people were different. They stood and kept silent. I have never heard so many people be silent."[10] Jesenská credited Czech Radio, based in Prague, for keeping the citizens safe with "its concise objectivity, reporting patiently every five minutes without fail: the German army is proceeding from the borders to Prague." Czech radio announcers advised citizens to carry on with their daily lives: to go to work and send their children to school. Yet, according to Jesenská, "In two days' time, the image of the city has changed beyond recognition."

The day following the invasion, March 16, 1939, the Nazi state declared that it had absorbed "the Protectorate of Bohemia and Moravia" into the Reich. Hácha received the title of state president of the Protectorate, but all real authority was transferred to the *Reichsprotektor* Konstantin von Neurath, one of Hitler's chief foreign policy advisers. Hácha defended his capitulation as the only way to safeguard the nation. In an interview with writer Karel Horský, Hácha took credit for saving Prague: "As you know, Saint Wenceslas is still standing in his place. Charles Bridge is standing, too, the Castle district was not blown 'into the air,' and hundreds of thousands of our young people are still breathing and living."[11] Indeed, most Prague residents' daily activities continued undisturbed. The grand opening of the long-awaited New Town department store, Bílá Labuť (White Swan), took place as planned on March 19, 1939, only four days after the Nazi occupation of Prague. Equipped with Prague's first escalator, the largest glass facade in Central Europe, and a neon rotating swan on its roof, the eleven-story shopping paradise was supposed to represent Czech modernity, but the opening was anything but festive in the newly occupied city.

Within weeks of the invasion, the Reich confiscated the former government's foreign currency and gold reserves and subordinated Czechoslovak finances to the new regime. The German government took charge of Czechoslovakia's largest industries, which could directly support the German war effort. The profitable armament and transportation sectors represented the biggest prize of the Nazi incorporation of Bohemia and Moravia into the Reich. Mining and metallurgy doubled their prewar productivity levels, and Czechs were conscripted to work in these and other war-related industries. The German occupiers even changed traffic laws, forcing Bohemians and Moravians to drive on the right side of the road.

The Germans granted the Czechs a degree of autonomy within the Protectorate. Most government bureaucrats retained their roles in the state apparatus subsumed within Hácha's anti-democratic, anti-Semitic government. A report from Prague to Berlin indicated that four hundred thousand Czechs retained their positions in the civil service, and an additional two thousand Germans joined the bureaucracy to ensure compliance with Nazi goals. Former Czech citizens justified their cooperation as a way to maintain some Czech autonomy and argued that the situation would be even worse if Germans occupied their posts. Many Czechs felt that doing their jobs protected their families.

Several hundred thousand German personnel staffed police and paramilitary organizations in Bohemia and Moravia. Nazis increasingly infiltrated public and private institutions and asserted themselves in people's daily lives. The Gestapo (Secret State Police) set up its headquarters in the New Town's Petschek Palace, which housed offices, interrogation rooms, and criminal

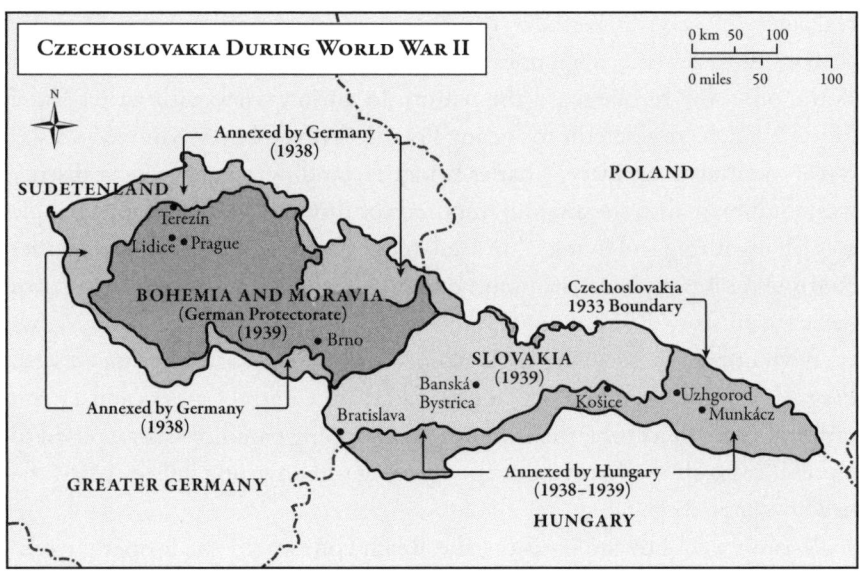

FIGURE 12.1   Czechoslovakia during World War II. In March 1939, Prague became the principal city of the Nazi-occupied Protectorate of Bohemia and Moravia.

courts. The SS (Schutzstaffel, Protection Squads), an elite paramilitary organization, and its subsidiary, the SD (Sicherheitsdienst, security service), also had branches in Prague. On March 27, 1939, General Johannes Blaskowitz, commander of the Werhmacht's occupation forces, led a military parade on Wenceslas Square. Blaskowitz visited the Tomb of the Unknown Soldier on Old Town Square and tenth-century archaeological sites at Prague Castle. The burial mounds discovered during the castle renovations in the 1920s suggested possible Baltic and Viking influence in Bohemia. The Nazi leadership used this as evidence of Prague's Germanic origins and threatened to arrest and incarcerate scholars who pointed to Slavic artifacts at the sites. The ultimate goal was the Germanification of Prague's past and present.

In the summer of 1939, Nazi laws took effect. The Regulation of Jewish Property Law declared that Jewish property belonged to Germany, and the 1935 Nuremberg Laws enforced racial definitions for Jews and *Mischlinge* (mixed race). Citizens could not travel in large groups, and itinerants—mainly Roma and Sinti—had to settle in permanent residences. In 1940, the Protectorate government began to construct concentration camps for these so-called "wandering gypsies." Jews' access to professions was radically curtailed, and they could no longer work in the civil service. The popular Czech Radio announcer Zdenka Walló, a gifted journalist who presented radio programs in several languages, was removed from her post for being half Jewish.

FIGURE 12.2 Visit of the commander in chief of the German army in Czechoslovakia, General Johannes Blaskowitz in Prague, March 27, 1939. National Digital Archives, State Treasury of Poland. Public domain, via Wikimedia Commons.

Czech authorities enforced the Nazis' "ghetto without walls," which isolated Jews from society, forbidding them to enter public swimming pools, cinemas, and parks. Novelist Jiří Weil recalled the confusion and fear: "I was forbidden to walk certain streets on certain days.... I had the names of all the streets and the days mixed up, and some of the streets I didn't even know. I imagined entering some street by chance...and suddenly a policeman would appear and arrest me."[12] Jewish survivors later described their shock that these rules existed in a city that had become rather tolerant of Jewish assimilation during the First Republic.

Meanwhile, most Prague residents tried to carry on with their normal lives as best they could. Journalist Milena Jesenská expressed disappointment in her fellow Czechs' ability to "behave wonderfully" amid an invasion. "They are polite on the tramways as they go to their jobs and schools as their nation falls apart." Dismayed, Jesenská wrote an article titled simply "March 15, 1939."

> In the German newspapers there was a story about the German soldiers who drove to Prague: a quiet city in a pre-spring dawn, a line of German vehicles and in them men with beating hearts: what will it be

like inside the city? How will people behave in these foreign streets? In the suburbs, they stop the first pedestrian, a laborer on his way to work.... He behaves calmly; quietly and peacefully he points the way.

Jesenská quoted a German officer who asked her why her countrymen greeted him so politely, as she warned her readers: "Servile behavior provokes only an ironical smile in the German of today, believe me." Jesenská took a different path. Through her friend Count Joachim von Zedtwitz, a Viennese medical student in Prague, she joined a resistance group that helped political fugitives and pilots cross into Poland. Jesenská's apartment became a meeting place for assembling paperwork and organizing the escapes. She encouraged Jewish friends to leave the country and provided shelter for individuals before they left Prague. The Jewish communist journalist Eugen Klinger hid at Jesenská's apartment before his escape. He begged his friend to escape with him, but she carried on her resistance work.

World War II began on September 1, 1939. The German invasion of Poland cut off the escape route used by Jesenská and Zedtwitz. Edvard Beneš came out of his self-imposed retirement and declared a Czechoslovak government in exile located in France. Several interwar politicians joined Beneš's group, including the moderate Catholic priest and People's Party leader Jan Šrámek and Jan Masaryk, a diplomat and the son of the former president.

Prague citizens took to the streets on October 28, 1939, the twenty-first anniversary of Czechoslovak statehood. Czech patriots from various political parties and civic organizations organized mass protests against the Nazi occupation. Thousands of citizens, wearing their Sunday clothes and black armbands, gathered on Wenceslas and Old Town Squares. Although the protests were relatively peaceful, four Czech university students died in confrontations with German soldiers. The Nazis arrested prominent interwar politicians and eighteen hundred teachers and students. Two weeks after the protests, a medical student, Jan Opletal, succumbed to wounds he sustained that day. His funeral on November 15 inspired more protests, and two days later, the Nazi regime shut down all universities and colleges in the Protectorate. Officials arrested and executed eight student leaders and a professor, all without trial. An additional twelve hundred students were arrested and sent to the Sachsenhausen concentration camp. Several newspapers and journals were shut down, and the rest were subjected to strict censorship. On the first anniversary of the reprisals, Beneš spoke from London, the new home of Czechoslovakia's government in exile, and declared November 17 "International Students Day."

The new regime targeted several of Prague's interwar cultural leaders that autumn. In November, the Nazi police apparatus targeted the liberal journal *Přítomnost*. Jesenská was arrested and sent to the Ravensbrück women's prison camp, where she died in 1944. The editor Ferdinand Peroutka, a close friend of Beneš and the Masaryk family, was also arrested in 1939. Peroutka refused the offer of freedom in exchange for collaborating with the Nazi press and survived imprisonment at Buchenwald. The Catholic theologian Alfred Fuchs, who had converted from Judaism, died in Dachau. The war claimed both Čapek brothers. Karel, devastated by the Munich Agreement, succumbed to illness in December 1938, and Josef died at Bergen-Belsen only weeks before the war's end. In a poem written during his imprisonment, Čapek assured his loved ones that his spirit remained in Prague: "I was there in body, but in spirit, with all of you... Oh yes—it is me. Only my body stayed behind, there in the foreign land."[13]

Small signs of resistance appeared in Prague in the first months of the war. Citizens marked public places with the letter "V," a nod to Winston Churchill's famous gesture, as well as the first initial of the Czech word for victory, *vítězství*. The campaign enraged Nazi leaders, and propaganda minister Joseph Goebbels ordered the Nazi leadership in Prague to take control of the propaganda. Claiming that the signs stood for the Latin phrase *veni, vidi, vici* (I came, I saw, I conquered), the regime added *V*s to buildings and signs throughout Prague. However, they could not erase the Czechs' intended meaning, and their efforts became the butt of Czech jokes. The Germans suspected Czech workers of sabotaging industrial production, but work slowdowns were infrequent. Czechs tuned in to short-wave radio broadcasts by Jan Masaryk and members of the London government in exile. Listening to foreign radio programs was illegal and could result in harsh prison sentences.

Most Czechs felt they had little choice but to accept the occupation and avoid violent reprisals. Daily life had become increasingly difficult as the German occupiers co-opted the entire economy for the war effort. Heavy industry replaced consumer goods, and stringent food rationing forced Czechs to improvise nutritious meals. One conservative women's group published a recipe book that taught women how to make soups and meatloaf without meat. Once Germany invaded the Soviet Union in June 1941, Czech rations dropped significantly as supplies and food were sent to the Eastern Front. Factory workers and others deemed essential to the war effort received higher ration amounts, but Prague's office workers could buy only ten ounces of meat per week. The average amounts of flour, fats, potatoes, and eggs consumed during the war dropped to about half of prewar levels.

Life became increasingly difficult for Prague Jews, and few Christians extended aid to their Jewish neighbors. Some clergy provided Jews with falsified baptismal certificates, but the Roman Catholic Church in the former Czechoslovakia did not have a good record of rescue compared to other European countries. There were exceptions to the passive acceptance of German anti-Semitic policy, with individuals sheltering friends or organizing escapes and *Kindertransports*. Beneš's London government in exile tried to inspire resistance activities at home. Domestic opposition groups consolidated under the banner ÚVOD (Ústřední vedení odboje domácího, Central Leadership of Home Resistance) to facilitate communication with the London government. ÚVOD published and distributed propaganda, communicated with allies abroad, and organized sabotage activities in industry, transportation, and civil society. The most common form of resistance was sending information to the London government through couriers or shortwave radios. Alois Eliáš, the prime minister in Hácha's Prague government, provided secret information to Beneš while feigning loyalty to Germany.

The Communist Party maintained its own resistance movement, which provided intelligence to Moscow once the war had spread to the Soviet Union. Prominent Communist leaders, such as Klement Gottwald and Zdeněk Nejedlý, spent the war in the Soviet Union. Prague's Communist daily newspaper *Rudé právo* temporarily abandoned the call for class struggle and supported a national coalition against fascism that included members of the Sokol, supporters of Beneš, liberals, socialists, and communists. The attack on the Soviet Union inspired acts of sabotage throughout the Protectorate—resistors burned railway cars, destroyed rail tracks, severed air brakes on trains, and cut telephone wires. Although most public gatherings were forbidden, Czechs attended mass, church festivals, and funerals wearing national costumes.

Once Germany had invaded the Soviet Union in June 1941, the Nazis needed to ensure their conquered territories were subdued. Hitler believed his Prague regime treated the Czechs too leniently and sought to solve the "Czech question." In September 1941, Hitler appointed Reinhard Heydrich as acting *Reichsprotektor* of Bohemia and Moravia. One of the most brutal leaders in the Nazi regime, Heydrich had been an SS member since 1931, directed the SD, and masterminded the Kristallnacht pogrom of November 1938. Tall and handsome, he represented the Aryan physical ideal. Some have speculated that Hitler feared Heydrich's charisma and ambition and wanted him out of Berlin. Or he may have merely selected the most ruthless of his upper echelon to subdue the Czechs. In preparation for Heydrich's arrival in

Prague, Goebbels ordered that "full Jews" over age six wear a Star of David starting on September 19, 1941.

Heydrich took office ten days later and soon earned the moniker "the Butcher of Prague." Within hours of his arrival in Prague, the Nazi government arrested and imprisoned Prime Minister Eliáš for sending information to the government in exile. A year later, he was executed at the Kobylisy firing range. Heydrich ordered the public hanging of two hundred Czechs and announced plans to transport Jews from Prague. In January 1942, Heydrich called the Wannsee Conference, where Nazi Party leaders planned the implementation of the "Final Solution to the Jewish Question."

The acting *Reichsprotektor* used a carrot-and-stick approach to leading the Protectorate: "I need peace in this territory in order that the Czech worker may devote all his working energy to the German war effort, so that the enormous war industry which exists here works smoothly and expands itself," Heydrich announced to his officers. He increased fat rations for workers and maintained high employment in industry while also threatening reprisals for any infraction against the state. As he explained, "We do not want to win over these people, we do not want this, and we would not succeed in it anyway. We shall only explain very clearly in practical life to everybody, by propaganda, measures, et cetera, that for the Czech it is really advantageous if at this moment he works a lot."[14] The Czechs' place in a Nazi racial framework preoccupied Heydrich. He and Hitler believed that some Czechs—especially those with Nordic features—could be Germanized, as they had long benefited from German leadership. Heydrich ordered racial studies on Protectorate citizens under the pretext of tuberculosis screenings, but the regime never followed through on bringing worthy Czechs into the German fold.

Heydrich intended to make the Protectorate *Judenrein* (free of Jews) as soon as possible. Transports of Jewish citizens from Prague began a month after Heydrich's arrival. Between October 1941 and March 1945, 46,067 members of Prague's Jewish population were forcibly deported from the city. Writer Heda Margolius Kovály recalled the day in October 1941 when her transport to an unknown destination left Prague. "The order was to report to the Exposition Hall, to bring food for several days, and essential baggage. No more." Holešovice's functionalist Trade Fair Palace, which symbolized modernity when it opened in 1928, became a "medieval madhouse" where people were organized for captivity and death. Kovály and thousands of fellow Jews walked to the Bubný Train Station, carrying up to fifty kilograms of belongings. After an agonizing journey, Kovály arrived at the Łódź Ghetto in Poland. Toward the end of the war, Kovály and some friends escaped during a death march from Auschwitz. Yet when she returned to Prague, several old friends refused to help her hide, fearful of Nazi reprisals, apartment searches, and identity checkpoints. "During those years Prague had changed, perhaps even more than I had," she wrote.[15]

Most Prague Jews first went to Theresienstadt (Terezín), a former Habsburg military fortress less than forty miles from the city. There the Nazis had created a Jewish ghetto to serve as a forced-labor and transit camp. Of the 140,000 Jews who lived in Theresienstadt during the war, at least 90,000 were sent to Auschwitz, Treblinka, and other death camps. Another 33,000 died of starvation and disease in Theresienstadt. The Nazis used Theresienstadt as a model camp for propaganda purposes and allowed inmates to perform music and take art classes. Prague-based musicians Viktor Ullman, Rafael Schächter, Gideon Klein, and many others gave concerts. The Prague Jewish composer Hans Krása reworked *Brundibar,* a Czech children's opera he had written in 1938. Krása gave singing classes in Theresienstadt and produced fifty-five performances of the opera. In 1944, the Nazis succumbed to pressure by the Danish government and hosted a delegation from the International Red Cross. Prisoners were forced to clean the camp, erect swing sets, and pretend to be happy and well fed. The Red Cross representatives watched a performance of *Brundibar*, which the Nazis filmed for use in propaganda. The completed film depicted joyful, healthy residents, and referred to the ghetto a "spa town" and Hitler's "gift" to the Jews. Following the Danish visit, the pace of deportations from Theresienstadt accelerated. The great majority of children who sang in *Brundibar* perished. Krása was murdered in Auschwitz in 1944.

The Bauhaus artist Friedl Dicker-Brandeis taught children's drawing classes until she was deported to Auschwitz, where she died in 1944. Helga Hošková (née Weissová), who survived the war and became a professional artist, considered her drawings a documentation of life in Theresienstadt. Her father told her, "Draw what you see." Her pictures captured daily life in the ghetto: women carrying heavy bags as a sneering German soldier looked on, a group of prisoners bathing at a sink under a sign warning "Save Water," and children waiting in line for meager rations.[16]

A small number of Prague Jews remained in Prague during the war. Some Jewish men performed forced labor: digging ditches, building roads, clearing snow, or staffing the city's cemeteries. A few Jewish women were retained for menial jobs. Yad Vashem, the Holocaust Memorial in Israel, has accounted for 227 survivors who hid or stayed "underground" in Prague. Only 5,000 Prague Jews survived the war. In Jiří Weil's semi-autobiographical novel *Life with a Star*, the protagonist Josef Roubíček does not report for his transport order. He spends the war working at a cemetery and hiding in an attic flat with only a cat for a companion. When Josef ventures out, he notices people sitting at the restaurants and cafés he had once enjoyed. In his mind, a policeman waits around every corner to check his identity card.

Weil himself was assigned to work at Prague's Jewish Museum. In 1942, the Nazi regime restored its management to the Prague Jewish community and tasked the Jewish art historian Josef Polák and his small staff with cataloging the museum's holdings and valuing objects stolen from synagogues throughout the Protectorate. Stories arose that Hitler planned to use Prague to build a museum of the "extinct race," but there is little evidence to support this. Few Jewish museum workers survived the war. When Weil received deportation orders, he staged his own suicide and went into hiding. The museum specialist Hana Volavková also survived and later recalled her colleagues' efforts:

> They had no illusions they were carrying out great work. They formed a very modest picture of their efforts and managed to see that it was an act of desperation that was nevertheless secretly underlined by an element of resistance and an element of free-will that stood up to a monstrous mechanism, which was heading in an unknown direction, but which was grinding them down.... The establishment and existence of the Jewish Museum in Prague was paid for by the lives of nearly all those who worked there during the war. It was these people—people who were to die without burial—who documented most of the material. It was these people who laid the foundations for the post-war museum and its future programme.[17]

While Czech Jews faced deportation and death, Heydrich envisioned making Prague the cultural center of the new Reich. He revived the city's German heritage and sponsored operas and orchestral performances of Mozart operas and Beethoven symphonies. He outlawed Czech cultural groups and celebrations, as well as any public acknowledgment of the Hussite heritage. Czechs could attend approved sporting and cultural events, and the two Prague football teams, Sparta and Slavia, attracted large crowds. Theaters staged preapproved Czech plays, and Barrandov studios released apolitical comedies and romance films. The studio head Miloš Havel cooperated with the regime by making newsreels and propaganda for the German government. Publishing houses continued to operate but could only print books approved by the censorship boards.

FIGURE 12.3 Jewish women sort confiscated textiles for the Jewish Museum of Prague. Report on the Year 1943, Council of Elders of the Jews (Bericht über das Jahr 1943, Ältestenrat der Juden). Creative Commons CC0 License via Wikimedia Commons.

Life in the Protectorate became a surreal blend of terror and diversion. Anti-fascist artists met secretly in Prague. Skupina 42 (Group 42) included poets, painters, sculptors, and photographers who promoted civilism: observations of everyday life enhanced by magical realism. Member Jiří Kolář published his first collection of poetry, *Křestný list* (Baptismal certificate), declaring, "You are as heavy as thunder, Poetry." In Kamil Lhoták's 1942 painting, *The Man Free of Gravity*, a man strolls through the sky oblivious to the bleak landscape beneath.

In London, the Czechoslovak government in exile wanted to spark the resistance movement at home, and with the assistance of Royal Air Force commandos, Beneš approved an assassination plot against acting *Reichsprotektor* Heydrich. The Royal Air Force trained Czech and Slovak pilots, who parachuted into Bohemia and met up with resistance members. On May 27, 1942, Jan Kubiš and Josef Gabčík stationed themselves in Holešovice, where Heydrich rode each morning on his way to work. When Heydrich's green open-topped Mercedes 320 Cabriolet B stopped to make a sharp turn, Gabčík jumped into the street and aimed his weapon. When the gun jammed, Heydrich made the fatal mistake of standing up and firing at the assassin with his own pistol. Kubiš took the opportunity to hurl a grenade, damaging Heydrich's vehicle and blowing out the windows of a nearby tramcar. Shrapnel from the Mercedes and the tram entered Heydrich, damaging his spleen and liver and causing internal bleeding. Heydrich's condition appeared to improve, but sepsis set in. He died in Prague on June 4, 1942.

The *Reichsprotektor* received two state funerals, one in Prague and one in Berlin. Hitler ordered a wave of reprisals. Over two thousand members of the Czech elite were arrested and executed. The SS executed 550 prisoners at Prague's Kobylisy Shooting Range, including interwar feminist politician Františka Plamínková and filmmaker Vladislav Vančura. Their bodies were taken to the Strašnice Crematorium in a Prague suburb, and their remains were never found. In the meantime, Kubiš, Gabčík, and five resistance members took refuge in the crypt of the Orthodox Church of Cyril and Methodius near the National Theater. An anonymous tip led the Gestapo to the church, where three fugitives were shot and four men took their own lives with cyanide pills. The Gestapo arrested and executed Bishop Matthias Goražd, two priests, and ten congregation members.

The Nazi leadership was determined to stamp out all resistance in the Protectorate. Karl Hermann Frank, a German Sudeten politician who had risen to head of the Protectorate's police forces, organized the destruction of Lidice, a Bohemian village close to Prague. Its 173 men were murdered, and its women and children were taken to concentration camps. A handful of Lidice's children were selected for Aryanization and adopted into German families, but the majority were murdered in mobile gas vans. The Nazi police razed the village and even diverted the nearby river so that Lidice would be wiped off the face of the earth. Two weeks later, the nearby village of Ležáky met the same fate. The Nazi regime flaunted its crimes, publishing pictures of the victims and their destroyed villages on newspapers' front pages. Czechoslovakia's London government in exile declared the violence in Prague, Lidice, and Ležáky "the most dastardly German act since the Dark Ages." The reprisals succeeded in curtailing Czech resistance in the Protectorate. A few Czechs with contacts abroad continued to pass information to London and Moscow, but most Prague citizens kept their heads down, went to work, and hoped the war would end soon.

The atrocities of June 1942 became fodder for allied propaganda. American and British leaders expressed shock and outrage, and prominent writers and artists addressed the murders in their work. American poets

Edna St. Vincent Millay and Langston Hughes wrote about Lidice, and British writer Cecil Day-Lewis read his stirring ode on the BBC radio: "Cry to us, murdered village while your grave arches raw on history, make us understand what freedom asks of us."[18] In 1943, the Museum of Modern Art in New York curated an exhibition of Czech anti-fascist art. Its centerpiece was the iconic poster "Wanted in Prague" by the exiled Czechoslovak artist Adolf Hoffmeister. A caricature of Hitler on a blood-red background depicted a frightened Führer holding his hands in the air as if surrendering for his crimes. (See Color Plate 16.)

Prague was far from Europe's battlelines, and the city's infrastructure remained unscathed for most of the war. On February 14, 1945, US pilots made a navigational error en route to Dresden and dropped over 150 tons of explosives on Prague's residential neighborhoods. The bombs destroyed the Gothic towers of the Emmaus Monastery on the Vltava's right embankment. The Palacký Bridge, which the Germans had renamed for Mozart, was also hit. Myslbek's statues of Czech mythological heroes toppled into the river. The bombs also struck the neo-Renaissance synagogue in Vinohrady, one of the largest Jewish temples in the world. The Valentine's Day bombing raid caused 701 civilian deaths and 1,184 injuries. Just over a month later, on March 25, the United States intentionally bombed Prague factories. The Palm Sunday raid killed 235 civilians, but the United States chose a holiday to minimize human casualties.

In the last months of the war, as the Red Army pushed westward, Beneš worked closely with Slovak leaders, setting up a temporary government in Košice, Slovakia. In March 1945, he and members of the London government traveled to Moscow to negotiate a reconstitution of Czechoslovakia. Beneš believed that Czechoslovakia could create a bridge between the East and West, and he planned to maintain strong relations with Britain and the Soviet Union after the war ended. Whether the new Europe would allow that remained to be seen. The armed uprising, which the poets Halas and Seifert had called for in 1939, came in the waning days of the war. Hitler had already killed himself, and German troops were retreating west, hoping to surrender to the Allies rather than the Red Army. On May 5, 1945, Czech policemen entered the Nazi-occupied radio building in Prague, killing German guards and taking over the broadcast. Upon hearing the rebels shout, "Calling all Czechs! Calling all Czechs!" over the radio, citizens grabbed rifles, constructed barricades on Prague streets, tore down German symbols, and hung Czech flags. A National Council occupied the basement of Old Town Hall, and on May 7, the German army destroyed much of the building. Four days of

FIGURE 12.4 The Vinohrady Synagogue, built in 1896, was hit during a US air raid in February 1945. William A. Rosenthall Judaica Collection—Postcards, College of Charleston Libraries, Charleston, SC, USA. Courtesy of Special Collections, College of Charleston Library.

fighting on the streets of Prague and at the Masaryk train station claimed the lives of at least one thousand German soldiers and about three thousand Czech civilians.

When Germany surrendered in France, the National Council agreed to a ceasefire, and the German army and Nazi staff retreated west. When the Red Army arrived in Prague on May 9, most German troops had evacuated, and Prague's residents flooded to Wenceslas Square to greet the liberators. After the war, different groups characterized the May uprising according to their political ideologies: a national revolution, a spontaneous demonstration by Czech workers, or the Red Army's liberation of Prague. The young Czech writer Josef Škvorecký challenged these myths. In his ironic novel *The Cowards*, young men join the Czech resistance to impress their girlfriends rather than to stand for democratic or socialist ideals.

Beneš returned to Prague on May 16. Crowds welcomed him at the station, just as they had greeted Masaryk twenty-seven years earlier. Beneš had high hopes for the future of his beloved country. He advocated cooperation with the Soviet Union and compromise with the Communist Party of Czechoslovakia. During the summer of 1945, Beneš honored two war heroes: General Ivan Konev, commander of the Red Army troops that liberated Prague, and General George S. Patton, whose Third Army drove the Germans out of the westernmost region of Czechoslovakia. These state visits reasserted Beneš's hope that Czechoslovakia could become a bridge between Eastern and Western Europe.

Although the Czechoslovak constitution provided only a limited role for the country's president, Beneš followed Masaryk's example and asserted executive power. In his first months back in Prague, he signed several decrees that changed the direction of Czechoslovak history. These included nationalizing much of the country's economic sector: Mines, fourteen large banks, six hundred smaller financial institutions, and insurance companies were brought under state control. Factories and large industries were likewise taken over, converting 62 percent of the industrial workforce to state employment. In October 1945, the National Assembly confirmed Beneš as Czechoslovak president, and the following June, he was reelected by popular vote.

Beneš also signed off on procedures for punishing war criminals and collaborators. Czechoslovaks were encouraged to denounce suspected Nazi collaborators. This pitted neighbor against neighbor and sometimes led to petty accusations. Yet thousands of war criminals were brought to justice.

FIGURE 12.5 General George S. Patton Jr. is awarded the Order of the White Lion and the Military Cross, First Class, by President Beneš of Czechoslovakia, during Patton's visit to Prague, Czechoslovakia, July 27, 1945. Photo by Norbie, 165th Signal Photographic Company, National Archives Photo no. 276537120.

Hácha died in prison awaiting trial, Henlein died by suicide while in American captivity, and von Neurath served fifteen years in prison. Walter Schmitt, head of the SS personnel office in Prague, and Karl Hermann Frank, the mastermind of the Lidice and Ležáky massacres, were executed in Prague. The Czechoslovak government held the entire German population of Bohemia and Moravia responsible for the Nazi occupation. Beneš ordered the confiscation of German property and the expulsion of the country's three million Germans. Bent on revenge, groups of Czech vigilantes violently forced out German families whose connection to Bohemia went back centuries. Approximately three million German speakers were expelled, and over twenty thousand Germans died during the so-called "wild expulsions." Although provisions existed for anti-fascist Germans to stay in Czechoslovakia, it was difficult to prove one's wartime loyalties.

In 1946, Czechoslovakia held elections for the newly created federal parliament. The Communist Party of Czechoslovakia outperformed all other

FIGURE 12.6 Marshal of the Soviet Union I. S. Konev and Army General A. I. Eremenko were inducted into the Czechoslovak Order of the White Lion on June 6, 1945. The ceremony at Prague Castle acknowledged Czechoslovakia's debt to the Soviet Union and Red Army for liberating most of the country. Photo by Alexander Ustinov. Mil.ru, CC BY 4.0, https://creativecommons.org/licenses/by/4.0, via Wikimedia Commons.

parties, earning 38 percent of the vote. Prague's electoral outcome mirrored the country's results, with 36 percent of citizens voting for the Communist Party. A left-leaning coalition of Communists, Social Democrats, and Czechoslovak socialists formed a government with Klement Gottwald as prime minister. Before the war, the Communist Party usually received about 10 percent of the votes, but its popularity skyrocketed during the war. The perception that Britain and France had abandoned Czechoslovakia and the Red Army's role in defeating the Germans led to unprecedented support for the Communist Party.

◆

The demographics of Prague's Jewish community changed significantly following the war. Prague Jews who survived the war often came home to find their apartments looted or occupied by new people. Artist Helga Hošková (née Weissová) and her mother had to fight with Prague city housing authorities to move back into their prewar apartment. Other survivors testified that neighbors refused to return their possessions, and Czechoslovak authorities sometimes refused to repatriate property to German-speaking Jewish survivors. Some returnees, however, reported receiving help settling back into Prague.[19]

In the years following the war, over two hundred thousand Jews crossed into Czechoslovakia from Poland en route to refugee camps in Germany and Austria. A small number of these survivors stayed in Prague. Thousands of Jews from the eastern provinces of Slovakia and sub-Carpathian Ruthenia migrated to Bohemia, and many settled in Prague. When asked about their reasons for migrating, Slovak Jews cited the anti-Semitism they faced under the Slovak fascist regime, while Ruthenians wanted to attach themselves to Czechoslovakia since the Soviet Union had annexed their region. Many of the new settlers practiced Orthodox Judaism, which had not been common among Prague Jews. With help from Jewish organizations abroad, the new community in Prague acquired ritual objects and installed *mikvot* (ritual baths).

Prague struggled to recover from its six-year occupation. Heda Margolius Kovály recalled the skyrocketing prices on the black market and the endless lines for ration cards and residence permits. The city survived the war with little physical damage, especially compared to Warsaw, Berlin, and Dresden, but its citizens were exhausted from their ordeal. The city assessed the landmarks bombed in February 1945. The Palacký Bridge was rebuilt, but Myslbek's statues of ancient Czech heroes were relocated to Vyšehrad. Emmaus Monastery's new modern steeples served as a memorial of the occupation and the bombing. The city decided not to rebuild the damaged sections of Old Town Hall as a reminder of the sacrifices of May 1945. Various groups in Prague debated the fate of the Vinohrady Synagogue, which an incendiary bomb had hit. The Czech city council proposed renovating the damaged building to create a new gym and cultural center for the Sokol. At the same time, the Jewish community petitioned to build a small prayer hall and a residence to house Holocaust survivors. The debate reflected the unanswered questions about what Jewish life would look like in postwar Prague.

Prague made it through the war, but the situation was tenuous. Other countries in the region—Poland, Romania, and Yugoslavia—had declared themselves "People's Democracies." Europe was swiftly dividing along a Cold War fault line. With pressure from Moscow, Czechoslovak leaders declined the United States' offer of Marshall Plan funds. Rather than a bridge between East and West, Prague was moving further toward Moscow. Postwar economic recovery was slow, and many citizens had lost trust in the prewar democratic parties. The city's residents remained divided about the best course for their capital and country.

13

Prague Winter, Prague Spring

IN EARLY 1948, the Communist Party intensified its drive to overtake the Czechoslovak government. Prime Minister Klement Gottwald boasted that the Party would win 51 percent of the national vote in the next election, but the Communist leadership knew its popularity had been slipping. Tensions within the fragile coalition government came to a head in February when Václav Nosek, the Communist minister of the interior, illegally purged noncommunist officers from the national police force. Twelve noncommunist cabinet ministers resigned in protest, believing that President Beneš would call for a new coalition. The ministers had miscalculated. Representatives of sympathetic left-wing parties, such as the influential Social Democrat Zdeněk Fierlinger, threw their support toward Gottwald, and Foreign Minister Jan Masaryk remained neutral.

Party leaders took advantage of the chaos. Communist action committees and leftist student groups filled Prague's streets on February 21, as Gottwald told trade unions to prepare for a general strike. The novelist Milan Kundera described the frigid Saturday in February: "Gottwald stepped out on the balcony of a Baroque palace in Prague to harangue hundreds of thousands of citizens massed in Old Town Square.... Gottwald in a fur hat, surrounded by his comrades, spoke to the people. On that balcony the history of Communist Bohemia began."[1]

Gottwald pushed Beneš to accept the ministers' resignations and appoint the slate the Party had prepared. He warned him of Moscow's growing impatience. On February 25, fearing civil war or a Soviet invasion, the weakened and sickly president capitulated. Later that afternoon, Gottwald greeted his followers on Wenceslas Square: "I have just returned from the castle from meeting the President....[He] accepted all my proposals as they were submitted."[2] The jubilant crowd celebrated its "Victorious February" in Prague's cold night air. The Communist Party would rule in Prague for the next four decades.

Upon Gottwald's announcement on Wenceslas Square, opponents and supporters of the new government assembled on Prague's streets. The liberal

French newspaper *Le Monde* compared Prague that evening to the 1938 Nazi invasion:

> Yesterday, you felt that you had been transported ten years back in time. The same unspoken emotions are shown, in women by tears, in men by the way in which they saluted.... But the police quickly dispersed the "reactionary" groups which vanished as soon as the columns mobilized by the Communist Party branches appeared. During the evening, the city was entirely given over to this crowd, not particularly revolutionary but perfectly disciplined, which walked up and down Wenceslas Square, the main city thoroughfare.[3]

Only two weeks after the February events, the foreign minister and son of Tomáš Masaryk was found dead. Jan Masaryk's body was discovered in the courtyard of the Baroque Černín Palace, which housed the Foreign Ministry. Authorities ruled that Masaryk, who suffered bouts of severe depression, had jumped to his death from his private apartment window. Yet, some anti-communists believed that the secret police had thrown Masaryk from the window; they referred to the death as the Third Defenestration of Prague.

Beneš suffered health setbacks and resigned in June 1948, clearing the way for Gottwald to become president. Isolated anti-communist protests broke out in the spring and summer, the most notable led by the Sokol association, but the state police apparatus swiftly quelled any dissent. Gottwald and his family moved to Prague Castle, "where the 'first proletarian president' lived surrounded by aristocratic opulence."[4] Other high-ranking Party members claimed luxurious villas on the left bank. The capital of a worker's democracy was becoming a kleptocracy that privileged only a select few Party leaders. Gottwald modeled his cult of personality on Stalin, and his image dominated May Day parades and other state holidays.

Edvard Beneš died on September 3, 1948, and the Communist Party honored him with a state funeral. Beneš's body lay in state on Vítkov Hill, where citizens queued for hours to pay their respects. Following the public visitation, Beneš's flag-draped coffin was taken to the National Museum on Wenceslas Square for the funeral and then to his burial place in southern Bohemia. The Communist daily newspaper *Rudé právo* lauded the deceased leader:

> Honorable President!
> During these days all the people of Prague bid you farewell with this manifesto.... On Vítkov hill, the site of the most celebrated

FIGURE 13.1 Members of the military and other Czechoslovak citizens march in a May Day parade in Prague carrying posters with Gottwald's image, early 1950s. Photo by Bauer Sándor for Fortepan, CC BY-SA 3.0, https://creativecommons.org/licenses/by-sa/3.0, via Wikimedia Commons

battle in the history of the Czech people—fought by the ancestors of today's democratic order—you symbolize the culmination of this centuries-long national struggle, not only as a spiritual leader, but as an intrepid warrior.[5]

The Communist Party had tried to demonstrate its legitimacy by honoring the popular former president. By tying themselves to Beneš, the Communist leadership communicated that the February takeover had been a legal transfer of power. Their plan backfired. Prague citizens took advantage of the public commemorations to protest the new government. Soon after, the Party changed its tactic and cast Beneš as a member of the interwar elite bourgeoisie. Before the 1948 coup, the Communist leadership promoted a moderate "Czechoslovak road to socialism" and promised to find a place for the urban middle class. Beneš's government had already carried out a large-scale nationalization of industry and transportation, but in 1948, the Czechoslovak Communists went after small business owners and so-called petty traders. A combination of pressure from Moscow and the Cominform and Gottwald's confidence pushed the Party in this radical direction. Propaganda blamed the "reactionary urban bourgeoisie" for class inequities in Czechoslovakia and called for the nationalization of even the smallest businesses.

In 1948, fashion designer Hana Podolská, known as the Czech Coco Chanel, saw her design studio nationalized and subsumed under the state enterprise Fashion House Prague. Karel Pačes's small liquor manufactory in Prague's Strašnice district, Jaroslav and Linda Vašata's popular restaurants in the Municipal Hall and on Wenceslas Square, and hundreds of other stores, bakeries, and workshops were seized. Entrepreneurs were expected to transition into state employees and run the firms they had founded. Podolská continued to work as a designer at her former firm until her sudden retirement in 1954. Other business owners refused to comply, and a wave of arrests shook the business sector. Pačes and Vašata joined sixty thousand fellow citizens who fled Czechoslovakia during the first two years of Communist rule.

The Czechoslovak state did not have the capacity to absorb the personnel and equipment from the private sector, and the economic repercussions were dire. Prague residents later recalled the difficult first years of communism, when supplies were low and prices skyrocketed. Heda Margolius Kovály described Prague in the early 1950s: "The city once again looked like an anthill that someone had stirred up with a stick. People were rushing nervously through the streets and forming long lines on the sidewalks in front of every store."[6] The new command economy favored large-scale industry over consumer goods, and the first Five Year Plan (1949–1953) focused on metallurgy and defense.

Small business owners were not the only citizens to face persecution. The Communist Party's political enemies, both inside and outside the Party, were victims of purges and trumped-up accusations. Show trials modeled on the Stalinist terror in the Soviet Union were broadcast on the radio and covered extensively in the press. The trial of Milada Horáková, a feminist politician in the Czechoslovak Socialist Party, garnered worldwide attention. A member of the anti-Nazi resistance, Horáková spent much of the war in concentration camps, only to be arrested and tortured by the new Czechoslovak regime. Luminaries such as Albert Einstein, Winston Churchill, and Eleanor Roosevelt petitioned for her release to no avail. Her execution at Prague's Pankrác prison on June 27, 1950, was the first and only political execution of a woman in Czechoslovak history. Moments before her death, Horáková stated, "I have lost this fight, but I leave with honor. I love this country; I love this nation. Strive for their wellbeing."[7]

Roman Catholic leaders also faced mass arrests and show trials. Article 17 of the new constitution stated, "Everyone is free to practice his religion, or to be without confession. The practicing of this must however not be in discord with public order or with good morals." This caveat enabled the Party to imprison hundreds of bishops, priests, and nuns in jails or work camps. In October 1949, the parliament gave the state authority to monitor the Catholic Church and other religious groups. *Rudé právo* warned that "Western capitalists" had imposed anti-communist activities and "villainous aims" upon the Catholic clergy. The archbishop of Prague, Josef Beran, opposed the parliamentary decree. He was placed under house arrest and then imprisoned from 1950 to 1963. Nine members of Roman Catholic religious orders were found guilty of conspiring with foreign powers to overthrow the state. The abbot of Břevnov Monastery, Anastáz Jan Opasek, served a multiyear prison term and became a bricklayer following his release. Church property was nationalized, and only priests deemed sufficiently loyal retained their positions and state salaries.[8]

The Party also took control of the Jewish community. In 1951, the Party demolished the Vinohrady Synagogue, which had been damaged in the 1945 air raid. When the Jewish community asked to use the salvaged bricks to renovate the synagogue in Prague's Libeň district, the Party refused, indicating that these were strategic materials owned by the state. The Party nationalized the Prague Jewish Museum, which comprised five historic synagogues and the Old Jewish Cemetery. Art historian and Holocaust survivor Hana Volavková returned to the museum as its director and spearheaded a project to renovate the Pinkas synagogue and turn it into a memorial for the nearly eighty thousand Bohemian and Moravian Jews who perished in the Holocaust. From 1955 to 1960, artists painted the names and hometowns of every victim onto Pinkas's walls. The entire nave was covered with names from Prague alone. As Volavková explained, these individuals once "degraded to numbers and transports during the war" have "obtained their homes and human faces again."[9] Prague Jewish writer and survivor Jiří Weil worked as a senior librarian at the museum and composed *Lamentations for 77,297 Victims*, which featured vignettes of individual Jewish lives cut short by the murderous regime: a starving old man who spills the soup he waited for, a woman who discovers her stolen thermos in a Terezín shop window, a laborer pushed off a tramcar who breaks his leg and lacerates his face. Weil juxtaposed his stories alongside verses from the Hebrew Bible: "The psalmist cries out 'My tears have been my bread, day and night.'"[10] Each March, the Jewish community held a commemoration for the four thousand Czech Jews who were murdered at Auschwitz in a single night.

FIGURE 13.2 Prague. Pinkas Synagogue. *Memorial to the 77,297 victims of Nazi persecution*. Praha. Pinkasova synagoga—Památník 77.297 obětí nacistického pronásledování. William A. Rosenthall Judaica Collection—Postcards, College of Charleston Libraries, Charleston, SC, USA. Courtesy of Special Collections, College of Charleston Library.

Mistrust and rivalry within the Czechoslovak Communist Party leadership manifested in a virulent anti-Semitism. In November 1951, General Secretary Rudolf Slánský, who grew up in a Jewish family, was arrested and accused of treason. Almost overnight, Slánský went from the second most important man in the state to the accused ringleader of a treasonous group in the Party's upper echelons. The following year, the Party named another thirteen high-ranking government officials in Prague as Slánský's co-conspirators. Of the fourteen Slánský trial defendants, eleven were Jews. The Party newspaper accounts listed the defendants who were "of Jewish origin," implying this was evidence of their disloyalty. Cold War political tension drove much of the era's anti-Semitic hysteria. The new Israeli state had allied with the United States, giving the West a strong foothold in the Middle East. The Czechoslovak Party attacked Zionism and investigated Party members with foreign ties. Among the defendants in the Slánský case were veterans of the Spanish Civil

War, members of the Czechoslovak government in exile, Holocaust survivors, and husbands of West European women.

Former concentration camp prisoners Rudolph Margolius and Artur London were accused of using their status as survivors to infiltrate the Party. London's memoir, written in exile many years later, provided a window into the anti-Semitism directed at the defendants. London claimed that a secret police interrogator told him, "We'll get rid of you and your filthy race!... Not everything Hitler did was right, but he destroyed the Jews, and he was right about that." London's mother, sister, and dozens of other relatives had died in concentration camps, but London reported that the interrogators taunted him: "Too many of you escaped the gas chamber. We'll finish what [Hitler] started."[11] While London's book has been criticized for fabrications and omissions, few can doubt the anti-Jewish underpinning of the trial. The prosecutors called the accused "Jewish bourgeois nationalists... Jewish racketeers, industrialists, and bourgeois elements."

All fourteen defendants pleaded guilty to charges of conspiracy and treason. The state broadcast parts of the eight-day trial on the radio, enabling Prague residents to hear the testimonies of well-known Communist leaders. The edited broadcasts were so compelling that even some of the defendants' wives—Lise London and Marion Šling—doubted their husbands' innocence. Defendant Otto Šling testified, "As an enemy inside the Czechoslovak Communist Party and in my hatred of the USSR, I spread mistrust of the Soviet Union among the members of the Czechoslovak Communist Party in London."[12] The court sentenced eleven defendants to death, while three escaped with a life sentence. When Rudolph Margolius's widow expressed disbelief in the outcome, his lawyer replied, "What did you expect? After all, your husband confessed." The eleven men were hanged just before dawn on December 3, 1951. Their ashes, mingled together, were scattered on an icy road just outside Prague.

Decades later, Margolius, London, and Šling's widows spoke out against the anti-Semitism that pervaded the proceedings. Czechoslovak citizens did not learn about the forced, rehearsed, and memorized confessions until the late 1960s. In his semi-autobiographical story, "A Race Through Prague," the Jewish writer Ota Pavel revealed his father's distraught reaction to the trial. An ardent Communist who escaped from a concentration camp, Pavel's father weeps while he reads the Party newspaper. He tells his son,

> "They're killing Jews again. They're looking for someone to blame it on all over again.... I can forgive murder—even judicial murder, even political murder. But a Communist newspaper should never print 'of

Jewish origin.' The Communists are dividing people up all over again, into Jews and non-Jews." And then he punched *Rudé právo* again, and it fell apart as though it had been made of rotten winter leaves.[13]

◆

Even during the repressive era of early communism, the Party leaders sought to portray themselves as legitimate and patriotic governors of Czechoslovakia. They emphasized their ties to the nation's history of rebellion and workers' activism. In 1950, Party leaders decided to complete the National Memorial on Vítkov Hill, which had not been used since the Nazi occupiers converted the building for munitions storage.

In a city replete with architectural reminders of feudalism and Catholicism, the memorial's functionalist architecture suited the Communist aesthetic. The site of the Hussite battle also resonated with the Communists, who appreciated the medieval rebels' anticlericalism and advocacy of communal property. In July 1950, Bohumil Kafka's equestrian statue of General Jan Žižka was unveiled in front of the memorial. The minister of national defense, Alexej Čepička, connected the contemporary Communist program to "the revolutionary legacy of the Hussite warriors." Max Švabinský's interwar mosaics of the Czechoslovak Legionnaires remained in the Hall of the Fallen Soldiers, but Communist posters, poetry, and artwork were added. A new hall honored the Red Army and featured Vladimir Sychra's 1953 mosaics of Soviet soldiers. Josef Malejkovský's bronze friezes for the monument's main doors juxtaposed scenes from the Hussite era with images of the Red Army liberation of Prague.

The Communist Party also embraced the Hussite legacy by rebuilding the Bethlehem Chapel, where Jan Hus had preached five centuries earlier. Zdeněk Nejedlý, the minister of education and public enlightenment, spearheaded the project. An ardent Communist who spent the war in the Soviet Union, Nejedlý was also a musicologist, an expert on medieval Bohemian songs, and an admirer of Jan Hus. Several homes on Bethlehem Square were destroyed to make room for the chapel, despite residents' protests. Very little of the fourteenth-century structure remained, so architects modeled the new building on an early drawing of the chapel. The Party proudly asserted that the builders used medieval building methods to connect to the city's medieval laborers. Representatives of the Czechoslovak and Prague governments, the Soviet embassy, and loyal Protestant churches attended the chapel opening in July 1954. Nejedlý spoke about Hus's proto-socialism, while Czechoslovak and Soviet anthems interspersed Old Czech Protestant hymns.

Socialist realist architecture, which Czechs called "Sorela," never gained widespread use in Prague. The Hotel Družba, which opened in 1957, did represent the style associated with Stalin's aesthetic preferences. The minister of defense (and Gottwald's son-in-law), Alexej Čepička, commissioned the hotel to house important military and state leaders visiting the Czechoslovak capital. He dreamed that Stalin would visit Prague to inaugurate the socialist realist building named for Soviet-Czechoslovak friendship. Inspired by the Seven Sisters skyscrapers in Moscow, the architects used modern building materials and construction techniques to create a Renaissance and Gothic design. Even before the building opened in 1957, army leaders deemed the hotel too massive and expensive. By this time, Čepička had been removed from his position as minister of defense, and Stalin had fallen out of favor The state travel bureau Čedok took over the building and renamed it the International Hotel Prague.

The Communist Party's project to erect a monument to Stalin, the "liberator of Czechoslovakia," also had a tumultuous history. In 1949, a jury awarded sculptor Otakar Švec the prestigious commission to design the Stalin memorial to stand on Letná Plain above the Vltava River. The jury's decision surprised many in the art world. Whereas Švec's interwar sculptures, *Sunbeam Motorcycle* and the *Speed Skater,* conveyed dynamism and motion, his design

FIGURE 13.3 Hotel Družba (now Grand Hotel International Prague) in Dejvice, Prague, represented the Socialist Realist (Sorela) style of architecture, ca. 1959. Photo by Nagy Gyula for Fortepan, CC BY-SA 3.0, https://creativecommons.org/licenses/by-sa/3.0, via Wikimedia Commons.

for Prague's massive Stalin Monument was static and domineering. The proposed design depicted Stalin leading two columns of Soviet and Czechoslovak workers, farmers, scientists, and soldiers. At over fifty feet tall, it would become the largest representation of Stalin in the world.

In April 1949, Gottwald led the groundbreaking ceremony. Holding a gold hammer, the president proclaimed, "With Stalin—for peace, socialism, happiness, and the prosperity of our people." Yet the project seemed doomed from the start. The enormous size and weight of the granite behemoth strained an ever-growing budget. Engineers worked to create a foundation sturdy enough to hold the massive structure, and new staircases from the riverbank to Letná doubled as reinforcements for the hill. Stalin, Gottwald, and Švec did not live to see the completed memorial. Both Stalin and Gottwald died in March 1953. Gottwald fell ill while attending Stalin's funeral in Moscow and died in Prague eleven days after Stalin's death. Švec died by suicide in 1955, two months before the memorial's May 1 unveiling. The Party, suffering political embarrassment, rescinded Švec's nomination as a national laureate and sent the secret police to destroy any art found in his apartment.

Less than a year after the Stalin Memorial opened to the public, Soviet Premier Nikita Khrushchev criticized the cult of personality that surrounded his predecessor. In February 1956, he held a closed-door meeting with a select group of delegates at the Twentieth Party Congress. His "secret speech" called attention to the purges of the 1930s and 1950s and declared that "Stalin showed in a whole series of cases his intolerance, his brutality, and his abuse of power."[14] Khrushchev denounced his predecessor and called on fellow Communist leaders to eschew their cults of personality. With Stalin out of favor, the looming statue on Letná Plain no longer reflected the Party philosophy.

Six years after Khrushchev's speech, the Czechoslovak Communist Party decided to destroy the Stalin Memorial. Fearing that a large explosion might damage the Čechův Bridge and the steeples and towers in historic Old Town, they blasted the monument in sections over a month. Prague writer Bohumil Hrabal discussed the destruction of the Stalin Monument in a short story: "'Why don't they leave the Prague statues alone?' said the sexton, taking out his binoculars and looking at the clock. 'There'd be statues galore from these almost thousand years. You couldn't even fall if you were coming home drunk; there'd always be some marble or sandstone hands to lean on. That's how many statues there'd be in Prague.'"[15]

The destruction of the Stalin Monument became symbolic of the Party's quiet reexamination of communism's early years in Czechoslovakia. The

FIGURE 13.4 Visitors at the Joseph Stalin Monument in Prague, Letná Plain ca. 1955–1962. Photo by Szent-tamási Mihály for Fortepan, CC BY-SA 3.0 via Wikimedia Commons.

Party created secret commissions to review cases that involved, in the words of President Novotný, "the sentencing of leading communists." The Slánský trial defendants Artur London and Vavro Hajdů were released from prison in 1956, as was Eduard Goldstücker, a Slovak Jew and Party member who had been forced to testify against Slánský. Goldstücker had served as ambassador to Israel from 1948 to 1951 but was then accused of trading secrets to the Jewish state on Slánský's behalf. In a subsequent espionage trial, Goldstücker received a multiyear sentence, performing heavy labor in the uranium mines. Though not formally rehabilitated, Goldstücker requested to return to his academic career and became a professor of German literature at Charles University. A few years later, on May 9, 1960, First Party Secretary Antonín Novotný issued a broad decree that freed over five thousand political prisoners.

In the post-Stalin and post-Gottwald era, the Czechoslovak leadership had to come to terms with a new direction in Soviet policy. Prague did not experience the popular protests and upheavals that preoccupied Poland, East Germany, and Hungary in the mid-1950s, but citizens suffered from economic uncertainty. A currency reform in May 1953 wiped out most individuals' savings, and the Party continued to set unattainable production targets within heavy industry. Gottwald's successor, Antonín Zápotocký, was called to Moscow and returned with a "New Economic Course" that focused on manufacturing consumer goods, staving off inflation, and improving living standards. Yet the country remained in a deep recession.

With a change in leadership, the Party sought to create a meaningful shared culture in Prague and beyond. In 1955, the first Spartakiad festival took place on Letná Plain. The mass gymnastics festival, modeled on prewar Sokol Slets, featured thousands of Czechoslovaks. The carefully choreographed movements represented a unified society of workers, farmers, and intelligentsia but avoided the Stalinist symbolism of a primary leader. In the finale of the adult performances, the gymnasts created an illusion of rotating cogwheels, while in the junior festival, children represented firing pistons and airplanes. Prague newspapers celebrated the children as future workers who would build dams, create new technology, and lead society. The Spartakiads took place in Prague's Strahov Stadium every five years and became national celebrations that Czechoslovaks eagerly anticipated. While some resented the ideological implications of the event, most citizens enjoyed the opportunity to come to the capital for two weeks and spend time with their families away from work. In the months leading up to a Spartakiad, Prague's stores were filled with goods not always available to the masses, and art exhibitions and musical entertainment coincided with the gymnastics demonstrations. The Spartakiads' celebrations of patriotism and unity linked communist culture to the popular prewar Sokol movement. As poet Vitěslav Nezval wrote, somewhat ironically, in 1955, "If a thousand people can on a single command… create a garden patch, there's no reason to despair, my friend, my comrade, over that which gave us our most challenging tomorrow."[16]

Postwar economic challenges and the increasing urbanization of the population contributed to housing shortages in Prague and other cities. Czechoslovakia had already experimented with prefabricated architecture in the interwar period, most notably at the Baťa Shoe Company in Zlín, Moravia. Communists embraced the prefab movement's symbolic equality as identical apartments cropped up in new developments. The "pioneering phase" of state-supported housing reached Prague in 1955. Czechs called the prefabricated apartments *paneláks*, named for the precut panels that composed the building. The first prefab apartments in Prague were modest in size and integrated into existing neighborhoods, such as Karlín and Pankrác. As time went on, increasingly larger buildings and neighborhoods were erected on Prague's outskirts. The Party touted the project as a socialist solution to housing that offered modern amenities and abundant natural light, while others abhorred the bleak, repetitive landscapes of Prague's periphery.

When Zápotocký died in 1957, the first secretary of the Communist Party, Antonín Novotný, succeeded him as president. Although Novotný had been a hardliner when Stalin was alive, he recognized the need for reform. In 1958, he promised that, within four years, the state would make an apartment available to anyone on a waiting list. To make this possible, the Party entertained discussions of cooperative housing schemes. A bill passed in 1959 allowed groups of citizens to form collectives to finance and build their own homes with oversight by national committees. The first such neighborhood was the Petřiny housing estate near the Prague airport. Half of the four thousand units were owned by citizen co-ops, and the rest were financed and rented through a state agency. The abbot-turned-bricklayer Opasek recalled, "It was typical on construction sites at the time for there to be only a few bricklayers or construction workers and their relatives."[17] Prague citizens spent weekends and vacations on these building projects, which offered the only possibility of homeownership. The Party was adamant that the units were not private but cooperative property.

Novotný was preoccupied with the country's reputation and sought to expand Czechoslovakia's influence abroad. Prague designers received permission to participate in the Brussels World Expo of 1958, where they displayed their innovative prefabricated housing. In keeping with the Expo's theme, "Evaluation of the world for a more humane world," the contributors demonstrated their country's technological and scientific progress. The Czechoslovak pavilion, called "A Day in Czechoslovakia," won first prize. The layout featured a raised rotunda and three cubes connected by glass wings. Inside, visitors saw modern textile designs and stylish porcelain dinner sets purportedly available to all citizens. The inventive architecture and interior designs suggested that the Communist East rivaled the West in living standards and modern amenities.

The Brussels Expo marked a turning point for Prague culture during communism. František Kahuda, the minister of education who chaired the Expo committee, allowed contributors tremendous artistic freedom. Following the Expo, Kahuda had the modular building's center hall transferred to Letná, where Prague families could stroll, see an exhibition, and eat in the restaurant overlooking the river. The exposition also introduced an innovative blacklight theater production to the world. The Magic Lantern was a multimedia production that combined movement, dance, mime, film, storytelling, and music. The first production in Prague was staged at the Adria Theater on Jungmann Square in New Town, and the company soon became affiliated with the National Theater. Director Alfred Radok hired a young Miloš Forman to assist him in set design; a decade later, Forman would go on to international fame as a film director.

De-Stalinization encouraged Prague's intellectual and artistic communities to broaden the scope of their work. In 1963, Eduard Goldstücker was formally rehabilitated and got permission to organize the first Communist-era conference on Franz Kafka. The Communist Party had dismissed Kafka as a decadent, bourgeois writer, but scholars from Czechoslovakia, East Germany, Austria, and France met at Liblice Castle, north of Prague, to reassess his contributions. Goldstücker was careful not to criticize the state, but he encouraged scholars to interpret Kafka through different lenses. Conference participants discussed Kafka as a Prague writer who experienced a "double or triple ghetto" of alienation as a Jew, a German speaker, and an intellectual in an age of anti-Semitic imperialism. Goldstücker provided a Marxist reading of Kafka's short story "Der Heizer" (The stoker), in which the author found "the way to the working class." The Kafka conference's success became a litmus test for further creative and scholarly work on once-forbidden topics. President Novotný opposed the rehabilitation of Kafka, whom he considered representative of "defeatism, weakness, and resignation," and he blamed the 1963 conference for "having a negative effect on the economy." Still, the conference's authorization felt like a miracle to Prague's scholarly and literary community.[18]

The Czechoslovak film industry, based in Prague, experienced a renaissance in the early 1960s. Filmmakers inspired by the French New Wave pushed the boundaries of subject matter and tone. The two Czechoslovak films to win an Academy Award during the 1960s, *The Shop on Main Street* and *Closely Watched Trains*, addressed issues of resistance and complicity during World War II and the Holocaust. Other young directors, such as Miloš Forman and Věra Chytilová, used satire to question conformity and privilege. The nationalization of the film industry after World War II created opportunities for daring filmmakers to apply for state funding and create experimental projects. They had access to world-renowned film studios at Barrandov and instruction at FAMU, a cinematic arts university that opened in Prague in 1946 near the National Theater. More tolerance for avant-garde art did not mean the end of government surveillance. Forman recalled, "Everything I did…meant an endless struggle against censorship, which was ubiquitous. The need to struggle, to be cunning day in and out, made me realize early on that film plays a social role, and that it even can help to change the world, even if only to a slight extent."[19]

The Prague theater scene was likewise invigorated in the 1960s. With nineteen theaters, Prague audiences enjoyed a range of productions unavailable in most of the Communist bloc. Václav Havel emerged as the most exciting young playwright in Prague. Havel's grandfather founded the Lucerna complex on Wenceslas Square; his uncle started the Barrandov Film Studios; and his father was a successful real estate developer. His wealthy bourgeois background meant that he was forbidden to study humanities at the university level. He enrolled in a technical college but soon quit. Havel secured a job as a stagehand at the Theater of the Balustrade and reveled in its productions of absurdist plays. He began to write scripts that explored the loss of individuality in a world of technocrats. *The Garden Party* and *The Memorandum* opened at the Balustrade in 1963 and 1965, before the writer turned thirty. In *The Garden Party*, a middle-aged Prague couple worries about their son Hugo, who can't seem to find a place in society, while their bright son Peter is already a lost cause. Early in the play, the parents fret about their family's position in society:

> MRS. PLUDEK: Everybody says Peter looks like a bourgeois intellectual. Why should you get into trouble because of him?
> MR. PLUDEK: Quite right, Berta. I'm the grandson of a poor farmhand, damn it! One of six children. I've five proletarian great uncles!
> MRS. PLUDEK: Peter is the black sheep of the family.[20]

In 1965, the American beat poet Allen Ginsberg visited Prague. An impromptu stopover in the city led to a longer stay and a residency at the Writers' Union, thanks to the intervention of novelist Josef Škvorecký. Ginsberg gave readings and wrote several poems that were translated and appeared in *Literární noviny*, the foremost literary journal in the country. The poet's long hair and bushy beard, not to mention his prolific drinking and sexual liaisons, attracted the attention of the youth as well as the secret police. On May 1, 1965, Ginsberg attended a student festival. May Day celebrations had been popular among Prague youth since the nineteenth century, but during the Communist era, the state emphasized the workers' holiday. In 1965, though, the Party permitted a student-organized event following the annual morning workers' parades. Students gathered at the exhibition grounds, where they chose the flamboyant Ginsberg as their "King of May." A week later, the poet was deported by the Czechoslovak secret police and put on a plane to London. Ginsberg memorialized his experience in *Král majales*, a poem that equally criticized the deceptions of capitalists who "proffer Napalm and…drink gin and whiskey on airplanes but let Indian brown millions starve" and communists who "create heavy industry but the heart is also heavy." He ended his poem by lamenting his lack of power and admitting to "trembling in fear while in police custody":

> And tho' I am the King of May, the Marxists have beat me upon the street,
> kept me up all night in Police Station, followed me thru Springtime Prague, detained me in secret and deported me from our kingdom by airplane.
> Thus I have written this poem on a jet seat in mid Heaven.[21]

In the mid-1960s, Prague's creative scene teetered between repression and reform. The official Party organ, the Writers' Union, oversaw the country's authors. The union controlled the state literary fund and several important journals, whose readership totaled over three hundred thousand. Its main journal, *Literární noviny*, began to publish anonymous opinion pieces that addressed political and economic issues, and the union meetings included discussions of censorship and artistic freedom. The Party management of the country's writers had the unintended consequence of bringing together intellectuals who would not have ordinarily met. Faithful Communists mingled with dissidents and influenced one another's attitudes and tactics.

At the 1965 congress, Havel gave an impassioned speech that criticized the Writers' Union as a stale bureaucracy. Some reform Communists agreed with Havel, but the organization was not yet ready to take action. Two years later, in June 1967, the Writers' Union Congress met in Prague and released a daring statement: "The Congress of Czechoslovak Writers does not agree with the contemporary practice of press supervision." Novelist and former Communist Milan Kundera opened the Congress by declaring that freedom of expression was "the basic moral principle of modern civilization."[22] His remarks described the importance of literary expression in a small nation, which required continual regeneration to remain relevant. The Party representatives at the Congress were horrified at the outspokenness of Ludvík Vaculík, Pavel Kohout, Ivan Klíma, and Havel, all of whom were forced off the ballot for the Writers' Union Central Committee. In September, *Literární noviny* was placed under the direct control of the Ministry of Culture, but most writers refused to contribute to the censored journal.

Later that year, a student demonstration called attention to the living conditions in Prague dormitories. The police used tear gas to disperse the peaceful crowd of fifteen hundred students, who demanded repairs to the electricity and heating. Reformers in the Party decried the brutality of police attacking young students carrying candles and chanting, "We want light." The unrest spread to other social sectors as citizens pushed for more attention to their everyday needs.

Fissures opened within the Party. Novotný's 1965 plan to decentralize the economy had not succeeded. In 1967, Alexander Dubček, the secretary of the Communist Party in Slovakia, called for more meaningful changes in the country's economy and culture. Popular protests against Novotný broke out in Prague and other major cities. In January 1968, the Czechoslovak Party Central Committee passed a vote of no confidence in the government, and Dubček replaced Novotný as the Party's general secretary. As the first Slovak to head the Czechoslovak Communist Party, Dubček came to Prague with the zeal of a reformer. A youthful forty-seven and with a quick smile, Dubček had a charisma not seen in Prague politicians since before the war. Dubček declared that the country would implement a reform program called "Socialism with a human face." Citizens could criticize the government, and newspapers investigated corruption and reported on controversial issues such as housing, transportation, and the standard of living. Individuals and trade unions were given more say in their workplaces, and farmers could form independent cooperatives.

Artistic freedom became the hallmark of the era, which became known as the Prague Spring. Censorship was eased in March 1968, and Dubček declared, "We shall have to remove everything that strangles artistic and scientific creativeness."[23] Banned writers were rehabilitated and even published; religious groups saw increased freedom; and travel restrictions were eased. The reinvigorated Czechoslovak Writers' Union chose former political prisoner Eduard Goldstücker as its president. Journals and newspapers, including the Party organ *Rudé právo*, championed the reforms, and dozens of publications were stocked in Prague's kiosks. The state released reports on the 1950s show trials, which admitted that defendants had been tortured into false confessions and forced to memorize their testimony.

Heda Margolius Kovály, whose husband Rudolph Margolius had been posthumously exonerated in 1963, recalled, "The spring of 1968 had all the intensity, anxiety and unreality of a dream come true. People flooded the narrow streets of Prague's Old Town and the courtyards of Hradčany Castle and stayed out long into the night." Kovály reveled in "the sound of laughter" echoing on Prague's ancient walls. The filmmaker Jan Němec captured images of Prague youth singing the American civil rights hymn "We Shall Overcome" and adding the lyrics, "We are the children of Dubček."[24] In June, seventy writers and other public figures issued the "2000 Words," a manifesto aimed at bolstering the reforms occurring in their country. Vaculík penned the document, which censured the Czechoslovak Communist Party's corruption and totalitarianism and called upon reform Communists to build a true democracy.

While Prague residents celebrated their newfound freedom, the Warsaw Pact countries grew concerned with the developments in Czechoslovakia. On July 29, 1968, Dubček was ordered to report to a small town on the Soviet-Slovak border, where Warsaw Pact leaders insisted that he roll back his domestic reforms. Dubček stood firm in his resolve. While he promised his loyalty to the Warsaw Pact, he refused to retreat from his reform agenda. Not all Czechoslovak Communists favored the reforms. On August 4, five members of the Czechoslovak Presidium presented a handwritten letter to Warsaw Pact leaders warning that the socialist order was under threat and requesting military aid. Two weeks later, Leonid Brezhnev, general secretary of the Soviet Communist Party, spoke directly to Dubček and demanded that he curtail the excesses of the Prague press: "The newspapers...have been doggedly [publishing] defamatory ravings about the Soviet Union and the other fraternal countries."[25] Dubček insisted that his program strengthened socialism and expanded popular support for the Party. As negotiations brought little change, Moscow ordered Warsaw Pact training exercises close to the Czechoslovak border, and the Warsaw Pact countries of Hungary, Poland, East Germany, and Bulgaria committed to aiding the Soviet Union in its actions against the rogue state. Only Romania, led by a young Nicolae Ceaușescu, refused to participate. Three years earlier, Allen Ginsberg wrote, "The Kingdom of May is too beautiful to last more than a month." The poet seemed to anticipate the fragility of Czechoslovakia's socialist experiment. By late August 1968, the region appeared poised for war.

On August 21, 1968, Prague citizens awoke to the news that their city had been invaded. The night before, Soviet aircraft landed at the Prague airport and seized control. The Warsaw Pact troops stationed at the border invaded Czechoslovakia and arrived in Prague before sunrise. Led by the Soviet army, the coalition included a smaller number of Hungarian, Polish, East German, and Bulgarian troops. In all, five hundred thousand soldiers crossed the border by ground or air. Ondřej Neff, a twenty-three-year-old journalist for Radio Prague, later recalled, "I'd been woken up by the sound of the aircraft overhead: Antonovs carrying troops. It was a very scary sight—this dark night, and all these planes without lights, like huge dark crosses flying over our heads."[26]

Wenceslas Square was the epicenter of violence in Prague. Soviet tanks rolled across tramway lines, and snipers fired at the National Museum. Fighting took place at the Czech Radio building, east of the square. Employees at the radio station continued to broadcast and attempted to hold off the invaders. One journalist recalled the early morning of August 21: "When I got to work there were already about 10 or 15 people there.... We were helpless, because the minister of telecommunications had switched off the radio and television transmitters, but the technicians managed to find a way of broadcasting via the telephone lines." Students and other citizens attempted to defend the building. They constructed barricades and lit city buses on fire to prevent troops from getting closer, but Soviet tanks relentlessly slammed into the blazing buses. By the following morning, the invading forces had taken over the radio station, and fifteen Czechoslovaks had died. Journalists managed to broadcast from secret locations in the city and provided information to the citizenry until mid-September.

The mounted figure of Saint Wenceslas became an inspiring sight for the beleaguered Prague citizens. *Rudé právo* supported the Prague Spring movement and commented: "The inscription on the statue, which normally is unnoticed, is endowed today with new and vital meaning: 'Do not let us perish, nor our heirs!'" Protesters plastered the monument with handmade signs in Russian and Czech reading, for example, "Soldiers, go home! Quickly!" and "Dubček, Hurrah," sentiments that *Rudé právo* claimed "expressed the opinion of us all." Weary citizens sat "dejectedly on the pedestal" staring at the National Museum, damaged with heavy artillery fire. One citizen described it this way: "Against the dark background shine hundreds of white spots, as if evil birds pecked at the façade."[27] Smaller demonstrations occurred on Old Town Square against the backdrop of the Jan Hus Memorial. Students and Czechoslovak soldiers climbed onto the statue carrying the national flag and led the national anthem and the Hussite warrior hymn. Despite the chaos during the invasion, the newspaper *Práce* proudly reported, "Flags still flutter over the head of the majestic Hus."[28]

Kovály watched as "tens of thousands of people with transistors to their ears milled around in streets filled with crushed automobiles and pieces of masonry that had been shot down from the surrounding buildings. Walls were covered with painted slogans. Trucks draped with Czechoslovak flags rammed into the Russian tanks and the air rang with the sound of intermittent gunfire."²⁹ *Rudé právo* reported, "Smoke from burning houses rises into the sky. We pass a smoke-smudged youth carrying a sad souvenir—the shell of an 85mm gun." Fewer than one hundred Czechoslovak citizens died in the invasion, but the fighting took a steep emotional toll on the country.

Loyal Communist Party members expressed disbelief at the turn of events, especially the news that Dubček and fellow reformers Josef Smrkovský, Ludvík Svoboda, and Oldřich Černík had been detained and brought to Moscow. Journalist, screenwriter, and playwright Jan Drda, who had criticized the outspoken Writers' Union members in 1967, wrote in *Rudé právo* on August 27, 1968, "The pen is shaking in my hand, my voice is breaking. For 45 years I have taught children to love the Soviet Union, to regard Moscow as the guarantee of our national and state independence. All this now lies in ruins.... The number of crimes committed in these days in the streets of Prague call to high heaven.... They have given rise to something dreadful in our hearts: hatred against ruse and betrayal, the burning sentiment of humiliation, the inextinguishable flame of hate."³⁰ Radio journalist Neff recalled, "I can remember the sense of desperation I felt in those early days of the

FIGURE 13.5 Warsaw Pact invasion of Czechoslovakia, 1968. Czechoslovaks carry their national flag past a burning Soviet tank in Prague. Central Intelligence Agency. Public domain, via Wikimedia Commons.

occupation. I felt my future had been lost." Indeed, Neff and hundreds of his fellow radio journalists lost their jobs following the invasion.

On August 27, the detained Czechoslovak leaders returned to Prague. Dubček and Svoboda addressed the nation on the radio. Despite their reassuring words, the leaders were devastated. Dubček fought back tears as he explained to the country, "We are convinced that we will find ways and means of developing with you all a policy that will eventually lead to a normalization of the situation."[31] The word "normalization" would become the name given to the era that followed the defunct Prague Spring. Within weeks, censorship returned to Czechoslovakia. Dubček retained his position in name, but the Soviet Union held the reins of power.

In September 1968, the Moscow newspaper *Pravda* published a justification for the invasion, which later became known as the Brezhnev Doctrine of Limited Sovereignty: "The measures taken by the Soviet Union, jointly with other socialist countries, in defending the socialist gains of the Czechoslovak people are of great significance for strengthening the socialist community, which is the main achievement of the international working class." Calling the Czechoslovak reformers "anti-socialists," the doctrine declared that "each Communist Party is responsible not only to its own people, but also to all the socialist countries, to the entire Communist movement."[32]

Although Prague had been subdued by the invasion, isolated protests continued. In January 1969, Prague university student Jan Palach immolated himself on Wenceslas Square to protest the continued presence of Soviet and Warsaw Pact troops in Prague. Thousands of students and citizens attended his funeral, processing through the streets of Prague with wreaths and photographs of the young martyr. Another student, Jan Zajíc, followed Palach's example. However, these singular acts could not effect real change.

In March 1969, Czechoslovaks and Soviets came face to face once more, this time on the ice. Prague's citizens tenaciously followed the ice hockey world championship in Stockholm. When the Czechoslovak team won its first game against the Soviet Union on March 21, citizens came to Wenceslas Square with signs reading, "They had no tanks, so they lost." A US diplomat, Kenneth Skoug Jr., reported that he "had never seen Czechs so happy. The city had not experienced such joy since the defeat of the Nazis in 1945."[33] A week later, the teams met again, and Czechoslovakia beat the Soviets by a single goal. Prague erupted into celebrations and protests. The police reported vandalism throughout the city, particularly attacks against the Soviet-based Aeroflot and Intourist offices in Prague. Considerable evidence suggested that Soviet agents carried out the attacks to provoke a regime change in

Czechoslovakia. Brezhnev responded to the hockey riots by demanding permanent changes in Prague.

A new government was in place by April 1969. Gustav Husák, a Slovak politician who had been a victim of the 1950s purges and spent six years in prison, replaced Dubček as the first secretary of the Communist Party. During the early days of the Prague Spring, he supported Dubček's reforms, but he soon became one of Moscow's chief allies in East-Central Europe. Svoboda, who had served as Dubček's president, also reversed course and joined the pro-Soviet government. Dubček left Prague and returned to Slovakia, and the following year, he was expelled from the Communist Party. He worked as a clerk in the Forestry Service for the next eighteen years.

The realigned Communist Party of Czechoslovakia reversed most reforms implemented during the Prague Spring. Dubček's plan to federalize Czechoslovakia did survive. As a Slovak, he recognized the inequities in the country and pushed for amendments to the 1960 constitution. The Czech Socialist Republic comprised Bohemia and Moravia, and the Slovak Socialist Republic lay in the eastern part of the country. The Federal Assembly became the highest governing body in the country. The Party renovated its building, a former stock exchange built in the 1930s. Karel Prager's unpopular 1973 addition, known as the Extension, wrapped the original building in a brutalist glass and concrete structure. The Assembly's location between the National Museum and the State Opera led Prague residents to joke that the Federal Assembly was "something between a theater and a museum."

14

Communism's Gray Zone

IN THE SPRING of 1969, the Czechoslovak government announced a new program: normalization, the term Dubček uttered during his tearful radio address the previous year. After the Prague Spring, the state's normalization policy signified an inward turn. Husák called for "a quiet life for the people... favorable conditions for the development of economic activity, stability... social and existential certainty.... It all creates conditions to live well and quietly, so that life is worth living."[1] The goal of normalization was to make everyday life more comfortable for the average citizen. Czechoslovakia became one of the most conservative but also one of the wealthiest countries in the Eastern bloc. The Party guaranteed employment and addressed the lack of consumer goods, available housing, and leisure activities.

During normalization, the state made concerted efforts to improve housing, infrastructure, transportation, and shopping in Prague. The district Jižní Město, located on the southern edge of Prague, took a holistic approach to housing by creating a small-town atmosphere with stores, parks, schools, and cultural events. Building began in the early 1970s and continued throughout the decade. The neighborhood quickly gained a terrible reputation: building materials were inferior, production was continually delayed, and there were frequent problems with heating, electricity, and elevator service. The rows of identical buildings created a drab gray suburb, and Jižní Město became a symbol of socialist incompetence.

Věra Chytilová's 1979 film *Panelstory* provided a lighthearted look at the trials and tribulations of life in Jižní Město. Characters in the film moved into unfinished buildings and watched rain pour into their new apartments. Family members and neighbors fought over the limited space. Chytilová hinted at a changing Prague by creating the character of an African doctor who lived alongside Czech families. The film critiqued a mainstay of normalization-era Prague, the corrupt petty bureaucrat. Daycare administrators and construction overseers in *Panelstory* take advantage of unsuspecting residents and further delay the creation of a rationalized, modern community.

Despite the problems depicted in Chytilová's ironic film, thousands of Prague families joined the waiting lists and happily moved into flats. Jižní Město and other microdistricts enabled Prague residents to leave the crowded city center and access convenient shopping, schools, and transportation.

Women still bore the double burden of work and family in the new socialist neighborhoods. The expectation that all citizens work outside the home led to a decline in the birth rate in the 1950s and 1960s, and the Party launched a pronatalist campaign in the 1970s. The state emphasized the strength of the nuclear family, and the era's socialist realist art glorified motherhood. The Party installed the sculpture *New Life* by Karel Lidický at the National Monument on Vítkov Hill. The site, replete with masculine symbolism, now included a rather conservative image of women's contribution to society.

Women's experiences under normalization were mixed. Long lines at stores and insufficient housing exacerbated the stresses of their daily lives, but in the 1970s, women benefited from childcare allowances, paid maternity and sick leave, increased childcare facilities, and rent subsidies. Some women remained frustrated that working hours in Czechoslovakia were the highest

FIGURE 14.1 Karel Lidický, *New Life* sculpture installed at the National Monument on Vítkov Hill ca. 1975. Photo by the author.

in Europe and that part-time employment was nearly impossible to find. While traditional gender roles were rarely questioned, the sociologist and dissident Jiřina Šiklová argued, "Women and men saw one another as allies, struggling against a repressive state."[2]

By 1980, Czechoslovakia had one of the highest birth rates among industrialized countries. The government incentives played a role, but so did periodic shortages of birth control and negative perceptions of oral contraceptives. In 1977, only 5 percent of Czech and 2 percent of Slovak women took birth control pills, compared to 37 percent in the Netherlands and 19 percent in Germany.[3] Abortion became the most common form of family planning, and most women who sought the procedure were married mothers of multiple children.

The state invested in modern shopping centers to accommodate the growing population. Two Prague landmarks, the Máj and Kotva department stores, opened in 1975 within two months of each other. Both featured experimental architecture, the newest consumer goods, and modern approaches to shopping. Máj stood on Národní třída, only a short walk away from the neoclassical National Theater and the candy-colored Baroque convent of St. Ursula. In contrast, Czech architect Martin Rajnis's Máj combined brutalist and high-tech design. Boxy, repetitious shapes filled a grid facade, and large glass panes enclosed exposed escalators. Near the art nouveau Municipal House, on the border of the Old and New Towns, stood Kotva. As the largest store in Czechoslovakia, Kotva showcased the abundance of socialism. The husband-and-wife team Vladímir Machonín and Věra Machonínová created a floor plan with interlocking hexagons connected by ten escalators. Each floor featured individual kiosks to mimic shopping in markets or small shops. A sign atop the building proudly announced: "Hail to the Communist Party of Czechoslovakia!" While the Party worked to respond to citizens' needs, the new stores' high prices and impractical goods frustrated eager consumers. (See Color Plate 17.)

Prague's transportation infrastructure could no longer accommodate the growing city. A new bridge spanned the Nusle Valley and connected Prague's New Town to Pankrác and the Jižní Město housing developments. The road led to a modern highway to Brno in Moravia. The bridge opened in 1974 and accommodated both car traffic and two tracks of a new public metro system. Named for the first Communist president, Klement Gottwald, the bridge acquired an unfortunate nickname. The "Suicide Bridge" became more associated with a high number of deaths than a feat of socialist engineering.

A major accomplishment of the 1970s was the Prague Metro. Soviet engineers helped Prague design an underground transport system. The red track (now track C) opened in 1974 to serve the city's southern sector. The green and yellow tracks (A and B) opened in 1978 and 1985, forming a triangle with exchange stations in the city center. Metallic panels in a rainbow of colors lent a futuristic look to the Prague Metro, and lines were continually extended to reach the expanding housing developments on the outskirts of the city. Budova ČKD, a new headquarters for the transportation company that designed and manufactured Prague's Tatra tramcars, opened in 1983 at Můstek, the lower end of Wenceslas Square. Husband-and-wife team Jan Šrámek and Alena Šrámková designed the postmodern glass-and-iron building. The round glass clock and curved facade echoed the modernist and art nouveau buildings already on the square, unlike the Máj and Kotva buildings, which clashed with their surroundings. ČKD represented an approach to architecture and transportation that connected the Communist era to Prague's past.

Normalization schemes promised to improve leisure activities in the city. In 1983, a new theater opened on Národní třída, forming a courtyard with the National Theater. Nová scena (the New Scene), designed by Stanislav Libenský, became the venue for the Magic Lantern Theater. The apolitical and accessible multimedia productions, popularized in the late 1950s, suited the normalization culture. The banal Magic Lantern shows contrasted with Václav Havel's description of his craft: the "very special, conspiratorial sense of togetherness that to me is what makes theater."[4] Yet many Prague citizens appreciated the state-funded entertainment. Operas and classical concerts were affordable for anyone with an interest, and the Palace of Culture, which opened in 1981 near Vyšehrad, hosted contemporary performances and family events. Prague families could also find entertainment at home through the state media's captivating television serials, such as *The Hospital at the Edge of Town* and *The Woman Behind the Counter.* Citizens were encouraged to pursue "the quiet life" among friends and family. Prague residents seeking to escape city life embraced the *chata* movement, in which families invested in rural cottages and spent weekends gardening and socializing in the country.

The state's planned economy still emphasized industry but expanded the production of consumer goods and services. The economy did grow significantly, and by the mid-1970s, Czechoslovakia and East Germany were the most prosperous countries in the Eastern bloc. While countries like Poland suffered food shortages and long lines for necessities, Czechoslovak citizens enjoyed a quality of life similar to many West Europeans. Prague was, by far, Czechoslovakia's wealthiest city.

Czechoslovakia faced a severe labor shortage due to high industrial and consumer production demand. In 1976, the *New York Times* reported a new phenomenon: "The sight of newly arrived Vietnamese taking weekend strolls around this old city has become common, and most of them apparently are working in the Prague area."[5] By 1983, thirty thousand Vietnamese guest workers were in the country, many living in the most inferior of Prague's housing developments. Throughout the normalization era, Czechoslovakia participated in the Soviet bloc's outreach to Communist countries in Africa, Asia, and Latin America. Several thousand foreign students—from Egypt, Somalia, Ethiopia, Guinea, Vietnam, Cuba, and several other countries—won scholarships to Prague's top engineering and technology schools, and language institutes welcomed foreigners to the capital city. While Prague remained rather homogeneous, students and workers from allied countries began to diversify the city's spaces.

―――― ◆ ――――

Following the Warsaw Pact invasion, a purge targeted the country's dissidents, including uncooperative reform communists, academics, theologians, and artists. Some critics of the regime left the country, including Heda Margolius Kovály, Milan Kundera, Miloš Forman, and Eduard Goldstücker. Novelist Josef Škvorecký and his wife fled to Canada, where they established '68 Publishers, which brought banned writings from Eastern Europe to an international audience. At home, a small group of Prague artists and intellectuals formed a nonconformist community and challenged the idea that normalization was normal. Most of the dissidents had already lost their careers or educational prospects after the Prague Spring and felt they had little more to lose. Havel was banned from theater and took a job in a southern Bohemian brewery. Ivan Klíma became a hospital orderly. Philosopher Jan Patočka took a forced early retirement from his full professorship at Charles University.

Intellectuals and artists frequented Café Slavia across from the National Theater or met at Havel's sizable apartment on the Vltava embankment. The secret police set up a surveillance center in the Renaissance water tower near the Mánes art center, and police officers followed the playwright on his walks through the city. Havel's semi-autobiographical play *Largo Desolato* traced the growing neurosis of a Prague writer who dreads the random knocks at his door, wondering if he will be questioned by the secret police or pressured by friends and family to give up his oppositional activities.

Dissidents discussed forming a parallel society within an oppressive regime. Patočka, who had studied with the renowned philosophers Edmund

Husserl and Martin Heidegger, guided fellow intellectuals in discussions of "being" within a modern society structured by science and technology. While normalization promised predictability through conformity, Patočka proposed a "solidarity of the shaken," composed of people "who had realized there are no certainties to hold one's life in place."[6] The deeply shocking experiences of the past several years—the Warsaw Pact invasion, constant surveillance, and bans of creative work—forced people to choose between conformity or authenticity. Havel considered Patočka a mentor and expressed the philosopher's ideals as "living in truth."

Creative and intellectual writers created an intricate network of self-publishing, known as *samizdat*. Former Communist Party member Jiřina Šiklová lost her position as a sociology professor for supporting the Prague Spring reforms. First employed as a janitor, she later found work as a researcher and social worker. She and other dissidents smuggled illicit texts out of the country to call attention to the issues facing the country. Friends and exiles in neighboring countries helped to get the works translated and published abroad. Samizdat writers contributed creative work, research projects, and essays on issues like the housing shortage in Prague and the environmental degradation of Bohemia. They maintained underground libraries of banned writings and held discussion groups on a variety of interests, from Christianity to punk rock to reformed Marxism. However, these individuals often remained detached from the everyday struggles of working people. Šiklová admitted that dissidents become "sometimes too focused on their own courage...[and] underrate" the contributions of ordinary citizens.[7]

Rock music became a language of dissent that could speak to a broader audience. After the Prague Spring, English-language lyrics and Western songs were censored, yet poet and essayist Ivan Martin Jirous explained, "Soon after the August invasion, the phenomenon of a real musical underground emerged in Prague." Jirous was the artistic director of Plastic People of the Universe, a psychedelic rock band inspired by Frank Zappa, the Fugs, and the Velvet Underground. While other important experimental Prague rock groups like the Primitives disbanded in the early months of normalization, the Plastics kept playing at secret venues. In an important samizdat essay, Jirous declared that 1973 witnessed a "third revival in Czech rock and roll music."[8] Jirous called for artists to form a parallel society that would defy the state's arbitrary rules. The Plastics' psychedelic music was not overtly political but had elements of nostalgia and mystery. In a concert recorded at Václav Havel's cottage in the early 1980s, the band performed "Delirium":

> The time of magic
> Night has come...
> Delirium
> We live in Prague
> That's where the spirit itself will
> One day appear
> We live in Prague
> That is where.[9]

In 1976, Jirous was arrested at his own wedding celebration, which doubled as a music festival. At least nineteen musicians from five bands faced charges, and their instruments and recording equipment were confiscated. A subsequent trial in Prague focused on four defendants: two Plastic People affiliates, a member of the rock band DG 370, and a Protestant minister who performed folk music. Jirous served an eighteen-month sentence. In response to the trial, which became known as the Trial of the Plastic People, leading dissidents issued the famous document Charter 77. The manifesto, published in January 1977, was signed by two hundred citizens. The authors described their organization:

> Charter 77 is a loose, informal, and open association of people of various shades of opinion, faiths and professions united by the will to strive individually and collectively for the respecting of civic and human rights in our own country and throughout the world.... Freedom of public expression is inhibited by the centralized control of all the communication media and of publishing and cultural institutions. No philosophical, political, or scientific view or artistic activity that departs ever so slightly from the narrow bounds of official ideology or aesthetics is allowed to be published; no open criticism can be made of abnormal social phenomena; no public defense is possible against false and insulting charges made in official propaganda.[10]

A subgroup of the Charter 77 association, the Committee for the Defense of the Unjustly Persecuted (VONS), took it upon itself to protest when Czechoslovakia broke international human rights agreements. Within weeks of the manifesto's release, the police questioned nearly every signatory. Patočka, already in poor health, faced a ten-hour interrogation. He died a few days later, at age sixty-nine.

Several women played leading roles in the Charter movement. The folk singer Marta Kubíšová, whose "Prayer for Marta" became an anthem of resistance during the Warsaw Pact invasion, served as a Charter spokesperson. Journalist Eva Kantůrková spent close to a year in prison under suspicion of sedition. She was never charged and eventually was released for lack of evidence. Her samizdat book *My Companions in the Bleak House* profiled twelve fellow prisoners, including prostitutes, pickpockets, and runaways. Petruška Šustrová served three years in prison for her activities in the Revolutionary Youth Movement, a leftist group that protested the Warsaw Pact invasion. Forbidden from finishing her studies in history and Czech, Šustrová worked as a postal clerk while writing and editing samizdat literature. Both Kantůrková and Šustrová served as Charter spokespersons. One of the most creative members of the Charter group was the popular television actress Barbora Štěpánová. A co-founder of the Society for a Merrier Present, she secretly staged guerrilla theater events in Prague. Projects included building a huge papier mâché whale and floating it down the Vltava River and dressing as police officers wearing watermelon-rind helmets and waving salami batons. Through contacts with Radio Free Europe, Štěpánová got some of the group's "happenings" covered in the Western press.[11] Women outside the Charter movement also joined together to advocate for their families. The pollution in Prague had led to high incidents of asthma and other respiratory ailments, and women used their power as working mothers to demand changes to environmental policy.

The government sought to draw attention away from the Charter activists and demonstrate the loyalty of the country's cultural sector. At a state-sponsored event at Prague's National Theater, prominent actors, singers, and other artists signed the "anti-Charter" and pledged their loyalty to the state. Among the seven thousand signatories was Jan Werich, who had co-founded the avant-garde Liberated Theater during the First Republic. His collaborator Jiří (later George) Voskovec had taken a different path, emigrating to the United States and pursuing an acting career in Hollywood. Upon signing, the prominent writers Bohumil Hrabal and Vladímir Neff regained publishing privileges they had lost after the Prague Spring. Other well-known signers were director Jiří Menzel, actor and screenwriter Zdeněk Šverák, and pop star Karel Gott. Years later, several signatories described the coercion the government applied, while others apologized for their part in the anti-Charter movement.

In October 1979, the state charged the members of VONS with subversion. Havel received a sentence of four and a half years without parole. Several codefendants received similar sentences. While imprisoned, Havel developed his philosophical ideas about the dissident movement in a series of letters to his wife, Olga Havlová. Havel was released in 1983 in ill health. A heavy smoker, he suffered from lung issues and bouts of pneumonia for the rest of his life.

While Havel served his longest prison term, news arrived of John Lennon's murder in New York. Shocked Prague students, who listened surreptitiously to the Beatles' music, marched to the "Crying Wall" on Kampa Island under the Charles Bridge. Already known for anti-state graffiti, the wall was surveilled and frequently whitewashed. In December 1980, days after the murder, someone painted a picture of Lennon on the wall as a symbol of peace. Havel wrote to his wife Olga from prison about the significance of Lennon's death. "You can't help feeling that the shot was fired by the reality of the eighties at one of the departing dreams—the dream of the sixties for peace, freedom, and brotherhood, the dream of the flower children."[12] The spot on Kampa Island soon became known as the Lennon Wall, a gathering place for students and dissidents who remembered their Czechoslovak version of 1960s hope.

FIGURE 14.2 The John Lennon Wall in 1981. Students and other Prague residents marked the wall with protest graffiti through the 1980s. Neptuul, CC BY-SA 3.0, https://creativecommons.org/licenses/by-sa/3.0, via Wikimedia Commons.

In 1984, poet and Charter signatory Jaroslav Seifert won the Nobel Prize for Literature, the only Czechoslovak ever to receive the honor. Seifert began his career in the early 1920s as a co-founder of Devětsil. Although he spent much of his career writing about the plight of the working class, his own socialist country failed to recognize its Nobel laureate. The news received only a small paragraph in Prague's Communist daily newspaper. Seifert's daughter Jana accepted the award for her father, who was too ill to travel, and she expressed the honesty of her father's poetry. "What my father wrote, he always wrote without great pretensions.... By his words he only tried to grab hold of life, and it was life itself that grabbed hold of him, always and in spite of everything."[13]

Most Czechoslovaks did not belong to the opposition or the Party leadership. Jiřina Šiklová's samizdat essays analyzed this "gray zone" of educated citizens and predicted that these individuals would become the leaders in a post-authoritarian Czechoslovakia. "Because their political involvement was minimal, they also had a lot more time for their own education and training, both personally and professionally. And so today Czechoslovakia's very best experts in their fields fall inside the gray zone."[14]

The small but active Charter movement continued through the 1980s. Havel gained international attention as Czechoslovakia's most important dissident. His essays were published abroad in multiple languages, and theaters from New York to Vienna produced his plays to call attention to the plight of Czechoslovak artists. In 1985, an American journalist asked Havel why he refused to leave the country. The playwright replied, "The solution in this human situation does not lie in leaving it.... Fourteen million people can't just go and leave Czechoslovakia empty." Havel saw his mission as carrying out the ideas of Patočka and Jirous and fighting for freedom of expression. He, too, employed a term discussed by Šiklová, though Havel defined it in a somewhat different way: "This is very important, working on the periphery of the official scene.... This is the 'gray zone.'"[15]

The Czechoslovak economy remained relatively stable during the 1980s. Prague residents continued to have a high standard of living, although Roma citizens and foreign guest workers struggled more than their Czech counterparts. Czechs had robust diets, with high levels of eggs, meat, and bread. Still, citizens were frustrated with the quantity and quality of many consumer goods. Car ownership was low, and the waiting list for a domestic Škoda family car was fifteen years. Foreign luxury goods could only be procured at state-run Tuzex shops, which used a coupon system available only to those with Party connections. Hormonal contraceptives remained difficult to obtain. A black market emerged as a shadow economy, with individuals trading materials they had taken from work. Prague's centrality in Europe gave residents illegal access to Western media markets. Some Czechoslovaks resented that they lacked access to the luxury goods advertised in West German and Austrian media. Whereas the Czechoslovak per capita gross domestic product had only doubled since 1938, Austria's and Italy's had increased tenfold.

Mikhail Gorbachev became the first secretary of the Soviet Communist Party in 1985. Citizens of the Warsaw Pact countries were intrigued by his rhetoric of perestroika (rebuilding) and glasnost (openness). The Czechoslovak Party insisted Gorbachev's goals had nothing in common with the Prague Spring. Zdeněk Mlynář, an exiled architect of Prague Spring's reform program, disagreed: "Every unbiased person can easily discern a congruence between many fundamental notions of the two reform concepts."[16] Gorbachev and Mlynář had been close friends while students in Moscow during the 1950s, and Gorbachev later acknowledged his debt to the Czechoslovak reformer.[17]

In 1987, several thousand Czechoslovaks waited in a cold April drizzle to catch a glimpse of the charismatic Soviet premier, who had become an international celebrity. In preparation for the visit, the municipal government had spruced up the city by replacing cobblestones on Wenceslas Square and cleaning building facades. A black car pulled up to the square's lower end, and the crowd cheered as Gorbachev stepped out, accompanied by Czechoslovak president Gustáv Husák. Only nineteen years earlier, Warsaw Pact tanks and soldiers had come to the same place to suppress the Prague Spring reform movement, but in 1987, Gorbachev promoted his reform programs.

The *New York Times* characterized most Prague residents' reaction to Gorbachev as "curious" but "guarded."[18] Prague's dissidents pointed out the contrast between the youthful Gorbachev, age fifty-six, walking alongside Husák, two decades his senior. Gorbachev smiled, waved, and shook hands like a Western politician. He told a Czech university student, "Young people have to take the initiative." As a woman waved enthusiastically from behind the barriers on Wenceslas Square, Gorbachev called out, "Women, they understand the need for reform!" An older man told a *New York Times* reporter, "Things are changing.... Even a year ago, it would be impossible to imagine so many people cheering for a leader from Moscow."[19]

That day, Gorbachev addressed Party leaders and trade union activists at the Palace of Culture, which had opened near Vyšehrad earlier that decade.

Gorbachev defended his programs: "Our rockets can locate Halley's Comet with utmost precision... and yet... we are seriously lagging behind in how we apply science and technology in the national economy, and our consumer goods are of poor quality.... Experience tells us that socialism can only develop with criticism and self-criticism."[20] Although the audience received his advice with rapturous applause, Czechoslovakia's Communist leadership resisted reform more than any other country in the region except Romania.

While Gorbachev's Soviet Union reduced censorship, Czechoslovakia continued to prosecute cultural and intellectual outsiders. Only a month before Gorbachev's visit, the state convicted five leaders of the Jazz Section, a cultural group banned by the Interior Ministry, for producing illegal publications and newsletters. Even the judge appeared beleaguered by the arbitrary accusations. Before issuing relatively light or suspended sentences, he commended the plaintiffs for their high level of music criticism.[21]

The normalization state had forged a bureaucratic dictatorship but not a totalitarian regime. People found alternate spaces to express their ideas and creativity—the household, sports, recreation, and local councils. Czechoslovakia did not face Hungary's spiraling debt or Poland's food shortages, and the standard of living in Prague was among the highest of any city in the Eastern bloc. The entertainment sector was well funded, and the state was erecting an enormous television tower in Prague's Žižkov neighborhood to improve TV reception.

Still, intellectuals, artists, and students desired change and embraced a nostalgia for the Prague Spring era that the younger generation only knew through their parents and teachers. On a chilly January afternoon in 1989, university students marked the twentieth anniversary of Jan Palach's self-immolation by gathering in front of the National Museum. After a quiet vigil, students moved toward Wenceslas Square's center. The crowd swelled to almost one thousand participants, singing the national anthem amid calls for "Freedom!" or "Gorbachev!" Miloš Jakeš, the secretary of the Communist Party, maintained his conservative stance against dissidents. Police officers responded to reports of a demonstration by blocking the side streets leading to Wenceslas Square and attacking the crowds with riot sticks, dogs, and water cannons. A West German camera crew was caught in the melee, and at least one Czech student suffered serious injuries.

That day, Václav Havel, accompanied by a small group of Czechoslovak artists and intellectuals, also visited the makeshift shrine to Palach. As they laid bright yellow daffodils on the ground, policemen swooped in and accused the dissidents of hooliganism and organizing the student demonstration on

Wenceslas Square. Despite the arrests, protests continued for the next few weeks. About eight hundred citizens were arrested during the last two weeks of January 1989. The state released most of the young protesters and aimed their reprisals at the more established dissident community. A Prague court sentenced Havel to a one-year prison term, and his seven associates received punishments ranging from small fines to incarcerations. Ota Veverka, a jazz musician, Charter 77 signatory, and the founder of the John Lennon Peace Group, told the court, "Laying flowers is not a punishable crime, and I hope it never will be."[22] The judge disagreed, sentencing him to a year in jail.

By 1989, Havel had gained popularity in the West, especially among writers and artists. While he served his prison term, international newspapers decried the jailing of a "major playwright." The Frankfurt Book Fair awarded him its International Peace Prize, and the Public Theater in New York City staged his play *Temptation*, a modern reworking of *Faust*. Protests to release Havel even took place in Poland and Hungary. The Czechoslovak government scolded its more liberal Communist neighbors for allowing the demonstrations and lambasted the Polish prime minister's attendance at a Havel play in a Warsaw theater. Havel was released on early parole on May 18 and emerged from prison noticeably thinner and weaker. He remained determined to push the movement forward and hosted a party on the night of his release. To the great surprise of Havel's colleagues and the Western journalists in attendance, Alexander Dubček arrived at Havel's apartment and embraced his host. The ousted Prague Spring leader never participated in public functions and rarely came to Prague.

Much had changed in the Soviet bloc during Havel's four months in prison. In Poland, Communist leaders met with representatives of the opposition group Solidarity. Two months of round-table talks led to an agreement to open elections, scheduled for June. Hungary dismantled the electrified fences on its Austrian border, and the Soviet Union completed its withdrawal from Afghanistan. Farther away, Chinese students occupied Tiananmen Square, demanding democratic reforms in the People's Republic. Like Prague citizens two years earlier, the Chinese protesters greeted a visiting Mikhail Gorbachev with enthusiastic cheers.

Over the summer and early autumn, new developments occurred in the region every day, but Prague remained quiet. After Solidarity's shocking victory in June, Havel and his associates secretly met with Polish activists for a picnic in a remote border area. Meanwhile, the Hungarian Socialist Workers' Party issued sweeping reforms and then abolished itself. East German asylum seekers applied for travel visas in record numbers, hoping to travel to Western

Europe. Over twenty-five thousand East Germans left the country that summer, many taking refuge at the West German embassy in Prague. A popular joke suggested that there should be a sign at the border announcing, "Leaving East Germany. Would the last one out please turn off the lights?"

By the fall, several thousand East Germans had arrived in Prague. Families camped in the embassy gardens, waiting for their turn to request asylum in West Germany. Prague students and other volunteers brought water and blankets to their German comrades. With Western media attention focused on protests in East Berlin, Leipzig, and Dresden, the Czechoslovak Communist Party leaders recognized the risks of blocking all reforms. The Party reversed some censorship decrees, and for the first time in two decades, works by Franz Kafka and Milan Kundera appeared in Prague's bookshops. Yet, there were few signs of real change in Czechoslovakia. The region's fellow hardliners, Nicolae Ceauşescu of Romania and Erich Honecker of East Germany came to Prague to meet with Czechoslovak leaders. Western observers speculated that these conservative states had allied to block meaningful reform in their respective countries. Once the dominos began to fall, however, the Communist authorities had little recourse. On November 9, thousands of Germans rushed to both sides of the Berlin Wall after a Party spokesman prematurely announced that the borders between East and West had opened. East German border guards, once under a shoot-to-kill order, laid down their weapons and helped people scale the wall.

On Friday, November 17, students throughout Czechoslovakia celebrated International Students' Day, the holiday Edvard Beneš declared fifty years earlier. The Communist Party supported the holiday that honored the student Jan Opletal, who was killed by the Nazis in 1939. Opletal became a symbol of anti-fascism during the Communist era, and the Party sanctioned a student vigil organized by the Socialist Youth Union at Vyšehrad cemetery. When someone called out, "To Wenceslas Square," the crowd began an impromptu walk to the Vltava River. At the National Theater embankment, the crowd turned onto Národní třída, where riot police stood waiting. Side streets were barricaded, and policemen beat young demonstrators with batons. About six hundred students were injured, and a rumor spread that a Prague student named Martin Šmíd had been killed by police. Even though Šmíd appeared on television to reassure fellow citizens that he was alive, rumors persisted, and the protests continued to swell. Over the next few days, more and more Prague residents headed to the city center, chanting, "Do not hurt our children!" University and high school students poured into Wenceslas Square, where cries of "Jan Opletal" met chants of "Jan Palach." The memories of 1939 and 1969 flooded the streets of 1989 Prague. Citizens sang the national anthem and the hymn of St. Wenceslas, accompanied by the chimes of marchers' jangling keys. Students distributed candles as tears streamed down the protesters' faces. The Velvet Revolution had begun.

On Sunday, November 19, Havel returned to Prague from his country cottage. He and fellow dissidents gathered at the Magic Lantern Theater, temporarily housed at the Adria Palace just off Wenceslas Square, and founded the Civic Forum. Actors, writers, and students sat on a stage and improvised their revolution, issuing demands for the release of political prisoners and an independent investigation of the state's violence against peaceful protesters.

British journalist and historian Timothy Garton Ash had been traveling throughout the region all summer and fall and managed to get entry to the Magic Lantern Theater. He speculated to an amateur television crew, "In Poland it took ten years, in Hungary ten months, in East Germany, ten weeks. Perhaps here in Czechoslovakia it will take ten days!"[23] Czech-American activist Rita Klímová used the word "velvet" to describe the peaceful and smooth movement that unfolded in Prague over the next week. Some say that Havel embraced Klímová's moniker because of his admiration for Lou Reed and the Velvet Underground.

Over the next few days, demonstrations in Prague grew, and similar gatherings took place in all of Czechoslovakia's major cities. On November 22, surrounded by fellow dissidents, Havel spoke to two hundred thousand people from the balcony of the Melantrich publishing house, an art nouveau building on the corner of Wenceslas Square. The crowd's clanging keys signaled the unlocking of freedoms. Two days later, on November 24, Alexander Dubček came to Prague from the Slovak capital, Bratislava, and joined Havel on the balcony, surprising a jubilant crowd. Protesters held up their fingers in victory signs and held signs reading "Svoboda" (Freedom), "Nežít ve lže!" (Don't live a lie!), "At' žije Dubček" (Long live Dubček), and "Václav Havel na Hrad" (Václav Havel to the Castle). Protesters recalled the popular myth that Saint Wenceslas—in Czech, Svatý Václav—would rescue his people at their greatest time of need. They embraced the symbolic coincidence of their leader's first name with that of the beloved medieval duke. The idealism and camaraderie on the square captivated the international media and influenced scholars to call the events in Prague effervescent, festive, and magical.

Tensions rose when the revolution moved to the Sparta Praha sports arena on Letná Plain. Between six hundred thousand and eight hundred thousand citizens gathered at the outdoor arena, and the Civic Forum invited the Communist prime minister, Ladislav Adamec, to address the crowd. Though he promised reforms, the crowd heckled and whistled, demanding resignations. The dissident Catholic priest and Charter 77 spokesman Václav Malý recalled, "By that time, people had sensed that the regime was collapsing, and they started to show their restlessness and disapproval.... But although some moments were very tense, there were no foul words or calls for violence. Still, I really struggled at times to keep the crowd calm."[24]

In the meantime, students formed work groups and organized a general strike. Some made flyers, while others visited factories, where they spoke to workers about supporting a unified action against the government. The state television and radio stations joined the opposition and spread news about the rapidly changing situation. On Monday, November 27, 75 percent of the Czechoslovak population left work in support of a two-hour general strike. The Party issued a series of reforms, but the die had been cast. Within two days of the strike, the Communist Party amended the constitution, removing the clause about its "leading role" in the state. Prague's citizens continued to demonstrate and organize into December.

Four days after Christmas, the National Assembly gathered in Vladislav Hall at Prague Castle. Alexander Dubček, the newly named speaker of the federal parliament, announced: "I hereby proclaim that Václav Havel has been elected president of the Czechoslovak Socialist Republic."[25] Nostalgia for the First Republic pervaded the city. Tomáš Masaryk's image hung in shop windows, and publishers printed commemorative books filled with photo-

FIGURE 14.3 Demonstrators gather at Můstek, the lower end of Wenceslas Square, on December 1, 1989. Photo by Josef Šrámek ml., CC BY 4.0, https://creativecommons.org/licenses/by/4.0, via Wikimedia Commons.

FIGURE 14.4 Václav Havel and Alexander Dubček greet Hungarian President Árpád Göncz at Prague Castle, 1990. Photo by Szalay Zoltán for Fortepan, CC BY-SA 3.0 via Wikimedia Commons.

graphs of the first president. Citizens and the international media embraced Havel as a philosopher president modeled on Masaryk.

Havel's inauguration on January 1, 1990, was a historic day that no one could have imagined a year earlier. Havel entered St. Vitus Cathedral and stopped for a short prayer in the medieval chapel of his namesake, Saint Wenceslas / Svatý Václav. Later, he and his wife Olga stood on the balcony at Prague Castle facing St. Vitus Cathedral and welcomed in a new year and a new era. He addressed the citizenry as their president and spoke the words written by Comenius, proclaimed in 1918 by Tomáš Masaryk, and etched onto the Jan Hus Memorial: "My people, the government has returned to your hands."

15

Post-Communist Prague

THE MOOD IN Prague was euphoric in the months following Václav Havel's inauguration as president of Czechoslovakia. Yet there was considerable work ahead. As Czech sociologist Jiří Musil explained, "The task was nothing less than to reconstruct completely a whole society."[1] After forty years of one-party rule and a centralized, planned economy, the new government needed to hold elections, reorganize the state, privatize the economy, and rebuild outdated infrastructure. In June 1990, the Czechoslovak citizenry participated in the first free parliamentary elections since 1946. Havel's Civic Forum movement and its Slovak counterpart, Public Against Violence, won in a landslide and formed a coalition government. The former dissident Petr Pithart, a close ally of Havel, was affirmed as prime minister. The word "socialist" was removed from the country's name, which became the Czech and Slovak Federative Republic. Prague remained the capital city.

Although the presidency was largely ceremonial, Havel used his platform to assert a moral framework for the nation. During the 1991 state visit of Israeli President Chaim Herzog, Havel hosted a concert in the Municipal House. Before the Czechoslovak Philharmonic performed music associated with the Theresienstadt ghetto, Havel addressed the audience. He acknowledged that many Czechs helped implement Nazi racial laws in the Protectorate and called these collaborators "the non-murdering murderers" of World War II. Havel attested to "a deep—perhaps even a metaphysical—feeling of shame. I am ashamed, if I may put it this way, of the human race." Havel recalled that as a boy, he admired the yellow stars worn by other children and only later learned their true significance. "If it is never to happen again that any children be compelled to wear on their clothes a brand designed to warn others against them and to indicate that they are inferior, we need to remind ourselves over and over again of the horrors that befell the Jewish people." Havel asserted that the country must take responsibility for its complicity in the Holocaust: "We need to talk about the suffering of the Jewish people even though it is so difficult."[2]

Havel's apologies for blemishes in Czech history did not always sit well with the citizenry or fellow politicians. Havel remarked in 1990, "I personally condemn the expulsions of Germans after the war—and so do many of my friends. I consider it as a deeply immoral act which did moral as well as material harm not only to Germans but also, and maybe even more so, to Czechs."[3] Czechoslovakia's political elite criticized Havel's apology, fearing that former citizens would seek economic reparations. In 1997, Germany and the Czech Republic signed a joint declaration apologizing for each country's mid-century crimes, but most Czechs resented the implication that the Sudetenland expulsions were equal to the dismemberment of Czechoslovakia in 1938.

Havel spoke frequently against the prejudices still central to Czech culture, especially toward the Roma population. The newfound freedoms following the Velvet Revolution enabled the rise of skinhead organizations that embraced fascist and racist ideologies. On the first anniversary of the Velvet Revolution, the *Washington Post* reported, "In the absence of the Communist era's police control, attacks on the Gypsy minority and Vietnamese workers by gangs of young skinheads are growing."[4] Havel condemned what he called "manifestations of intolerance, xenophobia, racism, and nationalism" and insisted that Romani people should "enjoy the same rights and responsibilities as all other citizens of our state...and the principles of collective blame or collective liability are not allowed to be applied against them." He reminded his fellow citizens, "Of the almost 6,000 Romani people from Bohemia and Moravia, fewer than 1,000 survived. Roma, too, were victims of the Holocaust."[5]

Prague's Jewish population—once the largest in Europe—numbered under two thousand by the end of the Communist period. Yet, the city was filled with reminders of its Jewish past. In 1994, the state returned the buildings of Prague's Jewish Museum to the Prague Jewish community. Tourists and school groups flocked to the five historic synagogues and the Old Jewish Cemetery. Artists repainted the names and hometowns of 77,297 Bohemian and Moravian Jews who perished during the Holocaust on Pinkas Synagogue's interior walls, which had fallen into disrepair under the Communist regime. The memorial had closed after the Warsaw Pact invasion in 1968 and reopened to the public in 1996. Another small memorial, designed by artist and Holocaust survivor Helga Hošková, marks the spot in Holešovice where Prague Jews assembled before their forced journeys to ghettos and concentration camps. Throughout the city, *Stolpersteine* (stumbling stones)—small bronze plaques placed among cobblestones—mark the places where Jewish families lived before the Nazi deportations. These memorials came from individual initiatives rather than an effort by the city government or the Czech state.

Prague's leaders also reckoned with reminders of communism. As in the post-Habsburg era, when city authorities took down double-headed eagles from public buildings, the post-communist Prague government removed the ubiquitous red stars from its buildings. Between December 1989 and April 1990, the city government announced new names for dozens of streets, squares, and transportation stations. The road leading to Prague's airport was changed from Vladimir Ilych Lenin to Edvard Beneš Boulevard. The space in front of Charles University's philosophical faculty no longer celebrated Red Army soldiers but instead commemorated martyred student Jan Palach. Defenders of Peace Street was renamed for the executed politician Milada Horáková. The name of Masaryk Station, which was called the Prague Central Railway Station during the Communist era, was restored. Fourteen metro stops were rechristened, ridding the city of Moscow, Gottwald, and Cosmonaut stations. Regarding the name of the Vltava River embankment where Havel's family home stood, the president remarked, "As a citizen, I do care whether I live on a quay named after a relatively unimportant philosopher of the past century like Friedrich Engels, or on a quay of Alois Rašín, a man who has contributed to this state to an extent equal to Tomáš Garrigue Masaryk.... I care about it. I confess it."[6] Calling Marx's collaborator unimportant and naming the quay for Rašín, the interwar minister assassinated by a Communist in 1923, tangibly demonstrated the city's rejection of state socialism.

In 1991, art student David Černý called attention to Prague's complex history and identity in a bold stunt. He and a group of friends snuck to the site of the Monument to Soviet Tank Crews in Prague's Smíchov district and painted it bubble-gum pink. The addition of an erect middle finger on the "Pink Tank" sent an obvious message to the former regime. Although the monument celebrated Prague's liberation in May 1945, it assumed a more sinister meaning following the 1968 Warsaw Pact invasion. Černý later remarked, "Having to pass this symbol of the Russian dictatorship which was here since I was born, I did not take the tank as a symbol of freedom—the end of the Second World War." Černý was arrested for destroying federal property, and the tank was repainted green after protests by the Soviet embassy. In turn, a group of Civic Forum politicians repainted it pink to protest Černý's arrest. While this color war played out in Prague, the last Soviet tanks pulled out of the country. Černý was at the forefront of Prague's post-communist creative culture. About the "Pink Tank," the artist recalled, "Of course, it was a political statement, and at the same time, it was an artistic action. And it was a lot of fun."[7]

The empty plinth on Letná Plain that had once supported the Stalin Memorial also reminded citizens of the authoritarian past. Although the monument to Stalin stood for only seven years, Prague residents still called the area U Stalinu (at Stalin). In the early 1990s, skateboarders practiced on the memorial's smooth granite surface, and the area underneath its base housed a pirate radio station and an unofficial rock club called Bunker. In 1991, the city marked the centennial of the 1891 Jubilee Exhibition by commissioning the Czech artist and professor Vratislav Novák to create a monument for the site. Novák designed the Prague Metronome, a functioning apparatus with a triangular base and a red needle that counts four beats per minute. Novák's inscription, "In time, all things pass," reminded observers that historical change is inevitable.

A palpable energy pulsed on the streets of Prague in the early 1990s. As early as February 1990, the *New York Times* proclaimed Prague one of the world's "hot travel spots."[8] A Czech Dixieland band performed daily on the

FIGURE 15.1 Vratislav Novák, Prague Metronome, 1991. Photo by the author.

Charles Bridge, and youths with guitars sang John Lennon's "Imagine" on Old Town Square. Yet the city lacked the infrastructure to accommodate significant numbers of wealthy North American and West European tourists. In 1990, there were only fifteen thousand hotel beds available in Prague. Foreign hotel chains and investment groups poured in to fill gaps in the tourism sector. Within a decade, fifty thousand hotel beds lodged over five million annual visitors. Holiday Inn acquired the International Hotel, built in the 1950s to honor Stalin, and replaced the rooftop's red star with the company's signature green emblem.

In 1992, UNESCO recognized Prague's historical core as a World Heritage site. The designation awarded Czechoslovakia financial resources to renovate city landmarks and historical sites. The Municipal House and its Smetana Concert Hall were remodeled, and its café became a popular destination for tourists. Houses in the Old Town Square and Lesser Town received new facades and fresh coats of candy-colored paint. The renovations displaced shops and services used by Prague's citizens, as souvenir merchants replaced hardware stores and butcher shops. In March 1992, Prague's first McDonald's opened near Wenceslas Square. Although some protested the addition of the golden arches to their golden city, an estimated eleven thousand people turned up for the opening. Independent journalist Ivan Hoffman surmised that history and modernity would coexist: "Both Saint Wenceslas and hamburgers are here to stay."[9] Prague became one of the 1990s' top European tourist destinations, ranking behind only Paris, Berlin, Rome, Barcelona, and Madrid. Foreign tourism boosted the economy, but prices in the city center rose considerably. Czechs often complained about the "tourist takeover of Prague."

Prague became known as a destination for West European and North American post-college expatriates, who taught English or waited tables and idealized Prague as a city of cheap beer and free music. Other expats stayed longer and founded businesses that catered to the young, international community—the Globe Bookstore and Café, Little Glen's Jazz and Blues Club, and Laundry Kings. The English-language weekly newspaper *Prague Post*, founded by Americans in 1991, called Prague the Left Bank of the 1990s. In its review of an eclectic exhibit at the Mánes Gallery, the *Los Angeles Times* declared: "Forget the Paris of the '90s. Prague is the New York of the '90s."[10]

The economic and social transformation took its toll on the local population, which had enjoyed a modest yet comfortable standard of living before the revolution. Younger Prague citizens benefited most from the economic and social changes that followed state socialism. They hurried to learn English

FIGURE 15.2 Tourists on the Charles Bridge, 2015. Photo by the author.

and German—taking evening or lunchtime classes or changing their university course of study—and looked for career opportunities in the new foreign enterprises that poured into the capital city. Aid from the International Monetary Fund and World Bank and investment by Western corporations pushed Prague toward neoliberalism and a globalized economy. Individuals participated in the economic overhaul through a complex voucher privatization scheme that enabled them to purchase small shares of state-owned enterprises or to buy their state-owned homes and apartments. Residents formed condominium associations to facilitate private ownership of modular *panelák* units, which housed 44 percent of Prague's residents. Small businesses were restituted to their former owners or auctioned off to citizens. Some émigrés returned to Prague, but few realized their dream to restart businesses that had closed four decades earlier.

Multinational corporations rushed in to invest and build modern office buildings. The Dutch insurance company ING acquired land on the Vltava embankment north of the National Theater, which had stood empty since the American bombing raid of February 1945. Václav Havel, whose family apartment was near the site, advocated for a new cultural center and gathering space for the Prague public. Croatian-Czech architect Vlado Milunić partnered with renowned Canadian-American architect Frank Gehry to design the Dancing Building, two adjoining towers, one concrete and angular and the other rounded and made primarily of glass. The Czech media dubbed the proposed design "Fred and Ginger," after the American dance partners and movie stars. One newspaper complained that "Frank Gehry was bringing Hollywood kitsch to Prague." Gehry insisted, "Of course, I never intended this.... Czechs are very against representation and proud of the sense of the abstract." Gehry explained that the second tower's resemblance to a female figure was unintentional: "I pinched it in at one point because the window in the building next door has a view of the castle across the river and we didn't think our tower should block it; that wouldn't be very neighborly. So, we made this cut, and the model looked like a dancing figure."[11] Despite the initial criticism, the Dancing House soon became popular with residents and tourists, who enjoyed its restaurants, gallery, and hotel.

FIGURE 15.3 Frank Gehry and Vlado Milunić, Dancing House on the Rašínovo Embankment, opened in 1995. Photo by the author.

While Prague garnered international attention, some Czechoslovak citizens resented the capital city, whose economic recovery was more rapid and stronger than in other cities and regions. Prague's political predominance in the Czech and Slovak Federative Republic did not sit well with citizens in Slovakia, who felt that the eastern province played a tertiary role behind Bohemia and Moravia. In July 1992, Slovaks elected populist politician Vladimir Mečiar as prime minister of the Slovak parliament. Mečiar ran on a platform of Slovak sovereignty. He met several times with his Czech counterpart, Václav Klaus, a free-market economist overseeing the transition to capitalism, to forge a new power-sharing law. The tense Czech-Slovak relationship developed against the backdrop of wars in the former Yugoslavia. While Havel strongly opposed a breakup of the state, he promised that he would not go to war to keep the regions united: "I have said many times that I am a supporter of a common state, but if life together in one state is not possible, I favor a constitutional separation."[12] It soon became clear that Mečiar would not agree to any compromise that maintained a central government, while Klaus insisted that the federal government must oversee diplomacy, the military, and the economy for the whole state. Klaus became increasingly frustrated and began to favor the split himself. The two prime ministers agreed to create separate states. In November 1992, the Federal Assembly in Prague disbanded the federation, and Havel resigned the presidency of a now-defunct state. The split became known as the Velvet Divorce.

The Czech Republic formed on January 1, 1993, with Prague as its capital. The city's population was just over 1.2 million, and about 10 percent of citizens lived in the confines of greater Prague. The constitution created a parliamentary democracy with a bicameral legislature composed of the Senate and the Chamber of Deputies. Klaus, the leader of the Civic Democratic Party, was selected as the prime minister. Havel ran for president without a party affiliation and received 54.5 percent of the parliamentary votes, while a leftist coalition led by Communist Party representative Marie Stiborová claimed nearly a quarter. For the country's first two decades, the largest government parties were the Civic Democrats and the Social Democrats, representing the moderate right and left, respectively. Prague also functioned as an independent city overseen by a mayor, the Prague City Council, and the Prague Assembly. In the first month of the new state, January 1993, the inflation rate soared above 20 percent, and older citizens saw the value of their pensions decline. Prague professionals and civil servants found that their salaries could not keep up with the cost of living.

As the president of a new country, the Czech Republic, Havel pledged to restore Prague Castle as the seat of a democracy. In 1996, a glass pyramid was placed atop the obelisk in the Castle's third courtyard to evoke the Czech Republic's new transparency. International celebrities were inspired by Prague's transformation. Britain's Prince Charles, a connoisseur of historical architecture, funded the restoration of the lower Prague Castle gardens. The Rolling Stones provided funds from their 1996 Prague concert to modernize lighting in several interior spaces in the castle.

Nostalgia for the Masaryk era pervaded the capital city. In the 1996 film *Kolya*, which depicted Prague in the final years of communism, the anxious main character asks his mother to put away her small bust of Tomáš G. Masaryk, fearful of anything that might draw attention to the family. Now, Masaryk's image was everywhere. On March 7, 2000, the 150th anniversary of his birth, a statue of Masaryk was unveiled near the entrance to Prague Castle. US Secretary of State Madeleine K. Albright, born in Prague in 1937, spoke at the ceremony. Albright's father, Josef Korbel, worked in Edvard Beneš's London government in exile and eventually became a professor of international relations in the United States. The Korbel family had converted to Christianity, and Albright had only recently rediscovered her family's Jewish heritage.

> It is especially moving to see this likeness of the living Masaryk so near to the Castle, where he served as President. And—on a personal note—so near to my family's former home, where I was born and where I played as a child. For me...the memories are strong. I was only four months old when President Masaryk died, but in every other sense I grew up with him....I would look at his picture and think to myself, "this is how a President should look." I would study his writings and think "this is how a President should inspire." I would research his actions and think, "this is how a President should lead."[13]

Prague's residents are divided about how to represent the Communist past. The Museum of Communism debuted in 2001. Founded by an American businessman, the heavy-handed exhibition has three sections: the Dream, the Reality, and the Nightmare. While popular with tourists, few Czechs visit the private museum. In 2002, the Prague City Council and the Confederation of Political Prisoners unveiled Olbram Zoubek's *Memorial to the Victims of Communism* in Petřín Park. The memorial has been at the center of several controversies. The organizers neglected to invite the country's most famous political prisoner, President Havel, to the ceremony. Some speculated that the anti-communist confederation viewed Havel as too soft on the former regime. The country's lustration laws forbid former members of the Czechoslovak secret police from holding a variety of civil service positions, but they were not prosecuted through the judiciary system.

The memorial features several nude male figures on a staircase. Each one has more pieces of his body missing until the last seems to disappear altogether. While the sculptor attempted to convey prisoners' loss of identity and individuality, some artists decried the repetitive and decomposing figures as kitschy and distasteful. Feminist groups resented the absence of female bodies and reminded the public that women, too, had been victims of the regime. In the memorial's first few years, it suffered attacks of graffiti, vandalism, and two small explosions.

Artist David Černý takes a less didactic approach with his public art. His sculptural installations in Prague provoke conversations about history and challenge concepts of national identity and memory. In 1999, Černý questioned the idealization of national heroes by creating a statue of Saint

FIGURE 15.4 Olbram Zoubek, *Memorial to the Victims of Communism* in Petřín Park, unveiled in 2002. Photo by the author.

Wenceslas astride an upside-down dead horse. Following its display on the eponymous square, *Horse* was permanently hung from a stained-glass dome in the Lucerna Palace shopping arcade. Near the Franz Kafka Museum at the Herget Brickyard, Černý installed a fountain named *Piss*, in which two nude male figures stand in a base shaped like the Czech Republic. Their torsos and penises move mechanically and spew toward each other. Some have interpreted the figures as representing a competition between Prague and Brno, the country's second city, while others wonder if Černý's work alludes to Czech apathy.

Artists continue Prague's tradition of avant-garde and experimental art. In 2001, Černý founded the Meet Factory, in an abandoned meatpacking plant, as a space for innovative contemporary artists. Following the devastating floods of 2002, the art space moved to Prague's Smíchov neighborhood, where artists, musicians, and filmmakers can apply for residencies. Several years later, the Dox Centre for Contemporary Art opened in Holešovice. Beyond formal galleries, Prague artists experimented with street art almost as soon as the revolution ended. While technically illegal, graffiti art has become more accepted and tolerated. An unspoken agreement that artists do not deface historical monuments has allowed exciting public art to flourish on old factory building facades, on *panelák* housing, and near the Florenc Bus Station.

Franz Kafka has become a ubiquitous symbol of post-communist Prague. Černý's kinetic sculpture of Kafka's head was unveiled in 2014, steps away from the British department store Tesco. Forty-five layers of stainless-steel pieces change direction and alter the writer's appearance. Some interpret Černý's work as a commentary on Kafka's struggles with anxiety and melancholy, but perhaps the artist suggests that we manipulate Kafka for our needs. Another monument to Kafka stands in Old Town Prague's Jewish quarter, in front of a Roman Catholic Church and a Jewish synagogue. The sculptor Jaroslav Róna saw his work's placement near the two religious edifices as a symbol of healing. On Róna's monument, a diminutive Kafka sits on the shoulders of a man whose body has disappeared into a large suit. The monument imagines a scene from Kafka's short story "Description of a Struggle," in which the narrator rides through Prague on the back of a mysterious companion.

In 2000, the Prague City Council debated a proposal to name an area in the Old Town for Kafka. Prague's mayor, Jan Buergermeister, opposed the measure and insisted, "Kafka would hate to be a square." The Kafka scholar and former dissident Eduard Goldstücker disagreed: "[Kafka] was a very modest man, but that doesn't mean he wouldn't like to have had his name attached to something."[14] The motion passed. In twenty-first-century Prague, cafés, restaurants, and a museum bear Kafka's name. Tourists can purchase T-shirts, postcards, and magnets with the writer's image. Kafka's remark to his friend Oskar Pollák—"Prague won't let go!"—seems prescient today.

After 1989, Prague's leaders, artists, and intellectuals have sought to define their place in a post-Soviet world, and the rhetoric of "returning to Europe" pervaded political discourse. Many Czechs pursued integration with Western and Central Europe, but the memory of the Munich betrayal had not vanished. The Czech Republic, along with Hungary and Poland, joined NATO in 1999, and three years later, Prague hosted the NATO summit that expanded the treaty alliance by seven former Warsaw Pact countries or Soviet republics: Slovakia, Romania, Bulgaria, Slovenia, Latvia, Lithuania, and Estonia.

Discussions about the Czech Republic's entry into the European Union stirred national debates. The new president, Václav Klaus, who took office in 2003, cautioned that the larger, wealthier EU states would dominate the

FIGURE 15.5 David Černý, *K.* (rotating head of Franz Kafka), 2014. Photo by Ondřej Vasiluk, CC BY-SA 4.0 via Wikimedia Commons.

small, former Communist countries. He likened Czech membership in the EU to dropping "a lump of sugar...into a cup of coffee."[15] At a Prague rally in June 2003, days before the national referendum on membership in the European Union, former president Havel retorted, "Those who fuss about losing our sovereignty [are] misguided." To remind citizens to cast their votes on joining the European Union, the words "YES" and "NO" were placed on either side of the Prague Metronome. Despite President Klaus's Euroskepticism, over 75 percent of the Czech population chose yes. A year later, Klaus followed the will of the people and signed the agreement that made the Czech Republic a member state. Along with nine other European countries, the Czech Republic pledged to participate in the common European market and the European Parliament and to uphold democratic institutions and human rights. On May 1, 2004, the EU's blue flag with a circle of golden stars rose alongside the national flag in buildings throughout Prague.

◆

Václav Havel died in his country home on December 17, 2011. He succumbed to the lung ailments that plagued him following years of chain smoking during his incarcerations. At age seventy-five, he had come to represent the moral opposition to late socialism as well as the triumphs and challenges of postcommunism. Tributes poured in from around the world. President Barack Obama remarked, "His peaceful resistance shook the foundations of an empire, exposed the emptiness of a repressive ideology, and proved that moral leadership is more powerful than any weapon."[16] Prague's citizens brought flowers, candles, and remembrances to the National Museum steps, the public areas at Prague Castle, and Havel's Prague residence. Havel did have his critics. Some Czechs believed that he treated former Communists too leniently, demanded an unattainable moral framework from the citizenry, and favored philosophy over practicality. Others critiqued his personal life and disparaged his 1997 marriage to thirty-nine-year-old actress Dagmar Veškerová, only a year after his wife Olga's death. Still, he was a popular and respected figure, and a genuine outpouring of grief overtook his city that December.

In an annual survey, Havel consistently places as the third most influential Czech, behind Charles IV and Tomáš Masaryk. Like these esteemed predecessors, Havel received an elaborate state funeral and procession through Prague. On December 21, 2011, the horse-drawn carriage used for Masaryk's funeral brought Havel's casket to Prague Castle's sixteenth-century Vladislav Hall, where current president Václav Klaus spoke. "As a writer and playwright, he believed in using the power of words to change the world, and he did not hesitate to use his words openly and sharply whenever he deemed it necessary." Klaus, who often clashed with Havel on policy and style, now called on the nation to carry out his work:

> It has been stated repeatedly in recent days that his death marks the end of one chapter in the history of our country. I would like for this not to be the case. The struggle for freedom and democracy and the discussion about the values of our society and its direction, which he has influenced so much over the past several decades, have not ended. I would like for everyone who is not indifferent about the future of our country to be willing to stand for their opinions and convictions with the same courage and determination with which Václav Havel did.[17]

Two days before Christmas, on December 23, 2011, thousands of onlookers lined Prague's streets and watched the funeral on large video monitors placed throughout the city. A photograph of Havel hung on the National Museum's facade overlooking the site of the Velvet Revolution. World leaders filled St. Vitus Cathedral. Madeleine Albright presented her eulogy in Czech, remarking that Havel "injected light to places of deepest darkness." One Prague citizen expressed the feelings of many Czechs, telling a *New York Times* reporter, "Our hopes from 1989 were fulfilled only partly. Not everything we wished for happened. But our children are growing up in a completely different society than we did, and that is why we are here to thank him."[18] The Czech Philharmonic performed Dvořák's *Requiem* in Havel's honor, but the fan of the Rolling Stones and Lou Reed might have preferred a rock concert. Indeed, his friends organized a tribute at Lucerna Music Bar, inside the Wenceslas Square landmark founded by Havel's own grandfather. Rock musicians, including Ivan Král, the Plastic People of the Universe, Suzanne Vega, and the Velvet Underground Revival Band, performed Havel's favorite tunes.

Somewhat shy, Havel might have balked at the many commemorations in his honor. In 2012, the Prague airport was named for him, though Havel famously hated flying. The following year, the airport installed a French Aubusson tapestry, *The Flying Man: Hommage à Václav Havel*. Designed by the Czech-born American artist Peter Sís and funded by five musicians—Bono, The Edge, Peter Gabriel, Sting, and Yoko Ono—the playful scene depicts a man floating among the clouds above the City of One Hundred Spires. Sís, known for his elaborately illustrated children's books, suggested that Havel's spirit has endured. Four Václav Havel Benches were installed in different parts of Prague to encourage citizens to sit and engage in open conversations. Kurt Gebauer installed the whimsical sculpture *A Heart for Václav Havel* in the pedestrian courtyard between the National and New Scene Theaters. The glowing red heart bursting from a cage represents Havel's commitment to peace and his penchant for heart-shaped symbols. Havel often added a small heart to his signature, and in 2002, the president welcomed NATO representatives to the Czech capital by illuminating a red neon heart above Prague Castle. (See Color Plate 18.) Václav Havel's death, of course, is not the end of the story, but it represents the end of an era. Havel was born during the First Republic, and his early childhood coincided with the Nazi occupation. He experienced communism through the lens of a dissident and artist, and, as president, he presided over a new democratic era.

Democracy has not been without its challenges. In the decade following Havel's passing, the country elected leaders who did not often live up to Havel's moral idealism or Václav Klaus's erudition and statesmanship. President Miloš Zeman, a Social Democrat, became known for his public gaffes. The billionaire technocrat Andrej Babiš, who was prime minister between 2017 and 2021, embraced a populist agenda that included increased pensions and child tax credits. His party, ANO (Dissatisfied Citizens' Action), opposed EU-established quotas for migrants entering the Czech Republic and embraced nationalist slogans. During his term, hate crimes against Roma and Vietnamese citizens rose.

A wave of scandals led thousands of citizens to protest the Babiš government in 2019. In June, a demonstration on Wenceslas Square called for an end to corruption, and in November, over 250,000 citizens marked the thirtieth anniversary of the Velvet Revolution with a protest on Letná Plain. Accusations that his government mishandled the COVID-19 global pandemic, which claimed the lives of thirty-five thousand Czech citizens, brought Babiš's government down in 2021. Two years later, Babiš lost a presidential bid by sixteen percentage points, a landslide in Czech politics. The new president, Petr Pavel, a liberal internationalist and former NATO general, visited a Václav Havel Bench soon after his presidential victory, signaling his plan to embrace the ideals of pluralism and an open society. Yet, a shaky coalition government in Prague leaves open the question of the Czech Republic's future. A challenge Havel posed in 1978 still resonates in a city where past, present, and future intersect in the streets, buildings, and landscapes:

> The real question is whether the brighter future is really always so distant. What if, on the contrary, it has been here for a long time already,

and only our own blindness and weakness has prevented us from seeing it around us and within us, and kept us from developing it?[19]

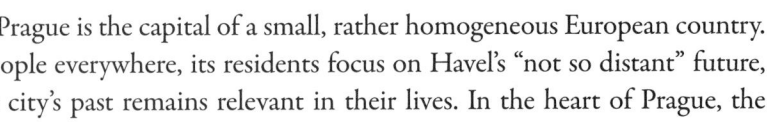

Today, Prague is the capital of a small, rather homogeneous European country. Like people everywhere, its residents focus on Havel's "not so distant" future, but the city's past remains relevant in their lives. In the heart of Prague, the Charles Bridge spans the Vltava River and connects eleven centuries of history. Romanesque churches, Renaissance synagogues, art nouveau apartments, and functionalist office buildings remind us that history shapes the present.

In 2020, the Prague 6 district commissioned a statue of Habsburg Empress Maria Theresa, but a century earlier, Prague residents tore down reminders of the Austrian past. Protesters objected to the placement of Maria Theresa in a park where anti-Nazi resistance leader Václav Morávek died in 1942. They suggested a World War II memorial would be more appropriate there. This and other similar debates evoke questions about how places assert communal values. Can a "Czech" capital both celebrate the Germanic Austrian past and condemn the Nazi German occupation? Has Prague adequately reckoned with the Jewish past when there is still not a museum or public monument dedicated to the Holocaust? Can the legacy of communism be addressed in a nuanced way?

New Prague monuments speak to some of these questions—or perhaps merely raise new ones. A replica of the Marian Column that was torn down in 1918 was erected on Old Town Square in 2020. The Society for the Recovery of the Marian Column had advocated for this since 1993, but many in Prague objected, believing a new column would celebrate "three hundred years of Habsburg subjugation of the Czech nation." An art historian of the Baroque era proclaimed, "Old Town Square cannot be turned into a museum."[20] Indeed, Prague is one of the most secular cities in Europe, and few residents attend religious services. Nearly three decades after the Society had laid a commemorative plaque that announced, "Here did lie—and will lie again—the Marian Column of Old Town Square," the Prague City Assembly narrowly approved the reinstallation proposal. The new column was unveiled with little fanfare in June 2020 amid the COVID-19 global pandemic. Today, it blends into a landscape already bursting with historical relics. Prague tourists, who sit on its base to rest from a day of sightseeing, seldom realize how new the "historic" monument is.

Also in 2020, Prague workers renovating Wenceslas Square discovered cobblestones emblazoned with Hebrew letters. Researchers concluded that the stones were hewn from a Jewish cemetery in northern Bohemia, which the Communist government had demolished. The state had installed the cobblestones in 1987 to prepare the square before Mikhail Gorbachev's visit. Once the archaeologists concluded their study, Prague's city government presented six thousand excavated cobblestones weighing seven tons to Prague's Jewish community.

Jaroslav Róna, the sculptor of Old Town's Kafka Memorial, was asked to find a use for them. Róna and his wife, Lucie Rónová, designed the *Return of the Stones* memorial, which was installed in September 2022 in Žižkov's Old Jewish Cemetery. This place of "meditation and commemoration for those people who know that the cemeteries where their relatives lay were destroyed" lies in the shadow of Prague's TV tower.[21] Most of the cemetery had been razed in the mid-1980s to make room for the seven-hundred-foot transmitter.

Although the *Return of the Stones* does not directly confront the Holocaust, the memorial recalls millions of European Jews who did not receive proper burials. Róna called *Return of the Stones* a transition from the physical to the spiritual world. More than a century ago, novelist Gustav Meyrink made a similar comment about the origin of Prague's name: "Prague does not have its name for no reason—in truth, Prague is a threshold between the life on Earth and Heaven, a threshold much thinner and narrower than in any other place."[22]

Few contemplate the meaning of Prague's TV tower, but for some, it stands as a symbol of historical insensitivity and erasure. František Bányai, chairman of Prague's Jewish community, called the desecration of Jewish cemeteries evidence of "barbarism, rudeness and archaic ruthlessness."[23] The Prague writer Irena Dousková reflected on the desecrated space in her short story "All's Well in the End." In it, a young man searches for a burial place for his Jewish mother. "She picked out the one beneath Žižkov Tower. The one that was now less than a third in size because of the tower.... The second oldest cemetery in Prague, no burials had been allowed there in a long time. But that didn't matter."[24] The grieving son brings his mother's ashes to the spot and illegally buries them there. In a story about growing up in Žižkov, the Czech-Roma writer Patrik Banga also pondered the destruction of the old cemetery: "I still wonder who had the stomach to make that decision, entirely humiliating the ancestors of the Jewish people buried there."[25]

Prague is a city that holds onto its history even through centuries of political and cultural transitions. In the 1930s, the poet Josef Hora reflected on the enduring reminders of Prague's past:

> The stone road flows
> Prague Castle behind me, the wall of the castle on which I lean,
> is mighty, centuries old, firm.
> You couldn't move it a millimeter.[26]

FIGURE 15.6 Jaroslav Róna and Lucie Rónová, *Return of the Stones Memorial* in the Old Jewish Cemetery in Žižkov, 2022. Photo by the author.

Prague Castle's looming presence inspired Franz Kafka, too. He located his novel *The Castle* in a fictional town, but Prague's imposing landscape inspired his setting. The protagonist K. steps "out into the beautiful winter morning. Now he saw the Castle above, sharply outlined in the clear air." As in Prague, Kafka's Castle "was neither an old-style knight's stronghold, nor a modern palace, but an extensive complex…of buildings."[27] Even when dense fog shrouds the Castle Mount, K. can feel its presence. "Prague won't let go."

Throughout Prague, sites of memory may blend into their surroundings, but they hold stories about the past. Plaques on buildings mark where famous artists lived. Stumbling blocks bear witness to the lives of Prague's murdered Jews. Statues of saints, German writers, and Czech musicians instruct us on who our heroes should be. They can expose fractures in collective memory, promote healing, or save a historical figure from relative obscurity. The meanings of these places expand beyond their original intentions and come to represent multiple, even conflicting, moments in history.

Notes

INTRODUCTION

1. Vítěslav Nezval, "Prague Panorama," in *Prague with Fingers of Rain*, trans. Edwald Osers (London: Bloodaxe Books, 2009), 41.
2. Quotations by Ripellino are all from Angelo Maria Ripellino, *Magic Prague*, trans. Michael Henry Heim (Berkeley: University of California Press, 1993), 9–10 and 67.
3. Albert Camus, *A Happy Death*, trans. Richard Howard (New York: Knopf, 1972), 66.
4. Peter Demetz, *Prague in Black and Gold* (New York: Hill and Wang, 1993), xiii.
5. Ivan Klíma, "The Spirit of Prague," in *The Spirit of Prague and Other Essays*, trans. Paul Wilson (New York: Granta Books), 45.
6. Christian Norberg-Schulz, *Genius Loci: Towards a Phenomenology of Architecture* (New York: Rizzoli, 1984).
7. Alfred Thomas, *Prague Palimpsest* (Chicago: University of Chicago Press, 2010).
8. Gustav Meyrink, "The City with the Secret Heartbeat," in *The Dedalus Meyrink Reader*, ed. and trans. Mike Mitchell (Sawtry, Cambridgeshire: Dedalus Books, 2010), 112–114.
9. Quoted in Erica Smeltzer, "The Metropolis and the Attic: Spatial Representations of Jewish Identity in Kafka and the Golem of Prague," *Partial Answers* 14, no. 2 (2016): 343.
10. Umberto Eco, *The Prague Cemetery*, trans. Richard Dixon (Boston: Houghton, Mifflin, Harcourt, 2011), 355.
11. Jeremy Adler, "What Was Lost? The Czech Jewish Community," *European Judaism* 38, no. 2 (2005): 76.

CHAPTER 1

1. Nicholas J. Saunders, Jan Frolík, and Volker Heyd, "Zeitgeist Archaeology: Conflict, Identity and Ideology at Prague Castle, 1918–2018," *Antiquity* 93, no. 370 (2019): 1009–1025.

2. Quotations by Ibrahim are taken from Dmitrij Mishin, "Ibrahim Ibn-Ya'qub At-Turtushi's Account of the Slavs from the Middle of the Tenth Century," in *Annual of Medieval Studies at the CEU 1994–1999*, ed. M. B. Davis and M. Sebők (Budapest: Central European University, 1996), 186.
3. Peter Charvát, "Notes on the Social Structure of Bohemia in the 11th–12th Century," *Památky archeologické* 73 (1992): 312–384.
4. Lenka Kováčiková et al., "Livestock as an Indicator of Socioeconomic Changes in Medieval Prague (Czech Republic)," *Archaeological and Anthropological Sciences* 12: 283 (2020), https://doi.org/10.1007/s12520-020-01229-5 (accessed February 10, 2025).
5. All quotations from Cosmas are taken from *The Chronicle of the Czechs*, trans. Lisa Wolverton (Washington, DC: Catholic University of America Press, 2009).
6. Martin Homza, *Mulieres suadentes—Persuasive Women: Female Royal Saints in Medieval East Central and Eastern Europe* (Leiden: Brill, 2017).
7. Quotations from the Latin and Slavonic hagiographies are taken from Marvin Kantor, *The Origins of Christianity in Bohemia: Sources and Commentary* (Evanston, IL: Northwestern University Press, 1990).
8. Otakar Odložilík, "Good King Wenceslas, a Historical Sketch," *Slavonic and East European Review* 8, no. 22 (1929): 121.
9. Jan Klápště, *The Archaeology of Prague and the Medieval Czech Lands, 1100–1600* (Sheffield, UK: Equinox Publishing, 2016).
10. Quoted in Rachel Greenblatt, *To Tell Their Children: Jewish Communal Memory in Early Modern Prague* (Palo Alto, CA: Stanford University Press, 2014), 14–15.
11. Quoted in Stephen M. Donovan, "Agnes of Bohemia," in *The Catholic Encyclopedia: An International Work of Reference on the Constitution, Doctrine, Discipline, and History of the Catholic Church*, ed. Charles G. Herbermann (New York: Robert Appleton, 1907), 213.
12. Joan Mueller, *Clare of Assisi: The Letters to Agnes* (Collegeville, MN: Liturgical Press, 2003), 3. See also Joan Mueller, *The Privilege of Poverty: Clare of Assisi, Agnes of Prague, and the Struggle for a Franciscan Rule for Women* (University Park: Pennsylvania State University Press, 2006).
13. Klápště, *Archaeology of Prague*, 115.
14. Quoted in Roman Jakobson, *Selected Writings*, vol. 2, *Uncollected Works*, part 2, *1934–1943*, ed. Jindřich Toman (Berlin: de Gruyter Mouton, 2013), 371.

CHAPTER 2

1. In the interest of clarity, I will refer to him as Charles throughout.
2. Attributed to Beneš Krabice of Weitmile, *Chronicle of the Prague Church*. The quotation is discussed by historian Eva Doležalová in "The Story of John of Luxembourg, Bohemia's Foreigner King," Radio Prague International, April 12, 2020, https://english.radio.cz/story-john-luxembourg-bohemias-foreigner-king-8701987 (accessed January 2, 2025).

3. Guillaume de Mauchaut, *The Judgement of the King of Bohemia*, trans. R. Barton Palmer (London: Routledge, 2019).
4. Quoted in Éloïse Adde, "The Justification of Tyrannicide in the Chronicle of Dalimil: The Czech Nobility as the 'Mystical Body' of the Realm," *Medivalista* 23 (2018): 15.
5. Quoted in Alfred Thomas, *Reading Women in Late Medieval Europe: Anne of Bohemia and Chaucer's Female Audience* (New York: Palgrave Macmillan, 2016), 55.
6. All quotations in this chapter that are attributed to Charles IV come from *Karoli IV Imperatoris Romanorum Vita Ab Eo IPSO Conscripta: Et Hystoria Nova De Sancto Wenceslao Martyre = Autobiography of Charles IV: And His Legend of St. Wenceslas*, ed. Nagy Balázs and Frank Schaer (Budapest: Central European University Press, 2001).
7. Ondřej Frinta and Dita Frintová, "Cathedral of Sts. Vitus, Wenceslas, and Adalbert—the Melting Pot of Czech Religious, National, and State Identity and Its Legal Status," *Laws* 12, no. 2 (2023): 25, https://doi.org/10.3390/laws12020025 (accessed February 10, 2025).
8. Quoted in Barbara Drake Boehm and Jiří Fajt, eds., *Prague: The Crown of Bohemia, 1347–1437* (New Haven, CT: Yale University Press, Metropolitan Museum of Art, 2005), 5.
9. Jan Royt, *The Prague of Charles IV, 1316–1378* (Prague: Karolinum Press, 2016), 19.
10. Attributed to Beneš Krabice of Weitmile, *Chronicle of the Prague Church*. The quotation is discussed in Pit Péporté, "John of Bohemia: Constructing a National Hero," in *Constructing the Middle Ages: Historiography, Collective Memory and Nation-Building in Luxembourg* (Leiden: Brill, 2011), 161–219.
11. David C. Mengel, "Emperor Charles IV (1346–1378) as the Architect of Local Religion in Prague," *Austrian History Yearbook* 41 (2010): 15–29.
12. Quoted in Royt, *Prague of Charles IV*, 180.
13. Quotations from Beneš Krabice of Weitmile come from *Chronicle of the Prague Church* excerpted in Jan Bažant, Nina Bažantová, and Frances Starn, eds., *The Czech Reader: History, Culture, Politics* (Durham, NC: Duke University Press, 2011), 35–38 (hereafter *Czech Reader*).
14. Quoted in Royt, *Prague of Charles IV*, 24.
15. Quoted in Royt, *Prague of Charles IV*, 25.
16. David C. Mengel, "From Venice to Jerusalem and Beyond: Milíč of Kroměříž and the Topography of Prostitution in Fourteenth-Century Prague," *Speculum* 79, no. 2 (2004): 416.
17. Quoted in Irene Malfatto, "John of Marignolli and the Historiographical Project of Charles IV," *Acta Universitatis Carolinae—Historia Universitatis Carolinae Pragensis* 55, no. 1 (2015): 133.
18. Jiří Špička, "Francesco Petrarca Travelling and Writing to Prague's Court," *Verbum Analecta Neolatina* 12, no. 1 (2010): 30.

19. Quoted in Petr Uličný, "The Choirs of St Vitus's Cathedral in Prague: A Marriage of Liturgy, Coronation, Royal Necropolis and Piety," *Journal of the British Archaeological Association* 168, no. 1 (2015): 212.

CHAPTER 3

1. Quoted in Barbara Newman, "The Passion of the Jews of Prague: The Pogrom of 1389 and the Lessons of a Medieval Parody," *Church History* 81, no. 1 (2012): 3.
2. Quoted in Isabel Scheltens, "Silver and Spices in the Runtinger Trade with Prague," *Hungarian Historical Review* 11, no. 3 (2022): 622.
3. Kara's elegy was translated in Miri Rubin, *Gentile Tales: The Narrative Assault on Late Medieval Jews* (Philadelphia: University of Pennsylvania Press, 2004), 196–198.
4. John M. Klassen, *The Nobility and the Making of the Hussite Revolution* (Boulder, CO: East European Quarterly, 1978), 22.
5. Klassen, *Nobility*, 23.
6. Pavel Soukup, *Jan Hus: The Life and Death of a Preacher* (West Lafayette, IN: Purdue University Press, 2019), 84–85.
7. Quotations from Hus's sermons are from František Šmahel and Ota Pavlíček, eds., *A Companion to Jan Hus* (Leiden: Brill, 2015).
8. John Klassen, "Women and Religious Reform in Late Medieval Bohemia," *Renaissance and Reformation / Renaissance et Réforme* 5, no. 4 (1981): 203–221.
9. Pavlína Rychterová, "The Vernacular Theology of Jan Hus," in Šmahel and Pavlíček, *Companion to Jan Hus*, 189.
10. Translated by the author.
11. T. R. Grundy, "Sigismund 'super grammaticam,'" *Notes and Queries*, Issue 261 (December 28, 1872): 524.
12. Jan Hus, "Letters to the Czechs," in *Czech Reader*, 51–53.
13. Quotations from Peter of Mladoňovice's account are from *John Hus at the Council of Constance*, ed. and trans. Matthew Spinka (New York: Columbia University Press, 1968), 229–230.
14. Hus, "Letters to the Czechs," 51–53.
15. Thomas A. Fudge, ed., *The Crusade Against Heretics in Bohemia, 1418–1437: Sources and Documents for the Hussite Crusades* (Oxfordshire, UK: Routledge, 2002), 17–19.
16. Thomas A. Fudge, *Heresy and Hussites in Late Medieval Europe* (Farnham, UK: Variorum Ashgate, 2014), 13.
17. Fudge, *Crusade Against Heretics*, 21–24.
18. Howard Kaminsky, *A History of the Hussite Revolution* (Eugene, OR: Wipf and Stock, 2004).

CHAPTER 4

1. All quotations from Lawrence of Březová are from Thomas A. Fudge, *Origins of the Hussite Uprising: The Chronicle of Laurence of Březová, 1414–1421* (London: Routledge, 2020).
2. Thomas A. Fudge, "Proclamation of the Crusading Bull," in *The Crusade Against Heretics in Bohemia, 1418–1437: Sources and Documents for the Hussite Crusades*, ed. Fudge (Oxfordshire, UK: Routledge, 2002), 51.
3. Quoted in Kaminsky, *A History*, 369. See also Kamila Veverková, *The Four Articles of Prague Within the Public Sphere of Hussite Bohemia: On the 600th Anniversary of Their Declaration (1420–2020)*, trans. Angelo Shaun Franklin (Lanham, MD: Lexington Books, 2021).
4. "Women Among the Hussite Armies," in Fudge, *Crusade Against Heretics*, 73.
5. "Crusaders and Heretics," in Fudge, *Crusade Against Heretics*, 81.
6. "Hussite Manifesto from Prague," in Fudge, *Crusade Against Heretics*, 58–59.
7. Howard Kaminsky, "Chiliasm and the Hussite Revolution," *Church History* 26, no. 1 (1957): 43–71.
8. Thomas A. Fudge, *The Magnificent Ride: The First Reformation in Hussite Bohemia* (New York: Routledge, 1998), 189.
9. "Žižka Calls for Army Conscription," in Fudge, *Crusade Against Heretics*, 123.
10. "The Blind General of the Hussite Armies," in Fudge, *Crusade Against Heretics*, 126.
11. Thomas A. Fudge, "Želivský's Head: Memory and New Martyrs Among the Hussites," in *The Bohemian Reformation and Religious Practice: Papers from the Sixth International Symposium on the Bohemian Reformation and Religious Practice*, ed. David R. Holeton (Prague: Academy of Sciences of the Czech Republic, 2007), 113–114.
12. "Žižka's Drum," in Fudge, *Crusade Against Heretics*, 106.
13. "Ye, Who Are God's Warriors," in *Czech Reader*, 54–55.
14. "Letter from Joan of Arc," in *Czech Reader*, 56–57.
15. Quoted in Václav Žůrek, "Indigenous or Foreign? The Role of Origin in the Debate About the Suitable Candidate in Electing Bohemian Kings in the Fifteenth Century," *Historical Studies on Central Europe* 2, no. 2 (2022): 55.
16. Preserved Smith, *The Life and Letters of Martin Luther* (London: Frank Cass, 1911), 72.
17. Quoted from Luther's preface to *The Letters of John Huss, Written During His Exile and Imprisonment*, trans. Campbell Mackenzie (Edinburgh: William Whyte, 1846), 3.
18. Eliška Fučíková, *Renaissance Prague*, trans. Derek Paton (Prague: Karolinum Press, 2018), 27.
19. Fučíková, *Renaissance Prague*, 98.

20. All quotations from the anonymous Hebrew chronicle are taken from Abraham David, ed., *A Hebrew Chronicle from Prague*, c. 1615, trans. Leon J. Weingerger and Dena Ordan (Tuscaloosa: University of Alabama Press, 2006).

CHAPTER 5

1. Fučíková, *Renaissance Prague*, 15.
2. Pierre Bergeron, "Description of Prague During the Time of Rudolph II," in *Czech Reader*, 77–79.
3. Quoted in Eliška Fučíková, *Prague in the Reign of Rudolph II: Mannerist Art and Architecture in the Imperial Capital, 1583–1612*, trans. Derek and Marzia Paton (Prague: Karolinum Press, 2015), 43.
4. Quoted in Fučíková, *Prague in the Reign*, 43.
5. Quoted in Fučíková, *Prague in the Reign*, 45.
6. Noah J. Efron, "'Our Forefathers Did Not Tell Us': Jews and Natural Philosophy in Rudolfine Prague," *Endeavour* 26, no. 1 (2002): 15–18.
7. Jan Campanus, "To the Memory of Tycho Brahe," in *Czech Reader*, 76.
8. Bergeron, "Description of Prague," 78.
9. Quotations from Weston are taken from Elizabeth Jane Weston, *Collected Writings* (Toronto: University of Toronto Press, 2000).
10. Tracy Guren Klirs, ed., *The Merit of Our Mothers: A Bilingual Anthology of Jewish Women's Prayers* (New York: Hebrew Union College Press Reprints, 1992), 3.
11. Hillel J. Kieval, "Pursuing the Golem of Prague: Jewish Culture and the Invention of a Tradition," *Modern Judaism* 17, no. 1 (February 1997): 7.
12. Quotations by Loew are taken from "Maharal of Prague," in *The Jews in Christian Europe: A Sourcebook, 315–1791*, ed. Jacob Rader Marcus and Marc Saperstein (Pittsburgh: Hebrew Union College Press, University of Pittsburgh Press, 2015), 443–450.
13. Quotations by Gans are taken from "Mordecai Meisel, Financier and Philanthropist Prague, 1592–1601," in Marcus and Saperstein, *Jews in Christian Europe*, 452–453.
14. "Mordecai Meisel (From the Fugger Newsletter, 1601)," in Marcus and Saperstein, *Jews in Christian Europe*, 454.
15. Quoted in Anna Parker, "Ester, a Missing Clasp, and Jewish Pawnbroking Networks in Renaissance Prague," *Austrian History Yearbook* 52 (2021): 56.
16. Rudolph II, "Letter of Majesty," in *Czech Reader*, 80–81.

CHAPTER 6

1. "The Defenestration of Prague, 23 May 1618," in *The Thirty Years War: A Sourcebook*, comp. Peter H. Wilson (New York: Palgrave Macmillan, 2010), 35–36.
2. All quotations from the rebels come from "The Bohemian 'Apology,' 25 May 1618," in Wilson, *Thirty Years War*, 37–40.
3. Joseph Davis, *Yom-Tov Lipman Heller: Portrait of a Seventeenth Century Rabbi* (Oxford: Littman Library of Jewish Civilization, 2016), 101.

4. Wilson, *Thirty Years War*, 285.
5. Charles Andrew Weeks, "Jacob Boehme and the Thirty Years' War," *Central European History* 24, no. 3 (1991): 216, http://www.jstor.org/stable/4546211 (accessed February 10, 2025).
6. David Kachlik et al., "The Life and Work of Jan Jesenský (1566–1621), the Physician of a Dying Time," *Journal of Medical Biography* 21, no. 3 (2013): 160.
7. Quotations from the anonymous Hebrew chronicle and the writings of Rabbi Yom-Tov Lipman Heller are taken from Davis, *Yom-Tov Lipman Heller*.
8. Alexander C. Putík, "The Origin of the Symbols of the Prague Jewish Town: The Banner of the Old-New Synagogue, David's Shield, and the 'Swedish Hat,'" *Judaica Bohemiae* 29 (1993): 4–37.
9. Barbora Klipcová and Petr Uličný, "Domenico Pugliani: A New Face in the History of Wallenstein Palace in Prague," *Umění Art* 3, no. 61 (2013): 212.
10. Putík, "Origin of the Symbols," 23.
11. Bohuslav Balbín, "Jan of Nepomuk," in *Czech Reader*, 96–99.
12. Suzanna Ivanič, *Cosmos and Materiality in Early Modern Prague* (Oxford: Oxford University Press, 2021), 26–27.
13. Joshua Teplitsky, "Heroes and Victims Without Villains: Plague in Early Modern Prague," *Jewish Social Studies: History, Culture, Society* n.s. 26, no. 1 (2020): 69–70.
14. See Rachel L. Greenblatt, "Saint and Counter Saint: Catholic Triumphalism and Jewish Resistance in Baroque Prague's Abeles Affair," *Jewish History* 30, nos. 1–2 (2016): 61–80.
15. Michael Laurence Miller, "Rabbi David Oppenheim on Trial: Turks, Titles, and Tribute in Counter-Reformation Prague," *Jewish Quarterly Review* 106, no. 1 (2016): 51.

CHAPTER 7

1. Quotations from Voltaire are from *The History of the War of 1741*, vol. 33 in *The Works of M. de Voltaire: A Contemporary Version* (London: E. R. DuMont, 1901).
2. Lucien Wolf, *Notes on the Diplomatic History of the Jewish Question: With Texts of Protocols, Treaty Stipulations and Other Public Acts and Official Documents* (London: Spottiswood, Ballantyne, 1919), 10.
3. Quoted in Aubrey Newman, "The Expulsion of the Jews from Prague in 1745 and British Foreign Policy," *Transactions & Miscellanies* (Jewish Historical Society of England) 22 (1968): 3.
4. Gottfried August Bürger, *Lenore*, trans. Dante Gabriel Rossetti (London: Ellis and Elvey, 1900), 19.
5. Kathryn L. Libin, "Prague," in *Mozart in Context*, ed. Simon P. Keefe (Cambridge: Cambridge University Press, 2018), 124.
6. Quotations about Mozart are from Daniel Freeman, *Mozart in Prague* (Tyrone, PA: BearClaw Press, 2013).
7. Hugh Agnew, *Czechs in the Lands of the Bohemian Crown* (Stanford, CA: Hoover Institution Press, 2004), 149.

CHAPTER 8

1. Richard Georg Plaschka, "The Political Significance of Frantisek Palacky," *Journal of Contemporary History* 8, no. 3 (1973): 37–38.
2. Johann Gottfried Herder, "On Slav Nations," in *Czech Reader*, 123–125.
3. František Palacký, "History of the Czech Nation in Bohemia and Moravia," in *Czech Reader*, 133–136.
4. Chad Bryant, *Prague: Belonging in the Modern City* (Cambridge, MA: Harvard University Press, 2021).
5. Josef Kajatán Tyl, "Where Is My Home?," in *Czech Reader*, 142.
6. Rudolf Kučera, "Marginalizing Josefina: Work, Gender, and Protest in Bohemia 1820–1844," *Journal of Social History* 46, no. 2 (2012): 436.
7. Quoted in Hillel J. Kieval, "Imperial Embraces and Ethnic Challenges: The Politics of Jewish Identity in the Bohemian Lands," *Shofar* 30, no. 4 (2012): 11.
8. Agnew, *Czechs in the Lands*, 116.
9. Plaschka, "Political Significance," 47.
10. Quotations about the Sokol are from Claire E. Nolte, *The Sokol in the Czech Lands to 1914: Training for the Nation* (Basingstoke: Palgrave Macmillan, 2003).
11. Martyn Rady, "Reviews," *Slavonic and East European Review* 72, no. 3 (1994): 553–556.
12. Karel Hynek Mácha, *May*, trans. Marcela Sulak (Prague: Twisted Spoon Press, 2005).
13. Jan Neruda, "What Shall We Do With It?" in *Prague: A Traveler's Literary Companion.*, ed. and trans. Paul Wilson (Berkeley, CA: Whereabouts Press, 1995), 24–30.
14. Quoted in Michal Frankl, "'The Enchantment Has Gone': Anti-Jewish Views of Jan Neruda in the Context of Czech Liberal Journalism in the 1860s," *Judaica Bohemiae* 46 (2011): 16.
15. Christopher Campo-Bowen, "'We Shall Remain Faithful': The Village Mode in Czech Opera, 1866–1928," PhD dissertation, University of North Carolina–Chapel Hill, 2018. Campo-Bowen originated the term "village mode" to describe the prevalent rural themes in Czech opera.
16. Bedřich Smetana, *Vltava (The Moldau): Study Score*, ed. Hugh Macdonald (Kassel: Bärenreiter, 2015).
17. Otakar Sourek, ed., *Antonin Dvorak Letters and Reminiscences* (Alplaus, NY: Artia, 1954), 116.
18. Brian Large, *Smetana* (Boston: de Capo Press, 1985), 191.
19. "History," *Rudolfinum*, https://www.rudolfinum.cz/en/history/ (accessed June 18, 2024).
20. Gary Cohen, "Cultural Crossings in Prague, 1900: Scenes from Late Imperial Austria," *Austrian History Yearbook* 45 (2014): 4.
21. Catherine Albrecht, "Pride in Production: The Jubilee Exhibition of 1891 and Economic Competition Between Czechs and Germans in Bohemia," *Austrian History Yearbook* 24 (1993): 102.
22. Although semantically similar, the party platform of the National Socialist Party in Bohemia was not comparable to that of the German National Socialist Party, which was founded two decades later.

CHAPTER 9

1. Jiří Karásek ze Lvovic, *A Gothic Soul*, trans. Kirsten Lodge (Prague: Twisted Spoon Press, 2015).
2. "Introduction," in Rainer Maria Rilke, *Poems*, trans. Jessie Lemont (New York: Tobias A. Wright, 1918), xvi.
3. Quoted in Stephan Delbos, "Bust of R.M. Rilke Unveiled in Prague," *Prague Post*, December 8, 2011.
4. Karla Machová, "The Bohemian Woman as a Factor in Industry and Economy," in the *World's Congress of Representative Women*, vol. 2, ed. May Wright Sewall (Chicago: Rand, McNally, 1894), 564.
5. František (Franz) Urban, *Zdravotní desatero proti tuberkulose* (1904), reproduced in *Health for Sale: Posters from the William H. Helfand Collection*, ed. William H. Helfand, John Ittmann, and Innis Howe Shoemaker (Philadelphia, PA: Philadelphia Museum of Art, 2011), 31.
6. Quoted in Cathleen M. Giustino, *Tearing Down Prague's Jewish Town: Ghetto Clearance and the Legacy of Middle-Class Ethnic Politics Around 1900* (Boulder, CO: East European Monographs, 2003), 124.
7. Giustino, *Tearing Down Prague's Jewish Town*, 281.
8. Gustav Janouch, *Conversations with Kafka: Notes and Reminiscences*, trans. Goronwy Rees (London: Derek Verschoyle, 1953), 80.
9. Alois Jirásek, *Legends of Old Bohemia*, trans. Edith Pargeter (London: Paul Hamyln, 1963), 223–228.
10. Meyrink, "City with Secret Heartbeat," 112.
11. Guillaume Apollinaire, *Zone: Selected Poems*, trans. Ron Padgett (New York: New York Review Books, 2015), 3–16.
12. Quoted in Carolin Duttlinger, ed., *Franz Kafka in Context* (Cambridge: Cambridge University Press, 2018), 149.
13. Janouch, *Conversations with Kafka*, 80.
14. All quotations from this story are taken from Franz Kafka, "Description of a Struggle," in *The Complete Stories*, trans. Tania Stern and James Stern (New York: Schocken Books, 1971), 25–73.
15. Scott Spector, *Prague Territories: National Conflict and Cultural Innovation in Franz Kafka's Fin de Siècle* (Berkeley: University of California Press, 2002), 36.
16. Franz Kafka, *Letters to Family, Friends, and Editors*, trans. Richard Winston and Clara Winston (New York: Schocken Books, 1977), 58.
17. Cynthia Paces, *Prague Panoramas: National Memory and Sacred Space in the Twentieth Century* (Pittsburgh, PA: University of Pittsburgh Press, 2009), 40.

CHAPTER 10

1. Manfried Rauchensteiner, *The First World War and the End of the Habsburg Monarchy, 1914–1918* (Berlin: de Gruyter, 2014), 83.

2. Jaroslav Hašek, *The Good Soldier Švejk and His Fortunes in the World War*, trans. Cecil Parrott (London: Penguin Classics, 2005), 3–4.
3. R. W. Seton-Watson, *A History of the Czechs and Slovaks* (Hamden, CT: Archon Books, 1965), 285.
4. "The Great War in the Life of Prague Citizens," Museum of the City of Prague. Online exhibit. https://www.muzeumprahy.cz/en/education-museum-on-line-on-line-exhibitions-great-war-in-the-life/ (accessed June 26, 2024).
5. Claire Morelon, *Streetscapes of War and Revolution: Prague 1914–1920* (Cambridge: Cambridge University Press, 2024).
6. Todd Wayne Huebner, "The Multi-National 'Nation-State': The Origins and Paradoxes of Czechoslovakia, 1914–1920," PhD dissertation, Columbia University, 1994, 24.
7. Claire Morelon, "Staging the Austrian War Effort in Public Space: Prague During the First World War," in *Städte im Krieg—Erlebnis, Inszenierung und Erinnerung des Ersten Weltkriegs*, ed. Ernst Otto Bräunche and Stephan Sander-Faes (Ostfildern, Germany: Jan Thorbecke Verlag, 2016), 95–110.
8. Paces, *Prague Panoramas*, 24.
9. Paces, *Prague Panoramas*, 75.
10. Paces, *Prague Panoramas*, 83.
11. Alice Garrigue Masaryk, *Alice Garrigue Masaryk, 1879–1966: Her Life as Recorded in Her Own Words and by Her Friends*, ed. Ruth Crawford Mitchell (Pittsburgh, PA: University Center for International Studies, University of Pittsburgh, 1980), 81.
12. Claire Morelon, "Sounds of Loss: Church Bells, Place, and Time in the Habsburg Empire During the First World War," *Past & Present* 244, no. 1 (2019): 220.
13. Rauchensteiner, *First World War*, 727.
14. Rudolf Kučera, *Rationed Life: Science, Everyday Life, and Working-Class Politics in the Bohemian Lands, 1914–1918* (New York: Berghahn Books, 2016), 12–14.
15. See Morelon, *Streetscapes*, chapter 5.
16. Rauchensteiner, *First World War*, 981.
17. Rauchensteiner, *First World War*, 996.
18. *Declaration of Independence of the Czechoslovak Republic: Printed for the Czechoslovak Arts Club of New York City* (New York: Marchbanks Press, 1918).
19. *Národní listy*, November 5, 1918.
20. Andrej Tóth et al., "On the Issue of the Spanish Flu in the First Czechoslovak Republic," *Canadian Journal of Health History* 39, no. 2 (2022): 397–418.
21. Derek Sayer, *The Coasts of Bohemia* (Princeton, NJ: Princeton University Press, 2000), 270.

CHAPTER 11

1. Paces, *Prague Panoramas*, 93.
2. Ruth Crawford, "Pathfinding in Prague," *The Survey*, June 11, 1921, 327–328.

3. Rudolf Kučera, "Exploiting Victory, Sinking into Defeat: Uniformed Violence in the Creation of the New Order in Czechoslovakia and Austria, 1918–1922," *Journal of Modern History* 88, no. 4 (2016): 827–855.
4. "Masaryk's First Presidential Message," *Czechoslovak Review: The Official Organ of the American Czechoslovak Board (Chicago)* 3, no. 2 (1919): 43–48.
5. Alpha Buse, "Occupations of Women. Main Findings of the Report," *The Survey*, June 11, 1921, 342.
6. Quoted in Kathleen Hayes, ed. and trans., *The Journalism of Milena Jesenská: A Critical Voice in Interwar Europe* (New York: Berghahn Books, 2003), 11.
7. Bruce R. Berglund, *Castle and Cathedral in Modern Prague: Longing for the Sacred in a Skeptical Age* (Budapest: Central European University Press, 2017), 175.
8. "Plečnik and Prague Castle: Apartment for the First President of Czechoslovakia," *Museum and Galleries of Ljubljana* (2017), https://mgml.si/en/plecnik-house/exhibitions/18/plecnik-and-prague-castle-apartment-for-the-first-president-of-czechoslovakia/ (accessed June 20, 2024).
9. Paces, *Prague Panoramas*, 143.
10. Quoted in Roman Szporluk, *The Political Thought of Thomas G. Masaryk* (Boulder, CO: East European Monographs, 1981), 84. See also Tomáš G. Masaryk, "The Czech Question," trans. Peter Kussi, in *Modernism: The Creation of Nation-States*, ed. Ahmet Ersoy, Maciej Górny, and Vangelis Kechriotis (Budapest: Central European University Press, 2010), 199–209.
11. Ladislav Holý, *The Little Czech and the Great Czech Nation: National Identity and the Post-Communist Social Transformation* (Cambridge: Cambridge University Press, 1996), 40.
12. Paces, *Prague Panoramas*, 122.
13. Paces, *Prague Panoramas*, 133.
14. Apollinaire, *Zone*, 3–16.
15. Meghan Forbes, "Devětsil and Dada: A Poetics of Play in the Interwar Czech Avant Garde," *ARTMargins* 9, no. 3 (2020): 8.
16. Jaroslav Seifert, "Opening Poem," in *The Poetry of Jaroslav Seifert*, trans. Ewald Osers (New Haven, CT: Catbird Press, 1998), 28.
17. Forbes, "Devětsil and Dada," 13.
18. Brian Locke, *Opera and Ideology in Prague: Polemics and Practice at the National Theater, 1900–1938* (Rochester, NY: University of Rochester Press, 2006), 201.
19. Matthew Rampley, "Metaphors of Progress: Hygiene and Purity in Czechoslovak Architecture," *Craace. Continuity/Rupture: Art and Architecture in Central Europe 1918–1939*, April 10, 2020, https://craace.com/2020/04/10/metaphors-of-progress-hygiene-and-purity-in-czechoslovak-architecture/#_ftnref7 (accessed June 20, 2024).
20. Nezval, *Prague with Fingers*, 62.
21. Paces, *Prague Panoramas*, 147.
22. *Prague Panoramas*, 170.

23. Jonathan Bolton, "Mourning Becomes the Nation: The Funeral of Tomáš G. Masaryk in 1937," *Bohemia* 45, no. 1 (2004): 115.

CHAPTER 12

1. "Text of Chancellor Adolf Hitler's Speech on the Czechoslovak Situation Yesterday," *New York Times*, September 29, 1938, 17.
2. "Text of Hitler's Speech."
3. František Halas, "Prague," in *From a Terrace in Prague*, ed. Stephan Delbos (Prague: Litteraria Pragensia Books, 2011), 94.
4. Jaroslav Seifert, "At the Tomb of the Old Kings," in *Poetry of Jaroslav Seifert*, 57.
5. Vojtech Mastny, *The Czechs Under Nazi Rule: The Failure of National Resistance, 1938–1945* (New York: Columbia University Press, 1971), 23.
6. Benjamin Frommer, "The Holocaust in Bohemia and Moravia," in *Prague and Beyond: Jews in the Bohemian Lands*, ed. Kateřina Čapková and Hillel J. Kieval (Philadelphia: University of Pennsylvania Press, 2021), 199.
7. Laura E. Brade and Rose Holmes, "Troublesome Sainthood: Nicholas Winton and the Contested History of Child Rescue in Prague, 1938–1940," *History and Memory: Studies in Representation of the Past* 29, no. 1 (2017): 3–40.
8. Frommer, "Holocaust," 196.
9. Quoted in Chad Bryant, *Prague in Black: Nazi Rule and Czech Nationalism* (Cambridge, MA: Harvard University Press, 2009), 29.
10. All quotations by Jesenská are taken from Hayes, *Journalism of Milena Jesenska*.
11. Bryant, *Prague in Black*, 43.
12. Jiří Weil, *Life with a Star*, trans. Rita Klímová and Roslyn Schloss (Evanston, IL: Northwestern University Press, 1997), 28.
13. Josef Čapek, "Miserable," quoted in Lenka Pichlikova-Burke, "Josef Čapek, Czech Modernist Innovator," Frick Art Reference Library, NYARC, https://nyarc.org/blog/josef-capek-czech-modernist-innovator (accessed June 21, 2024).
14. Reinhard Heydrich, "On the Elimination of the Czech Nation," in *Czech Reader*, 321–326.
15. All quotations from Heda Margolius Kovály in Chapters 12 and 13 are from *Under a Cruel Star: A Life in Prague, 1941–1968*, trans. Helen Epstein (New York: Holmes & Meier, 1997).
16. Helga Weissová, *Draw What You See: A Child's Drawings from Theresienstadt/Terezín* (Göttingen: Wallstein Verlag, 1998).
17. Leo Pavlát, "The Jewish Museum in Prague during the Second World War." *European Judaism* 41, no. 1 (2008): 124–130.
18. C. Day Lewis, *The Complete Poems of C. Day Lewis* (Palo Alto, CA: Stanford University Press, 1992), 336.
19. Kateřina Čapková, "Periphery and Center: Jews in the Bohemian Lands from 1945 to the Present," in *Prague and Beyond*, 247–248.

CHAPTER 13

1. Milan Kundera, *The Book of Laughter and Forgetting*, trans. Adam Asher (New York: HarperCollins, 2023), 3.
2. *Rudé právo*, February 26, 1948.
3. "Le président Bénès a capitulé devant les exigences de M. Gottwald," trans. CVCE. EU by UNI.LU, *Le Monde*, February 26, 1948.
4. Igor Lukes, "Rudolph Slanský: His Trials and Trial," *Woodrow Wilson Working Papers*, Cold War International History Project, 2008, 44.
5. *Rudé právo*, September 9, 1948.
6. Kovaly, *Under a Cruel Star*, 106.
7. "Monument Dedicated to Milada Horáková to Be Unveiled in Prague," *Embassy of the Czech Republic in Washington D.C. Newsletter*, Ministry of Foreign Affairs, September 16, 2020, https://mzv.gov.cz/washington/en/culture_events/news/monument_dedicated_to_milada_horakova_to.html (accessed January 3, 2025).
8. Quotations in this section are from Paces, *Prague Panoramas*, 190–191.
9. Sarah Cramsey, "Saying Kaddish in Czechoslovakia: Memorialization, the Jewish Tragedy and the *Tryzna*," *Journal of Modern Jewish Studies* 7, no. 1 (2008): 44.
10. Jiří Weil, *Lamentations for 77,297 Victims*, trans. David Lightfoot (Prague: Karolinum Press, 2020), 23.
11. Artur London, *The Confession*, trans. Alistair Hamilton (New York: William Morrow, 1970), 38.
12. *Proceedings of the Trials of Slansky, et al, in Prague, Czechoslovakia, November 20–27, 1952 as Broadcast by the Czechoslovak Home Service*, 1953. Publication information not identified. https://archive.org/details/ProceedingsOfSlanskyTrialPrague1952/mode/2up (accessed June 25, 2024).
13. Ota Pavel, "A Race Through Prague," in *Prague: A Traveler's Literary Companion*, 180–192.
14. Nikita Sergeevich Khrushchev, *The "Secret" Speech: Delivered to the Closed Session of the Twentieth Congress of the Communist Party of the Soviet Union* (Nottingham, UK: Spokesman Books for the Bertrand Russell Peace Foundation, 1976).
15. Quoted in Hana Pichová, "The Lineup for Meat: The Stalin Statue in Prague," *PMLA* 123, no. 3 (2008): 629.
16. Quoted in Petr Roubal, *Spartakiads: The Politics of Physical Culture in Communist Czechoslovakia* (Prague: Karolinum Press, 2019), 11.
17. Quoted in Marta Edith Holečková, "On Cooperative Housing in Socialist Czechoslovakia, 1959–1970," *Architektúra & urbanizmus* 56, nos. 3–4 (2023): 194.
18. Quoted in Veronika Tuckerová, "Reading Kafka, Writing Vita: The Trials of the Kafka Scholar Eduard Goldstücker," *New German Critique* 42, no. 1 (2015): 138.
19. "Interview with Milos Forman," *UNESCO Courier: A Window Open on the World* 48, nos. 7–8 (1995): 18–20.
20. Václav Havel, "The Garden Party," excerpt in *Czech Reader*, 364.
21. Allen Ginsberg, *The Collected Poems, 1947–1997* (New York: HarperCollins, 2007), 363.

22. Jerome Karabel, "The Revolt of the Intellectuals: The Origins of the Prague Spring and the Politics of Reform Communism," UC Berkeley: Institute for Research on Labor and Employment, May 1990, 49.
23. Quoted in Miloslav Rechcígl, *On Behalf of Their Homeland: Fifty Years of SVU. An Eyewitness Account of the History of the Czechoslovak Society of Arts and Sciences (SVU)* (Berkeley: University of California Press, 2008), 58.
24. *Oratorium pro Prahu* (Oratorio for Prague), dir. by Jan Němec, Czechoslovakia, 1968, 26 min.
25. Jaromir Navratil, *The Prague Spring '68* (Budapest: Central European University Press, 2006), 345–356.
26. "Eyewitness: Prague Spring Crushed," BBC News, August 21, 2008, http://news.bbc.co.uk/2/hi/europe/7572276.stm (accessed February 10, 2025).
27. Quoted in Robert Littell, ed., *The Czech Black Book* (London: Pall Mall Press, 1969), 56.
28. Paces, *Prague Panoramas*, 212.
29. Kovály, *Under a Cruel Star*, 187.
30. Quoted in Hana Beneš, "Czech Literature in the 1968 Crisis," *Bulletin of the Midwest Modern Language Association* 5 (1972): 97–114.
31. "Text of Speeches by Svoboda and Dubcek on Moscow Talks," *New York Times*, August 27, 1968, 16, https://nyti.ms/4eESh56 (accessed June 25, 2024).
32. "Brezhnev Doctrine on Limited Sovereignty," in *The Rise and Fall of the Soviet Union*, ed. Richard Sawka (New York: Routledge Sources in History, 1999), 357.
33. Oldřich Tůma et al., "The (Inter-Communist) Cold War on Ice: Soviet-Czechoslovak Ice Hockey Politics, 1967–1969," CWIHP Working Paper 69, February 2014, 8.

CHAPTER 14

1. Quoted in Kieran Williams, The Prague Spring and Its Aftermath: Czechoslovak Politics, 1968–1970 (Cambridge: Cambridge University Press, 1997), 40. See also Zuzana Poláčková and Pieter C. van Duin, "Gustáv Husák and the Foundations of 'Normalization': Slovak, Czechoslovak and Federative Perspectives, 1968–1970," *Slavonica* 24, nos. 1–2 (2019): 1–16.
2. Emily Thompson, "The Women of Charter 77 and the New Dissenters," Radio Free Europe / Radio Liberty, https://www.rferl.org/a/28217006.html#nav (accessed June 23, 2024).
3. Alena Heitlinger, "Passage to Motherhood: Personal and Social 'Management' of Reproduction in Czechoslovakia in the 1980s," in *Women, State, and Party in Eastern Europe*, ed. Sharon L. Wolchik and Alfred G. Mayer (Durham, NC: Duke University Press, 1985), 287.
4. Quoted in Paul Berman, *Tale of Two Utopias. The Political Journey of the Generation of 1968* (New York: W. W. Norton, 1996), 230. See also Jarka M. Burian, *Modern*

Czech Theatre: Reflector and Conscience of a Nation (Iowa City: University of Iowa Press, 2000).
5. Malcolm W. Browne, "Czechoslovakia Is Importing Vietnamese Workers," *New York Times*, April 25, 1976, 10.
6. Quoted in Martin Palouš, ed., *The Solidarity of the Shaken: Jan Patočka's Legacy in the Modern World* (Washington, DC: Academia Press, 2019).
7. Jiřina Šiklová, "The 'Gray Zone' and the Future of Dissent in Czechoslovakia," trans. Káča Poláčková-Henley and Gerald Turner, *Social Research* 57, no. 2 (1990): 352.
8. All Jirous quotations are from Tony Mitchell, "Mixing Pop and Politics: Rock Music in Czechoslovakia Before and After the Velvet Revolution," *Popular Music* 11, no. 2 (1992): 187–203.
9. Plastic People of the Universe, "Delirium," *Co Znamená Vésti Koně*, remastered, reissued 2010, liner notes (translated by the author).
10. "Czech Republic/Slovakia: Text of Charter 77," Radio Free Europe / Radio Liberty Archive, January 1, 1997, https://www.rferl.org/a/1083022.html (accessed June 25, 2024).
11. Thompson, "Women of Charter 77."
12. Václav Havel, *Letters to Olga*, trans. Paul Wilson (New York: Knopf, 1988), 167.
13. Jana Seifertová, "Jaroslav Seifert: Banquet Speech," *The Nobel Prize*, December 10, 1984, https://www.nobelprize.org/prizes/literature/1984/seifert/speech/ (accessed June 25, 2024).
14. Šiklová, "The 'Gray Zone' and the Future of Dissent in Czechoslovakia," 352.
15. David Storey, "Witness: Vaclav Havel: Moral Force at the End of a Long Staircase," Reuters, December 11, 2011, https://www.reuters.com/article/idUSTRE7BH0N9/ (accessed February 10, 2025).
16. Zdeněk Mlynář, "The Lessons of the Prague Spring," *Labour Focus on Eastern Europe* 10, no. 2 (1988): 34–40.
17. Mikhail Gorbachev and Zdeněk Mlynář, *Conversations with Gorbachev: On Perestroika, the Prague Spring, and the Crossroads of Socialism* (New York: Columbia University Press, 2002).
18. Michael T. Kaufman, "Gorbachev on a Prague Stroll: The Cheers and the Curiosity," *New York Times*, April 10, 1987.
19. Kaufman, "Gorbachev on a Prague Stroll."
20. "Mikhail Gorbachev's Speech at Rally in Prague," Joint Soviet-Czechoslovak Communique, *Soviet Weekly Supplement*, April 1987.
21. Peter Bugge, "Normalization and the Limits of the Law: The Case of the Czech Jazz Section," *East European Politics and Societies* 22, no. 2 (2008): 282–318.
22. John Tagliabue, "7 More Dissidents Convicted in Prague," *New York Times*, February 23, 1989.
23. Timothy Garton Ash, *The Magic Lantern: The Revolutions of '89 Witnessed in Warsaw, Budapest, Berlin, and Prague* (New York: Penguin Random House, 1993), 78.

24. "Places of the Velvet Revolution 3: Wenceslas Square and Letná Plain," *Radio Prague International*, November 13, 2019, https://english.radio.cz/places-velvet-revolution-3-wenceslas-square-and-letna-plain-8115621(accessed February 10, 2025).
25. "Places of the Velvet Revolution 5: Prague Castle," *Radio Prague International*, November 15, 2019, https://english.radio.cz/places-velvet-revolution-5-prague-castle-8115416 (accessed February 10, 2025).

CHAPTER 15

1. Jiří Musil, "Czechoslovakia in the Middle of Transition," *Sociologický Časopis / Czech Sociological Review* 28 (1992): 5–21.
2. Václav Havel, *The Art of the Impossible: Politics as Morality in Practice. Speeches and Writings, 1990–1996* (New York: Knopf, 1997), 75–77.
3. Judith Renner, "'I'm Sorry for Apologising': Czech and German Apologies and Their Perlocutionary Effects," *Review of International Studies* 37, no. 4 (2011): 1588.
4. Mary Battiata, "A Year Later, Prague Loses Its Euphoria," *Washington Post*, November 17, 1990.
5. "Václav Havel's 1995 Speech at the Unveiling of the Lety Memorial," *Roma.cz*, May 22, 2015, https://romea.cz/en/czech-republic/vaclav-havel-s-1995-speech-at-the-unveiling-of-the-lety-memorial#google_vignette (accessed February 10, 2025).
6. Jaroslav David and Jana Davidová Glogarová, "President Václav Havel as an Inspiration for Czech Urbanonymy," *Onomastica* 65 (2021): 265.
7. "The Complicated History of Prague's Tank No. 23," *Radio Prague International*, May 8, 2005, https://english.radio.cz/complicated-history-pragues-tank-no-23-8098701(accessed February 10, 2025).
8. Terry Trucco, "Suddenly It's Eastern Europe!," *New York Times*, February 11, 1990, 19.
9. Paces, *Prague Panoramas*, 240.
10. Susan Muchnic, "Checking Prague's Post-Revolution Artistic Pulse," *Los Angeles Times*, June 30, 1992.
11. Frank O. Gehry, "Architectural Projects: Current and Recently Completed Work," *Bulletin of the American Academy of Arts and Sciences* 49, no. 5 (1996): 44.
12. Henry Kamm, "As Slovak Separatism Gains, Havel Faces the Unthinkable," *New York Times*, November 20, 1991.
13. Secretary of State Madeleine K. Albright, Remarks at Tomas Masaryk Statue Unveiling Ceremony, Prague Castle, Prague, Czech Republic, March 7, 2000. As released by the Office of the Spokesman, US Department of State. https://1997-2001.state.gov/statements/2000/000307a.html (accessed February 10, 2025).
14. Kate Connolly, "Kafka Would Hate to Be a Square, Say Prague Officials," *The Guardian*, February 15, 2000.
15. Wayne C. Thompson, *Nordic, Central, and Southeastern Europe, 2015–2016* (Lanham, MD: Rowman & Littlefield, 2016), 357.

16. "Statement of President Obama on the Death of Vaclav Havel," December 18, 2011, The White House of Barack Obama, https://obamawhitehouse.archives.gov/the-press-office/2011/12/18/statement-president-obama-death-vaclav-havel (accessed January 1, 2025).
17. "President Klaus Paying Tribute to President Havel," December 21, 2011, Embassy of the Czech Republic in Washington, DC, https://mzv.gov.cz/washington/en/czech_u_s_relations/news/speech_by_the_president_of_the_czech.html?force_format=mobile (accessed June 25, 2024).
18. "Mourners in Prague Honor Havel," *New York Times*, December 23, 2011 https://www.nytimes.com/2011/12/24/world/europe/mourners-in-czech-republic-honor-vaclav-havel.html (accessed February 10, 2025).
19. Václav Havel, "The Power of the Powerless," in *The Power of the Powerless: Citizens Against the State in Central-Eastern Europe*, ed. John Keane (Abington, UK: Routledge, 2010), 59.
20. Paces, *Prague Panoramas*, 232.
21. Ruth Fraňková, "Jewish Tombstones Broken Up for Paving Stones Made into New Prague Monument," Radio Prague International, September 8, 2022, https://english.radio.cz/jewish-tombstones-broken-paving-stones-made-new-prague-monument-8760913#:~:text=The%20Return%20of%20the%20Stones%20was%20made%20by%20sculptor,and%20his%20artist%20wife%20Lucie.&text=%E2%80%9CThe%20centre%20is%20a%20convex,cube%20walls%20are%20gradually%20receding (accessed July 9, 2024).
22. Meyrink, "City with Secret Heartbeat," 112–114.
23. Fraňková, "Jewish Tombstones Broken Up."
24. Irena Dousková, "All's Well in the End," trans. Melvyn Clarke, in *The Book of Prague: A City in Short Fiction*, ed. Ivana Myšková and Jan Zikmund (Manchester, UK: Comma Press, 2023), 59–76.
25. Patrik Banga, "Žižkovite," trans. Alex Zucker, in Myšková and Zikmund, *Book of Prague*, 101–108.
26. Josef Hora, "Prague," trans. Stephan Delbos and Ester Fleicherová, in Delbos, *From a Terrace*, 49.
27. Franz Kafka, *The Castle*, trans. J. A. Underwood (New York: Penguin Books, 1997), 8–9.

Bibliography

Abrams, Bradley F. "The Marshall Plan and Czechoslovak Democracy: Elements of Interdependence." In *The Marshall Plan: Fifty Years After*, edited by M. Schain, 93–116. New York: Palgrave Macmillan, 2001.

Adde, Éloïse. "The Justification of Tyrannicide in the Chronicle of Dalimil. The Czech Nobility as the 'Mystical Body' of the Realm." *Medievalista Online* 23 (2018). https://doi.org/10.4000/medievalista.1606. Accessed February 10, 2025.

Adler, Jeremy. "What Was Lost? The Czech Jewish Community." *European Judaism* 38, no. 2 (2005): 70–76.

Agnew, Hugh. *The Czechs and the Lands of the Bohemian Crown*. Stanford, CA: Hoover Institution Press, 2004.

Agnew, Hugh. *Origins of the Czech National Renascence*. Pittsburgh, PA: University of Pittsburgh Press, 1994.

Albrecht, Catherine. "Pride in Production: The Jubilee Exhibition of 1891 and Economic Competition Between Czechs and Germans in Bohemia." *Austrian History Yearbook* 24 (1993): 101–118.

Albright, Madeleine K. *Prague Winter: A Personal Story of Remembrance and War, 1937–1948*. New York: HarperCollins, 2012.

Albright, Madeleine K. "Remarks at Tomas Masaryk Statue Unveiling Ceremony, Prague Castle." U.S. Department of State. March 7, 2000. https://1997-2001.state.gov/statements/2000/000307a.html. Accessed February 10, 2025.

Altshuler, David, ed. *The Precious Legacy: Judaic Treasures from the Czechoslovak State Collections*. New York: Summit Books, 1983.

Antonín, Robert. *The Ideal Ruler in Medieval Bohemia*. Translated by Sean Mark Miller. Leiden: Brill, 2017.

Apollinaire, Guillaume. *Zone: Selected Poems*. Translated by Ron Padgett. New York: New York Review Books, 2015.

Asbach, Olaf, and Peter Schröder, eds. *The Ashgate Research Companion to the Thirty Years' War*. London: Routledge, 2016.

Bažant, Jan, Nina Bažantová, and Frances Starn, eds. *The Czech Reader: History, Culture, Politics*. Durham, NC: Duke University Press, 2011.

Becker, Edwin, et al. *Prague 1900: Poetry and Ecstasy*. Amsterdam: Van Gogh Museum, 1999.

Beckerman, Michael, ed. *Dvořák and His World*. Princeton, NJ: Princeton University Press, 1993.

Bečková, Kateřina. *Prague: The City and Its River*. Translated by Derek and Marzia Paton. Prague: Karolinum Press, 2016.

Bede, Jarrett. *Charles IV, Holy Roman Emperor*. London: Eyre and Spottiswoode, 1935.

Benda, Vilém, and the State Jewish Museum. *The Prague Ghetto in the Renaissance Period*. Prague: Orbis, 1965.

Berend, Nora, Przemysław Urbańczyk, and Przemysław Wiszewski. *Central Europe in the High Middle Ages Bohemia, Hungary, and Poland c.900–c.1300*. Cambridge: Cambridge University Press, 2013.

Berglund, Bruce R. *Castle and Cathedral in Modern Prague: Longing for the Sacred in a Skeptical Age*. Budapest: Central European University Press, 2017.

Berman, Paul. *Tale of Two Utopias. The Political Journey of the Generation of 1968*. New York: W. W. Norton, 1996.

Blaive, Muriel. "The Czech Museum of Communism: What National Narrative of the Past?" In *Museums of Communism*, edited by Stephen N. Norris, 218–243. Bloomington: Indiana University Press, 2020.

Boehm, Barbara Drake, and Jiří Fajt, eds. *Prague, the Crown of Bohemia, 1347–1437*. New York: Metropolitan Museum of Art, 2005.

Bolton, Jonathan. *Charter 77, The Plastic People of the Universe, and Czech Culture Under Communism*. Cambridge, MA: Harvard University Press, 2014.

Bolton, Jonathan. "Mourning Becomes the Nation: The Funeral of Tomáš G. Masaryk in 1937." *Bohemia* 45, no. 1 (2004): 115–131.

Brade, Laura E., and Rose Holmes. "Troublesome Sainthood: Nicholas Winton and the Contested History of Child Rescue in Prague, 1938–1940." *History and Memory: Studies in Representation of the Past* 29, no. 1 (2017): 3–40.

Bren, Paulina. *The Greengrocer and His TV: The Culture of Communism After the 1968 Prague Spring*. Ithaca, NY: Cornell University Press, 2010.

Březová, Laurence of. *Origins of the Hussite Uprising. The Chronicle of Laurence of Březová (1414–1421)*. Translated and edited by Thomas A. Fudge. Abington, UK: Routledge, 2020.

Brod, Max. *Franz Kafka: A Biography*. Translated by G. Humphreys Roberts. New York: Schocken Books, 1947.

Bryant, Chad. *Prague: Belonging in the Modern City*. Cambridge, MA: Harvard University Press, 2021.

Bryant, Chad. *Prague in Black: Nazi Rule and Czech Nationalism*. Cambridge, MA: Harvard University Press, 2009.

Bryant, Chad, Kateřina Čapková, and Diana Dumitru. "Undone from Within: The Downfall of Rudolf Slánský and Czechoslovak-Soviet Dynamics under Stalin." *The Journal of Modern History* 95, no. 4 (2023): 847–886.

Bugge, Peter. "Normalization and the Limits of the Law: The Case of the Czech Jazz Section." *East European Politics and Societies* 22, no. 2 (2008): 282–318.

Bürger, Gottfried August. *Lenore*. Translated by Dante Gabriel Rossetti. London: Ellis and Elvey, 1900.

Burian, Jarka M. *Modern Czech Theatre: Reflector and Conscience of a Nation*. Iowa City: University of Iowa Press, 2000.

Buse, Alpha. "Occupations of Women. Main Findings of the Report." *The Survey*, June 11, 1921, 342.

Campo-Bowen, Christopher. "'We Shall Remain Faithful': The Village Mode in Czech Opera, 1866–1928." PhD diss., University of North Carolina–Chapel Hill, 2018.

Camus, Albert. *A Happy Death*. Translated by Richard Howard. New York: Vintage Books, 1995.

Čapek, Karel. *R.U.R. Rossum's Universal Robots*. Translated by Claudia Novack. New York: Penguin Books, 2004.

Čapek, Karel. *Talks with T. G. Masaryk*. Translated by Dora Round. Edited by Michael Henry Heim. North Haven, CT: Catbird Press, 1995.

Čapek, Karel, and Josef Čapek. *R. U. R. and the Insect Play*. Translated by Paul Selver. Oxford: Oxford University Press, 1923.

Čapková, Kateřina. *Czechs, Germans, Jews? National Identity and the Jews of Bohemia*. New York: Berghahn Books, 2012.

Čapková, Kateřina, and Hillel J. Kieval, eds. *Prague and Beyond: Jews in the Bohemian Lands*. Philadelphia: University of Pennsylvania Press, 2021.

Carter, F. W. "The Cotton Printing Industry in Prague 1766–1873." *Textile History* 6, no. 1 (1975): 132–155.

Carter, F. W. "The Industrial Development of Prague 1800–1850." *Slavonic and East European Review* 51, no. 123 (1973): 243–275.

Cerman, Ivo, Rita Krueger, and Susan Reynolds, eds. *The Enlightenment in Bohemia*. Liverpool: Voltaire Foundation in association with Liverpool University Press, 2011.

Charvát, Peter. "Notes on the Social Structure of Bohemia in the 11th–12th Century." *Památky archeologické* 73 (1992): 312–384.

Cohen, Gary B. "Cultural Crossings in Prague, 1900: Scenes from Late Imperial Austria." *Austrian History Yearbook* 45 (2014): 1–30.

Cohen, Gary B. "Jews in German Society: Prague, 1860–1914." *Central European History* 10, no. 1 (1977): 28–54.

Cohen, Gary B. *The Politics of Ethnic Survival: Germans in Prague, 1861–1914*. 2nd ed. West Lafayette, IN: Purdue University Press, 2006.

Cohen, Gary B., and Franz A. J. Szabo, eds. *Embodiments of Power: Building Baroque Cities in Europe*. New York: Berghahn Books, 2008.

Cooper, David L. *The Czech Manuscripts: Forgery, Translation, and National Myth*. Dekalb: Northern Illinois University Press, 2023.

Cramsey, Sarah. "Saying Kaddish in Czechoslovakia: Memorialization, the Jewish Tragedy and the *Tryzna*." *Journal of Modern Jewish Studies* 7, no. 1 (2008): 35–50.

Crawford, Ruth. "Pathfinding in Prague." *The Survey* 46 (June 11, 1921): 327–332.

Czepczyński, Mariusz. *Cultural Landscapes of Post-Socialist Cities: Representation of Powers and Needs*. Farnham, UK: Ashgate, 2008.

David, Abraham, ed. *A Hebrew Chronicle from Prague, c. 1615*. Translated by Leon J. Weingerger and Dena Ordan. Tuscaloosa: University of Alabama Press, 2006.

David, Jaroslav, and Jana Davidová Glogarová. "President Václav Havel as an Inspiration for Czech Urbanonymy." *Onomastica* 65 (2021): 255–269.

Davis, Joseph. *Yom-Tov Lipman Heller: Portrait of a Seventeenth Century Rabbi*. Oxford: Littman Library of Jewish Civilization, 2016.

Day Lewis, C. *The Complete Poems of C. Day Lewis*. Palo Alto, CA: Stanford University Press, 1992.

Deák, István. *Beyond Nationalism: A Social and Political History of the Habsburg Officer Corps, 1848–1918*. New York: Oxford University Press, 1990.

Dee, John. *John Dee: Essential Readings*. Berkeley, CA: North Atlantic Books, 2003.

Delbos, Stephan. "Bust of R.M. Rilke Unveiled in Prague." *Prague Post*, December 8, 2011. https://www.praguepost.com/blogs/blog/2011/12/08/rilke-bust-unveiled/. Accessed February 10, 2025.

Delbos, Stephan, ed. *From a Terrace in Prague*. Prague: Litteraria Pragensia Books, 2011.

Demetz, Peter. *Prague in Black and Gold: Scenes from the Life of a European City*. New York: Hill and Wang, 1997.

Duttlinger, Carolin, ed. *Franz Kafka in Context*. Cambridge: Cambridge University Press, 2017.

Eco, Umberto. *The Prague Cemetery*. Translated by Richard Dixon. Boston: Houghton, Mifflin, Harcourt, 2011.

Efron, Noah J. "'Our Forefathers Did Not Tell Us': Jews and Natural Philosophy in Rudolfine Prague." *Endeavour* 26, no. 1 (2002): 15–18.

Evans, R. J. W. *Rudolph and His World: A Study in Intellectual History, 1576–1612*. Oxford: Oxford University Press, 1973.

Feinberg, Melissa. *Communism in Eastern Europe*. New York: Routledge, 2022.

Feinberg, Melissa. *Elusive Equality: Gender, Citizenship, and the Limits of Democracy in Czechoslovakia, 1918–1950*. Pittsburgh, PA: University of Pittsburgh Press, 2006.

Filipová, Marta. "Artwork of the Month, December 2020: Bride with a Cigarette by Milada Marešová (1933)." December 21, 2020. *Craace. Continuity/Rupture: Art and Architecture in Central Europe 1918–1939*. https://www.researchgate.net/

publication/348755356_Artwork_of_the_Month_December_2020_Bride_with_a_Cigarette_by_Milada_Maresova_1933. Accessed February 10, 2025.

Filipová, Marta. *Modernity, HIstory, and Politics in Czech Art*. London: Routledge, 2020.

Flanagan, Brenda, and Hana Waisserová. *Women's artistic dissent: Repelling totalitarianism in pre-1989 Czechoslovakia*. Lanham, MD: Lexington Books, 2024.

Forbes, Meghan. "Devětsil and Dada: A Poetics of Play in the Interwar Czech Avant-Garde." *ARTMargins* 9, no. 3 (2020): 7–28.

Frankl, Michal. "'The Enchantment Has Gone': Anti-Jewish Views of Jan Neruda in the Context of Czech Liberal Journalism in the 1860s." *Judaica Bohemiae* 46 (2011): 7–22.

Frankl, Michal. "Free of Controversy? Recent Research on the Holocaust in the Bohemian Lands." *Dapim: Studies on the Holocaust* 31, no. 3 (2017): 262–270.

Freeman, Daniel. *Mozart in Prague*. Tyrone, PA: BearClaw Press, 2013.

Freeman, Daniel. *The Prague Theater of Count Anton von Sporck*. Hillsdale, NY: Pendragon Press, 1992.

Frinta, Ondřej, and Dita Frintová. "Cathedral of Sts. Vitus, Wenceslas, and Adalbert—the Melting Pot of Czech Religious, National, and State Identity and Its Legal Status." *Laws* 12, no. 2 (2023): 1–27.

Frommer, Benjamin. *National Cleansing: Retribution Against Nazi Collaborators in Postwar Czechoslovakia*. Cambridge: Cambridge University Press, 2004.

Fučíková, Eliška. *Prague in the Reign of Rudolph II: Mannerist Art and Architecture in the Imperial Capital, 1583–1612*. Translated by Derek and Marzia Paton. Prague: Karolinum Press, 2015.

Fučíková, Eliška. *Renaissance Prague*. Translated by Derek Paton. Prague: Karolinum Press, 2018.

Fudge, Thomas A., ed. *The Crusade Against Heretics in Bohemia, 1418–1437: Sources and Documents for the Hussite Crusades*. Farnham, UK: Ashgate, 2002.

Fudge, Thomas A. *Heresy and Hussites in Late Medieval Europe*. Farnham, UK: Variorum Ashgate, 2014.

Fudge, Thomas A. *Jan Hus: Religious Reform and Social Revolution in Bohemia*. London: I.B. Taurus, 2010.

Fudge, Thomas A. *The Magnificent Ride: The First Reformation in Hussite Bohemia*. Farnham, UK: Ashgate, 1998.

Fudge, Thomas A. *Origins of the Hussite Uprising: The Chronicle of Laurence of Březová, 1414–1421*. London: Routledge, 2020.

Fudge, Thomas A. "Želivský's Head: Memory and New Martyrs Among the Hussites." In *The Bohemian Reformation and Religious Practice: Papers from the Sixth International Symposium on the Bohemian Reformation and Religious Practice*, edited by David R. Holeton, 111–132. Prague: Academy of Sciences of the Czech Republic, 2007.

Garton Ash, Timothy. *The Magic Lantern: The Revolutions of '89 Witnessed in Warsaw, Budapest, Berlin, and Prague*. New York: Penguin Random House, 1993.

Garver, Bruce. *The Young Czech Party, 1874–1901, and the Emergence of a Multi-Party System*. New Haven, CT: Yale University Press, 1978.

Gehry, Frank O. "Architectural Projects: Current and Recently Completed Work." *Bulletin of the American Academy of Arts and Sciences* 49, no. 5 (1996): 36–55.

Ginsberg, Allen. *The Collected Poems, 1947–1997*. New York: HarperCollins, 2007.

Giustino, Cathleen M. "Rodin in Prague: Modern Art, Cultural Diplomacy, and National Display." *Slavic Review* 69, no. 3 (2010): 591–619.

Giustino, Cathleen M. *Tearing Down Prague's Jewish Town: Ghetto Clearance and the Legacy of Middle-Class Ethnic Politics Around 1900*. Boulder, CO: East European Monographs, 2003.

Glassheim, Eagle. *Noble Nationalists: The Transformation of the Bohemian Aristocracy*. Cambridge, MA: Harvard University Press, 2005.

Gorbachev, Mikhail, and Zdeněk Mlynář. *Conversations with Gorbachev: On Perestroika, the Prague Spring, and the Crossroads of Socialism*. Translated by George Shriver. New York: Columbia University Press, 2002.

Greenblatt, Rachel L. "Saint and Counter Saint: Catholic Triumphalism and Jewish Resistance in Baroque Prague's Abeles Affair." *Jewish History* 30, nos. 1–2 (2016): 61–80.

Greenblatt, Rachel L. *To Tell Their Children: Jewish Communal Memory in Early Modern Prague*. Palo Alto, CA: Stanford University Press, 2014.

Grundy, T. R. "Sigismund 'super grammaticam.'" *Notes and Queries*, no. 261 (December 28, 1872): 524.

Hájková, Anna. *The Last Ghetto: An Everyday History of Theresienstadt*. New York: Oxford University Press, 2020.

Hašek, Jaroslav. *The Good Soldier Schweik and His Fortunes in the Great War*. Translated by Cecil Parrott. London: Penguin Classics, 2005.

Havel, Václav. *The Art of the Impossible: Politics as Morality in Practice. Speeches and Writings, 1990–1996*. Translated by Paul Wilson and others. New York: Knopf, 1997.

Havel, Václav. *Letters to Olga*. Translated by Paul Wilson. New York: Alfred A. Knopf, 1988.

Havel, Václav. *Summer Meditations*. Translated by Paul Wilson. New York: Vintage Books, 1993.

Havel, Václav. *To the Castle and Back*. Translated by Paul Wilson. New York: Vintage Books, 2008.

Hayes, Kathleen, ed. *The Journalism of Milena Jesenská: A Critical Voice in Interwar Europe*. New York: Berghahn Books, 2003.

Heitlinger, Alena. "Passage to Motherhood: Personal and Social 'Management' of Reproduction in Czechoslovakia in the 1980s." In *Women, State, and Party in Eastern Europe*, edited by Sharon L. Wolchik and Alfred G. Mayer, 286–300. Durham, NC: Duke University Press, 1985.

Heymann, Frederick G. *George of Poděbrady, King of Heretics*. Princeton, NJ: Princeton University Press, 1965.

Heymann, Frederick G. *John Žižka and the Hussite Revolution*. Princeton, NJ: Princeton University Press, 1955.

Hojda, Zdeněk, and Jiří Pešek. *The Palaces of Prague*. New York: Vendome Press, 1994.

Holečková, Marta Edith. "On Cooperative Housing in Socialist Czechoslovakia, 1959–1970." *Architektúra & urbanizmus* 56, nos. 3–4 (2023): 187–195.

Holý, Ladislav. *The Little Czech and the Great Czech Nation: National Identity and the Post-Communist Social Transformation*. Cambridge: Cambridge University Press, 1996.

Homza, Martin. *Mulieres suadentes—Persuasive Women: Female Royal Saints in Medieval East Central and Eastern Europe*. Leiden: Brill, 2017.

Honisch, Erika Supria. "Encounters with Music in Rudolf II's Prague." *Austrian History Yearbook* 52 (2021): 64–80.

Horacek, Ivana. "Illuminating Methods, Picturing Instruments: Tycho Brahe's Instrumental Images." *Austrian History Yearbook* 52 (2021): 30–53.

Horníčková, Kateřina, ed. *Faces of Community in Central European Towns: Images, Symbols, and Performances, 1400–1700*. Lanham, MD: Lexington Books, 2018.

Huebner, Karla. *Magnetic Woman: Toyen and the Surrealist Erotic*. Pittsburgh, PA: University of Pittsburgh Press, 2021.

Huebner, Todd Wayne. "The Multi-National 'Nation-State.' The Origins and Paradoxes of Czechoslovakia, 1914–1920." PhD diss., Columbia University, 1994.

Insua, Juan, ed. *The City of K. Franz Kafka & Prague*. Barcelona: Centre Cultura Contemporania de Barcelona, 2002.

Ivanič, Suzanna. *Cosmos and Materiality in Early Modern Prague*. Oxford: Oxford University Press, 2021.

Ivanič, Suzanna. "Global Catholicism in Seventeenth-Century Prague." *Austrian History Yearbook* 52 (2021): 17–29.

Jakobson, Roman. *Selected Writings*. Vol. 9, *Uncollected Works*, Part 2, *1934–1943*. Edited by Jindřich Toman. Berlin: de Gruyter Mouton, 2013.

Jamison, Anne. *Kafka's Other Prague: Writings from the Czechoslovak Republic*. Evanston, IL: Northwestern University Press, 2018.

Janouch, Gustav. *Conversations with Kafka: Notes and Reminiscences*. Translated by Goronwy Rees. London: Derek Verschoyle, 1953.

Jirásek, Alois. *Legends of Old Bohemia*. Translated by Edith Pargeter. London: Paul Hamyln, 1963.

Judson, Pieter M. *Guardians of the Nation. Activists on the Language Frontiers of Imperial Austria*. Cambridge, MA: Harvard University Press, 2007.

Judson, Pieter M. *The Habsburg Empire. A New History*. Cambridge MA: Harvard University Press, 2016.

Kachlik, David, David Vichnar, Dana Kachlikova, Vladimir Musil, Kristian Szabo, and Josef Stingl. "The Life and Work of Jan Jesenský (1566–1621), the Physician of a Dying Time." *Journal of Medical Biography* 21, no. 3 (2013): 153–163.

Kafka, Franz. *The Castle*. Translated by J. A. Underwood. London: Penguin Books, 1997.

Kafka, Franz. *The Complete Stories*. Translated by Tania Stern and James Stern. New York: Schocken Books, 1971.

Kafka, Franz. *Letters to Family, Friends, and Editors*. Translated by Richard Winston and Clara Winston. New York: Schocken Books, 1977.

Kafka, Franz. *Letter to His Father*. Translated by Ernst Kaiser and Eithne Wilkins. New York: Schocken Books, 1966.

Kafka, Franz. *The Metamorphosis*. Translated by Stanley Corngold. New York: Bantam Books, 1972.

Kafka, Franz. *The Trial*. Translated by Breon Mitchell. New York: Schocken Books, 1998.

Kaminsky, Howard. "Chiliasm and the Hussite Revolution." *Church History* 26, no. 1 (1957): 43–71.

Kaminsky, Howard. *A History of the Hussite Revolution*. Eugene, OR: Wipf and Stock, 2004.

Kaminsky, Howard. "The Prague Insurrection of 30 July 1419." *Medieval et Humanistica* 17 (1966): 106–126.

Kantor, Marvin. *Medieval Slavic Lives of Saints and Princes*. Ann Arbor: Michigan Slavic Translations, 1983.

Kantor, Marvin. *The Origins of Christianity in Bohemia: Sources and Commentary*. Evanston, IL: Northwestern University Press, 1990.

Karabel, Jerome. "The Revolt of The Intellectuals: The Origins of the Prague Spring and the Politics of Reform Communism." University of California Berkeley, Institute for Research on Labor and Employment Working Paper Series, 1990.

Karásek, Jiří ze Lvovic. *A Gothic Soul*. Translated by Kristin Lodge. Prague: Twisted Spoon Press, 2015.

Keane, John, ed. *The Power of the Powerless: Citizens Against the State in Central-Eastern Europe*. Abington, UK: Routledge, 2010.

Keefe, Simon P., ed. *Mozart in Context*. Cambridge: Cambridge University Press, 2018.

Kelly, T. Mills. "Taking It to the Streets: Czech National Socialists in 1908." *Austrian History Yearbook* 29, no. 1 (1998): 93–112.

Kelly, T. Mills. *Without Remorse: Czech National Socialism in Late-Habsburg Austria*. Boulder, CO: East European Monographs, 2006.

Khrushchev, Nikita Sergeevich. *The "Secret" Speech: Delivered to the Closed Session of the Twentieth Congress of the Communist Party of the Soviet Union*. Nottingham, UK: Spokesman Books for the Bertrand Russell Peace Foundation, 1976.

Kieval, Hillel J. "Imperial Embraces and Ethnic Challenges: The Politics of Jewish Identity in the Bohemian Lands." *Shofar* 30, no. 4 (2012): 1–17.

Kieval, Hillel J. "Jewish Prague, Christian Prague, and the Castle in the City's 'Golden Age.'" *Jewish Studies Quarterly* 18, no. 2 (2011): 202–215.

Kieval, Hillel J. *Languages of Community: The Jewish Experience in the Czech Lands*. Berkeley: University of California Press, 2000.

Kieval, Hillel J. "Pursuing the Golem of Prague: Jewish Culture and the Invention of a Tradition." *Modern Judaism* 17, no. 1 (1997): 1–23.

Kimball, Stanley Buchholz. *Czech Nationalism: A Study of the National Theatre Movement, 1845–83*. Urbana: University of Illinois Press, 1964.

Klápstě, Jan. *The Archaeology of Prague and the Medieval Czech Lands, 1100–1600*. Sheffield, UK: Equinox, 2016.

Klápstě, Jan. *The Czech Lands in Medieval Transformation*. Leiden: Brill, 2012.

Klassen, John M. *The Nobility and the Making of the Hussite Revolution*. New York: Columbia University Press, 1978.

Klassen, John M. "Women and Religious Reform in Late Medieval Bohemia." *Renaissance and Reformation / Renaissance et Réforme* 5, no. 4 (1981): 203–221.

Klíma, Ivan. *The Spirit of Prague and Other Essays*. Translated by Paul Wilson. London: Granta Books, 1995.

Klipcová, Barbora, and Petr Uličný. "Domenico Pugliani: A New Face in the History of Wallenstein Palace in Prague." *Umění Art* 3, no. 61 (2013): 206–220.

Klirs, Tracy Guren, ed. *The Merit of Our Mothers: A Bilingual Anthology of Jewish Women's Prayers*. New York: Hebrew Union College Press, 1992.

Kováčiková, Lenka, Olga Trojánková, Petr Starec, Petr Meduna, and Petr Limburský. "Livestock as an Indicator of Socioeconomic Changes in Medieval Prague (Czech Republic)." *Archaeological and Anthropological Sciences* 12, no. 283 (2020). https://doi.org/10.1007/s12520-020-01229-5. Accessed February 10, 2025.

Kovály, Heda Margolius. *Under a Cruel Star: A Life in Prague, 1941–1968*. Translated by Helen Epstein. New York: Holmes & Meier, 1997.

Krapfl, James. *Revolution with a Human Face: Politics, Culture, and Community in Czechoslovakia, 1989–1992*. Ithaca, NY: Cornell University Press, 2013.

Krueger, Rita. *Czech, German, and Noble: Status and National Identity in Habsburg Bohemia*. New York: Oxford University Press, 2009.

Kučera, Rudolf. "Exploiting Victory, Sinking into Defeat: Uniformed Violence in the Creation of the New Order in Czechoslovakia and Austria, 1918–1922." *Journal of Modern History* 88, no. 4 (2016): 827–855.

Kučera, Rudolph. "Marginalizing Josefina: Work, Gender, and Protest in Bohemia 1820–1844." *Journal of Social History* 46, no. 2 (2012): 430–448.

Kučera, Rudolph. *Rationed Life: Science, Everyday Life, and Working-Class Politics in the Bohemian Lands, 1914–1918*. New York: Berghahn Books, 2016.

Kun, Miklós. *Prague Spring–Prague Fall: Blank Spots of 1968*. Translated by Hajnal Csatorday. Budapest: Akadémiai Kiadó, 1999.

Kundera, Milan. *The Book of Laughter and Forgetting*. Translated by Aaron Asher. New York: HarperCollins, 1996.

Large, Brian. *Smetana*. Boston: de Capo Press, 1985.

Little, Robert, ed. *The Czech Black Book*. New York: Frederick A. Praeger, 1969.

Locke, Brian S. *Opera and Ideology in Prague: Polemics and Practice at the National Theater, 1900–1938*. Rochester, NY: University of Rochester Press, 2006.

London, Artur. *The Confession*. Translated by Alistair Hamilton. New York: William Morrow, 1970.

Louthan, Howard. *Converting Bohemia: Force and Persuasion in the Catholic Reformation*. Cambridge: Cambridge University Press, 2011.

Louthan, Howard. "Global Prague: Renaissance and Reformation Crossroads: Introduction: Golden Prague—Beyond Rudolf." *Austrian History Yearbook* 52 (2021): 13–16.

Lukes, Igor. "Rudolph Slanský: His Trials and Trial." Woodrow Wilson Working Papers 50, Cold War International History Project, Washington, DC, 2008.

Lukes, Igor. "The Rudolph Slanský Affair—New Evidence." *Slavic Review* 58, no. 1 (1999): 160–187.

Macartney, C. A. *The Habsburg Empire, 1790–1918*. New York: Macmillan, 1961.

Mácha, Karel Hynek. *May*. Translated by Marcela Sulak. Prague: Twisted Spoon Press, 2005.

Machová, Karla. "The Bohemian Woman as a Factor in Industry and Economy." In *The World's Congress of Representative Women*, vol. 2, edited by May Wright Sewall, 564. Chicago: Rand, McNally, 1894.

Mackenzie, Campbell, trans. *The Letters of John Huss, Written During his Exile and Imprisonment*. Edinburgh: William Whyte, 1846.

Malfatto, Irene. "John of Marignolli and the Historiographical Project of Charles IV." *Acta Universitatis Carolinae—Historia Universitatis Carolinae Pragensis* 55, no. 1 (2015): 131–140.

Mamatey, Victor S., and Radomír Luža, eds. *A History of the Czechoslovak Republic*. Princeton, NJ: Princeton University Press, 1973.

Marcus, Jacob Rader, and Marc Saperstein, eds. *The Jews in Christian Europe: A Sourcebook, 315–1791*. Pittsburgh, PA: Hebrew Union College Press, University of Pittsburgh Press, 2015.

Masaryk, Tomáš G. "The Czech Question." In *Modernism: The Creation of Nation-States*, translated by Peter Kussi, 199–209. Budapest: Central European University Press, 2010.

Masaryk, Thomas G., Milan R. Stefanik, and Edward Benes. *Declaration of Independence of the Czechoslovak Republic*. New York: Marchbanks Press, printed for the Czechoslovak Arts Club of New York City, 1918.

Mastny, Vojtech. *The Czechs Under Nazi Rule: The Failure of Resistance, 1939–1942*. New York: Columbia University Press, 1971.

Mauchaut, Guillaume de. *The Judgement of the King of Bohemia*. Translated by R. Barton Palmer. London: Routledge, 2019.

Mengel, David C. "Emperor Charles IV (1346–1378) as the Architect of Local Religion in Prague." *Austrian History Yearbook* 41 (2010): 15–29.

Mengel, David C. "From Venice to Jerusalem and Beyond: Milíč of Kroměříž and the Topography of Prostitution in Fourteenth-Century Prague." *Speculum* 79, no. 2 (2004): 407–442.

Merseburg, Thietmar von. *Ottonian Germany: The Chronicon of Thietmar of Merseburg*. Translated by David Warner. Manchester: Manchester University Press, 2001.

Meyrink, Gustav. "The City with the Secret Heartbeat." In *The Dedalus Meyrink Reader*, edited and translated by Mike Mitchell. Sawtry, Cambridgeshire: Dedalus Books, 2013.

Meyrink, Gustav. *The Golem*. Translated by Mike Mitchell. Sawtry, Cambridgeshire: Dedalus Books, 1998.

"'Mikhail Gorbachev's Speech at Rally in Prague': Joint Soviet-Czechoslovak Communique." *Soviet Weekly Supplement*, April 1987.

Miller, Michael Laurence. "Rabbi David Oppenheim on Trial: Turks, Titles, and Tribute in Counter-Reformation Prague." *Jewish Quarterly Review* 106, no. 1 (2016): 42–75.

Miller, Paul, and Claire Morelon. *Embers of Empire Continuity and Rupture in the Habsburg Successor States After 1918*. New York: Berghahn Books, 2018.

"Miloš Forman: Interview." *UNESCO Courier* 48, nos. 7–8 (1995): 18–20.

Mishin, Dmitrij. "Ibrahim Ibn-Ya'qub At-Turtushi's Account of the Slavs from the Middle of the Tenth Century." In *Annual of Medieval Studies at the CEU 1994–1995*, edited by M. B. Davis and M. Sebők, 184–199. Budapest: Central European University Press, 1996.

Mitchell, Ruth Crawford, ed. *Alice Garrigue Masaryk, 1879–1966: Her Life as Recorded in Her Own Words and by Her Friends*. Pittsburgh, PA: University Center for International Studies, University of Pittsburgh, 1980.

Mitchell, Tony. "Mixing Pop and Politics: Rock Music in Czechoslovakia Before and After the Velvet Revolution." *Popular Music* 11, no. 2 (1992): 187–203.

Mladenovic, Petr z. *John Hus at the Council of Constance*. Translated and edited by Matthew Spinka. New York: Columbia University Press, 1965.

Mlynář, Zdeněk. "The Lessons of the Prague Spring." *Labour Focus on Eastern Europe* 10, no. 2 (1988): 34–40.

Morelon, Claire. "Sounds of Loss: Church Bells, Place, and Time in the Habsburg Empire During the First World War." *Past & Present* 244, no. 1 (2019): 195–234.

Morelon, Claire. "Staging the Austrian War Effort in Public Space: Prague During the First World War." In *Städte im Krieg—Erlebnis, Inszenierung und Erinnerung des Ersten Weltkriegs*, edited by Ernst Otto Bräunche and Stephan Sander-Faes, 95–110. Ostfildern, Germany: Jan Thorbecke Verlag, 2016.

Morelon, Claire. *Streetscapes of War and Revolution: Prague, 1914–1920*. Cambridge: Cambridge University Press, 2024.

Mueller, Joan. *Clare of Assisi: The Letters to Agnes*. Collegeville, MN: Liturgical Press, 2003.

Mueller, Joan. *The Privilege of Poverty: Clare of Assisi, Agnes of Prague, and the Struggle for a Franciscan Rule for Women*. University Park: Pennsylvania State University Press, 2006.

Museum of the City of Prague. "The Great War in the Life of Prague Citizens." https://www.muzeumprahy.cz. Accessed June 20, 2024.

Musil, Jiří. "Czechoslovakia in the Middle of Transition." *Sociologický Časopis / Czech Sociological Review* 28 (1992): 5–21.

Myšková, Ivana, and Jan Zikmund, eds. *The Book of Prague: A City in Short Fiction*. Manchester, UK: Comma Press, 2023.

Nagy, Balázs, and Frank Schaer, eds. *Karoli IV Imperatoris Romanorum Vita Ab Eo IPSO Conscripta: Et Hystoria Nova De Sancto Wenceslao Martyre = Autobiography* of Charles IV: And His Legend of St. Wenceslas. Budapest: Central European University Press, 2001.

Navratil, Jaromir. *The Prague Spring '68*. Budapest: Central European University Press, 2006.

Němcová, Božena. *The Grandmother*. Translated by Frances Gregor. Chicago: A. C. McClurg, 1891.

Němec, Jan, dir. *Oratorium pro Prahu* (Oratorio for Prague). Czechoslovakia, Facets Multi-Media, 1968, 26 mins.

Neruda, Jan. *Prague Tales*. Translated by Michael Henry Heim. Budapest: Central European University Press, 2011.

Newman, Aubrey. "The Expulsion of the Jews from Prague in 1745 and British Foreign Policy." *Transactions & Miscellanies* (Jewish Historical Society of England) 22 (1968): 30–41.

Newman, Barbara. "'The Passion of the Jews of Prague': The Pogrom of 1389 and the Lessons of a Medieval Parody." *Church History* 81, no. 1 (2012): 1–26.

Nezval, Vitěslav. *Prague with Fingers of Rain*. Translated by Edwald Osers. London: Bloodaxe Books, 2009.

Nolte, Claire E. *The Sokol in the Czech Lands to 1914: Training for the Nation*. Basingstoke, UK: Palgrave Macmillan, 2003.

Norberg-Schulz, Christian. *Genius Loci: Towards a Phenomenology of Architecture*. New York: Rizzoli, 1984.

Nummendal, Tara. *Alchemy and Authority in the Holy Roman Empire*. Chicago: University of Chicago Press, 2007.

Odložilík, Otakar. "Good King Wenceslas, a Historical Sketch." *Slavonic and East European Review* 8, no. 22 (1929): 20–30.

Oldřich, Tůma, Mikhail Prozumenschikov, John Soares, Mark Kramer, and James G. Hershberg. "The (Inter-Communist) Cold War on Ice: Soviet-Czechoslovak Ice Hockey Politics, 1967–1969." Woodrow Wilson Working Papers 69, Cold War International History Project, Washington, DC, 2014.

Opacic, Zoe, ed. *Prague and Bohemia: Medieval Art, Architecture and Cultural Exchange in Central Europe*. Leeds: British Archaeological Association, 2009.

Ort, Thomas. *Art and Life in Modernist Prague: Karel Čapek and His Generation, 1911–1938*. Basingstoke, UK: Palgrave Macmillan, 2013.

Orzoff, Andrea. *Battle for the Castle: The Myth of Czechoslovakia in Europe, 1914–1948*. New York: Oxford University Press, 2011.

Pacáková-Hošťálková, Božena. *Prague: Its Gardens and Parks*. Translated by David Short. Prague: Karolinum, 2017.

Paces, Cynthia. "Commemorating Jan Hus, Creating a Czechoslovak State: The 1915 Quincentenary." In *The Age of Anniversaries: The Cult of Commemoration, 1895–1925*, edited by T. G. Otte, 147–167. New York: Routledge, 2018.

Paces, Cynthia. "Czech Motherhood and Fin-de-Siècle Visual Culture." In *Gender in 20th-Century Eastern Europe and the USSR*, edited by Catherine Baker, 25–48. London: Palgrave, 2016.

Paces, Cynthia. "Fascism and Catholic Intellectuals in Czechoslovakia." In *Fascism and Catholicism in Europe*, edited by Jan Nelis, 319–333. Hildesheim: Olms, 2015.

Paces, Cynthia. *Prague Panoramas: National Memory and Sacred Space in the Twentieth Century*. Pittsburgh, PA: University of Pittsburgh Press, 2009.

Palmitessa, James R. *Material Culture & Daily Life in the New City of Prague in the Age of Rudolph II*. Krems: Medium Aevum Quotidianum, 1997.

Palmitessa, James R. "The Prague Uprising of 1611: Property, Politics, and Catholic Renewal in the Early Years of Habsburg Rule." *Central European History* 31, no. 4 (1998): 299–328.

Palouš, Martin, ed. *The Solidarity of the Shaken: Jan Patočka's Legacy in the Modern World*. Washington, DC: Academia Press, 2019.

Parker, Anna. "Ester, a Missing Clasp, and Jewish Pawnbroking Networks in Renaissance Prague." *Austrian History Yearbook* 52 (2021): 54–63.

Pavel, Ota. "A Race Through Prague." Translated by Paul Wilson. *Crosscurrents* 2 (1983): 295–298.

Pavitt, Jane. *Prague: The Buildings of Europe*. Manchester: Manchester University Press, 2000.

Pavlát, Leo. "The Jewish Museum in Prague During the Second World War." *European Judaism* 41, no. 1 (2008): 124–130.

Pech, Stanley Z. *The Czech Revolution of 1848*. Chapel Hill: University of North Carolina Press, 1969.

Péporté, Pit. *Constructing the Middle Ages*. Leiden: Brill, 2011.

Pichlikova-Burke, Lenka. "Josef Čapek, Czech Modernist Innovator." February 12, 2012. Frick Art Reference Library, NYARC. https://nyarc.org/blog/josef-capek-czech-modernist-innovator. Accessed February 10, 2025.

Pichová, Hana. "The Lineup for Meat: The Stalin Statue in Prague." *PMLA* 123, no. 3 (2008): 614–631.

Plaschka, Richard Georg. "The Political Significance of Frantisek Palacky." *Journal of Contemporary History* 8, no. 3 (1973): 35–55.

The Plastic People of the Universe. "Delirium." Liner notes. *Co Znamená Vésti Koně*. Plastic People of the Universe. Recorded 1981. Levné Knihy LK 1478-2, 2010. CD.

Poláčková, Zuzana, and Pieter C. van Duin. "Gustáv Husák and the Foundations of 'Normalization': Slovak, Czechoslovak and Federative Perspectives, 1968–1970." *Slavonica* 24, nos. 1–2 (2019): 1–16.

Polisensky, Josef V. *The Thirty Years War*. Berkeley: University of California Press, 1971.

Porter, Roy S., and Mikuláš Teich, eds. *The Enlightenment in National Context*. Cambridge: Cambridge University Press, 1981.

Putík, Alexander C. "The Origin of the Symbols of the Prague Jewish Town: The Banner of the Old-New Synagogue, David's Shield, and the 'Swedish Hat.'" *Judaica Bohemiae* 29 (1993): 4–37.

Rady, Martyn. "Reviews." *Slavonic and East European Review* 72, no. 3 (1994): 553–556.

Ragkos, Nikolaos. "On the Orientation of Czech Cities Founded During the 13th Century." *Mediterranean Archaeology and Archaeometry* 18, no. 4 (2018): 81–88.

Rampley, Matthew. "Metaphors of Progress: Hygiene and Purity in Czechoslovak Architecture." *OSF*. April 14, 2020. doi:10.17605/OSF.IO/SWHR7. Accessed February 10, 2025.

Rauchensteiner, Manfried. *The First World War and the End of the Habsburg Monarchy, 1914–1918*. Translated by Anna Guttel. Vienna: Böhlau Verlag, 2014.

Rechcígl, Miloslav. *On Behalf of Their Homeland: Fifty Years of SVU. An Eyewitness Account of the History of the Czechoslovak Society of Arts and Sciences (SVU)*. Berkeley: University of California Press, 2008.

Renner, Judith. "'I'm Sorry for Apologising': Czech and German Apologies and Their Perlocutionary Effects." *Review of International Studies* 37, no. 4 (2011): 1579–1597.

Rilke, Rainer Maria. *Poems*. Translated by Jessie Lemont. New York: Tobias A. Wright, 1918.

Ripellino, Angelo Maria. *Magic Prague*. Translated by David Newton Marinelli. Edited by Michael Henry Heim. Berkeley: University of California Press, 1994.

Rothkirchen, Livia. *The Jews of Bohemia and Moravia: Facing the Holocaust*. Lincoln: University of Nebraska Press, 2006.

Roubal, Petr. *Spartakiads. The Politics of Physical Culture in Communist Czechoslovakia*. Prague: Karolinum Press, 2019.

Royt, Jan. *The Prague of Charles IV*. Translated by Derek Paton and Marzia Paton. Prague: Karolinum Press, 2016.

Rubin, Miri. *Gentile Tales: The Narrative Assault on Late Medieval Jews*. New Haven, CT: Yale University Press, 1999.

Rudolfinum. "History." https://www.rudolfinum.cz/en/history/. Accessed June 18, 2024.

Saunders, Nicholas J., Jan Frolík, and Volker Heyd. "Zeitgeist Archaeology: Conflict, Identity and Ideology at Prague Castle, 1918–2018." *Antiquity* 93, no. 370 (2019): 1009–1025.

Sawicki, Nicholas. "Rodin and the Prague Exhibition of 1902: Promoting Modernism and Advancing Reputations." *Cantor Arts Center Journal* 3 (2002–2003): 185–197.

Sawka, Richard, ed. *The Rise and Fall of the Soviet Union*. New York: Routledge, 1999.

Sayer, Derek. *The Coasts of Bohemia: A Czech History*. Princeton, NJ: Princeton University Press, 1998.

Sayer, Derek. *Postcards from Absurdistan: Prague at the End of History*. Princeton, NJ: Princeton University Press, 2022.

Sayer, Derek. *Prague, Capital of the Twentieth Century: A Surrealist History*. Princeton, NJ: Princeton University Press, 2013.

Scheltens, Isabel. "Silver and Spices in the Runtinger Trade with Prague." *Hungarian Historical Review* 11, no. 3 (2022): 622–646.

Sebestyen, Victor. *Revolution 1989: The Fall of the Soviet Empire*. New York: Vintage Books, 2010.

Seifert, Jaroslav. *The Poetry of Jaroslav Seifert*. Translated by Ewald Osers. New Haven, CT: Catbird Press, 1998.

Seton-Watson, R. W. *A History of the Czechs and Slovaks*. Hamden, CT: Archon Books, 1965.

Shriver, Thomas, Alison Adams, and Rachel Einwohner. "Motherhood and Opportunities for Activism Before and After the Czech Velvet Revolution." *Mobilization* 18, no. 3 (2013): 267–288.

Šiklová, Jiřina. "The 'Gray Zone' and the Future of Dissent in Czechoslovakia." Translated by Káča Poláčková-Henley and Gerald Turner. *Social Research* 57, no. 2 (1990): 347–363.

Škvorecký, Josef. *The Cowards*. Translated by Jeanne Němcová. New York: Grove Books, 1970.

Šmahel, František, and Ota Pavlíček, eds. *A Companion to Jan Hus*. Leiden: Brill, 2015.

Smeltzer, Erica. "The Metropolis and the Attic: Spatial Representations of Jewish Identity in Kafka and the Golem of Prague." *Partial Answers* 14, no. 2 (2016): 343–360.

Smetana, Bedřich. *Vltava (The Moldau): Study Score*. Edited by Hugh Macdonald. Kassel, Germany: Bärenreiter, 2015.

Smetánka, Jaroslav František, ed. "Masaryk's First Presidential Message." *Czechoslovak Review: The Official Organ of the American Czechoslovak Board (Chicago)* 3, no. 2 (1919): 43–48.

Smith, Preserved. *The Life and Letters of Martin Luther*. London: Frank Cass, 1911.

Šmok, Martin. *Through the Labyrinth of Normalization: The Jewish Community as a Mirror for the Majority Society*. Prague: Jewish Museum in Prague, 2017.

Solomon, Maynard. *Mozart, a Biography*. New York: HarperCollins, 1996.

Soukup, Pavel. *Jan Hus: The Life and Death of a Preacher*. West Lafayette, IN: Purdue University Press, 2019.

Sourek, Otakar, ed. *Antonin Dvorak Letters and Reminiscences*. Alplaus, NY: Artia, 1954.

Spector, Scott. *Prague Territories: National Conflict and Cultural Innovation in Franz Kafka's Fin de Siècle*. Berkeley: University of California Press, 2000.

Špička, Jiří. "Francesco Petrarca Travelling and Writing to Prague's Court." *Verbum Analecta Neolatina* 12, no. 1 (2010): 27–40.

Spinka, Matthew, ed. and trans. *John Hus at the Council of Constance*. New York: Columbia University Press, 1968.

Stokes, Gale. *The Walls Came Tumbling Down: The Collapse of Communism in Eastern Europe*. New York: Oxford University Press, 1993.

Stolarik, M. Mark, ed. *The Czech and Slovak Republics: Twenty Years of Independence*. Budapest: Central European University Press, 2016.

Švácha, Rostislav. *Architecture of New Prague, 1895–1945*. Translated by Alexandra Buchler. Cambridge, MA: MIT Press, 1995.

Szelényi, Iván. "Jiří Musil and the East European Origins of the New Urban Sociology." *Sociologický Časopis / Czech Sociological Review* 48, no. 6 (2012): 1156–1163.

Szporluk, Roman. *The Political Thought of Thomas G. Masaryk*. Boulder, CO: East European Monographs, 1981.

Teich, Mikuláš, ed. *Bohemia in History*. Cambridge: Cambridge University Press, 1998.

Teplitsky, Joshua. "Heroes and Victims Without Villains: Plague in Early Modern Prague." *Jewish Social Studies* 26, no. 1 (2020): 67–76.

Teplitsky, Joshua. "A 'Prince of the Land of Israel' in Prague: Jewish Philanthropy, Patronage, and Power in Early Modern Europe and Beyond." *Jewish History* 29 (2015): 245–271.

Thomas, Alfred. *Anne's Bohemia: Czech Literature and Society, 1310–1420*. Minneapolis: University of Minnesota Press, 1998.

Thomas, Alfred. *Prague Palimpsest: Writing, Memory, and the City*. Chicago: University of Chicago Press, 2010.

Thomas, Alfred. *Reading Women in Late Medieval Europe: Anne of Bohemia and Chaucer's Female Audience*. New York: Palgrave Macmillan, 2016.

Thompson, Emily. "The Women of Charter 77 and the New Dissenters." Radio Free Europe / Radio Liberty. https://www.rferl.org/a/28217006.html#nav. Accessed June 23, 2024.

Thompson, Wayne C. *Nordic, Central, and Southeastern Europe, 2015–2016*. Lanham, MD: Rowman & Littlefield, 2016.

Tóth, Andrej, Inka Kratochvílová, Jakub Drábek, Lukáš Novotný, Věra Hellerová, Martin Červený, and Valérie Tóthová. "On the Issue of the Spanish Flu in the First Czechoslovak Republic." *Canadian Journal of Health History* 39, no. 2 (2022): 397–418.

Tuckerová, Veronika. *Reading Kafka in Prague: On Translation, Samizdat, Censorship, Export, S and Dissent*. London: Bloomsbury Academic, 2005.

Tuckerová, Veronika. "Reading Kafka, Writing Vita: The Trials of the Kafka Scholar Eduard Goldstücker." *New German Critique* 42, no. 1 (2015): 129–161.

Uličný, Petr. "The Choirs of St Vitus's Cathedral in Prague: A Marriage of Liturgy, Coronation, Royal Necropolis and Piety." *Journal of the British Archaeological Association* 168, no. 1 (2015): 186–233.

Urban, František. "Zdravotní desatero proti tuberkulose." 1904. In *Health for Sale: Posters from the William H. Helfand Collection*, edited by William H. Helfand, John Ittmann, and Innis Howe Shoemaker. Philadelphia, PA: Philadelphia Museum of Art, 2011.

Valley, Eli. *The Great Jewish Cities of Central and Eastern Europe: A Travel Guide and Resource Book to Prague, Warsaw, Cracow, and Budapest*. Northvale, NJ: Jason Aronson, 1999.

Veverková, Kamila. *The Four Articles of Prague within the Public Sphere of Hussite Bohemia: On the 600th Anniversary of their Declaration (1420–2020)*. Translated by Angelo Shaun Franklin. Lanham, MD: Lexington Books, 2021.

Vlnas, Vít. *The Glory of the Baroque in Bohemia*. Prague: National Gallery of Prague, 2001.

Volavková, Hana. *The Pinkas Synagogue: A Memorial to Our Past and to Our Days*. Prague: State Jewish Museum, 1955.

Voltaire. *The History of the War of 1741*. Vol. 33 of *The Works of M. de Voltaire: A Contemporary Version*. London: E. R. DuMont, 1901.

Wagenbach, Klaus. *Kafka*. Translated by Edward Osers. Cambridge, MA: Harvard University Press, 2003.

Weeks, Charles Andrew. "Jacob Boehme and the Thirty Years' War." *Central European History* 24, no. 3 (1991): 213–221.

Weil, Jiří. *Lamentations for 77,297 Victims*. Translated by David Lightfoot. Prague: Karolinum Press, 2020.

Weil, Jiří. *Life with a Star*. Translated by Rita Klímová and Roslyn Schloss. Evanston, IL: Northwestern University Press, 1997.

Weissová, Helga. *Draw What You See: A Child's Drawings from Theresienstadt/Terezín*. Göttingen: Wallstein Verlag, 1998.

Williams, Kieran. *The Prague Spring and Its Aftermath: Czechoslovak Politics, 1968–1970*. Cambridge: Cambridge University Press, 1997.

Wilson, Paul, ed. *Prague: A Traveler's Literary Companion*. Berkeley, CA: Whereabouts Press, 1995.

Wilson, Peter H. *The Thirty Years War: A Sourcebook*. New York: Palgrave Macmillan, 2010.

Wilson, Peter H. *The Thirty Years War: Europe's Tragedy*. Cambridge, MA: Belknap Press of Harvard University Press, 2009.

Wingfield, Nancy M. *Flag Wars and Stone Saints: How the Bohemian Lands Became Czech*. Cambridge, MA: Harvard University Press, 2007.

Wingfield, Nancy M. *The World of Prostitution in Late Imperial Austria*. New York: Oxford University Press, 2017.

Witkovsky, Matthew S. "Truly Blank: The Monument to National Liberation and Interwar Modernism in Prague." *Umění* 49, no. 1 (2001): 42–60.

Wittlich, Petr. *Art Nouveau Prague*. Translated by Petra Key. Prague: Karolinum Press, 2020.

Wittlich, Petr. *Prague Fin de Siècle, 1890–1914*. Translated by Maev de la Guardia. Paris: Flammarion, 1992.

Wolf, Lucien. *Notes on the Diplomatic History of the Jewish Question: With Texts of Protocols, Treaty Stipulations and Other Public Acts and Official Documents*. London: Spottiswood, Ballantyne, 1919.

Wolverton, Lisa, trans. *Cosmas of Prague: Chronicle of the Czechs*. Washington, DC: Catholic University of America Press, 2009.

Wolverton, Lisa. *Cosmas of Prague: Narrative, Classicism, Politics*. Washington, DC: Catholic University of America Press, 2014.

Wolverton, Lisa. *Hastening Toward Prague: Power and Society in the Czech Medieval Lands*. Philadelphia: University of Pennsylvania Press, 2001.

Zaracor, Kimberly Elman. *Manufacturing a Socialist Modernity*. Pittsburgh, PA: University of Pittsburgh Press, 2011.

Zeman, Zbyněk. *The Masaryks: The Making of Czechoslovakia*. London: Weidenfeld and Nicolson, 1976.

Zeman, Zbyněk, and Antonín Klimek. *The Life of Edvard Beneš, 1884–1948: Czechoslovakia in Peace and War*. Oxford: Oxford Academic, 1997.

Žůrek, Václav. "Indigenous or Foreign? The Role of Origin in the Debate About the Suitable Candidate in Electing Bohemian Kings in the Fifteenth Century." *Historical Studies on Central Europe* 2, no. 2 (2022): 43–59.

Index

Note: Color Plates and Figures are indicated by "*cp*" and "*f*" following the page number.

For the benefit of digital users, indexed terms that span two pages (e.g., 52–53) may, on occasion, appear on only one of those pages.

A
Abeles, Lazar, 141–142
Abeles, Simon, 141–142
Adalbert (Vojtěch) of Prague, Saint, 20–21, 41, 57, 154
Adamec, Ladislav, 300–301
Agnes, (Anežka) of Prague, Saint, 26–28, 28*f*, 30–31
Agrarian Party, 201–202, 209, 240–241
Albrecht of Habsburg (Holy Roman emperor), 33
Albrecht of Habsburg (son-in-law and heir of Sigismund), 92
Albright, Madeleine K., 311, 316
alchemy, 14, 113–114
Anna of Bavaria (Charles IV's second wife), 45, 51–52
Anna of Świdnica (Charles IV's third wife), 52–53
Anne of Bohemia and Hungary (Ferdinand I's wife), 100
anti-Semitism. *See also* Holocaust; Jewish community; Jewish quarter; Prague under Nazi rule
  blasphemy charges, 129–130, 142, 143*f*
  blood libel claims, 29–30, 186
  Catholic Church and, 63–64, 129–130, 140
  Communist Party and, 269–270
  crucifix on Charles Bridge and, 143*f*
  clearance of the ghetto motivated by, 190–191
  economic factors of, 22–23, 29, 63–64, 98, 223–224
  First Crusade and, 22–23
  ghetto clearance and, 190–191
  Hilsner Trial, 186
  historical accounts of, 7, 22–23, 65–66
  plagues and, 140
Apollinaire, Guillaume, 194, 231
archbishop of Prague, 20, 25, 42, 49, 68, 75, 86, 140, 145–146, 267–268
archdiocese of Prague, 41–42, 58
architecture
  avant-garde styles in, 205, 229
  Baroque style in, 4, 130–133, 131*f*, 136–139, 141, 144, 151, 191, 205, 288
  brutalism in, 285, 288
  functionalism in, 234–239, 253–254, 271, 318

architecture (*Continued*)
  Gothic style in, 4–6, 26, 28, 30–31, 35, 37, 48–49, 99, 118–119
  modernist style in, 204–205, 234–239, 288–289
  neoclassical style in, 155, 161, 181, 224, 229
  neo-Renaissance style in, 181–183, 188, 200–201, 258
  prefabrication in, 275–276
  Renaissance style in, 4, 97, 99–103, 108–111, 114–117, 181
  Rococo style in, 4, 139, 150–152, 163
  Romanesque style in, 20–24, 37, 44, 54–55, 318
  sgraffito technique in, 101
Arcimboldo, Giuseppe, 2, 108–109, 108–109*cp*
art. *See also* architecture; film; operas; painting; plays; Prague Spring
  Art Deco, 239–240
  art nouveau, 183–184, 192–193, 199–200, 204, 211, 231, 234, 288–289, 300, 318
  avant-garde movements in, 231–232, 277–278, 313
  collections of, 58–60, 68–69, 71, 107–109
  cubism, 204–205
  surrealism, 197, 238
  women artists, 227
Ash, Timothy Garton, 300
Astronomical Clock (Orloj) (Old Town Hall), 70, 70*f*, 175–176, 215
At the Castle District in Prague (Gurk), 151*cp*
Auschwitz, 253–254, 268
Austria. *See also* Habsburg monarchy; Vienna
  Ausgleich split into dual monarchy of, 173–174
  de-Austrianizing of Prague, 217, 221–222
  Empire of, 168–169, 242–243
  imperial diet in, 170–171
  protests against *Ausgleich* in Prague and, 173–174
Austria-Hungary
  Bosnia-Herzegovina annexed by, 207
  collapse of, 216–217
  Czech independence movement from, 201–202, 209, 212–215
  Great War participation of, 208–210, 212–213, 215–217

B

Babiš, Andrej, 317
Baroque Silver Tomb of St. John Nepomuk by Fischer von Erlach (Sedelmayr), 138*f*
Bach, Alexander von, 171–172, 209
Badeni, Kasimir, 185–186
Balbín, Bohuslav, 89–90, 136–137
Barrandov Studios, 238–239, 255, 277–278
Battle of Vítkov (1420), 85–86
Battle of White Mountain (1620), 126–128
Beethoven, Ludwig van, 182, 255
Bendl, Jan Jiří, 130–131, 136, 202
Beneš, Edvard
  as Foreign Minister 224–225, 241
  as President, 241–243, 260, 264
  Czechoslovak government in exile (World War II) led by, 250, 252, 256–260
  death and funeral of, 265–267
  during World War I, 212
  expulsion of Sudeten Germans ordered by, 260–261
  legacy of, 266–267, 299–300, 305
  photograph of, 261*f*
  resignations of, 244, 265
  war criminals punished under, 260–261
Beneš Krabice of Veitmile, 45–46, 48–49, 51, 53, 58
Benešová, Hana, 212
Beran, Josef, Archbishop of Prague, 267–268

Bergeron, Pierre, 101, 106–107, 110–111
Bethlehem Chapel, 72, 75–76, 271
Bifolium with Christ in Majesty in an Initial A, 69f
Bilá Labut' (White Swan) Department Store, 246–247
Black Death, 45–46, 63–64, 72
Blanche (Margaret of Valois), first wife of Charles IV, 39, 43–45
Blaskowitz, Johannes, 247–248, 249f
Bohemia. *See also* Bohemian Diet; Habsburg monarchy; Holy Roman Empire; Prague during the early Middle Ages; Přemyslid dynasty
  Boii influence on name of, 10–11
  Christianization of, 11, 16–20
  early history and expansion of, 10–15, 17–18, 27–29
  Holy Roman Empire's incorporation of, 2–3, 20–21
  Kingdom of, 3–4, 43, 52f, 67, 123–124, 148–149, 194–195, 197–198, 219
  overview of, 1–6, 10–11
Bohemian Diet, 33, 94–97, 100, 124, 168, 201–202
Bohemian Museum. *See* National Museum (formerly Bohemian Museum)
Bohemian reform movement, 71–73, 76, 78–79, 83–84. *See also* Hus, Jan; Hussite Wars; Taborites; Utraquism
Boleslav I, Duke, 17–18
Boleslav II, Duke, 18–20
Bořivoj, Duke, 11, 16
Brahe, Tycho, 2, 111–114
Brahms, Johannes, 180
Braunerová, Zdenka, 191
Brezhnev, Leonid, 281, 284–285
Břetislav I, Duke, 21
Břetislav II, Duke, 23

Břevnov Monastery, 20, 139, 154, 267–268
Brod, Max, 196–199, 223–224, 245
Bruegel, Pieter, 108–109
Brundibar opera (Krása), 254
Brussels World Expo (*1958*), 276–277
Buergermeister, Jan, 313–314
Bull Staircase (Prague Castle), 229, 230f
Bürger, Gottfried August, 149–150
Burial of Saint Wenceslas, The (Master of Eggenburg), 18cp

C
Calvinism, 125–126, 130, 136–137, 154
Café Arco, 196–197
Café Slavia, 239–240, 290
Camus, Albert, 1–2
Čapek, Josef, 251
Čapek, Karel, 230–232, 251
Carmelite Order, 44, 49, 130–131, 153–155
Castle District, 59–60, 96–97, 99, 102–103, 106, 126, 131, 150
Castle Town (Hradčany), 5–6, 5f, 55, 155, 194, 280–281
Catherine, Saint, 39–40, 50–51, 59–60, 60f
Catholic Church. *See also* Catholics; Counter-Reformation; Hussite Wars (1419–1437); Reformation; Thirty Years War (1618–1648)
  anti-Semitism of, 140
  archdiocese of Prague established by, 41–42
  bishopric of Prague bestowed by, 20
  Christianization of Bohemia under, 11, 16–20
  conciliar movement in, 76–77
  end of influence of, 174
  Papal Schism in, 67, 71, 74–77
  reform movements and, 50–51, 71, 76–77, 84, 90, 92–93
Catholic League, 124–126

Catholics
  culture of, 130
  fleeing of, 86
  forced conversions by, 130
  in nobility, 91–93, 123–124, 130–131, 137–138
  Protestants' rivalries with, 119–120
  under Communism, 268
  violence against, 120
Cattle Market (later Charles Square), 46
Černý, David, 305–306, 312–314, 314*f*
Chamberlain, Neville, 242–243
Chapel of Saint Wenceslas (St. Vitus Cathedral), 54–55, 94
Church of Saint Wenceslas (Vršovice), 239
Charlemagne, Holy Roman Emperor, 11, 20–21, 45, 58–60
Charles Bridge (Stone Bridge), 5–6, 56–57, 57*f*, 61, 142, 143*f*, 174, 308*f*
Charles-Ferdinand University. *See* Prague University
Charles IV, Emperor. *See also* Prague under Charles IV
  artistic interests of, 39, 50–51, 58–60, 83–84
  ascension of, 42–43, 45
  autobiography of, 38–41, 51
  childhood and upbringing of, 35–36, 38–39
  coronation of, 42–44
  Crown of Saint Wenceslas commissioned and used by, 43–44
  Jewish community and, 46–47
  leadership of, 46
  legacy of, 62, 315–316
  marriages of, 39, 45, 52–53
  military campaigns of, 38–41
  nobility's relations with, 40–41, 51–52, 61
  political rivals of, 41–43, 45
  relic collection of, 57–58
  statue of, 57
  vision for Prague of, 41, 45–46, 131
  university founded by, 47–48
  Wenceslas Square founded by, 6
Charles VI, Emperor, 67, 144–145, 148–149
Charter 77, 292, 297–298, 300–301
Chotek, Sophie, Archduchess, 207–208
Christianity. *See* Catholic Church; Counter-Reformation; Hussite Wars; Jesuits; Lutheranism; Protestants; Reformation
Christian of Anhalt, Prince, 125–126
Chronicle of Dalimil, 38
Chronicle of the Czechs (Cosmas of Prague), 13, 18
Chronicle of the Prague Church (Krabice), 51
church reform movements, 50–51, 71, 76–77, 84, 90, 92–93. *See also* Hus, Jan
Chytilová, Věra, 277–278, 286–287
Civic Forum, 300–301, 303, 305–306
Clare of Assisi, 26–27, 58
Clam-Gallas Palace (Old Town), 139
Clementinum University, 103, 130, 131*f*, 138–139, 153, 157–159
Clement VI, Pope (Pierre Roger), 39, 41–42, 45, 51
Club on Behalf of Old Prague, 191
Cominform, 266–267
Communist Party of Czechoslovakia. *See also* Prague under Communist rule; Prague under normalization
  announcement of new state under, 264–265
  anti-Semitism of, 269–271
  censorship eased by, 280
  economic challenges under, 266–267, 274–275, 280
  nationalization policies of, 266–267

normalization under, 286–291, 297
propaganda of, 266–267, 271
purges and accusations by, 264,
  267–268
realignment following invasion of
  1968 in, 285
rise to power of, 261–262
Stalin statue project of, 272–274
Compact of Prague (1433), 91–92
Compacts of Basel (1436), 93
Compacts of Prague (1436), 93
Confederation of Political Prisoners,
  311–312
Congress of Vienna (1515), 96
Congress of Vienna (1814–1815), 160
Conrad of Vechta, (archbishop of
  Prague), 86
Convent of St. Agnes (Old Town),
  28, 28f
Corvinus, Matthias, 93
Cosmas of Prague, 6, 13–16, 18,
  20–23, 43
Council of Basil (1431), 91–92
Council of Constance (1417), 79
Counter-Reformation, 97–98, 131,
  134–138, 143–144. *See also* Prague
  during the Thirty Years War and
  Counter-Reformation
Crown of Saint Wenceslas, 43–44,
  153–154
Czech and Slovak Federative Republic,
  303–304, 310
Czech community. *See* Czech-German
  relations; Czech language; Czech
  nationalism; Prague during Czech
  nationalization
Czech history, 13, 165, 230, 304
Czech independence movement from
  Austria-Hungary, 201–202, 209,
  212–215
Czech language. *See also* Prague during
  Czech nationalization

films in, 233–234
first achievements in, 23–24, 50–51,
  95–96, 159–160, 165–166,
  175–176, 232
folk stories, songs, and customs
  collected in, 175–176
and German language, 2–3, 165,
  174–175, 182–183, 187
historical chronicles in, 37–38,
  159–160
literature in, 32, 37–38, 90, 95–96,
  159–160, 175, 231–232
music in, 165–166, 168, 178–180
nobility's use of, 33, 74, 83
Old Czech, 30, 164, 181, 186, 271
plays in, 155–156, 255
Czech nationalism, 144, 186–187,
  190–191, 200–202, 211–213, 230,
  244. *See also* Prague during Czech
  nationalization
Czechoslovakia (First Republic). *See also*
  Prague in the Czechoslovak state
democracy of, 224–225, 229
ending of, 244
founding of, 215–217, 221–224
identity challenges in, 219–220,
  240–241, 244
Jewish community in, 224, 263
map of, 248f
population of, 219–220
Prague's function in, 3–4, 221, 228
Slovakia's secession from,
  245–246
women's equality in, 225–226
Czechoslovakia (Second Republic),
  244–250. *See also* Prague under
  Nazi rule
Czechoslovakia (Third Republic),
  260–264
Czechoslovak Legion's Bank
  (Legiobanka) (Gočár),
  234, 235f

Czechoslovak Women's National
    Council (ŽNR), 228
Czech Republic (modern). *See also*
    Czechoslovakia (First Republic);
    Czechoslovakia (Second Republic);
    Czechoslovakia (Third Republic);
    Prague in the Czech Republic
  constitution of, 310
  contemporary situation of,
    318–320
  democratic challenges in, 317–318
  EU membership of, 314–315
  formation of, 310
  NATO joined by, 314
  Prague as capital of, 3–4, 6
  Velvet Divorce leading to, 310

D
Dačický, Jiří, 111, 112*f*
Daladier, Édouard, 242–243
Daliborka prison, 110
Dancing House (Gehry and Milunić),
    308–309, 309*f*
Da Ponte, Lorenzo, 156–157
Dee, John, 114
Defenestration of Prague, First, 80–81
Defenestration of Prague, Second,
    122–124, 123*f*
Defenestration of Prague, Third, 265
Demetz, Peter, 2
Devětsil (art association), 232–238,
    243–244, 286–287
de Vries, Adriaen, 109, 132, 136
Dicker-Brandeis, Friedl, 254
Dientzenhofer, Christoph, 139
Dientzenhofer, Kilian Ignaz, 139, 150
Dio-Dato, Giorgio, 142
Dobrovský, Josef, 159–160, 163–164
Dominican Order, 25–26, 37, 49–50, 103
Drahomíra (mother of St. Wenceslas), 16
Drda, Jan, 283–284

Dubček, Alexander
  role in 1968–69 of, 280–286
  role in 1989 of, 298, 300–302, 302*f*
Dürer, Albrecht, 108–109
Duschek, Josefa, 157–158
Dvořák, Antonín, 175–176, 179–180, 182,
    200–201, 316

E
Eco, Umberto, 7
Edict of Tolerance (1782), 154, 161
Einstein, Albert, 196–197, 267
Elisabeth Přemyslová, 34–38, 40–41
Emmaus Monastery (Na Slovanech),
    44–45, 258, 263
Enlightenment Prague. *See* Prague
    during the Enlightenment
Erben, Karel Jaromír, 175–176, 178–180
Ernest (Arnošt) of Pardubice (first
    archbishop of Prague), 42, 49, 68
Estates Theater (formerly Nostitz
    National Theater), 155–157, 156*f*,
    166, 181–182*f*
Estates Theater (Morstadt), 156*f*
*Execution of Twenty-Seven Bohemian
    Rebels on Old Town Square,
    June 1621* (Hogenberg), 127*f*

F
Ferdinand I of Habsburg, Emperor
  Bohemian Diet under, 96–97, 100, 103
  Catholicism of, 97–98
  centralized rule favored by, 97
  Holy Roman emperor anointing of, 103
  installation as king of, 96
  Jews of Prague expelled under,
    100, 103
  legal reforms following uprising
    against, 103
  modernization projects of, 96–97,
    99–101

nobility's relations with, 96–98, 100, 103
Protestantism tolerated by, 97–98
siege of Prague by, 103
Ferdinand II of Habsburg, Emperor, 124–127, 129–131
film, 233–234, 238–239, 254–255, 276–278, 280–281, 286–287, 311
Forman, Miloš, 276–278, 290
France
Bavaria's conflict with, 146
French Revolution, 160
Great War participation of, 220
New Wave cinema, 277–278
Prague captured by, 145
Thirty Years War participation of, 133
Francis I of Lorraine, Emperor, 148, 153, 160, 185, 222
Francis Ferdinand, Archduke, 207–208, 210, 217
Francis Joseph I, Emperor, 170–172, 185, 201–202, 207
Frank, Karl Hermann, 257, 261–262
Frederick II, Emperor, 25–27, 145

G
Gabčík, Josef, 256–257
Gans, David, 112, 117–119
Gebauer, Jan, 186
Gebauer, Kurt, 316–317, 316–317*cp*
George of Poděbrady, King, 92–93, 94*f*
German Casino, 172–173, 178
German community. *See also* German language
expulsion of, 260–262, 304
judicial privileges granted to, 21
looting of businesses in 1919 of, 223–224
nationalism of, 7, 240–243
settlers and immigrants, 10–11, 28, 32–33

German-Czech relations. *See* Czech-German relations
Germanification, 247–248, 253
German language
and Czech language, 2–3, 174–175, 182–183, 187
codification as state language of, 162
Jews associated with, 190–191, 223–224
language ordinance on, 185
literature in, 37–38, 150
music in, 173, 233
newspapers in, 181
scholarship in, 175
sermons in, 49–50
German Theater (1888), 181–182, 186
Germany. *See also* Holy Roman Empire; Nazi Germany; Prussia
Berlin Wall falls in, 299
Czech Republic joint declaration on apologies for crimes by, 304
East Germany, 274–275, 277, 281, 289, 298–300
Great War participation of, 207, 215
reunification of, 168–169, 173
Ginsberg, Allen, 278–279, 281
Gočár, Josef, 204–205, 205*f*, 234, 235*f*, 239
Goebbels, Joseph, 251
Golden Bull of 1356, 52
Golden Lane (Prague Castle), 110, 110*cp*, 151*f*, 195, 212
Goldstücker, Eduard, 273–274, 277, 280, 290, 313–314
Golem legend, 1–2, 116–117, 192–194
Göncz, Árpád, President of Hungary, 302*f*
Gorbachev, Mikhail, 296–297
Gott, Karel, 293
Gottwald, Klement, 261–262, 264–265, 273
Great Comet of 1577 above Prague, The (Dačický), 112*f*

Greater Prague Act (1921), 6, 221
Great War, The. *See also* Prague during the Great War
    armistice in, 216–217
    battlefield defeats and casualties in, 211
    beginning of, 209
    Central powers in, 207, 215
    Entente countries in, 207
    refugees in Prague during, 209–210

H

Habsburg monarchy. *See also* Ferdinand I of Habsburg, Emperor; Ferdinand II of Habsburg, Emperor; Francis Joseph I, Emperor; Holy Roman Empire; Joseph II, Emperor; Maria Theresa, Empress; Prague during the Thirty Years War and Counter-Reformation; Rudolph II of Habsburg, Emperor; Thirty Years War (1618–1648)
    Czechoslovakia's Declaration of Independence from, 215–216
    fall of, 173
    Hungary compromise of, 174
    loyalty assertions to, 129–130, 144, 201–202, 208–209
    Wars of Austrian Succession in, 145
Hácha, Emil, 245–247, 260–261
Halas, František, 243–244, 258–260
Hášek, Jaroslav, 208
Havel, Miloš, 238–239, 255
Havel, Václav (President)
    apologies for Czech complicity in Holocaust and expulsions, 303–304
    executive approach of, 303, 308–309
    family and upbringing of, 278
    imprisonment of, 294
    legacy of, 315–316
    photograph of, 302f
    presidential election of, 301–302
    memorials to, 316–317
    theatrical approach of, 289
    Velvet Revolution participation of, 299–300
Havel, Václav Maria, (entrepreneur, father of President Havel), 238–239
Havel, Vácslav, (entrepreneur, grandfather of President Havel), 234, 238–239
Heart for Václav Havel, A (Gebauer), 316–317, 316–317*cp*
Heller, Yom-Tov Lippmann, 128–130
Henlein, Konrad, 240–242, 260–262
Heydrich, Reinhard, 253–254, 256–257
Hitler, Adolf, 242–243, 245–246, 252–253, 257–260
Hoffmeister, Adolf, 257–258
Holešovice (also Bubeneč-Holešovice) 162, 182–183, 234, 256–257, 304–305, 313
Hollar, Wenceslas, 57*f*, 133–134, 134*f*
Holocaust. *See also* anti-Semitism.
    Auschwitz in, 253–254, 268
    concentration and death camps of, 253–254
    deaths in, 254, 304–305
    Final Solution implemented in, 253–255
    memorials to, 268, 319
    survivors of, 254–255, 263
Holý, Prokop, 91
Holy Roman Empire. *See also* Charles IV, Emperor; Ferdinand I of Habsburg, Emperor; Ferdinand II of Habsburg, Emperor; Francis Joseph I, Emperor; Joseph II, Emperor; Maria Theresa, Empress; Rudolph II of Habsburg, Emperor
    Bohemia incorporated by, 2–3, 20–21
    Congress of Vienna replaces, 160
    establishment of, 20–21

map of, 52f
Prague as capital of, 3–4, 52–53
Horáková, Milada, 267, 305
Horowitz family, 98–99, 128
Horse Market (later Wenceslas Square), 6, 46, 169–170
Hošková (née Weissová), Helga, 254, 262, 304–305
Hotel Družba (later Grand Hotel International Prague), 272, 272f
House at the Black Madonna, The, 204–205, 205f
House at the Stone Bell (Old Town Square), 35, 36f
House at the Three Ostriches, 101, 142
Hrabal, Bohmil, 273, 293
Hradčany (Castle Town), 5–6, 5f, 55, 155, 194, 280–281
Hruban, Mořic, 221–222
Hungary. *See also* Austria-Hungary
  Austrian Empire's war against, 171–172
  Habsburg compromise with, 174
  Kingdom of, 76–77, 96, 160
  Munich Agreement's impact on, 243–244, 251
  Warsaw Pact participation of, 281
Hus, Jan
  arrest and imprisonment of, 77
  Bohemian reform movement led by, 71–73, 76, 78–79
  Czech language emphasized by, 73–74
  early life and education of, 71–72
  excommunication of, 75–76
  execution by immolation of, 78
  memorial of, 79–80, 211–212, 214f, 230–231, 282, 302
  nobility's relations with, 74, 76–77
  sainthood of, 92–93
  statue of, 211, 214f, 230–231, 246, 282, 302
  trial of, 77
Husák, Gustav, 285–286, 296

Hussites
  First Defenestration of Prague by, 80–81
  Four Articles of Prague as agreement among, 84
  imperial troop occupation against, 84–85
  internal conflict among, 90–91
  leadership of, 88
  manifesto of, 84, 88
Hussite Wars (1419–1437). *See also* Prague during Hussite Wars and new dynasties
  Battle of Vítkov in, 85–86
  end and effects of, 89, 91–92
  First Defenestration as first confrontation in, 81
  Plzeň battle in, 91
  Siege of Vyšehrad in, 86–89

I
illuminated manuscripts, 44–45, 68, 136
Infant of Prague, 130–131, 154
International Students Day 242, 299–300
Institute for Gentlewomen (Prague Castle), 151, 152f
intellectual developments. *See* Bohemian reform movement; Counter-Reformation; Prague during Czech nationalization; Prague during the Enlightenment; Prague Spring
Italy
  artistic and architectural influences of, 46, 58–59, 68, 99, 101–103, 107–109, 131, 138–139
  military campaigns in, 39–40, 172
  Munich Agreement signed by, 243
  Immigrants in Prague from, 21, 106

J
Jagiellonian dynasty, 93–94, 96. *See also* Vladislav Jagiellon, King

Jakeš, Miloš, 297
Jakoubek of Stříbro, 75–76, 79, 83
Jan Hus at the Stake from the Jenský Codex, 78*cp*
jazz music, 232–234, 297–298, 307
Jesenská, Milena, 227, 246, 249–250
Jesenský, Jan (Jesenius), 113, 128
Jesuit Order, 97–98, 106, 123–124, 130, 134–135, 144, 150, 153, 202
Jewish community. *See also* anti-Semitism; Holocaust; Jewish quarter; Old-New Synagogue; Prague under Nazi rule
  commercial activity of, 11–12, 23, 29–30, 63–64, 98, 116, 119, 161–162, 167, 185, 190
  conversion attempts against, 129–130, 141–142, 144
  Czech language embraced by, 190–191
  Edict of Tolerance and, 154, 161
  expulsions of, 100, 103–104, 140, 148–149
  Familiants Laws (Familiantengesetze) and, 148–149
  financial role in, 46–47, 63–64, 98, 129, 143–144
  fleeing of members of, 98–100, 209–210, 244, 250, 252
  German language associated with, 190–191, 223–224
  intellectual developments in, 116–117, 168, 196–197, 245, 277
  literary developments in, 116, 168, 194–197
  Nazi deportations of, 250–251, 253–255
  population of, 98, 100, 103–104, 140, 143–144, 148–149, 244, 262, 304–305
  poverty in, 98, 190
  refugees in, 209–212, 223–224, 244–245, 263

  violence against, 22–23, 64–66, 94, 167, 185–186, 223–224
Jewish Museum, 191, 195*f*, 255, 268, 304–305
Jewish quarter. *See also* Old-New Synagogue (Jewish quarter)
  architecture of, 30–31, 151–152, 191, 199
  clearance of ghetto in, 7, 190–191
  fire in, 100, 140–141
  ghetto period of, 7, 64, 98, 140, 143–144, 151–152, 190, 194–195, 254
  Golem legend developed in, 192–193
  map of, 195*f*
  photograph of, 192*f*
  Renaissance Jewish thought centered in, 116–117
  tourism to, 191, 304–305
  vandalism of synagogues in, 65–66, 185–186
Jewish Town Hall (Jewish quarter), 151–153, 191, 194, 223–224, 245,*f*
Ježek, Jaroslav, 233–234
Jirásek, Alois, 192–193
Jirous, Ivan Martin, 291–292
Jižní Město (housing development), 286–287
John Očko of Vlašim, Archbishop of Prague, 49, 58–59, 58–59*cp*, 61, 68
John of Luxembourg, King, 35–38, 41–42
Josel of Rosheim, 98–99
Joseph II, Emperor
  administrative uniting of the four towns by, 155
  Crown of Saint Wenceslas not received by, 153–154
  Edict of Tolerance of, 154, 161
  election of, 153
  German codified as state language by, 162
  Klostersturm order of, 153–154
  modernizing reforms under, 146–147, 153–154

nobility's relations with, 154–155
Patent of Tolerance of, 163
Patent on Serfdom of, 154–155
Prague as peripheral to, 155
Toleration Patent of 1783 by, 190
Judith Bridge, 24, 27, 56–57

K
Kabbalah, 116–117, 193
Kafka, Franz
birth and education of, 194–195
Czech and German used by, 194–195
family of, 194–195
ghetto's clearance and, 7, 191, 195
intellectual and philosophical interests of, 196–197
Jewish identity of, 197
photograph of, 198f
Prague as inspiration for, 1–2, 7, 194–197, 320
reception of, 198–199
sculptures of, 313, 314f
Kafka Museum, 312–313
Kaiserin Maria Theresia (Kilian), 147f
Kara, Avigdor, 65–66
Karlštejn Castle, 59–60, 59f, 86–88
"Kde domov můj?" (Where is my home?) (Czech national anthem), 166
Kelley, Edward, 114–115
Kepler, Johannes, 2, 111–112, 114
Khrushchev, Nikita, 273
Kingdom of Bohemia, 3–4, 43, 52f, 67, 123–124, 148–149, 194–195, 197–198, 219
Kingdom of the East Franks, 11, 20–21
Klíma, Ivan, 2, 279, 290
Klaus, Václav, 310, 314–316
Klausen Synagogue (Jewish quarter), 141, 141f, 195f
Klofáč, Václav, 186, 209, 213
Kollár, Jan, 164, 169
Konev, Ivan, 260, 262f

Kotěra, Jan, 199, 204–205
Kotva department store, 288, 288cp
Kovály, Heda Margolius, 253–254, 263, 267, 280–283, 290
Kramář, Karel, 209, 212–213
Krásnohorská, Eliška, 176
Kundera, Milan, 231–232, 264, 279, 290, 299
Kurz, Augusta, 228f
Kutná Hora (Kuttenberg), 32–34, 75, 89
Kutná Hora decrees (1409), 75

L
language and linguistic developments. *See* Czech language; German language
Langweil, Antonín, 165
Lawrence of Březová, 83–90
Legiobanka (Gočár). *See* Czechoslovak Legion's Bank
Lennon Wall, 294, 294f
Lesser Town
architecture of, 101
fire of 1541 in, 100, 102–103
founding of, 5, 28
German settlers to, 28, 32–33
Italian immigrants to, 106
prosperity of, 106
Royal Way through, 43–44
transformation of, 132, 133f
Letná Plain, 272–273, 275, 300–301, 306, 317
Libuše, 14–16, 15f
literary developments. *See also* Kafka, Franz; Havel, Václav; Prague Spring
avant-garde in, 235–238
Czech literature, 32, 37–38, 90, 95–96, 159–160, 175, 231–232
illuminated manuscripts, 44–45, 68, 136
Poetism movement in, 232–233

Loew, Judah ben (Maharal), 116–117, 118*f*, 192–193
London, Artur, 270, 273–274
Louis IV of Bavaria, Emperor, 42–43, 45
Lucerna Palace (Wenceslas Square), 227, 234, 312–313
Ludmila, Saint, 16–17, 58
Luther, Martin, 97
Lutheranism, 97–98, 106, 111, 125, 130, 136, 154

M
Mácha, Karel Hynek, 175
Magic Lantern, 276–277, 289, 300
Maisel Synagogue (Jewish quarter), 118–119, 195*f*
Maisel, Mordechai, 118–119
Malý, Václav, 300–301
Mánes, Josef, 173, 175–176, 199, 217
Mánes Union of Fine Artists, 199, 234–235, 237*f*
Manuscript on the Art of War (Wienner), 89–90*cp*
Marešová, Milada, 227
Margaret of Valois (Blanche), 39, 43–44, 71
Margolius, Rudolf, 270, 280–281
Marian Column, 136, 217, 218*f*, 219*f*, 221–222, 318
Maria Theresa, Empress, 145–150, 152–154, 318
Masaryk, Jan, 250–251, 264–265
Masaryk, Tomáš G.
  Declaration of Independence written by, 215–216
  election of, 220
  leadership approach of, 224–225, 230
  legacy of, 224, 315–316
  minorities, attitude toward, 224, 241
  photographs of, 220*f*, 224, 225*f*
  statue of, 311
Masaryková, Alice, 212, 225–226
Masaryková, Charlotte Garrigue, 212, 215–216, 225–226
Matthias, Emperor, 114, 120–122, 124, 132, 150
Matthias Gate (Prague Castle), 120–121, 121*f*, 151
Mauder, Josef, 200–201, 201*f*
Memorial to the Victims of Communism (Zoubek), 311–313, 312*f*
Methodius, Saint, 16, 182–183
Metternich, Klemens von, 160, 168
Meyrink, Gustav, 7, 193–194, 319
middle-class in Prague, 46, 111, 130, 152–153, 169–170, 178, 210, 226, 234
Milíč, Jan of Kroměříž, 49–50, 72, 92–93
Mlada, Princess (daughter of Bohuslav I), 18–20, 44
Moravia, xi, 21, 28, 31–32, 89, 91–93, 102–103, 116–117, 130, 148–149, 162–163, 167, 170–171, 173, 185, 199, 219–220, 229, 244–245, 275–276, 285, 288, 310
  Battle of Austerlitz in, 160
  Great Moravian Empire, 11, 16
  Margrave of, 27–28, 40–41, 66
  Nazi rule in, 246–248, 248*f*, 252–253, 304
Mozart, W. A., 2, 156–158
Mucha, Alfons, 199–200, 214, 231, 239, 239*cp*
Munich Agreement (1938), 243–244, 251
Municipal House (Obecní Dům), 199–200, 200*f*, 307
Museums. *See* Kafka Museum, Jewish Museum, Museum of Communism, National Museum (formerly Bohemian Museum)
Museum of Communism, 311–312

music. *See* Dvořák, Antonín; Estates Theater, German Theater, jazz music, Mozart, W. A.; National Theater; operas; plays; rock music; Smetana, Bedřich
Mussolini, Benito, 243
Myslbek, Josef Václav, 202–203, 203*f*

N
Napoleonic Wars (1803–1815), 160, 166
National Assembly, 220, 225–226, 228, 260, 301–302
National Committee (Great War), 215–217, 219–220
National Museum (formerly Bohemian Museum), 4*f*, 6, 163–165, 175–176, 182–183, 183*f*, 265, 282, 285, 297, 315–316
National (Czechoslovak) Socialist Party (founded 1897), 186, 201–202, 209, 215
National Theater, 178–181, 233
Nazi Germany, 240–245, 247–248, 251–253. *See also* Prague under Nazi rule
Nejedlý, Zdeněk, 252, 271
Němcová, Božena, 176, 200–201
Němec, Jan, 280–281
neo-Renaissance style, 181–183, 188, 191, 200–201, 258
Nepomuk, John of, 66, 136–140, 205, 221–222
Neruda, Jan, 176–178, 200–201
Neurath, Konstantin von, 246–247, 261–262
New Life (Lidický), 287, 287*f*
New Synagogue. *See* Old-New Synagogue
New Town. *See also* Wenceslas Square (New Town)
  architecture of, 205, 234
  founding of, 5, 46
  growth of, 47, 111
  Italy and France as model for, 46
  prostitution in, 50
  rights afforded to burghers of, 47
Nezval, Vitěslav, 1, 232–233, 238, 275
normalization period. *See* Communist Party of Czechoslovakia; Prague under normalization
Nostitz-Rieneck, Franz Anton, 155, 159–160
Nostitz National Theater (*See* Estates Theater)
Novotný, Antonín, 274–277, 280
Novotný, Otakar, 234–238

O
Old Czech Party (also Old Czechs), 174, 181, 185
Old Jewish Cemetery (Jewish quarter), 141*f*, 190–191, 268, 304–305, 319, 320*f*
Old-New Synagogue (Jewish quarter), 30–31, 32*f*, 65–66
Old Town. *See also* Old Town Square
  architecture of, 48–49, 101
  founding of, 5
  as intellectual center of Prague, 70
  plagues in, 64, 140
  public theater opened in, 155
  Royal Way through, 43–44
  Second Defenestration attacks in, 122–123
Old Town Square
  archaeology of, 30
  architecture of, 101
  astronomical clock in, 215
  building of, 25
  historical memory in, 318
  Thirty Years War execution site in, 127–128
  urban planning of, 25

operas, 156–158, 165–166, 175–176, 178–179, 233, 254
Opletal, Jan, 250, 299–300
Otakar I, Přemysl, King, 25–26
Otakar II, Přemysl, King, 27–31
Our Jubilee Exhibition (Kronbauer), 184*f*
Our Lady Before Týn (Old Town Square), 35, 49, 75–76, 92–93, 113, 127–128, 141–142, 168–169, 218*f*, 221–222
Our Lady of the Snows (New Town), 44, 56*f*, 80

P
painting, 58–59, 103, 107–109, 111, 115–116, 130, 138–139, 182–183, 188, 200–201, 204–205, 238–239, 256
Palace of Culture, 289, 296–297
Palach, Jan, 6, 284, 297–300, 305
Palacký, František, 163–165, 168–171, 171*f*, 174, 180, 203, 246
Palacký Bridge, 258, 263
Pan-Slav Congress (1848), 169–170, 201
Papal Schism, 67, 71, 74–77
Parler, Peter, 53–57
Patent of Serfdom (1781), 154–155, 161
Patočka, Jan, 290–292, 295
Patton, George S., 260, 261*f*
Pavel, Ota, 270–271
Pavel, Petr, 317
Payne, Peter ("Master English"), 73, 76
Peace of Augsburg (1555), 97–98, 106
Peace of Westphalia (1648), 136, 138
Pernštejn family, 102–103, 130–131
Peroutka, Ferdinand, 230, 241, 251
Petrarch, 52–53
Petřín Hill and Gardens (Laurenziberg), 4, 14–15, 31–32, 106, 130–131, 155, 165, 175–177, 183–184, 188, 311–312, 312*ff*
Pinkas Synagogue (Jewish quarter), 99, 268, 269*f*

plagues, 45–46, 63–64, 72, 140, 188
Plastic People of the Universe (band), 291–292
plays, 64–65, 144, 155–156, 197, 215, 255, 278, 295
Plečnik, Jože, 229–230, 230*f*, 239
Poland, 21, 98, 219–220, 243, 250, 253–254, 298
Polyxena of Pernštejn and Lobkowicz, 130–131, 195–196
Portrait of Saint Catherine (Master Theodoric), 60*f*
post-Communist Prague. See Prague post-Communism
poverty, 55, 64, 67–68, 90–91, 98, 110, 189–190, 210, 226
Powder Tower, 4*f*, 5–6, 200*f*, 204–205
Pragmatic Sanction (1713), 145
Prague. See also Castle Town; Lesser Town; New Town; Old Town; Prague at the turn of the twentieth century; Prague Castle; Prague during the early middle ages; Prague during the Enlightenment; Prague during the First Czechoslovak Republic; Prague during the Great War; Prague during the Hussite Wars; Prague during the nineteenth century; Prague during the Thirty Years War and Counter-Reformation; Prague in the Czech Republic; Prague post-Communism; Prague during the early Middle Ages; Prague under Charles IV; Prague under Communist rule; Prague under Nazi rule; Prague under normalization; Prague under Rudolph II; Prague under Wenceslas IV; Wenceslas Square
aesthetic of, 1–2, 4–5, 7

architectural styles of, 4–5
contradictions of, 2
dark side of, 1–2, 7–8
etymology of, 12
geography of, 4
maps of, 3–6f, 12f, 56f, 248
photograph of, 4cp
tourism to, 2
Prague at the turn of the twentieth century
   alienation of modernity in, 187,
     193–194, 199
   architecture in, 188, 191, 199–201,
     204–205
   artistic developments in, 188–189,
     191–192, 199–200, 202–205
   Czech-German relations in, 187,
     201–202, 205–206
   Czech nationalism in, 190–191,
     194–195, 200–202
   ethnic and religious diversity in, 187
   ghetto clearance in, 190–191
   intellectual developments in, 188, 191,
     196–197
   Jewish community in, 190–197
   literary developments in, 187–189,
     193–199
   modernizing projects in, 189–191
   political activism and reform in,
     189–190, 200–202
   population growth in, 187
   public health campaigns in, 189–190
   statues and memorials in, 192–193,
     202–203
   violence in, 197–198, 201–202
Prague Castle. *See also* Golden Lane;
     Matthias Gate; St. George Basilica
     and convent; St. Vitus Cathedral
     (Prague Castle); Summer Palace;
     Vladislav Hall
   archeological record of, 11–12, 247–248
   architecture of, 11–12, 100–101,
     150–151, 229

Bull Staircase of, 229, 230f
First Courtyard of, 151, 151f, 230f
map of, 151f
renovations of, 35, 40, 94, 100–101,
   150, 229, 247–248, 311
Spanish Riding Stables, 106–107
Theresian wing added to, 151
tourism to, 106–107
Prague during the early Middle Ages.
   See also Libuše; Ludmila, Saint;
   Přemyslid dynasty; Wenceslas,
   Saint
   archaeological records of, 10–13
   architecture in, 23–24, 26, 28, 30–31
   bilingualism in, 32–33
   Christianization of Bohemia in, 11,
     16–20
   Czech-German relations in, 32–33
   Czech history and identity in, 13, 32
   economic development in, 23–25,
     29–30, 33–34
   expansion in, 24–25
   founding accounts of, 13–16
   Jewish community in, 12, 21–24, 29–31
   limited information on, 10–11, 13, 18
   literary developments in, 32
   map of, 12f
   as meeting place of cultures, 11, 12f
   population of, 23–24, 33
   religious institutional development in,
     25–27
   right bank development in, 23–26
   trade route crossroads at, 11–12, 12f
   violence in, 33–34
Prague during the Enlightenment
   architecture in, 150–152, 155, 161
   artistic developments in, 155–159
   coronations in, 145–146
   Czech language in, 146, 159–160
   Edict of Tolerance in, 154
   intellectual developments in, 148, 150,
     159–160

Prague during the Enlightenment (*Continued*)
  Jewish community in, 148–150
  linguistic dimensions in, 159–160, 162
  literary developments in, 149–150, 159–160
  modernizing reforms in, 146–147, 153
  musical and theatrical developments in, 155–159
  population growth of, 162
  proto-industrial revolution in, 160–162
  religious toleration in, 154
Prague during the First Czechoslovak Republic
  architecture in, 234–240
  artistic developments in, 227, 231–240
  Catholic and Habsburg symbols attacked in, 221–222, 230–231
  Czech-German relations in, 221–224, 230, 240–241
  ethnic and linguistic minorities in, 221–224, 241
  Great Depression in, 238–240
  intellectual developments in, 230, 232–233
  Jewish community in, 223–224
  literary developments in, 231–233, 238–239
  market scene of, 226*f*
  musical and theatrical developments in, 233–234
  population of, 221
  shortages and rationing in, 221–222, 222*f*
  violence in, 221–224
  women's experiences in, 225–227
Prague during the Great War
  arrests in, 211–212
  censorship in, 209, 215
  Czech-German relations in, 219
  Czech nationalism in, 211–212, 216
  economic impacts in, 211, 213
  Jewish community in, 211
  patriotic displays in, 209–210
  rationing and food shortages in, 211, 211*f*, 213–214
  refugees arrive in, 209–211
  strikes and protests in, 213, 215
  support for war effort in, 209, 209*cp*
  women filling traditional male roles during, 210
Prague during the Hussite Wars
  archbishop in, 86
  Czech language in, 83, 88, 90
  nobility in, 83, 92
  violence in, 83–85, 90
Prague during the nineteenth century
  architecture in, 163, 175–176, 181–183
  artistic developments in, 175–176, 178–179, 181–183
  cultural life and civil society in, 171–172, 175
  Czech-German relations in, 169, 172–175, 178–179, 181–184
  industrialization in, 167–168, 177–178, 185–186
  intellectual developments in, 163–165, 168, 170, 175–176
  Jewish community in, 167–168, 178
  linguistic dimensions of, 163–166, 168, 174, 185
  literary developments in, 164–165, 168, 170, 175–177
  musical and theatrical developments in, 165–166, 168, 172–173, 178–183
  nationalist activity in, 164–165, 168–170, 173–176, 183–186
  political activism and reform in, 166–174, 185–186
  tourism in, 175–176
  violence in, 169–170, 185–186
Prague during the Thirty Years War and Counter-Reformation. *See also* Second Defenestration of Prague, Battle of White Mountain

architecture in, 130–133, 131*f*, 136–139, 141, 144
artistic developments in, 130, 131*f*, 132–133, 136, 138–139, 144
intellectual developments in, 130–131, 136, 144
Jewish community in, 128–130, 137–144
literary developments in, 128, 136
musical and theatrical developments in, 144
population of, 137–138
public executions in, 127–128
statues in, 130–131
Prague Ethnographic Exhibition (1895), 184–185, 184–185*cp*
Prague in the Czech Republic
elections in, 314–315, 317
European Union and, 314–315, 317
foundation of, 310
international relations in, 304, 307–309
NATO and, 314, 316–317
population of, 310
protests in, 317
secularism in, 318
Prague Metronome, 306*f*
Prague post-Communism
architecture in, 308–309, 318
artistic developments in, 311–314, 316–317
economic reform of, 307–310
ethnic minorities in, 304, 317, 319
historical memory in, 318–320
intellectual developments in, 314
Jewish community in, 304–305, 318–319
literary developments in, 319
musical and theatrical developments in, 303
renovations in, 305, 307, 311
statues and monuments in, 305–306, 312–313, 318–319

tourism in, 306–307, 308*f*
UNESCO recognition of, 307
Prague Spring, 6, 280, 282, 284–285, 290–291
Prague under Charles IV. See also *Charles IV, Emperor*; St. Vitus Cathedral
archdiocese in, 58
architecture in, 35, 37–38, 48–49, 53
artistic developments in, 45, 52–53, 55, 58–60
Black Death epidemic in, 45–46
Charles Bridge constructed in, 56–57, 57*f*
Czech-German relations in, 35, 38
growth during, 47, 53, 57
intellectual developments in, 50–51
Jewish community in, 46–47
language in, 37–38, 40, 47, 50–51
legal reforms in, 51–52
literary developments in, 50–51
map of, 56*f*
New Town founded in, 5, 46
as pinnacle of medieval Prague, 52–53, 62
population in, 47
Prague University established in, 48–49
religious reform in, 49–50
Prague under Communist rule. See also Prague Spring; Prague under normalization
architecture in, 271–273, 275–276
arrests in, 267–270, 283–284
artistic developments in, 268, 271, 280
censorship in, 277–280, 284
film in, 276–278, 280–281
housing shortages in, 275–276
intellectual developments in, 277–279
invasion of (1968), 281–284, 283*f*
Jewish community in, 268–271
literary developments in, 278–281
musical and theatrical developments in, 276–279

Prague under Communist rule (*Continued*)
  nationalization of businesses and
    property in, 267–268, 277–278
  Prague Spring in, 280, 282, 284–285
  protests in, 280, 282, 284
  show trials and political prisoners in,
    267–270
  Stalin statue project in, 272–274
  violence in, 280, 282
Prague under Nazi rule
  arrests in, 250–251, 253, 257
  artistic developments in, 257–258
  censorship in, 250–251, 255
  deportations to concentration camps
    in, 248, 250–251, 253–255
  executions in, 253, 257
  exile government support in,
    250–253, 256–258
  film in, 255, 257
  German nationalism in, 242–243,
    247–248, 253
  Jewish Museum and, 255, 256*f*
  Jewish refugees in, 244–245,
    254–255, 263
  literary developments in, 243–244, 256
  map of, 248*f*
  May uprising in, 258–260
  musical and theatrical developments
    in, 255
  propaganda in, 251, 255
  protests in, 243, 250
  resistance in, 243–244, 250–252,
    256–260
Prague under normalization
  architecture in, 288–289, 300
  arrests in, 292–293
  artistic developments in, 286–287,
    290–293, 295, 297–298
  censorship in, 291–294, 297
  Charter 77 movement in, 292–293,
    295
  dissidents in, 286–287, 290–292, 297

  economic development in, 289–290,
    295–296
  Gorbachev's visit to, 296–297
  intellectual developments in,
    290–291, 297–298
  literary developments in, 291–292
  musical and theatrical developments
    in, 289, 291–292, 294, 297
  population of, 287–288
  protests in, 297–298
  transportation infrastructure in,
    288–289
  Velvet Revolution demonstrations in,
    299–300
  violence in, 300–301
  women's experiences in, 287–288, 296
Prague under Rudolph II
  alchemy and astronomy in, 113–114
  architecture in, 118–119
  artistic developments in, 107–109
  diversity of, 106
  imperial court moved to, 105
  intellectual developments in, 105,
    108–109, 111, 113–114,
    116–119
  Jewish community in, 116–119
  literary developments in, 111, 114–116
  population of, 105
  religious toleration in, 106
  violence in, 110, 120
Prague under Wenceslas IV
  artistic developments in, 68–69
  Astronomical Clock installed in, 70
  Black Death in, 63–64, 72
  church reform movement in, 71–73,
    75–82
  Czech-German relations in, 63, 73
  First Defenestration in, 80–82
  growth during, 71
  intellectual developments in, 70–71, 76
  Jewish community in, 63–66
  language in, 72–74, 76

literary developments in, 68–69
popular preaching in, 72
violence in, 64–65, 81
Prague University
as Charles University, 274f, 290, 305
as Charles-Ferdinand University, 174–175, 188–189, 194–197, 210
establishment of, 48
Kutná Hora decrees and, 75
organization and buildings of, 48–49, 70
religious conflicts and, 71–75, 79, 83, 88–89, 111, 122, 128, 130, 140
Přemysl, Duke, 14, 15f
Přemyslid dynasty, 18–21, 25, 31–33.
See also Borivoj, Duke; Boleslav I, Duke; Boleslav II Duke; Charles IV, Emperor; Otakar I, Přemysl, King; Otakar II, Přemysl, King; Wenceslas, Duke; Wenceslas I, King
Princip, Gavrilo, 207
prostitution, 50, 110, 292–293
Protectorate of Bohemia and Moravia. See Prague under Nazi rule
Protestant Academy (formerly the Carolinum's Faculty of Arts), 130
Protestants, 2–3, 97–98, 106, 119–120, 122, 154, 161, 239. See also Calvinism, Lutheranism, Reformation, United Brethren
Prussia, 145–146, 148–150, 155, 160, 178–179

R
Radetzky, Joseph, 222, 223f
Rašín, Alois, 212, 224–225, 305
Red Army, 258–260, 271, 305
Red Cross, 210, 225–226, 254
Reformation, 68, 97, 111, 124, 159–160, 175, 212, 230
Regulation of Jewish Property Law (1939), 248

religious developments. See Bohemian reform movement; Catholic Church; Catholics; Counter-Reformation; Edict of Tolerance (1782); Hus, Jan; Hussites; Hussite Wars (1419–1437); Jewish community; Protestants; Reformation; Second Defenestration of Prague (1618); Taborites; Thirty Years War (1618–1648); Utraquism
Renaissance, 68, 97, 99, 111
Renaissance style, 99–103, 108–111, 114–117, 181
Return of the Stones (Róna and Rónová), 319, 320f
Rieger, František, 170–171, 171f, 181
Rilke, Rainer Maria, 188–189
Ripellino, Angelo Maria, 1–2
rock music. See also Plastic People of the Universe, Rolling Stones. 8, 291–292, 300, 306, 311, 316
Rodin, Auguste, 199
Roger, Pierre. See Clement VI, Pope
Rolling Stones, 8, 311, 316
Roma and Sinti communities, 7, 219–220, 224, 248, 295–296, 304, 317
Romanesque design, 20–24, 37, 44, 54–55, 318
Róna, Jaroslav, 313, 319, 320f
Rónová, Lucie, 319, 320f
Rudé právo (newspaper), 252, 265–266, 280, 282–284
Rudolph II of Habsburg, Emperor. See also Prague under Rudolph II
art collection of, 107–109
astronomical interests and court of, 111–113
crown of, 107–108
imperial court moved to Prague under, 105
imprisonment of, 120

Rudolph II of Habsburg, Emperor.
  (*Continued*)
  Letter of Majesty issued by, 119–120
  nobility's relations with, 119–120
  overthrow of, 120
  portrait of, 108–109, 109*f*
  religious toleration under, 106
Russia, 160, 171, 209–210, 220. *See also* Soviet Union

S

Sadeler, Aegidius, 95*f*, 106–107, 108*f*, 109*f*
Saints Procopius and Adalbert, 21cp
samizdat (self-publishing network), 291–293, 295
Second Czechoslovak Republic. *See* Czechoslovakia (Second Republic)
Second Defenestration of Prague. *See* Defenestration of Prague, Second
Seifert, Josef, 232, 243–244, 258–260, 295
Serbia, 44–45, 201–202, 207
"Siege of Prague" (Schleder, Osten, and Merck), 135*f*
Sigismund, Emperor
  ascension of, 81–82
  Bohemian throne claimed by, 83
  church council called by, 76–77
  Hussites attacked by, 85–88
  nobility's relations with, 83, 92
  refusal to negotiate with Hussites by, 88–89
Šiklová, Jiřina, 291, 295
Silesia, 26, 84–85, 93, 145–146, 148–149, 160–161, 219–220
Slánský, Rudolf, 269–270, 273–274
Slav Epic, The (Mucha), 239, 239cp
Slavín (mausoleum at Vyšehrad Cemetery), 200–201, 201*f*
Šling, Otto, 270
Slovakia
  Communist Party in, 280
  Hungarian period of, 219–220
  Munich Agreement, 243–244, 251
  autonomy of, 243, 245–246
  relations with Prague and, 217
  Velvet Divorce of, 310
Smetana, Bedřich, 168, 170, 176, 178–180
Sokol gymnastics association, 173, 204*f*, 210, 230–231, 263, 265
Sophia, Queen, 72, 79, 83–84
Soviet Union, 3–4, 266–267, 273–275, 280–284, 283*f*, 296–298
Sporck, Anton, 144
Stalin, Joseph, 265, 267, 272, 277
Stalin Monument (Prague), 272–274, 274*f*
Star Summer Palace (Letohrádek Hvězda, Stern Schloss), 101, 102*f*
St. Francis Church, 28*f*
St. George Basilica and convent (Prague Castle), 17–20, 19*f*, 32, 110, 153–154
St. John the Baptist Church, 23–24, 54
St. Martin's Church (Vyšehrad), 21–22, 22*f*
St. Martin in the Wall, 76
St. Nicholas (Prout), 177*f*
St. Nicholas Church (Lesser Town), 106, 131*f*, 139, 139cp, 158, 177*f*
St. Nicholas Church (Old Town), 139
Stone Bridge. *See* Charles Bridge (Stone Bridge)
Stříbrný, Jiří, 216–217
St. Vitus Cathedral (Prague Castle)
  architecture of, 44, 53–54, 231
  consecration of, 18
  Golden Gate of, 55
  photograph of, 54*f*
  reopening following renovation of, 231
  side chapels of, 54–55
  Wenceslas's tomb in, 42
St. Wenceslas Square. *See* Wenceslas Square
Sucharda, Stanislav, 199, 203
Sudetenland, 242–244, 304
Summer Palace (Anne's Summer Palace, Belvedere) (Prague Castle), 101, 102*f*, 111–113, 155

Šustrová, Petruška, 292–293
Švec, Otakar, 272–273
Světlá, Karolina, 173, 176, 178–179
Svoboda, Ludvík, 283–285

T
Taborites, 83–84, 91–92, 97
Teige, Karel, 232–233, 235–239
theatrical developments. See Mozart, W. A.; National Theater; operas; plays
Theresienstadt (Terezín), 207, 254, 303
Theodoric, Master, 59–60, 60f
Thirty Years War (1618–1648). See also Prague during the Thirty Years War and Counter-Reformation
  anti-Semitism resurgence during, 129–130
  Catholic League in, 125–126
  end of, 133–136
  Marian column erected to celebrate Habsburg victory in, 136
  Second Defenestration as sparking, 122, 133
  surrender of Bohemian troops in, 126
  trials and public executions in, 126–128
  White Mountain battle in, 126–128
Thun-Hohenstein, Franz, Count, 185, 209–210, 212–213
Toleration Patent (1783), 190
"Tower of Babel" from the *Wenceslas Bible*, 68cp
Toyen (Maria Čermínová), 238
Trade Fair Palace, 234, 236f, 253–254
turn of the century Prague. See Prague at the turn of the century
Týn Church (Old Town Square). See Our Lady before Týn Church

U
Upper classes, 11–12, 22–23, 37, 64, 79, 101–103, 106, 110–111, 137–138, 150, 188, 199, 239–240

Utraquism, 79–80, 83–84, 91–94, 98–99
United Brethren Church (also Bohemian Brethren), 90, 97, 130, 132, 154, 163

V
Vančura, Vladislav, 235–238, 257
Velvet Divorce (1992), 310
Velvet Revolution (1989), 299–302, 301f, 317
Vertumnus (Arcimboldo), 108–109cp
Vienna
  Congress of 1515 in, 96
  Congress of 1815 in, 160
  Great War's impact on, 214
  imperial center, 96–97, 103–105, 120, 125, 128, 132, 137–138, 145–146, 150, 152–153, 155, 168, 170, 173–174, 208–209, 212, 215–216
  imperial diet convened in, 170–171
  railroad connection between Prague and, 166
View of the City of Prague, A (Wechter, van der Bossche, and Sadeler), 107, 108f
Villa Müller, 235–238
Vinohrady, 188, 190, 221, 239, 258
Vinohrady Synagogue, 259f, 263, 268
Vítkov Hill, 85–86, 88–89, 239, 265, 271, 287
Vladislav Hall (Prague Castle), 94–95, 100, 106–107, 301–302, 315–316
Vladislav Hall During the Annual Fair (Sadeler), 95f
Vladislav Jagiellon, King, 93–96
Vladislav II, Přemysl, King, 24–25, 56
Vltava (Moldau) River, 4–6, 10–11
Volavková, Hana, 255, 268
Voskovec, Jiří, (later George), 233–234, 293
Votive Panel of John Očko of Vlašim, 58–59cp
Vyšehrad, 15–16, 22–23, 22f, 200–201

W
Wagner, Richard, 178–180
Waldhauser, Conrad von, 49–50, 92–93
Wallenstein, Albrecht von, 125–126, 132–133
Wallenstein Palace and Gardens, 4f, 131f, 132–133, 133f, 136, 210
"Wanted in Prague" (Hoffmeister), 257–258, 257–258cp
War–Bond Campaign Poster, 209cp
wars and conflicts. *See* Great War, The; Hussite Wars (1419–1437); Prague during Hussite Wars and new dynasties; Prague during the Great War; Prague under Nazi rule; Second Defenestration of Prague (1618); Thirty Years War (1618–1648); World War II
Warsaw Pact. *See also* Prague, invasion of (1968), 280–285, 283f, 290, 305–306
Weil, Jiří, 249, 255, 268
Wenceslas, Duke (Saint)
　Christian faith of, 16–18
　Crown of, 5–6, 43–44, 153–154
　"Good King Wenceslas" carol named for, 17–18
　hagiographies of, 16–18, 136
　legacy of, 17–18, 244
　monument to, 246
　murder of, 17
　rise to power of, 16–17
　statues of, 6, 17–18, 54–55, 136, 202–203, 203f, 282, 307–308
　as symbol of Prague, 17–18
Wenceslas I, King, 25–27
Wenceslas II, King, 31–32, 47
Wenceslas IV, King. *See also* Prague under Wenceslas IV
　artistic collection and personal library of, 68–69, 71
　capture and imprisonment of, 66–67
　Hussite War outbreak and, 81–82
　illuminated manuscripts of, 136
　imperial title lost by, 67
　Jewish community under, 63–64
　Kutná Hora decrees of, 75
　Nepomuk's execution ordered by, 66, 136–137
　nobility's relations with, 66
　Sigismund designated heir of, 66–67
Wenceslas Square (New Town)
　Baťa Shoe Store, 234–235
　Czechoslovak Republic celebration in, 6
　Czech Radio Building, 258–260, 282
　equestrian statue of St. Wenceslas in, 6, 17–18, 136, 202
　founding by Charles IV of, 6
　Grand Hotel Europa in, 199
　historical events at, 6
　International Students' Day protests in, 299–300
　Lucerna Palace in, 227, 234
　November 1989 regime change protests in, 6
　Palach's immolation protest in, 284
　Prague Spring stamped out in, 6
　renaming of, 6, 170
Werfel, Franz, 196–197
Werich, Jan, 233–234, 293
Weston, Elizabeth Jane (Westonia), 114–116
Wilson, Woodrow, 215–217
Windischgrätz, General Alfred I, Prince of, 166–167, 169–171
Winton, Nicholas, 244–245
Wohlmut, Boniface, 101, 106–107
Woman from Prague (Hollar), 134f
women's experiences, 50, 74, 176, 210, 225–228, 267, 296
working-class experiences, 166–167, 175, 182–183, 188, 190, 213–214, 217–219, 226, 239–240

World War I. *See* Great War, The; Prague during the Great War

World War II, 7–8, 248*f*, 250, 277–278, 303, 318. *See also* Holocaust, The; Nazi Germany; Prague under Nazi rule

Writers' Union, 278–280, 283–284

Wyclif, John, 69, 71, 73, 75, 77, 79

Y

Ya'qūb, Ibrahim Ibn, 11–13

Young Czech Party, 174, 185–186, 201–202

Z

Zahradník, Isidor, 216–217

Zanantoni, Eduard, 213, 215

Zap, Karel Vladislav, 165

Zápotocký, Antonín, 274–276

Zbraslav Monastery, 40, 58–59, 154

Zelená hora and Královský dvůr manuscript controversy, 164, 186

Želivský, Jan, 80–81, 90–91

Zeman, Miloš, 317

Žižka, Jan, 81, 85, 87*f*, 88–91, 239, 271

Žižkov, 162, 185–186, 188–189, 213–214, 221, 319, 320*f*